SEPA CREDIT TRANSFER

How to understand and add value to your SCT Payment Project

By Jean Paul Megue

ISBN 979-1-0947-1001-2

www.paiementor.com

Table of Contents

Introduction

The world of payments is broad and fascinating. Paying belongs to our everyday lives. Therefore we easily understand the concept of paying and value exchange. But when we talk about payments systems and how they work, things are not always that trivial. Payments systems, processes and products are various and multiple. There are retail (or low value) and wholesale (or large value) payments and payments can be performed domestically or internationally. This book is about a *domestic* payment instrument in Europe: the SEPA Credit Transfer or simply SCT. After reading it, you will understand how the payments systems involved in SCT processing work. I will introduce it by briefly telling you my own story with SEPA and then give an overview of its chapters.

The first SEPA payment instrument, the SEPA Credit Transfer, has been around since beginning 2008. It was officially launched on 28th January 2008, when the banks started to use it for funds transfer. The banks and clearing houses had to prepare in order to be ready for the exchanges of SCT messages by the launch date. Therefore they had to start projects many months or years before. I took part in one of those projects.

Working as a junior consultant in 2007, I started an assignment with a bank running a payment program. Two projects in the program consisted in connecting the bank to the local country Clearing System and to the Pan-European Clearing System. When I arrived, the projects were already in testing, so in pretty advanced stages. Since the projects were behind schedule, my team lead and other colleagues were busy catching up in order to deliver on time.

I was working as a junior tester and people were expecting me to prepare and execute test scenarios and test cases as soon as possible in a very short time. I went through all the existing documents with the aim of grasping rapidly what the project is all about and then ensure that I can write high quality deliverables. I faced two major problems: 1) The number of documents to read on SEPA and the project was just too high. I started reading project documents. But the more I read some of them, the more I got confused. Key information was available in several documents and it was difficult to connect the dots. 2) Sadly no one took the time to guide me in this sometimes awkward, but exciting SEPA journey. People were busy and I was left to myself.

I have an irresistible need to understand the big picture as well as the details. So I tried to find a book on the subject that will enable me to become skillful quickly and add value. My searches in physical and online libraries were unsuccessful. The books, which I saw, contained a presentation of the different means of payment, but did not mention the standards or the banking processes related to SEPA. I had to rely on people in the project team, but the information provided was incomplete and frankly baffling at times. Looking back I think all the people on the project were struggling as much as me. Many did not understand the basics and therefore couldn't help or could help me only partially. Little by little, I went from project to project and from team to team and with the time I was able to understand more and more. It took me around four to five years to put the puzzle together for the foundations. You may think that this is pretty long time. And I would agree with you. My case shows how essential training is. Knowledge is power and we should never underestimate knowledge, no matter how little it may seem to be. When I tell my story and people pretend it is too long, I always cite two examples to illustrate the importance of training and guidance.

The first one is the combination door lock. How long does it take to open a door equipped with such a combination? Well it depends. If you know the combination, you can open the door in seconds. But someone has to tell you. If you do not know the combination, you may spend hours, months and even years and you may still not be able to open the door. Knowing the combination may seem nothing, but it is a real power that can even save life in extreme emergency situations. The second example I take is about the laws of physics. Let's for example consider Newton's law of universal gravitation revealed in his book *the Principia* published in 1687. Today it is taught in schools in few hours. But it took centuries and many scientists who worked with patience and passion to get there. Without training and guidance, you may need much more time than necessary to become a subject matter expert. I have written this book to guide you in your SEPA journey and allow you to move faster to your destination.

Around three years ago after I started an assignment with another bank, fellow workers came to me and asked me if I could recommend a good book on SEPA Credit Transfer. I made a search on the Web and was unpleasantly surprised to see that the situation has not changed much compared to 2007. There was still no book I could recommend to people eager to quickly unravel the mysteries of SEPA. Then I said, initially joking, that I will write one book on SEPA Credit Transfer. The idea caught on and finally I decided to pause, sit down and write. The result is what you have in your hand. Personally I am very happy with it and I hope I had this book when I started my SEPA journey. It would have made my life much easier and things would have been completely different. The book is for people working on SEPA projects in the banking industry or who simply want to understand what SEPA is and how banks and clearing houses implement it. For people working on corporations, the book can be of great help in understanding the banking processes and tools and the type of services banks provide on SEPA Credit Transfer.

One of the main goal I pursue with this book is to help my readers connect the dots: ISO 20022 standards, SEPA standard and messages, clearing and settlement mechanisms, the banking processes, applications, channels and of course the customers, etc. While going through this book full of pictures and illustrations, you will get clear and concise explanations about all these topics. For the first time, you have all that information gathered at the same place and that makes this book truly unique.

Below short summaries of the content of the different chapters are provided.

The chapter 1 is about the four corner model of the SEPA Credit Transfer. After a brief introduction on payment systems models, a very detailed analysis of the SCT four corner model is made. All the actors involved are considered: the different types of customers and their needs, the banks and the Clearing and Settlement Mechanisms (CSM). Concepts like direct and indirect participants are explained in connection with CSM. After presenting the key players, we look at the messages exchanged between banks and customers and between banks themselves. Then we talk about the three options for a bank to exchange messages: first with itself; second directly with another bank inside the same bank group or with an indirect participant and third with another bank through a CSM. In the final part, we make a focus on the originator bank messages and beneficiary bank messages as a whole.

In chapter 2, you get acquainted with the SCT messages, which are based on ISO 20022 standard. It begins with an introduction to the ISO 20022 standard, after which the differences between ISO 20022 and SEPA are considered. As next step, we focus on SEPA standard and see how to distinguish between SEPA Core and SEPA Additional Optional Services message elements. The chapter continues with the presentation of all the SCT messages and their structures. The main building blocks of which the messages consist are illustrated and explained. And the gaps between ISO 20022 and SEPA standards are highlighted.

The chapter 3 is about the Additional Optional Services available in SEPA. I have tried to classify them from the simple to the more complex ones. For each of them, you see what the different AOS are, why they have been implemented and what they are used for. Some AOS are widespread and banks throughout the SEPA area can adhere to them. Others are used only inside certain communities and available only to banks which belong to those communities.

The chapter 4 decrypts the payment processing value chain for the SEPA Credit Transfer. It consists of three sub processes which are explained in detail: Payment Acquisition and Reporting, Payment Order management, Payment Exchange. The first paragraph, payment acquisition and reporting, talks about the channels through which banks and customer exchange information. A particular focus is made on file based channels. The main protocols used for the exchange of files are presented: EBICS and SWIFTNet protocols. The second major paragraph describes the payment order management. There we go through the main checks, validations and controls that happen at this stage during the payment processing. The payment exchange is analyzed in the next paragraph. It covers important concepts like routing, bulking and debulking of messages. After that, we look at the payment application architectures which support the functions and processes of the payment processing value chain. The last paragraph analyzes the payment status reports which contain information provided by the bank to the customers about the processing of their payments.

The chapter 5 provides the answer to the question: what is a SEPA Credit Transfer? This may sound strange and you may wonder why you have to get so far before getting the answer to this important question. The reason is simple. I want to make things easy for my readers. Some of the topics handled in this chapter are presented in the previous chapters, chapter 1 and 4 particularly. Reading them will help you to grasp the content of this chapter much faster. The chapter sheds light on many notions that are partially understood or even misunderstood in relation with the SEPA Credit Transfer: IBAN, BIC, execution time, ultimate debtor and ultimate creditor and so on.

In chapter 6, two key topics are handled: booking and the account balance management. At the end of day, processing payment is moving funds. And funds move through debits and credits on accounts. To give you a strong foundation, the chapter starts with the presentation of the double booking entry principle and accounting events. Few examples are provided and analyzed to illustrate that principle. After that we look at booking and non-booking transactions of the SCT Scheme. Then we focus on booking transactions for the SCT Creditor bank and SCT Debtor Bank. You see the different accounting events and how the funds flow from system to system until it reaches the final destination. In the next two paragraphs, we consider Nostro and Vostro accounts and shadow or mirror accounts respectively. They are explained in very simple manner with examples to make things intelligible even for people who are completely new to the subject. The last paragraph deals with account balance management for single and merged accounts.

The chapter 7 is about the Graphical User Interface of payment engines applications. First we present the navigation menus and what they generally contain. Then we look at payment transactions with an interest in the information displayed on the application GUI. The main subject addressed in this chapter are user actions. Since user actions depend on user rights and user roles, we first see what rights and roles are. The search, worklist items and audit trails are analyzed after that. The chapter ends with an analysis of 3270 screens which are still very widespread and bring few challenges. Some hints are provided to help you meet those challenges.

The chapter 8 talks about payment engines in the Bank IT environment. Payment engines use many interfaces to interact with other applications of the Bank. Therefore the first major paragraph presents the different types of interfaces with examples to help you understand synchronous and asynchronous messaging as well as transactional and batch mode. The second paragraph analyses the interfaces between payment engines and their surrounding systems and looks at the information exchange.

The annexes at the end the book provide additional details on the following subjects: List of SEPA countries, IBAN calculation and validation, how to read the SCT rulebooks and implementation guidelines.

There are a lot of topics addressed in the book. Some of them could have been treated with more depth. But I did not do that because I estimate that these details are not necessary to grasp the whole picture and connect the dots. However I am keen to see what my readers will think and would appreciate to receive feedback.
I wish you a very pleasant reading.

Chapter 1 The Four Corner Model of the SEPA Credit Transfer

LEARNING OBJECTIVES

After reading this chapter, you will be able to answer the following questions:

1. What are the underlying models on which payment systems operate?
2. What is the four corner model?
3. What is clearing? What is settlement?
4. What are the payment messages exchanged in the SEPA Credit Transfer scheme and what are they used for?
5. What are intrabank, intrabankgroup and interbank messages?

The Four Corner Model is a fundamental concept in payments. The SEPA Credit Transfer (SCT) and many other payment instruments operate with that model. However, before carrying out a thorough examination of the Four Corner Model for the SCT, it is essential to get an overview of payment systems models. They provide the keys to understand where the Four Corner Model comes from and to study any payment instrument.

1.1 Payment systems models

Payment systems operate essentially on two types of models: open loop models and closed loop models.

Open loop models

Open loop systems can be compared with a hub-and-spoke model. The system is connected to Banks or similar institutions which act as intermediaries. And the banks are connected to end parties, the senders and receivers of funds. There is no direct connection between end parties and the payments system. The picture below depicts an open loop payments system.

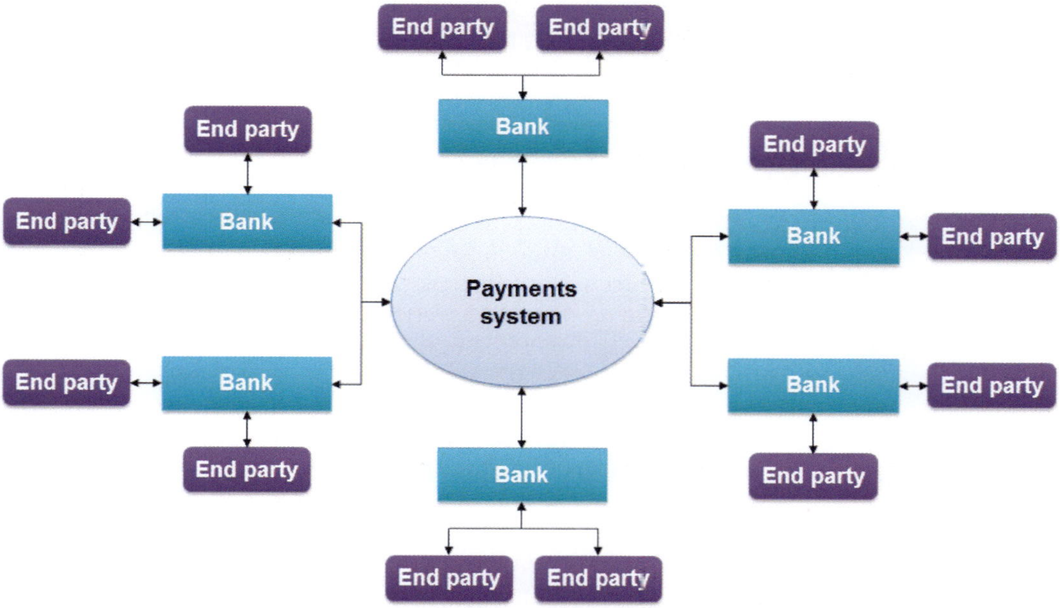

Figure 1.1: Open loop payments system model

The payments are sent from an end party to its bank, then from that bank to another bank through the payments system and finally the receiving bank delivers the payments to its end party customer. Open loop models yield the great advantage of allowing banks to transact with each other without direct relationships. When a bank joins the system, it can exchange transactions with all the banks that are already in the system and vice versa. This allows open loop systems to scale rapidly.

In an open loop system end parties send funds to one another without having direct relationship to the same bank. All end parties are in a way connected to each other through the payments system and the intermediary banks.

Banks that join a payment system are bound by the rules. Since they are independent entities, each bank has its own project and timelines to implement these rules. In general, they have a period of many months and sometimes even years to become compliant. The implementation of new rules takes time in open loop model. This is one of the drawback of these models. And even worse, banks may have different interpretations of the same rule with various implementations as a result.

Visa and MasterCard are open loop systems. If you possess either of these cards, you got it from your Bank and not directly from Visa or MasterCard. Your Bank is the intermediary between you and those payments systems. Merchants that accept Visa or MasterCard do not join them directly. They have to sign a contract with a Bank which is member of Visa or MasterCard.

For the transfer of funds, banks join payments systems at national or regional level. The bank customers cannot join these systems directly. In fact many are not even aware of their existence. Customers send and receive payments through their banks, the intermediaries between them and the payments systems. Payments systems for the SEPA Credit Transfer are open loop systems. You are certainly wondering yourself what closed loop systems are. The next paragraph is about closed loop models.

Closed loop models

Closed loop payments systems connect end parties directly to each other without banks as intermediaries. The end parties, merchants and consumers, join the payments system directly.

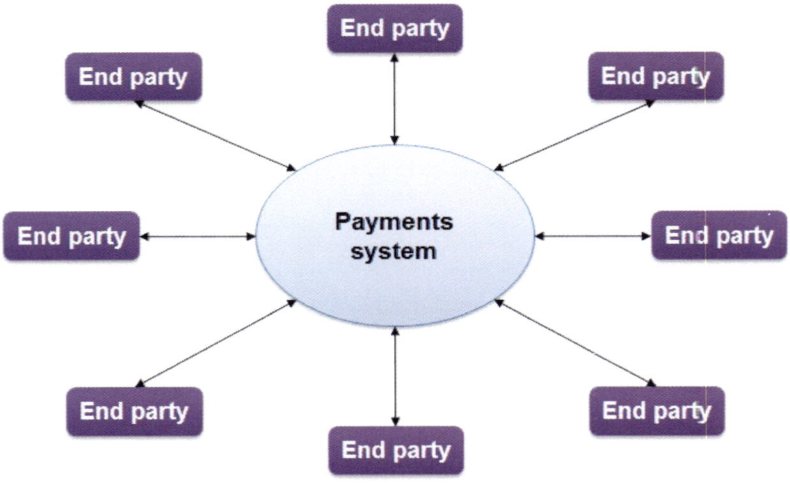

Figure 1.2 : Close loop payments system model

As we see on the above picture, there is no intermediary layer. The architecture of closed loop systems is therefore quite simple. End parties must both join the payments system before they can transact with each other. It can be consider as a centralized system with one entity operating it. Changes and new services can be implemented and delivered pretty fast to all the end parties. This is an advantage of these models.

American express network is an example of a closed loop system. End parties (Merchants and consumers) deal directly with American Express. Paypal operates a close loop payments system. To pay with his paypal information (email and password), a consumer first has to register with paypal. And merchants can accept payments via paypal only if they join the system. It is interesting to note that both AMEX and Paypal heavily rely on open loop systems to transfer funds to their end parties. Funds transfers happen ultimately through accounts held by banks. Amex and Paypal can access the accounts only through open loop systems. Therefore closed loop systems are not stand-alone systems. They need open loop systems to provide all the necessary services to their end users.

The closed loop payments systems do not grow as rapidly as open loop systems because merchants and consumers must join the system itself. This may sound a bit counter-intuitive. But it comes from the fact that setting up a distribution network to address consumers directly is expensive and takes time. On the other hand, with Internet, a product can gain traction quickly and become very popular. In just 20 years, Paypal has grown from zero to almost a quarter billion online users.

In open loop systems, customers of the systems are the banks which distribute the payment instruments related products to their own customers, the end parties. In closed loop systems, customers are the end parties. That makes a big difference at the end in terms of operations, management and growth.

After this brief introduction on payments systems models, let us now focus on the SEPA Credit Transfer and the underlying model.

1.2 The Four Corner Model of the SEPA Credit Transfer

Before diving into the four corner model, let's briefly define the terms SEPA and SEPA Credit Transfer. SEPA is the *area* where citizens, companies and other economic actors can make and receive payments in euro, within all the EU Member States, whether between or within national boundaries under the same basic conditions, rights and obligations, regardless of their location and local currency. The SEPA Credit Transfer is the payment instrument governed by the rules of the SEPA Credit Transfer Scheme for making credit transfer payments in euro throughout the SEPA from bank accounts to other bank accounts. The EPC defines a SEPA Scheme as "*a set of rules, practices and standards to achieve interoperability for the provision and operation of a SEPA payment instrument agreed at interbank level.*" The word SEPA is sometimes used to refer to the scheme and not to the SEPA area.

The Four Corner Model is at the basis of all SEPA payments. It is called the Four Corner Model because four main actors participate in the processes of sending and receiving funds. For the SCT, the actors are: the originator or debtor, the originator bank, the beneficiary or creditor and the beneficiary bank. The figure below depicts the Four Corner Model of the SEPA Credit Transfer with the main actors as it is presented in the SCT rulebook.

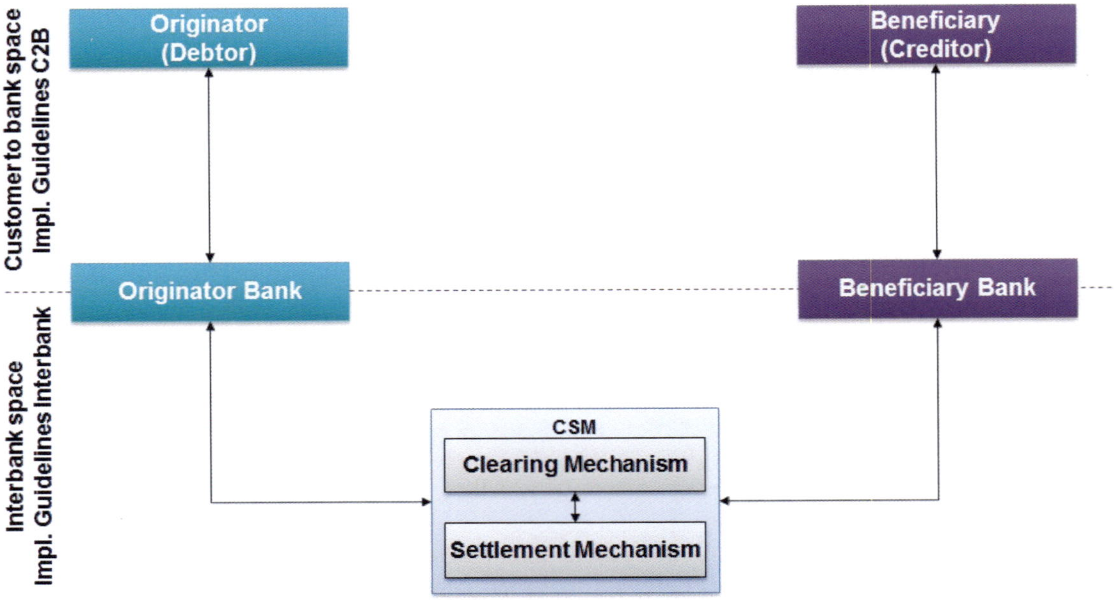

Figure 1.3: The Four Corner Model of the SEPA Credit Transfer

The Debtor originates a credit transfer by giving an order to his bank. The originator bank, after reception, makes the necessary checks to ensure that the order is complete and can be executed successfully. After the execution, the payment is sent to the clearing system (CSM), which after successful completion of its own checks and processing, forward it to the Beneficiary Bank. The Beneficiary bank informs its customer, the beneficiary, that his account has been credited. In this paragraph, we will see what and who these main actors really are, and what are their needs pertaining to the exchange of SCT.

When you look at the figure, something draws your attention immediately: the CSM box where you see the Clearing and Settlement Mechanisms between the originator bank and the beneficiary bank. They seem to be completely overlooked in the model since they don't belong to the "four corners" mentioned before. However, they play a crucial role as we will see later.

Another interesting thing to notice is the two different spaces highlighted on the left: the customer-to-bank space and the interbank space. The customer-to-bank space is about the exchanges of messages between the bank and its customers that can be either originator or beneficiary. The ordering customer sends instructions to his bank in general to ask the bank to execute transfers. And the bank sends information to its customer either to inform him that payments have been received on his accounts or to provide statuses about the execution of his orders. The interbank space is the space where banks exchange payment messages among themselves. Messages are sent from one bank to another directly or through a CSM.

Now let us look at the end parties: originator and beneficiary. The originator and the beneficiary are customers of the originator bank and beneficiary bank respectively. The same person can play the role of originator and beneficiary depending on him or her sending or receiving funds. This means that the same bank can play both the roles of originator bank and the beneficiary bank. As payment professionals, it is important to have a holistic view of the customers and banks and to understand what roles they play in the specific processes. The customers have different needs that banks must respond to by providing different kind of services. We will now illustrate through examples the type of needs that the different customers have: The private customer, the small and medium-sized business (SMB), the associations and non-governmental organizations (NGO) and the large companies.

1.2.1 The private customer

The private customer is an individual who has opened an account with a bank. He receives his salary or pensions and makes a couple of credit transfer per month. In the European Union, the mean number of credit transfers made by individual per year amounts to around 50. It means that we, as individuals, make between 4 and 5 transfers each month. Thus compared to other actors, private customers are not heavy users of payment services. In general, they use the Website of their Bank to manually input an order or they can go to a branch and complete a form with transfer information. They might also use their phone and other channels accepted by their bank to initiate payment orders. The bank will then send a confirmation, update their account balance and provide a statement in paper or electronic form.

As receivers of funds, private customers are keen to be informed quite rapidly, particularly through the mobile or the Internet banking applications that allow checking account balances anytime and anywhere. How many payments does a private customer receive each month? I could not find any statistic, but we all know that number is much smaller than the mean number of credit transfers made. Customers therefore appreciate when they receive a notification from their bank that their accounts have been credited.

In general, the private customer opens one current account with a bank for his banking operations including transferring and receiving funds. He may have other types of accounts, like saving accounts too. But the number of accounts is pretty limited compared to other types of end parties as we will see later. Because of the reduced number of accounts, the customer does not require sophisticated reporting. And the bank can satisfy his needs with basic reporting services.

Every coin has two sides. Technology enables the rapid access to information but has also been used to facilitate the initiation of fraudulent transactions. Fraudsters are constantly coming up with new ways to trick people out of their money. Despite the initiatives taken by banks to protect their customers, the cost of fraud continues to rise all over the world. Therefore, the fear of falling victim to payment fraud remains a concern for private customers. Maintaining the trust in payments and payments systems is vital for any economy and the banks must keep fighting fraud threats to reassure their customers. Security belongs to the top priority topics on the agenda of banks today and for the years to come.

The table below contains a summary of the private customer's needs.

<table>
<tr><th>Private customer as Debtor</th><th>Private customer as Creditor</th></tr>
<tr><td>• Initiates 4 to 5 credit transfers every month</td><td>• Receives salary, pensions and other revenues on his account.</td></tr>
<tr><td colspan="2">• Has limited number of accounts (one current account is in general sufficient).
• Wants to have access to payment and account reporting whenever and wherever he wishes, but reads account statements from time to time.
• Is concerned with security</td></tr>
</table>

Table 1-1 : Private consumer's main needs

1.2.2 The Small and Medium-sized Businesses

The small and medium-sized businesses (SMB) are companies with one to few dozens of employees. In many countries they represent over 90% of businesses. For that reason, SMB are seen as the backbone of the economy.

SMB have different needs than private customers, already by the number of payments to be made or received. They make transfers to their suppliers and employees and receive payments from their customers. The size of the business and the number of employees influence their needs and must be well-considered to better serve them. When the number of employees is very limited (less than 10 for example), the SMB can use the e-Banking portal of their bank to manually input payment orders like a private customer does for instance. For a company with few dozens of employees, it is cumbersome to manually input all accounts and employee information to initiate payments at the end of each month. Solutions to avoid inputting the same information every time are really appreciated. For example, templates for multi-beneficiary payment orders where all the information is kept are very useful. At the end of each month, no need to input everything again. Only the date, amounts and few references need to be updated to make the payments.

After a payment order is validated, the SMB wants to be informed rapidly in case an exception occurs during its processing. In business, delayed payments can have drastic consequences. Therefore, SMB may request to get one notification per mail and another one per SMS or even to be called directly so that they can handle the issue as quickly as possible.

As creditors, SMB may receive many payments during the day. It is very important for them to closely follow their financial situation. For young companies, it is a question of survival. That is the reason why they request and read account statements more often than a private customer. Many SMB receive account statements on a weekly or even daily basis.

SMB are dynamic structures. The number of employees will increase or decrease with the time. And so their needs will evolve with the changing structure. SMB may start the business with one current account, but with the time they will open many other accounts to better organize and easily follow their financials. A consolidated report including all accounts will be of great value in this case. Because of these reasons, the banks must build a closer relationship to their SMB customers to identify and respond to their evolving needs. And the solutions offered to SMB should be easily scalable and adaptable.

Like private customers, SMB fear to become victims of payment fraud which in their case may be caused by employees (internal fraud) or by external third parties (external fraud). Studies show that they are more vulnerable to fraud and yet fraud can have more devastating consequences on them, and may even mean the end of their business. Therefore, SMB look towards banks for suitable solutions and support. And security is clearly a topic to be taken very seriously for them.

The table below contains a summary of the SMB customers' needs.

<table>
<tr><th>SMB as Debtor</th><th>SMB as Creditor</th></tr>
<tr><td>• Makes periodic salary and supplier payments</td><td>• Receives payments from customers.</td></tr>
<tr><td colspan="2">• Must in general open many accounts to better manage the business finances
• Wants to have access to payment and account reporting whenever and wherever needed; hardly spends a day without reading account statements.
• Is very concerned with security and appreciates solutions to fight against internal and external fraud.</td></tr>
</table>

Table 1-2 : Small-and-Medium Business' main needs

1.2.3 The Associations and Non-governmental organizations (NGO)

Associations and Non-governmental Organizations (NGO) are non-profit organizations whose activities are usually towards charity or other social actions. They are run by volunteers or employees and get most of their funding from donations and government grants. To accept donations and perform other financial duties, they make use of bank account(s).

Although Associations and NGO do not pursue the goal of making profit, they have a lot in common with companies. First, they are both legal entities. Second, they have a mission statement. Third, they need money to run their operations. And fourth, they are run by people to provide goods or services. The number of people working for them varies with the size of their activities which can in some cases be carried out in many countries and regions. No wonder that in many countries, banks provide similar services to SMB, associations and NGO. Very big associations and NGO are treated by banks like *large companies* which will be the topic of the next paragraph.

Associations and NGO receive donations and grants from members, sympathizers, partners and the government. And this can happen through credit of their bank accounts. They make payments to suppliers, employees (if they have) and beneficiaries of their activities which can be individuals, households and/or communities. Like SMB, they are interested in solutions allowing not to input the same data again and again when they make payment orders.

Pertaining to reporting, statuses of payment orders do matter of course and information should be provided as fast as possible through mails and SMS and when requested through a website for example. They may operate many accounts for legal or practical reasons. The higher the number of accounts, the more important it becomes to get a consolidated view.

Like for SMB, security is a concern for Associations and NGO. They can be victims of internal and external fraud too with terrible consequences on their image and activities. Effective solutions to address these issues and fight against fraud are of great interest for them.

The table below contains a summary of the Association / NGO customers' needs.

<table>
<tr><th>Association / NGO as Debtor</th><th>Association / NGO as Creditor</th></tr>
<tr><td>• Makes payments to beneficiaries of their activities, suppliers and employees (if they have)</td><td>• Receives donations and grants from members, sympathizers, partners and the government.</td></tr>
<tr><td colspan="2">• May have to open many accounts for legal or practical reasons
• Wants to have access to payment and account reporting when requested and needed.
• Is very concerned with security and appreciates solutions to fight against internal and external fraud.</td></tr>
</table>

Table 1-3 : Association and NGOs' main needs

After considering private customers, SMB, associations and NGO, we start to see which different needs end parties have. We will further dig into that topic by looking at the case of large companies.

1.2.4 The Large companies

Large companies have many hundreds to thousands of employees and may operate their business in many countries all over the world. With multi-million-euro turnovers, their needs in payment services are very sophisticated. Big businesses can make and receive a very high number of payments every day. They are customers of several Banks which may be in many countries around the globe with different base currencies.

Like the other end parties, they can use bank secure web sites to follow what is happening on their accounts. But one bank web site is not enough to get the overview of what is going on in a multibank relationship. Getting a consolidated view of all accounts is of primary importance. Otherwise, it's impossible to know what the overall situation is. Yet, that is crucial for decision making and steering the activities. Large companies therefore look for solutions that can provide a centralized and consolidated view of all their accounts. The centralization of payments exchange with all their banks in a single solution also contributes to a better reporting.

For a large company, the manual input of payments for the salaries is just unthinkable. As already said, they may have thousands of employees and suppliers. That is the reason why their payments orders are transported to their banks in batch files (If you don't understand what it is now, don't bother. We will come back to that later on) generated and formatted in ERP systems or treasury solutions. After getting and processing of the Batch files, the banks send status reports (in files) back to the company. The reports contain execution status - success or failure - of sent orders. Ideally, they should be processed in the same application (ERP or treasury solutions) and automatically linked to the orders, so that people can see if something went wrong and take the necessary corrective actions.

Because of the huge number of transactions, large companies request banks to send account statements daily and sometimes even multiple times a day. The manual handling of the statements would be prone to error and won't be time and cost effective. IT applications are thus indispensable to carry out these tasks efficiently.

Now we get to the key point of this paragraph: *large corporations (and NGO) have to set up specific software solutions and infrastructures to exchange payments and related reporting in an effective and efficient way with their many banks.* The solutions should also provide the necessary consolidated view of all accounts. Integration and communication between banks' IT solutions and company's own solutions are crucial for the customer satisfaction. However, banks and companies should not lose sight of the main business issues because of the technical challenges. Banks develop many services and solutions to address large companies' needs. However, each company is unique and has its own specificities. Taking the time to talk to the customers to understand their specific needs is always a good investment to make.

Security is a major concern for large companies. But unlike smaller companies, their means allow them to implement systems and procedures to keep their payment operations secure. Nevertheless, Banks and large companies should keep on watch because fraudsters constantly find new ways to break security systems.

The table below contains a summary of the needs of a large company.

<table>
<tr><th>Large company as Debtor</th><th>Large company as Creditor</th></tr>
<tr><td>• Makes salary and supplier payments in huge number</td><td>• Receives payments from customers in huge number.</td></tr>
<tr><td colspan="2">• Has many accounts in different currency
• Wants to have access to payment and account reporting whenever and wherever needed; has people whose job is checking payments and account statements.</td></tr>
</table>

- Requires a consolidated view of all the accounts
- Is very concerned with security and appreciates solutions to fight against internal and external fraud.

Table 1-4 : Large company's main needs

The above examples illustrate the typical needs of the different end parties. It is important to understand those differences because they affect the offering the bank creates to serve specific customer segments and logically the processes that they implement to address those customers' needs. After having considered CSM and end parties, the time has come to look at the role of banks in the four-corner model.

1.2.5 Banks and the SEPA Credit Transfer

To exchange SEPA Credit Transfers, a Bank must adhere to the SEPA Credit Transfer Scheme. About the scheme, the rulebook states: "The Scheme establishes *a set of interbank rules, practices and standards to be observed* by Participants who adhere to the Scheme. It allows the payments industry in SEPA to offer a SEPA-wide core and basic credit transfer product to customers in euro."

The scheme is about the rules that banks must observe. The chapter entitled BUSINESS AND OPERATIONAL RULES in the SCT rulebook provides detailed information about what is expected from a Bank that wants to become participant in the Scheme. In the interbank space, the rules are binding. It means that they are mandatory and the banks must implement them as they are. There is no flexibility, except the ones provided by the rules themselves, because of one crucial word in the world of payments: *Interoperability*. In the context of SCT Scheme, interoperability is the capacity for a bank to:

- Send payments messages through the CSM towards any receiving bank connected to the CSM,
- Receive payments messages from the CSM no matter from which sending bank the CSM got it.
- Exchange payments directly with other banks without going through the CSM.

Interoperability is possible only if the messages exchanged are standardized. SCT messages are based on the standard ISO 20022 that will be extensively discussed later. For now, just keep in mind that standardization and interoperability are closely interrelated.

Even if the rules are now binding in the customer-to-bank space (Before they were recommended or optional), banks may still agree with their customers to apply specific rules to provide additional services. Since it is only between the bank and the customer, this gives more flexibility in terms of implementation. But things might become cumbersome when the number of customers increases and the bank wants to make each customer happy. On the long term, going beyond the standard brings more complexity and makes it difficult to streamline the processes.

One last point: We said before that the same bank can play both the roles of the Debtor Bank and Creditor Bank. Note also that a bank can choose to adhere to the scheme only as Creditor Bank or only as Debtor Bank. This can be done temporary or permanently depending of the bank's constraints and expectations.

After presenting the originators, beneficiaries and the banks, it is now time to look at the Clearing and Settlement Mechanisms. What are their functions and why are they so critical in the payments systems? The next paragraph will answer these questions.

1.3 Clearing and Settlement Mechanisms

Clearing and settlement mechanism plays a major role in the interbank exchange of payments. They are the cornerstone of payments systems. Therefore, it is important to understand what they are and why they are so crucial. I will present you these concepts step by step. And you will see that it is easy and straightforward.

Although generally mentioned together, Clearing and Settlement are two completely different things. In this paragraph, we first define clearing and illustrate it with some examples. After that settlement is presented in a general manner and then in the context of SEPA.

1.3.1 What is clearing?

The Bank for International Settlements (BIS) defines the term clearing as the process of transmitting, reconciling and, in some cases, confirming transactions prior to settlement, including the ***netting*** of transactions and the establishment of final positions for settlement. The key word in this definition is the word ***netting***, which is seen by the BIS as the offsetting of obligations between or among participants in the netting arrangement, thereby reducing the number and value of payments or deliveries needed to settle a set of transactions.

It takes at least two actors for the establishment of a clearing mechanism and the required netting process. When there are exactly two players, we talk about bilateral clearing. If there are more than two players, it is called multilateral clearing. Two Banks or a group of banks may decide to make clearing between them without going through an interbank system.

To make the things easier to understand, let us take an example of bilateral clearing. Bilateral clearing is the simplest case, since only two participants are involved. The two participants are you and me and we have to originate credit transfers because we live far away from each other. If you owe me 100 € and I owe you 25 €, then there are two options to resolve our debts with credit transfers:

1. You can make a transfer of 100 € from your account to my account and I can make a transfer of 25 € from my account to your account.
2. Or you can make only one transfer of 75 € (100 € – 25 €) to my account and everyone will be happy. 75 € is the final position after the netting. The final position is made by neutralizing the reciprocal commitments between you and me. That is the offsetting of obligations.

In the first option, two credit transfers are made. In the second option, only one transfer is made. And it is possible to make only one transfer because we first do the netting of amounts. Therefore, we can save one transaction. If we consider a netting process with a very high number of participants, we immediately see that clearing contributes to significantly reduce the number of transfers needed to settle a set of transactions.

Now if we transpose this example to two financial institutions, the number of transactions they exchange among each other may amount to hundreds of thousands or even to millions every day. The clearing allows them not to make a transfer each time a transaction is sent from one bank to another. They can decide at the end of each day for instance to do the netting and then the party which owns money to the other will make a single transfer.

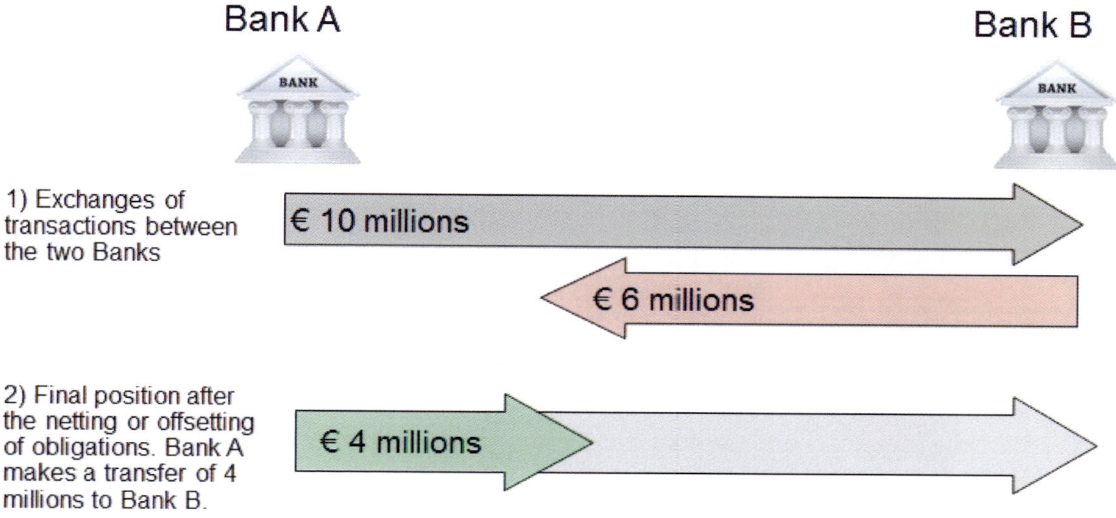

Figure 1.4 Bilateral Clearing

This example shows that bilateral clearing is already quite efficient. If the clearing is done for more than 2 banks, it will be even more efficient. The higher the number of banks involved in the clearing process, the more effective it is. We will discuss those benefits in detail by analyzing the multilateral clearing

1.3.2 Multilateral Clearing

In a multilateral clearing, a high number of financial institutions are involved. But the principle is the same as for bilateral clearing. All the banks will exchange payments among each other up to a certain time. Then the netting will happen after which the final position will be calculated for each of the bank. Since many transactions (thousands or even millions) are exchanged between the banks, the clearing allows avoiding the execution of a huge number of transfers.

To understand how effective multilateral clearing is, imagine a bank that is directly connected to several other banks and there is no CSM in between. In the following figure, a system with five participant Banks has been considered. To reach all the other banks, each bank must establish a point-to-point connection with each of them. This results in a fully connected network topology which is extremely impractical for large networks.

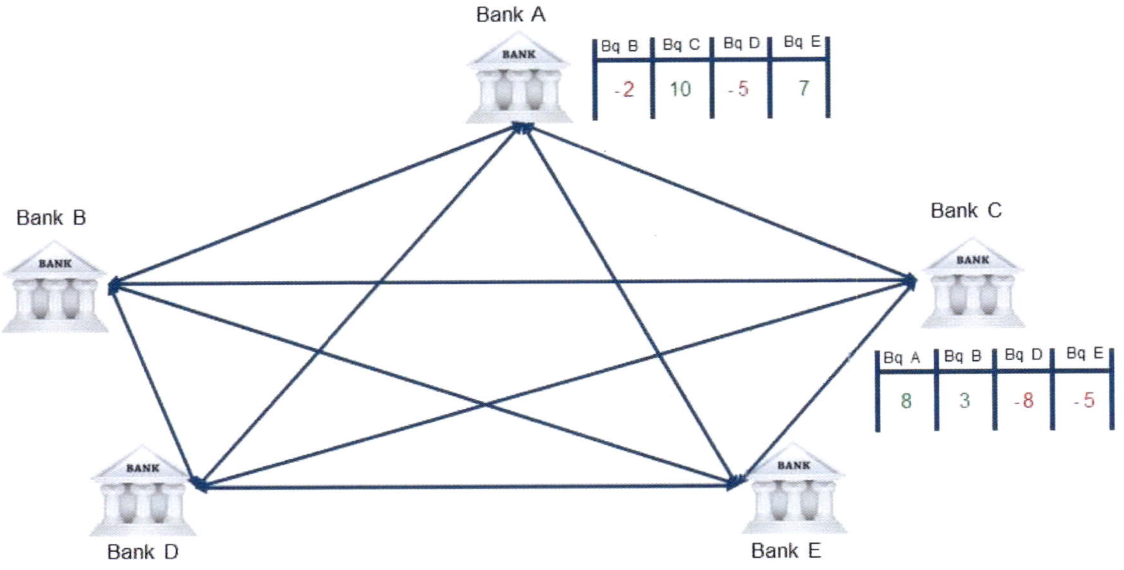

Figure 1.5: System with multiple bilateral clearing

In this configuration, many bilateral clearings should be performed. Below are the main issues with this topology:

1. Each bank in the system must take care of the netting of positions itself. It must do that for each of the bank it is connected to, which is quite cumbersome. On the drawing, netting is represented for Bank A and C. With several hundreds of Banks, the complexity will increase for the netting.
2. Every time a new bank comes to the market, it should set up a connection with all the other banks if it wants to reach them directly. This becomes also more and more difficult with the growing number of banks.
3. How to make sure that the other banks will really pay after the clearing process? Remember that the money is really transferred after the clearing.

These problems are solved by introducing a third party, the Clearing House, which implements the clearing mechanism. To reach all Banks connected to the CSM, a bank has to establish only one connection to the CSM. It is far much easier to implement and less costly than building links to each bank directly. A Bank does not have to implement the clearing with each counterparty since the Clearing House takes care of it. And the CSM can better manage the risk associated to the availability of funds than each bank by itself.

Below you see a picture with four participant banks which are connected to a Clearing House. And the clearing House is connected to the central Bank, the overseer of the banking market in a country, a region or an area. This is how things are in the reality. Banks are connected through a clearing house. The central bank comes into play because as overseer of the banking system in the economy, it implements the settlement mechanism that banks use to transfer funds among themselves. This is a crucial point to keep in mind: in almost all economies, banks do not exchange funds directly among themselves. They should do it through the central bank.

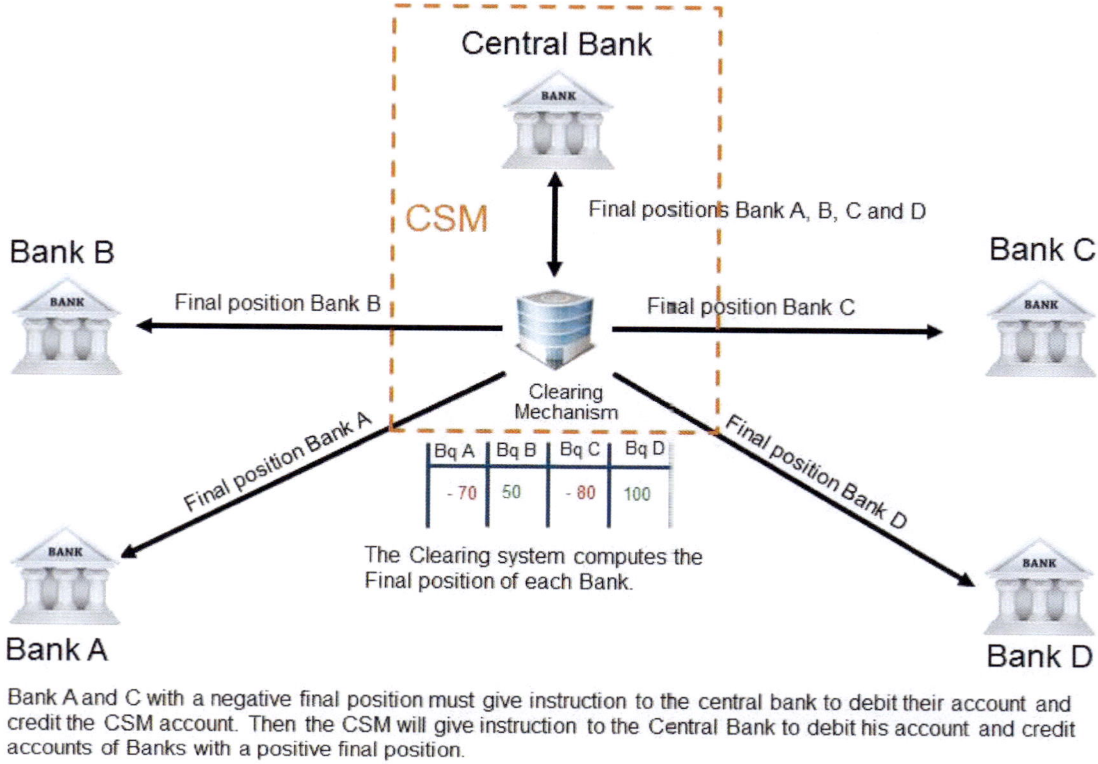

Figure 1.6: Multilateral Clearing

This configuration is like a star network. Participant Banks can be compared to nodes of the network and the clearing system acts like a central network hub or concentrator. In the real world, the number of banks connected to the CSM is much more important. This gives the CSM an even more crucial role. But the principles underlying clearing mechanism remain the same. The clearing system computes the final position of all the participant banks one or several times a day.

One might think wrongly that the clearing system computes the final position between each bank and each other participant bank. A clearing of this type certainly would limit the number of transfers of funds to carry out. But given the number of participant banks, the number of transfers would still be quite high. I have good news for you. The reality is much simpler. Each participant bank considers the clearing system as a single counterparty.

When a bank receives a credit transaction, it considers that the clearing system owes it money regardless of the bank that issued the operation. If it is a debit transaction, it considers that it owes money to the clearing system regardless of the bank that issued the operation. In the other direction, when a bank sends a debit transaction, it considers that it owes money to the clearing system regardless of the receiving bank of the operation. And if it is a credit transaction, then the clearing system owes money to the bank no matter which is the receiving bank of the operation. Therefore, the multilateral net position represents the bilateral net position between each participant and the central counterparty.

Each participant bank considers the clearing system as a single counterparty. In case a participant bank would fail to fulfill its obligations, the other banks will not ask that bank to pay. But they will ask the clearing system to pay. That is what it means for the CSM to be the single counterparty toward participant banks. We see, the clearing system does more than just exchanging transactions and computing the final position. It manages the risk related to the potential failure of a bank to fulfill his obligations toward the CSM and the banking community. The bigger the bank, the more important it is to manage the risk. A failure of a very big bank can cause the whole system to collapse (systemic risk). To avoid this, CSMs set up strict procedures related to risk management. But let us go back to the above figure again.

After the clearing, final position of Bank A and Bank C is -70 million € and -80 million € respectively. It is said in the financial jargon that they are short. Final position of Bank B and Bank D is +50 million € and +100 million € respectively. The banks with negative positions have to fulfill their obligations by transferring the funds to the CSM. The banks with positive positions get funds from the CSM. The process of moving funds is the settlement.

The CSM will debit the accounts of Bank A and C at the central bank and credit its own account. The Banks with a short position (negative final position) must ensure that sufficient amount is available on their accounts. After crediting its account with funds from Banks A and C, the CSM will debit its account and credit accounts of Banks with a long position (positive final position). Take note that the sum of all Banks' final positions is zero. The debit of one party is always the credit of another and vice versa. So, the total amount must be zero. This was a short introduction to the settlement. We will examine it in more detail in the next paragraph.

1.3.3 The settlement

The Bank of International Settlement (BIS) defines settlement as an act that discharges obligations in respect of funds or securities transfers between two or more parties. Thus, settlement is the funds transfer that is carried out by one party to fulfill its obligations towards the counterparty in a financial operation. The settlement happens in general after bilateral or multilateral clearing. In payments, there are basically two types of settlements: gross settlement and net settlement.

A **gross settlement system** is a system in which the settlement or funds transfer occurs individually after each payment transaction is processed in the system. Banks generally use this type of system to exchange urgent transfers or large amounts transfers. If the funds are not available, the transfer cannot be executed. However, when the funds are available, the instructions are executed instantaneously. That is why these systems are called RTGS, which stands for Real-Time Gross Settlement System. "Real-time" means that funds transfer happens right away if funds are available. In addition, when a funds transfer is made between two accounts at the central bank, it becomes final and irrevocable immediately after the transfer is made. The risk of default is therefore eliminated. An RTGS system is a critical infrastructure for a country's economy since it connects all the (participating) banks and facilitates fast transfer of funds among them. RTGS systems are usually operated by the central bank of a country or monetary zone. Remember that central bank plays the function of "Bank of banks" as overseer of the banking system.

Things are different in a net settlement system. Transactions are exchanged among participants without transfers of funds. Then the multilateral netting happens at specific time(s). The obligations are netted among all the participants and the multilateral net settlement positions are calculated. The net settlement position is the sum of the value of all the transfers a participant has received during a certain period of time less the value of the transfers made by that participant to all other participants. If the sum is positive, the participant is in a multilateral net credit position; if the sum is negative, the participant is in a multilateral net debit position.

Some time is needed to compute the net positions, send the information to the banks and proceed to the transfer of funds. This inevitably adds delays in the actual moving of funds. To reduce the delays and improve the liquidity in the overall system, many settlement cycles are generally carried out during the day after related multilateral clearings. If a participant wants a transaction to be settled at a specific time, it must send that transaction before the cut-off for that settlement cycle. The clearing system communicates the cut-off times of settlement cycles to all participants and the information about the settlement times. So, each participant is aware that transactions that reach the CSM after the cut-off time for a specific settlement cycle cannot be considered. They may be considered in the next settlement cycle depending on the CSM rules.

The settlement requires transfer of funds between participant banks. Payments between banks are made via their accounts with the central bank. The central bank for the euro area is the European Central Bank. TARGET2 is the real-time gross settlement (RTGS) system owned and operated by the Eurosystem, which comprises the European Central Bank and the national central banks of the Member States whose currency is the euro. TARGET stands for Trans-European Automated Real-time Gross Settlement Express Transfer system. Real-time means that funds are moved instantaneously.

The transfer of funds between participant banks is carried out in TARGET2. Participants with net debit position which need to pay, must ensure to have sufficient funds on their accounts at the central bank. If that is not the case, a participant must make a transfer to credit his account. As already explained, if a participant fails and cannot pay, the other participants awaiting the funds will not request anything from it... but from the single counterparty, the clearing house. That is why clearing houses require collateral deposits (also called "margin deposits") from participants before they join. Clearing houses also provide a guarantee fund that can be used to cover losses that exceed a defaulting participant's collateral on deposit.

1.3.4 Direct and Indirect Participants

You read above that the transfer of funds happens between participant banks in TARGET2. We can be more precise by stating that the transfer of funds is made between *direct* participants in TARGET2. Banks can join a clearing system as direct participant or as indirect participant. In this paragraph, we will see the differences between these two types of participants and why only direct participants settle in TARGET2.

The following figure depicts direct and indirect participants and the relationship they have to the Clearing System (CS), which itself is connected to the Settlement System (SS). Strictly speaking, the CSM is the combination of Clearing Mechanism and Settlement Mechanism as shown in the picture. In practice, people often say CSM and think only of the Clearing System. That is a partial view. When you talk about CSM, it is good to always have both clearing and settlement systems in mind.

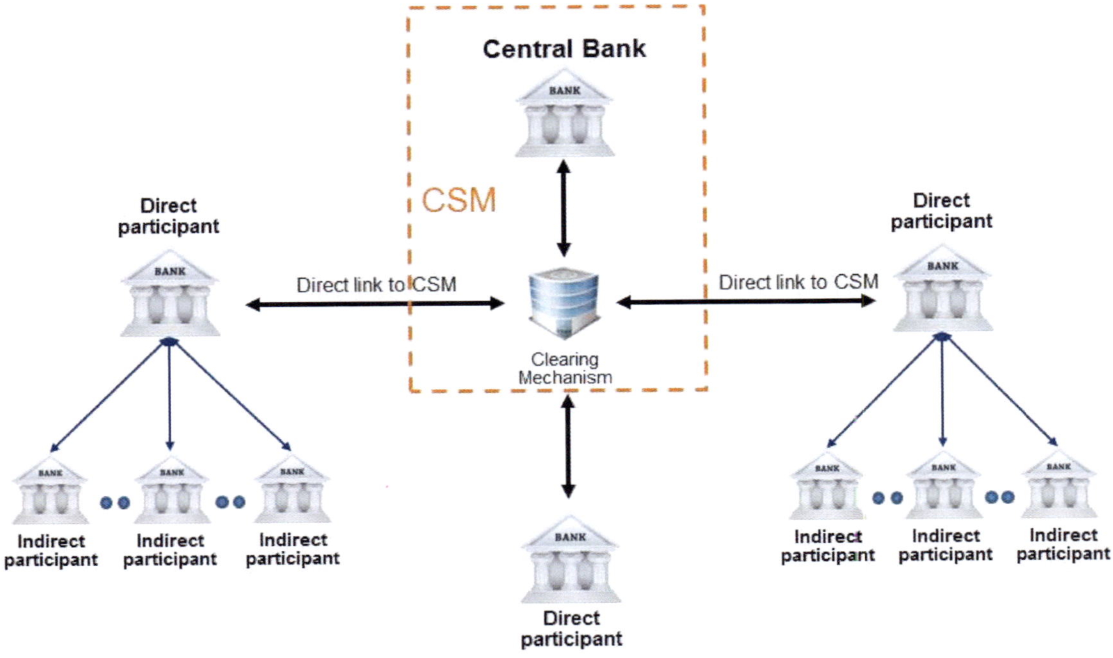

Figure 1.7: Direct and Indirect Participants to a CSM

Direct participants (DP) have a direct link to the CSM. They exchange payment transactions directly with the CS. Indirect participants do not have a direct link to the CSM. They have a connection to a direct participant which exchanges transactions with the CSM on their behalf. When the CSM receives a credit transfer from indirect participant through the direct participant, it expects the direct participant to pay the money not the indirect participant. And when the CSM sends a credit transfer to the indirect participant through the direct participant, it expects the direct participant to receive the money not the indirect participant.

The funds transfer between DP and CSM always happens through the Settlement System. The direct participant takes money from the indirect participant (IP) and gives it to the CSM and receives the money from the CSM and gives it to its indirect participant. Therefore, direct and indirect participants must have an account relationship. The indirect participant opens a so-called correspondent account with the direct participant, so that it can receive deposits from and make payments on behalf of the indirect participant. Correspondent accounts will be discussed in detail in an upcoming chapter.

Even if the CSM exchanges transactions only with DPs, it has the information about all indirect participants represented by a DP. The clearing system uses that information to route to the DP the transactions where the receiving bank is the IP. The payment transactions will ultimately reach the indirect participant. The money however will be debited or credited by the CSM on the DP account. It is the DP's responsibility to collect the funds from or give them to its IP.

Now why would a bank choose to be an indirect participant? In summary, there are two main reasons for that: cost and speed. First, becoming direct participant and setting up a connection to a CSM imply to carry out important projects. Without a minimal volume of transactions, there is no return on investment. Indirect participants are most of the time smaller banks which use the services of bigger banks to exchange their transactions. Thus, they can save the costs for running and maintaining a direct connection to a CSM. But a big bank with multiple subsidiaries in many SEPA countries can choose to have one direct participant and many indirect participants to lower the cost as well. Subsidiaries of that big bank can be of important size. But they remain indirect participant because the Bank Group has decided to have only one direct participant. The other reason is that it is easier and faster to establish a connection to a direct participant than to a CSM. A big American bank which creates a subsidiary in a SEPA country for example, may choose to start as an indirect participant and only builds its own connection to the CSM later.

Since indirect participants use the services of direct participants to access the clearing system, direct participants have the opportunity to get some revenue from their direct connection. But a direct participant must ensure a good level of quality and service to gain indirect participants as customers. There is theoretically no limit to the number of indirect participants that a direct participant can have. This makes the competition even tougher.

To conclude this paragraph, I want to stress the importance of understanding that indirect participants are banks like the others. They have their own customers and channels. They have their own IT systems. And please do not associate indirect participant with small size or direct participant with big size. A small bank can become a direct participant and a big bank can choose to be an indirect participant. Keep in mind that an indirect participant can connect to a CSM only through a direct participant.

1.3.5 Clearing systems in the SEPA zone

A list of SCT Scheme-compliant clearing systems in the SEPA zone is available on the EPC website[1]. This list is not exhaustive. Clearing systems of countries like Croatia, Great Britain or Switzerland are missing from list and it is well known that they do the clearing and settlement of SEPA payments as well. In spite of not having all CSMs on the EPC list, a study of the listed ones brought me to the following interesting observation. In terms of connection to participants, CSMs can be classified in three categories: National CSMs, Regional CSMs, Pan European CSMs.

A national CSM interconnects Banks within the boundaries of a country. Therefore , banks that are outside the country cannot become participants to that Clearing System. Examples of national CSMs are KIR of Poland and Iberpay of Spain. The Banks located in these countries exchange SCT among themselves primarily through the national CSM. Some national CSMs have the capacity to offer their services outside their boundaries and clear payments of foreign banks. But the proximity, the language barrier and national payments market specificities are major disadvantages preventing foreign banks to become their customers. It is hard to imagine a French Bank becoming direct participant to the Spanish CSM Iberpay or an English Bank becoming direct participant to KIR, the polish CSM. Obviously, the opposite is true in both cases.

A regional CSM interconnects Banks in many SEPA countries, but not in all the SEPA area. Banks located in all the countries where the CSM operate can become participants. An example of a regional CSM is Equens. Present in four countries of the SEPA zone, Equens has signed inter-CSM agreements with CSMs in more than 10 countries to clear transactions directly with these CSMs. It clears transactions through EBA as well. Due to all these connections, Equens can become a Single Point of Contact for Banks for the clearing of SCT and other types of payments toward all destinations in SEPA.
The CSM CORE of STET provides Clearing and Settlement Services to the French and Belgian banking communities. Belgian banks completed migration of SEPA and non-SEPA payment instruments to STET platform in March 2016. The future will tell us if STET is able to expand its services to other countries.

---

[1] http://www.europeanpaymentscouncil.eu/index.cfm/sepa-credit-transfer/sct-scheme-compliant-clearing-and-settlement-mechanisms-csms/

A Pan European CSM is a CSM to which Banks in all SEPA countries are connected. It is called a Pan European Automated Clearing House (PE-ACH). There is only one PE-ACH in the SEPA zone: STEP2. All banks in the SEPA area can exchange payment transactions through STEP2. From the beginning of SEPA with the Credit Transfer on 28 January 2008, STEP2 has been offering SCT processing services across all the SEPA countries. Euro Banking Association (EBA), the company that runs the STEP2 platform, has over 180 Members from the European Union and across the world. Two countries, Luxembourg and Finland, completed the migration of their domestic SEPA credit transfers to STEP2 in October 2006 and December 2011 respectively. Therefore, EBA STEP2 plays a key role in the clearing of SEPA payments not only in the whole SEPA area but also for specific countries in SEPA.

Many CSMs have established interoperability for SEPA with STEP2[2] and/or with other CSMs. This strategy enables them to provide full reach throughout SEPA. A participant connected to a national CSM can theoretically reach only banks located in the same country that are connected to the same CSM. The issue with this is that Banks of other SEPA countries are not reachable. There are essentially two ways to solve this problem:

1. The banks have to build a connection to another CSM to reach foreign Banks. This is the solution that has been chosen by the French banking community. In France, all big bank groups are direct participants to CORE, the national CSM and to STEP2, the PE-ACH. The direct participant banks must set up, run and maintain two connections to the clearing systems.
2. The national CSM can establish interoperability with STEP2 or with a CSM interoperable with STEP2. Direct participants can send all their transactions to the national CSM, a Single Point of Contact, which then routes them, either directly to the same country beneficiary bank or to the PE-ACH STEP2. This solution brings the following consequences: Each direct participant can save the costs related to building a direct connection to STEP2. The national CSM should become itself direct participant to STEP2.

The list of CSMs interoperating with STEP2 shows that at least, 15 countries have chosen the second solution. Big countries like Germany and Italy are among them. For the remaining countries, the solution 1 has been put in place. The rationale behind the decision of adopting the one or the other solution is not so easy to find out. There is very little communication and almost no articles about that subject.

One can think of risk mitigation for solution 1. The banks prefer multiple connections so that they can still be reachable in case one of the connections would fail. For solution 2, the cost reduction plays a more important role. The national CSM sets up a connection to STEP2, and all direct participants can save the cost to do the same.

What we have discussed above shows that Banks can be connected to one or multiple CSMs directly or through other CSMs. The next figure illustrates that.

---

2 Check this URL for more information: https://www.ebaclearing.eu/services/step2-t-platform/reachability/.

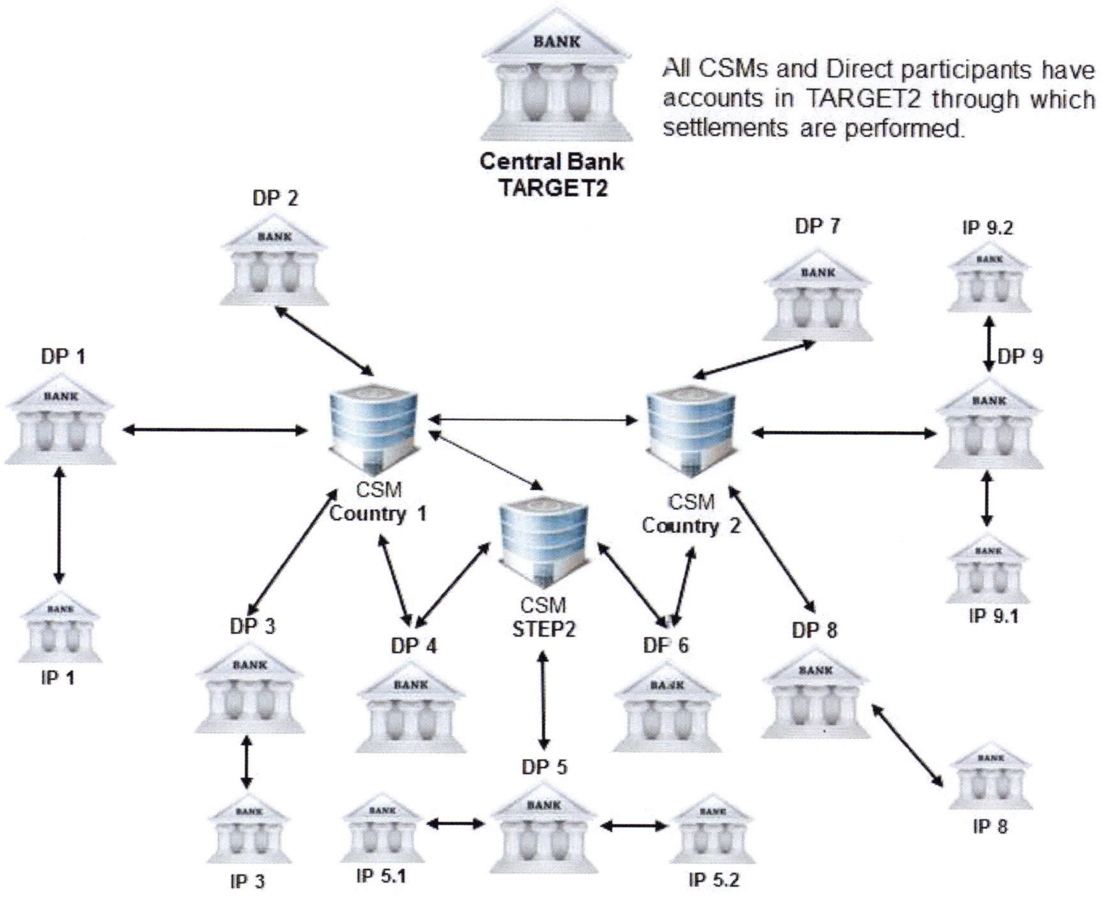

Figure 1.8: Interconnections of CSMs

Three CSMs are visible in the above figure: CSM of country 1, CSM of country 2 and STEP2. Direct Participants (DP) are connected to CSMs and Indirect Participants (IP) are connected to Direct Participants (DP). To make the drawing easy to understand, connections between CSMs, Banks and TARGET2 have been left out. But please remember that each bank has an account at the central bank and the settlements are carried out through accounts of CSMs and Direct Participants in TARGET2.

The CSM of country 1 is interoperating with CSM of country 2 and STEP2, each on a bilateral basis. The CSM of country 2 interoperates only with the CSM of country 1, but not with STEP2. Interoperability among CSMs is a very good thing for the reachability. Any participant can reach any other participant due to that. Let us take a couple of examples:

- IP 1 sends a transaction to IP 9.2: IP 1 first sends it to DP 1 which forwards it to the CSM it is connected to. The CSM of country 1 forwards the transaction to the CSM of country 2 since they have a bilateral agreement. In general it is less costly than going through STEP2. In any case, the CSM of country 2 sends the transaction to DP 9 which finally delivers it to IP 9.2. IP 1 can reach Banks in all the SEPA area even if its direct participant is connected to the country CSM. This is possible because of the bilateral agreement to interoperate.
- IP 3 sends a transaction to DP 5: IP 3 first sends it to DP 3 which forwards it to the CSM it is connected to. The CSM of country 1 forwards the transaction to STEP2. It cannot forward the transaction to the CSM of country 2 which does not have a connection to DP 5. STEP2 delivers the transaction to the final destination, DP 5.

- DP 4 sends a transaction to DP 6: There are multiple ways to reach DP 6. DP4 can send it to its national CSM. The CSM of country 1 then has to decide which way to take, if the transaction will be sent to the CSM of country 2 or to STEP2. Each of these CSM is connected to DP 6. As alternative DP 4 can send the transaction directly to STEP2 which will forward it to DP 6 to which STEP2 is directly connected.

Interoperability among CSMs drastically improves the reachability at network level. But the routing algorithms should be designed and implemented very carefully.

A last question remains. What do we really mean with interoperability at CSM level? You certainly think of CSMs that are able to exchange payments messages with other CSMs. And that is correct. The SEPA messages are well known and clearly described in standard. But why would CSMs still need to talk to each other? There are a least two reasons.

The first one is that CSMs do not wrap the SEPA messages in the same way. Let us take an image to illustrate this. Imagine that each CSM carries SEPA messages in its own kind of envelopes. The other CSMs must be able to open the envelopes before they can read the messages inside. The envelopes are not standardized. And CSMs have no choice than to talk to each other.

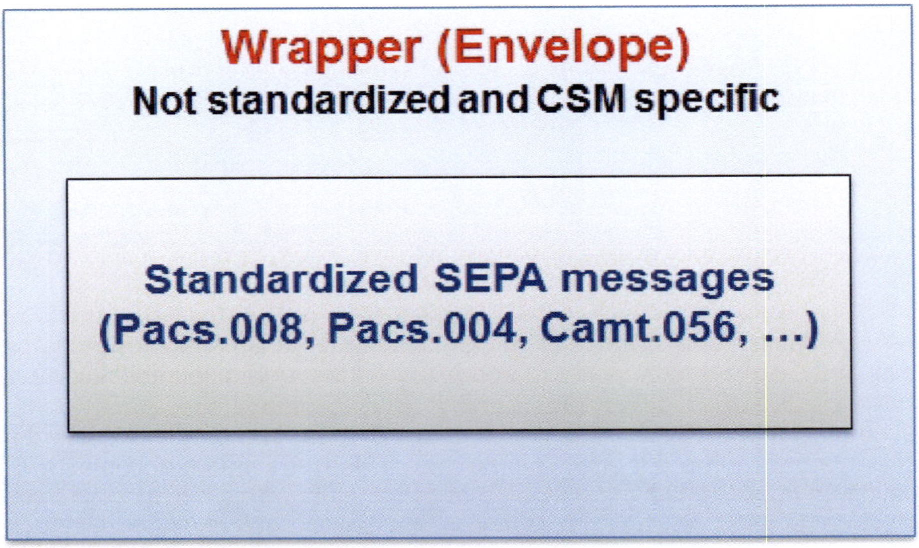

Figure 1.9: High level structure of a CSM Message

The second reason is that CSMs do not use the same protocol to transport their messages. Computer communication must follow very strict rules. And it is literally impossible to achieve it if CSMs do not agree on which rules they are going to follow. We will come back to protocol later. Just keep that in mind for now.

Finally, CSMs must align their clearing and settlement times, particularly for the beginning of the day and the end of the day. The end customer should not suffer because a national CSM is settling the transactions through STEP2. It means that the national CSM must ensure that the transactions reach STEP2 before it is too late, and can therefore be settled during the same day.

In conclusion, many clearing systems exist in the SEPA area. The majority operates in one country. Few of them are in two or more countries. And STEP2 is still the only real PE-ACH in

SEPA. Most of the CSMs have established interoperability with other CSMs and/or STEP2 to provide full reach throughout the SEPA area.

1.4 The messages exchanged in SEPA Credit Transfer Scheme

After having presented the four-cornel model and the clearing and settlement, let us now look at the messages exchanged between the different actors in SEPA. We will first limit ourselves to the messages mentioned in the EPC (European Payment Council) documents:

- EPC125-05 2017 SCT Rulebook version 1.1.pdf – SEPA Rulebook 2017 version 1.1
- EPC115-06 SCT Interbank IG 2017 V2.1.pdf– SEPA Interbank Implementation guidelines 2017 version 2.1
- EPC132-08 SCT C2B IG 2017 V1.0– SEPA Customer-to-bank Implementation guidelines 2017 version 1.0
- EPC188-09-Recommendation-on-Customer-Reporting-SCT-and-SDD

If you are not able to find these versions, just take the latest versions available.

The specifications of the messages are found in the implementation guidelines (IG). SEPA messages are all based on the ISO 20022 standard. In the Implementation guidelines, messages are presented as belonging to two spaces.

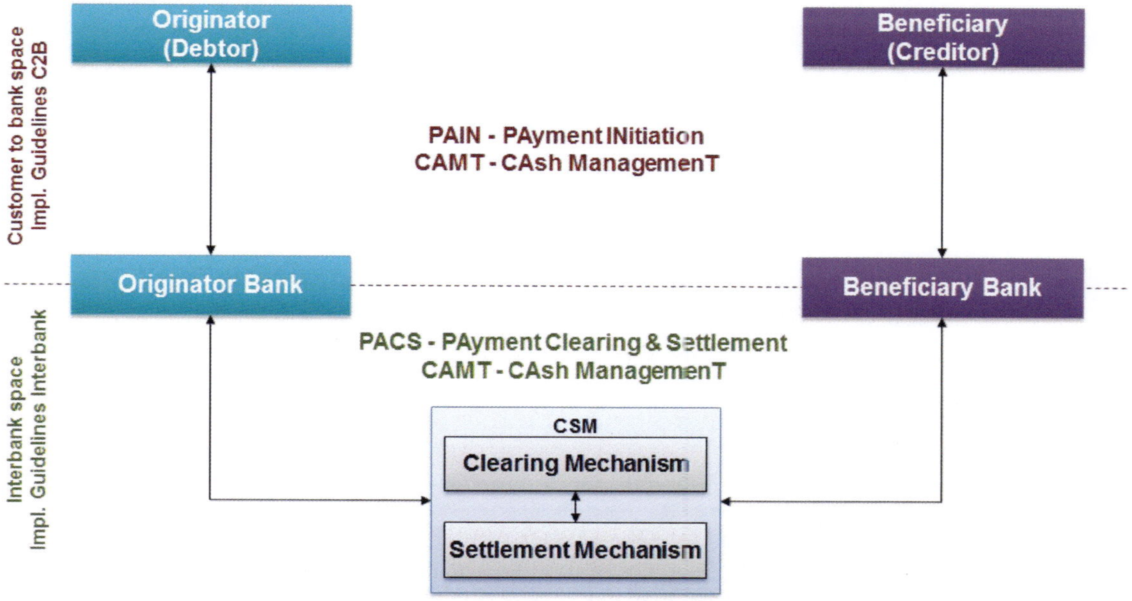

Figure 1.10: Customer-to-bank Space and Interbank Space of SCT

The spaces are depicted on the Figure 1.10: Customer-to-bank Space and Interbank Space of SCT: **Customer-to-bank** space on the top and **Interbank** space on the bottom:

- The customer-to-bank space refers to the area where customers and banks exchange messages. When the message goes from the Customer to the bank, it is called Customer-to-Bank messages. When it goes in the opposite direction, it is called Bank-to-Customer messages. In general, messages sent from customer-to-bank are orders or instructions while as messages sent from Bank-to-Customer fall under reporting.

- The Interbank space refers to the area where banks exchange messages among themselves. The exchange can be done either directly or through a CSM.

The picture below contains all the messages mentioned in the EPC documents and the direction in which they flow.

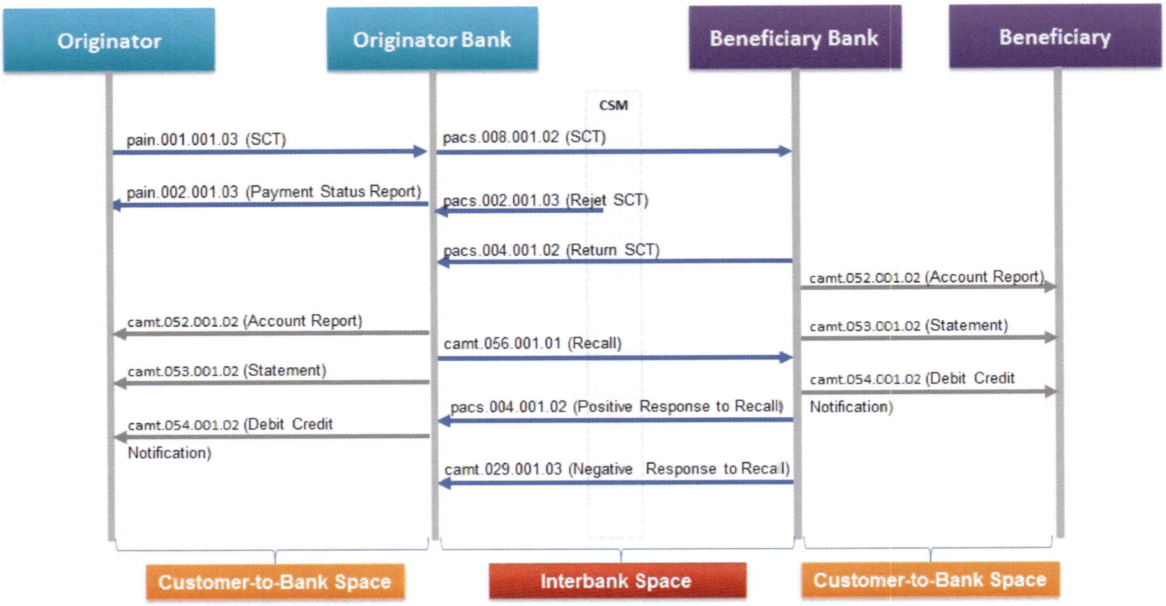

Figure 1.11: SEPA Messages available in the EPC documents

When we look at the naming of the messages, we see that they all begin with four letters:

- PAIN and CAMT in the Customer-to-Bank space
- PACS and CAMT in the Interbank space

These four letters are inherited from the ISO20022 standard:

- PAIN stands for **PA**yment **IN**itiation: Pain messages are used by originators to send instructions to the bank and received status report about their execution from the Bank. They are used exclusively in the C2B space.
- CAMT stands for **CA**sh **M**anagemen**T**: In the C2B space, Camt messages are used to inform the customer about his cash situation as a result of the execution of his instructions or reception of payments. Customers can also send camt messages to cancel orders or transactions. In the Interbank space, Camt messages are used to cancel orders or transactions as well, but also to reply on cancellation requests.
- PACS stands for **PA**yment **C**learing & **S**ettlement: Pacs messages are used to transfer money from one financial institution to another financial institution. They are used exclusively in the Interbank space.

Another interesting thing on messages' names is the series of numbers after the four letters. For instance, you may wonder when you see Pacs.**008.001.02,** why do we have the numbers **008.001.02**? And is there any meaning behind?

The explanation is found in the standard ISO 20022. The four letters and the three digits after Pacs, Camt or Pain identify a specific message. The pain.001 message is used to send **credit transfer** orders or instructions from a Customer to the Bank. The pacs.008 message is used for the clearing and settlement of **credit transfers** between financial institutions. Those messages cannot be used for direct debits. If the customer wants to send direct debit instructions, he has to use another message. He cannot use the pain.001 for that. Same thing applies for the pacs.008. It is used for the clearing and settlement of credit transfers. If a bank wants to clear and settle direct debits, it will have to use another type of message. So, every time you see pain.001, you know it is about **credit transfer** orders from a Customer to the Bank. And every time you see pacs.008, you know it is about **credit transfer** clearing and settlement between financial institutions.

What about the five last digits (Pain.001.**001.03**)? All of them are used for the versioning of the messages. Pain.001.001.03 means version 1.3 of the pain.001 message. When a new version of the message is published, only the last digit is increased. The next version after the Pain.001.001.03 is the Pain.001.001.0**4**. It means that we will have the Pain.001.**002.00** after the Pain.001.**001.99**. That will not happen before some time.

Now If you look at all the messages carefully, you see that the digits 4, 5 and 6 are always the same 001. Pain.001.001.03, Pacs.008.001.02, Pacs.004.001.02, Camt.054.001.02, and so on. This is the case because ISO 20022 has been around for a couple of years only. All the messages have the version **001**.0X. The 001 does not have an important meaning now since all the ISO 20022 messages have it at the same positions. That is why, the 001 is generally ignored when the message version is given and only the last two digits are considered. People would say: "Can you process the pain version 2 (instead of version 1.2)?", which would mean Pain.001.001.02.

After this brief presentation, it is now time to go through each message that appeared in SEPA Credit transfer EPC books and look at their meaning. In the following paragraph, I will first present the messages used in the customer-to-bank space and then those used in the interbank space.

1.4.1 Messages in the Customer-to-bank space

As introduction, let me stress an important point out of the EPC documents: the messages exchanged in the Customer-to-Bank space were initially *recommended*[3], but are now *mandatory*. It means that banks must accept messages from their customers that are formatted as specified the Implementation Guidelines. However, a bank and his customer can still agree to add specific rules or tags to the messages. The practice shows that it is better to stick to the standard. Bringing in specific rules and requirements that are not compliant with SEPA increases the complexity and the costs for all parties on the long term.

1.4.1.1 Pain.001.001.03 (SCT orders)

As already mentioned, the pain.001 message is used for transmitting customer credit transfer instructions to a Bank. The purpose is to request movement of funds from the debtor account to one or multiple creditor accounts. As private individual, you don't send a pain.001 message to your bank. In general, you will go to your bank website or to a branch and no one will ask you to provide the pain.001 message. Who then uses pain.001 messages? Enterprises, associations, non-governmental organizations and similar institutions do. In short, any company or institution that needs to initiate a sizable number of payment orders. Solutions for individuals are not appropriate for them.

Let us consider a large telecommunication company with thousands of employees. Manual entry of payment instructions for the salaries in a website provided by a bank will take a huge amount of time. In addition to that, the probability to make errors is very high. To avoid all those problems, the telecommunication company will create the pain.001 message directly from its ERP or treasury system and send it to the Bank. It requires the setting up of a secured

---

[3] You can download and check a previous version of the Implementation guidelines (Year 2015 for example)

connection to the bank since the information exchanged is very sensitive. We will come back to that later. For now, just keep in mind that pain.001 message is used by corporations to send customer credit transfer orders to their Banks.

Another interesting point about the pain.001 is that two versions are used in SEPA: Pain.001.001.02 and Pain.001.001.03. If you go to the ISO20022 website[4], you will see that there is already a version 8 of the pain.001 message (pain.001.001.08). It means that the standard ISO 20022 has evolved since the version 3. Obviously, the EPC has not recommended the use of recent versions because previous versions still fit the needs of corporations for SEPA payments well. If you are interested in the differences between the two pain.001 versions, I refer you the end of paragraph 2.4.2.

1.4.1.2 Pain.002.001.03 (Payment Status Report)

The pain.002 message is sent by the Bank to the customer to inform him about the positive or negative status of customer credit transfer orders. When Banks receive orders, they perform checks to ensure that they can accept and process the orders. If something goes wrong and the order cannot be accepted and processed for one reason or another, the customer must be informed. This reporting is critical for the customer. If he receives nothing, he can assume that the bank has correctly executed the orders. And if that assumption is wrong and your own salary was in the instruction, it will not be funny at all for you. ☺

In a later chapter, we will analyze the kind of problems that can occur during the processing of those instructions.

1.4.1.3 Bank to Customer Reporting messages

The EPC recommends three messages for the customer reporting. The bank can use one or many of them, according to client's needs, to provide account reports, account statements and debit/credit notification. It is important to understand that these reporting messages are for customers which can integrate and process them in own IT systems. They are not supposed to be read by humans. Therefore, banks deliver these reporting messages almost exclusively to corporate customers or important nongovernmental organizations.

Camt.052.001.02 (Bank To Customer Account Report): The account report is generally used for reporting *intra-day* transactions and balances. If you know customer reporting in SWIFT MT format, it is equivalent to MT941 Balance Report, and MT942 Interim Transaction Report. The term intraday needs some clarification. Intraday basically means "within the day". Intraday reporting's give information to the customers about what has happened on their account during a period of the day. It can be from early in the morning to 10:00 am, then from 10:00 am to 2:00 pm and so on. Some companies ask their banks to send many of these intraday reporting's because managing their business requires it. They can thus have a view on what is happening on the short term and make better financial decisions.

Camt.053.001.02 (Bank to Customer Account Statement): The Bank-to-Customer statement message is created by **the bank** to report balance data, debits and credits booked on the account. Debit or Credit transactions are specified in the statement. In the SWIFT MT world, it is equivalent to MT940 Customer Statement Message and MT950 Statement Message. An account statement contains an opening balance and a close balance. The difference between those balances is the sum of all credits and debits on the account during the timeframe considered for the statement. The debits and credits may come from the execution of credit transfer instructions or from other kind of transactions (direct debit,

---

[4] http://www.iso20022.org/payments_messages.page

international payments and so on). The bank relies on account management applications to provide all the information. In general, corporate customers will receive the statement each day. The periodicity is set in a bilateral agreement. Some customers may want to receive them on a weekly or biweekly basis.

Camt.054.001.02 (Bank to Customer Debit Credit Notification): The Bank-to-Customer Debit / Credit Notification includes transactions and related amounts, but no balance data. The customer gets information about the transactions which are debited or credited to his accounts and can act upon if needed. For customer reporting in SWIFT MT format, it is the equivalent of MT900 Confirmation of Debit and MT910 Confirmation of Credit. However, many debit and credit information can be bulked in the same camt.054 message. This report is generally delivered to the customer on an ad hoc basis.

1.4.2 Messages in the interbank space

The messages exchanged in the interbank space have always been and are *mandatory*. It means banks must comply with all the underlying SEPA rules. This is to ensure that their messages can be received and processed by any participant to the interbank space. Banks can exchange messages directly between themselves or through a Clearing and Settlement Mechanism. In this paragraph, each message used in the interbank space will be presented and analyzed.

1.4.2.1 Pacs.008.001.02 (SCT)

The ***Financial Institution to Financial Institution Customer Credit Transfer message*** is used to move the money from the sending bank to the destination bank. When the bank of the debtor sends the pacs.008, it is like it is saying to the bank of the beneficiary: “Here is money I have debited from my customer. Please take the money and credit your customer whose account information is available in the payment.” But the real movement of money happens only after clearing and settlement. Therefore, the credit transfer must have a settlement date, which is the date where the funds transfer is done from the originator bank to the beneficiary bank.

The pacs.008 is by far the message with the highest volumes in the interbank space. In an ideal world where nothing unwanted would happen during the processing of those messages, the other messages would not be needed at all. But we know that it is not the right way of thinking. Don’t we? *There is no process without exception.* Indeed, many exceptions can happen during the processing of the credit transfer either at Debtor bank or at Creditor bank. When an exception occurs, banks should be able to handle it properly and provide the correct information to their peers or customers.

The exceptions! The exceptions! Our lives would be much easier in the payment world without them. One message is required to move the money, but many are needed to handle the exceptions. Let us now look at the exception handling messages. They are also called related transactions or r-transactions because they all relate to the original pacs.008.

1.4.2.2 Pacs.002.001.03 (Payment Status Report or Reject SCT)

SEPA Credit Transfer and R-transactions messages can be rejected for many reasons: the message is not readable because the XML format is invalid. The IBAN or the BIC specified in the message is invalid, and so on. Rejections of pacs.008 messages can happen at many levels as we will see later. The pacs.002 provides the information about the level and the original message which has been rejected.

For two banks that exchange transactions through a CSM, the credit transfer message first must go through the CSM. The CSM rejects the message if it fails the checks, and sends a pacs.002 to the originator Bank. In the majority of the cases, the reject message is sent by the CSM and not by the beneficiary Bank. If a CSM creates a pacs.002, the rejected pacs.008 will obviously not be settled at settlement date.

A direct participant bank sends a pacs.002 to indirect participants to inform them about transactions that have been rejected. When that happens, the related transactions do not reach the CSM and thus cannot be settled.

According to the SCT rulebook, the CSM or the Bank, that sends a pacs.002 message, must do it either the same day where the pacs.008 was received or at the latest on the next business day.

1.4.2.3 Pacs.004.001.02 (Return SCT)

The Payment Return message is used to undo a payment previously settled. When a bank receives a pacs.008, it should process it and books the money to the beneficiary account. But what if the beneficiary closed his account two days ago? What if the account does not exist at all in the Bank? In those cases, the bank will not be able to credit the account. According to the SEPA rules, the beneficiary bank must *return* the money to the originator Bank. Besides the reasons mentioned above, there are numerous reasons why a bank might have to return the money. In any case, it will use the pacs.004 message to do that. The return has its own settlement date, the date at which the money will be paid back to the originator bank. The reason for returning the funds is indicated by a code in the return message.

A bank can only return the money that it has previously received. So the payment return message is initiated and sent after settlement. The SEPA rules oblige the Beneficiary Bank to send the Return message to the Originator Bank at the latest three Banking Business Days after Settlement Date. The underlying principle is that money should be return as soon as possible to the originator.

1.4.2.4 Camt.056.001.01 (Recall SCT)

The Debtor Bank makes use of the recall message to submit cancellation requests to the Beneficiary bank. But why would a Debtor bank want to cancel a previously sent credit transfer (pacs.008)? Several reasons exist. The credit transfer can be sent two times because of a human error for instance. Or a technical error may cause the sending of erroneous pacs.008 messages. In both cases, the debtor will try to get his money back by sending a cancellation request. Please notice that a cancellation request does not move money. It is not a booking message and therefore there is no settlement date in the camt.056 message.

According to the SEPA rules, the originator bank can send the cancellation request up to 10 days after the settlement of the credit transfer message. After reception of the request, the beneficiary bank has two choices: to accept or to refuse.

Remark: In the 2017 SCT Rulebook, the Request for Recall by the Originator was introduced and will enter into force as of 18 November 2018. It allows the debtor under certain conditions to claim the funds reimbursement of a settled credit transfer up to 13 months after settlement.

1.4.2.5 Pacs.004.001.02 (Positive Response to Recall)

The positive response to a recall is sent by the beneficiary Bank, when it *responds favorably* to the demand of the originator bank to cancel the original payment. The name of this message is familiar to us. We saw before that the Payment Return message, which is used by the beneficiary bank to return funds when they cannot be credited to the beneficiary account, is also a pacs.004. The positive response to a cancellation request is a payment return. But in this case the return is not made because the money cannot be credited. The funds are returned because the originator bank has requested to have them back. The beneficiary account has been credited and it has to be debited in order to give the funds back. In most countries, the law obliges beneficiary banks to explicitly get the consent of their clients before returning the funds. The bank must get the customer approval before returning the funds and that may take few days.

The positive response message is a return message with the particular reason code FOCR (Following Cancellation Request). A reason code indicates why the beneficiary bank returns the funds. For a positive response to a cancellation request, the only reason code allowed is FOCR. If there is another reason code in the pacs.004, it is considered a normal return, not a positive response to a cancellation request.

According to the SEPA rulebook, the beneficiary bank can send the positive response to a cancellation request up to 10 business days after the reception of the cancellation request message.

1.4.2.6 Camt.029.001.03 (Negative Response to Recall / Resolution of Investigation)

The negative response to a recall is sent by the beneficiary Bank, when it *responds unfavorably* to the demand of the originator bank to cancel the original payment. The negative response, also called resolution of investigation, informs the debtor bank that his request has been rejected and therefore it will not get the money back.

The camt.029 is not a booking message. It means that there is no movement of funds associated with it. It just gives the information that the beneficiary bank or the beneficiary refuses to give the money back.

According to the SEPA Business rules, the beneficiary bank can send the negative response to a cancellation request up to 10 business days after the reception of the cancellation request message.

Now let us look at the messages again and particularly at the periods during which the different types of messages can be exchanged in the interbank space. Those periods are visible in the diagram below where we have a timeline beginning at D-3 (3 business days before the settlement date) and ending at D+20 (20 business days after the settlement date).

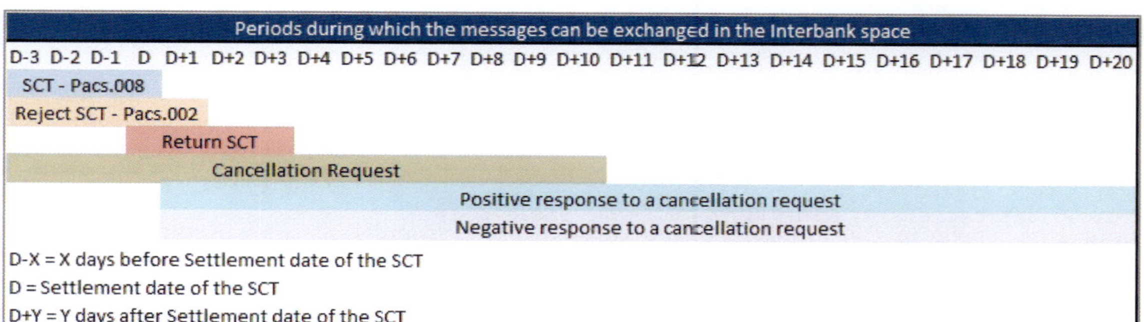

You may wonder why we start at D-3. It is simply because some ACHs allow the participants to transmit pacs.008 messages up to three business days in advance. The originator bank can therefore send the pacs.008 message for the Clearing and Settlement of SCT up to three days before settlement to the settlement date. In practice however, the pacs.008 message is forwarded to the CSM on settlement date or the day before. The reason is simple. The debtor bank executes the payment order and debits the customer before transmitting the message to the CSM. And *it can debit the customer only on settlement date or the day before.* It cannot debit the customer 2 or 3 days before. That would be against the rulebook which defines the SCT Maximum Execution Time to one banking business day: “Originator Banks are obliged to ensure that the amount of the Credit Transfer is credited to the account of the Beneficiary Bank within one Banking Business Day following the point in time of receipt of the Credit Transfer Instruction in accordance with the provisions of the Payment Services Directive.”

In case the CSM cannot process a message, it will send a reject SCT to the debtor bank. This is general done in the seconds following the reception of the SCT messages even if the SEPA rules allow the CSM to reply at the latest one day after it got the SCT. A reject SCT can therefore be sent from three days before settlement to one day after requested settlement.

When the beneficiary bank receives an SCT that cannot be credited to the customer account, it can return the money immediately, but at the latest three business days after the settlement. So the return SCT can be initiated and transmitted from D settlement date (after receiving the SCT) up to D+3.

The cancellation request can be sent as soon as possible after the SCT was sent, but at the latest 10 business days after the settlement of the SCT. If a recall is sent before the settlement, i.e. between D-3 and D before settlement, the CSM can cancel the SCT at the reception of the cancellation. That is what the PEACH STEP2 does. It does not forward the credit transfer and the recall to the beneficiary bank. It just informs the debtor bank that the cancellation of the original transaction was successful. If the SCT has already been settled, the CSM cannot cancel it. It has to forward it to the beneficiary bank which will then take the decision to respond positively or negatively.

The positive and negative response to cancellation request must be sent by the beneficiary bank as soon as possible but at the latest ten business days after the reception of the cancellation request message. So if the beneficiary bank gets the recall message exactly ten days after the settlement of the SCT, it can reply ten days later, which makes 20 days after the settlement of the SCT.

1.4.3 Intrabank and Intrabankgroup transactions

The word *Intra* is a prefix meaning "within something, inside something, on the inside". An intrabank transaction is a transaction exchanged inside or within the same bank. An intrabankgroup transaction is a transaction exchanged inside or within the same bankgroup. An intrabankgroup transaction can also be seen as an interbank transaction between two different banks of the same bankgroup. In the payments world, these two categories of transactions are called ***“on-us transactions”***. For someone working in a one bank of a bankgroup, “on-us” means intrabank while it may mean intrabankgroup for someone working at bankgroup level. It is important to have that distinction in mind to avoid misunderstandings. In any case, the exchange of on-us transactions does not require going through a CSM. They may go through a CSM, but it is not required. This paragraph is about *on-us transactions* at bank level or at bankgroup level.

1.4.3.1 Intrabank transactions

Intrabank transactions occur when the intermediary bank is the same on both sides of the credit transfer. Both debtor and beneficiary are customers of the same bank which holds their accounts. Consequently the debtor bank and the creditor bank are identical. In that case, there is no clearing needed and the transaction is settled directly through an internal book transfer. The bank debits the originator account and credits the beneficiary account. These transactions can be executed much faster than the ones which have to go through the clearing and settlement process in a CSM.

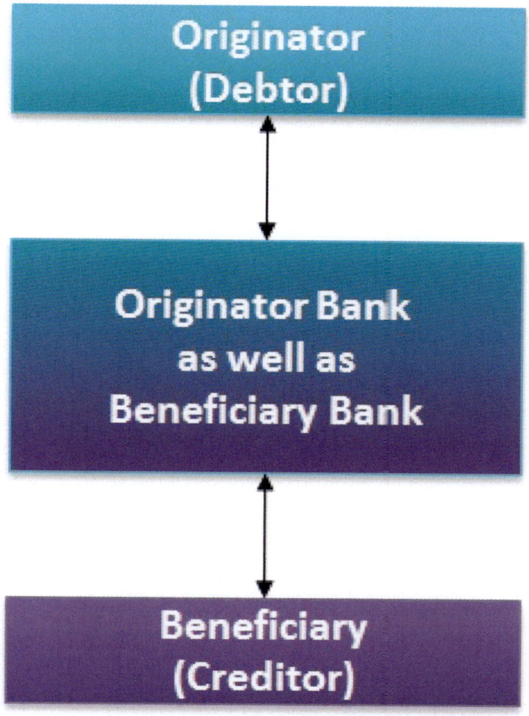

Figure 1.12: Model for intrabank transfer

The bigger the bank, the larger the customer base and the higher the percentage of on-us transactions because the probability of having transactions between the bank customers increases. Furthermore, many customers have multiple accounts (current accounts, saving accounts, etc) and need to move funds from one of their accounts to another. They initiate intrabank transactions for that purpose as well. As a matter of fact, the number of intrabank transactions between accounts of the same customer is much higher than between accounts of two different customers in a bank.

On-us transactions at bankgroup level bring other challenges. We will now take a closer look at them.

1.4.3.2 Intrabankgroup transactions

In a wider sense on-us transactions occur where the originator bank and the beneficiary bank are separate entities but belong to same bankgroup. A bank group consists of many banks located in the same country or in different countries. Below are some examples:

- In France, large mutualist bank groups like Credit Agricole and BPCE are composed of dozens of regional banks each. And they have subsidiaries located in other SEPA countries as well.
- Many bank groups in SEPA like Deutsche Bank, ING and Nordea have subsidiaries in many SEPA countries.

In general, the banks within the same group exchange payment transactions directly among themselves without going through a CSM. These transactions, the intrabankgroup transactions, are settled directly by moving the funds inside the group. But more steps are needed here. It is not the same as for intrabank transactions, where the bank can just debit the debtor account and credit the beneficiary account in its own book. Since two different banks are involved, funds have to go through many internal accounts before reaching the beneficiary account. In Chapter 6 , you will understand how this is done.

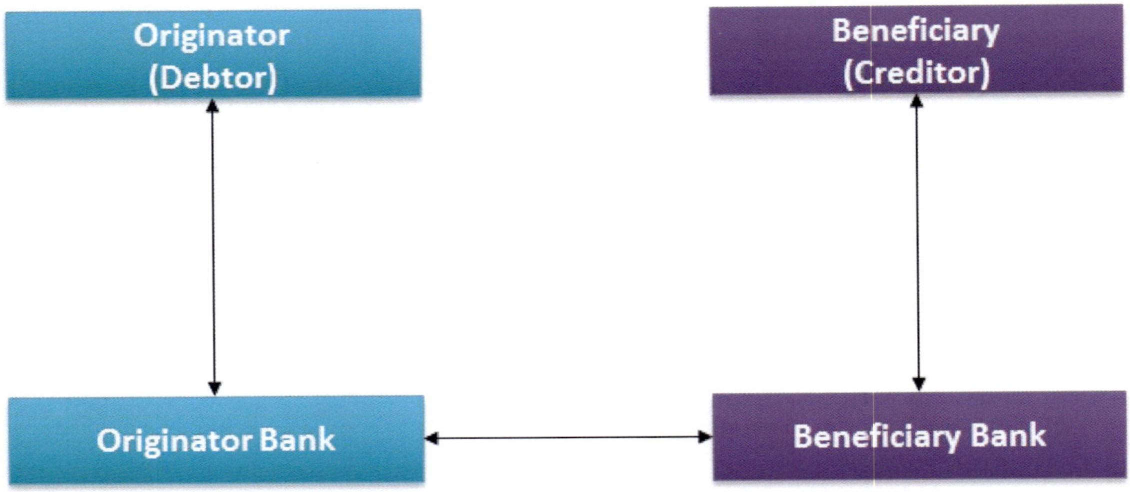

Figure 1.13: Model for Intrabankgroup transfer

This looks like a real four corner model. Doesn't it? There are exactly four actors and there is no CSM between the banks involved. The reality is slightly different because banks are not connected directly to each other but through a platform as we see in the next figure. The platform belongs in general to the major office of the bankgroup.

An exchange platform is put in place to avoid the creation of many bilateral links between the different banks of the bank group. The platform not only allows all banks of the group to connect to each other but also to share same connection(s) to one or several CSM through which external banks can be reached.

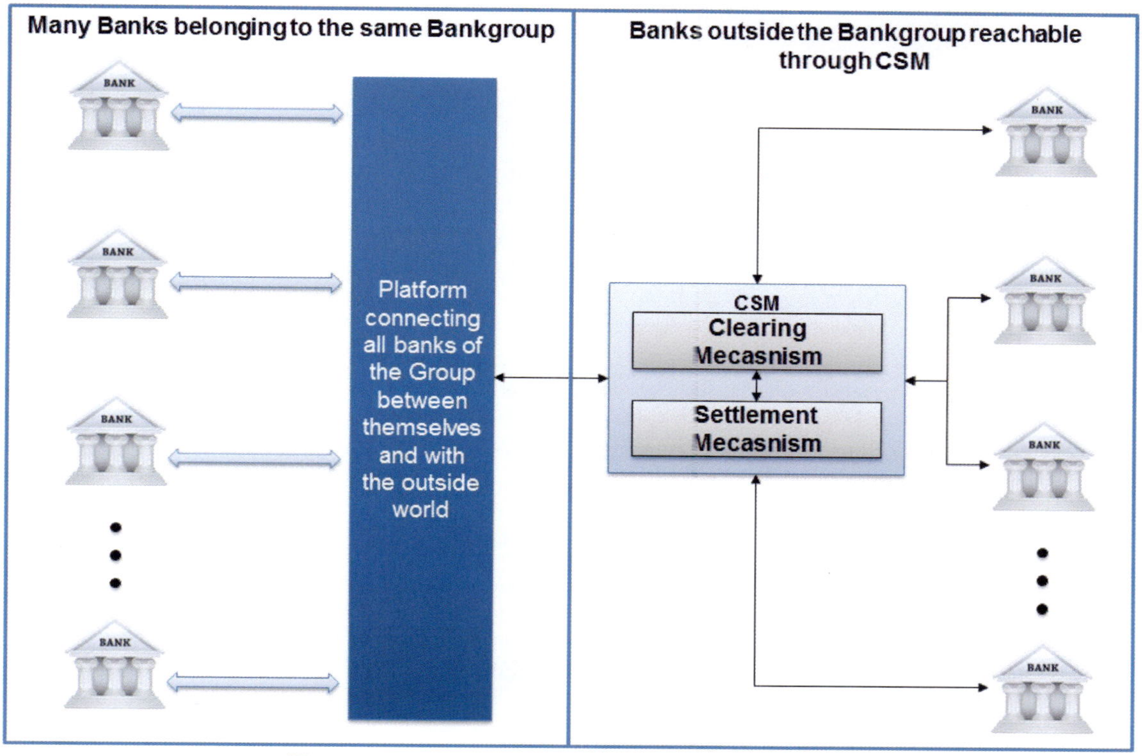

Figure 1.14: Exchange platform of a Bankgroup

The routing intelligence is implemented in the exchange platform. It is quite simple in principle. If a payment coming from one bank of the group has another bank of the group as destination, the platform will route it directly to that bank. But if a payment coming from one bank of the group has as destination a bank outside the group, then the platform will route it to the CSM which will do the final routing to the correct destination.

The volumes of on-us transactions at bank and bankgroup level are not negligible in large bank group. They can amount to several thousand or even millions daily. This makes the platform an essential system for the payment services provided by the bank group. In the next paragraph, I will come back to the messages exchanged between originator and beneficiary bank and draw your attention to a key point. Read on.

1.4.4 Originator bank and Beneficiary bank messages

There is a trap to avoid at the beginning of your journey in the exiting world of payments. Beginners tend to think that:

- the Debtor Bank only sends credit transfer to move the funds from the debtor to the beneficiary. And it is not supposed to receive any message.
- the Creditor Bank only receives messages with the funds from the debtor bank and credit the beneficiary account. It is not supposed to send any message.

One reason why beginners tend to think that way is because they have probably skipped that part in the SEPA rulebooks (it comes a bit far in the document) or they have not received a proper training on what SEPA Credit transfer is about and the different messages. This book is supposed to help you overcome these obstacles. But this book is not intended to replace the EPC documents or to make a summary of them. Reading this book will help you understand them faster. So please do take the time to go through them. Another reason, I think, comes from beginners' personal experience with credit transfers that they make or receive. People give instructions to the bank to move the funds and that is what happens almost all the time. Or their account is credited when a credit transfer arrives and they have never received a cancellation request to return the funds. As originator or beneficiary, customers barely see the exceptions.

Yes the originator bank sends the credit transfer to move the funds. But it does much more as we can see in the picture below. It receives all the messages resulting from exception handling like the reject from the CSM, the payment return or the responses to a cancellation request. The debtor bank must evidently send a cancellation request before it can receive the related responses.

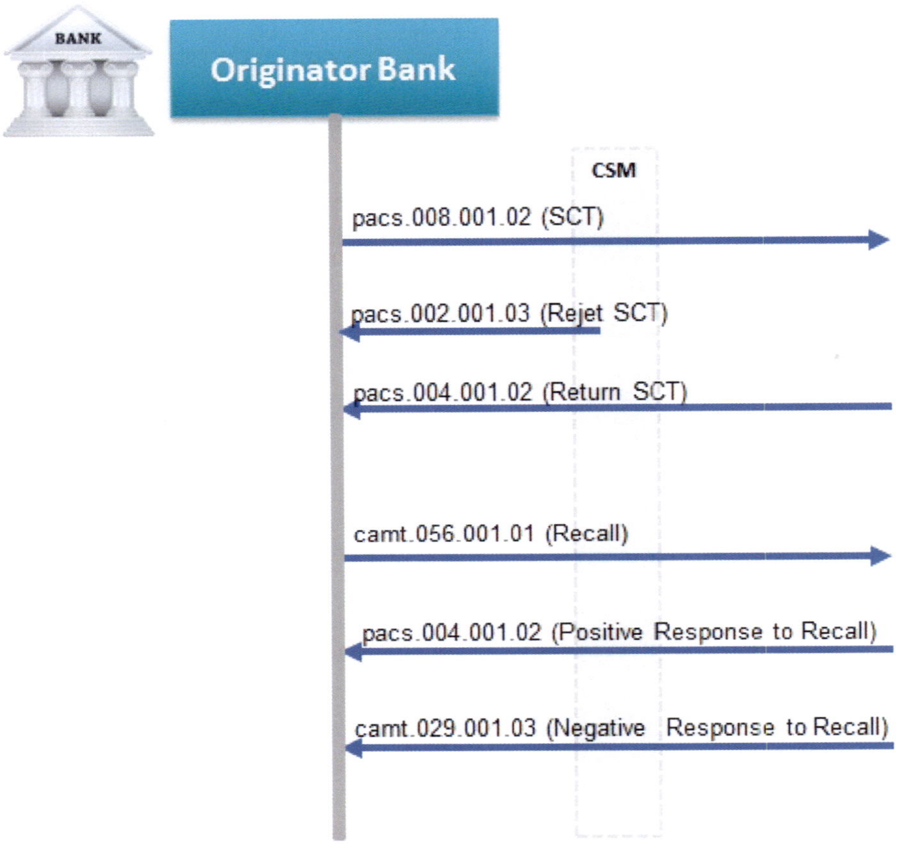

Figure 1.15: Debtor bank outgoing and incoming mandatory messages

So as a debtor bank, it is not sufficient just to send the credit transfer. The debtor bank must be able to send and receive all the other messages. Remember that all the messages are mandatory in the interbank space. A bank that can only send credit transfers, but not receive payment returns is not SEPA compliant and cannot adhere to the Scheme. The banks must have the ability to process all the messages to become member of the SEPA community.

The same thing applies for the beneficiary bank. Yes it receives the credit transfers. But it does much more that. It sends all the messages resulting from exception handling like the payment return or the responses to a cancellation request. The beneficiary bank may also receive a cancellation request. And if it happens, it must of course handle it and reply correctly.

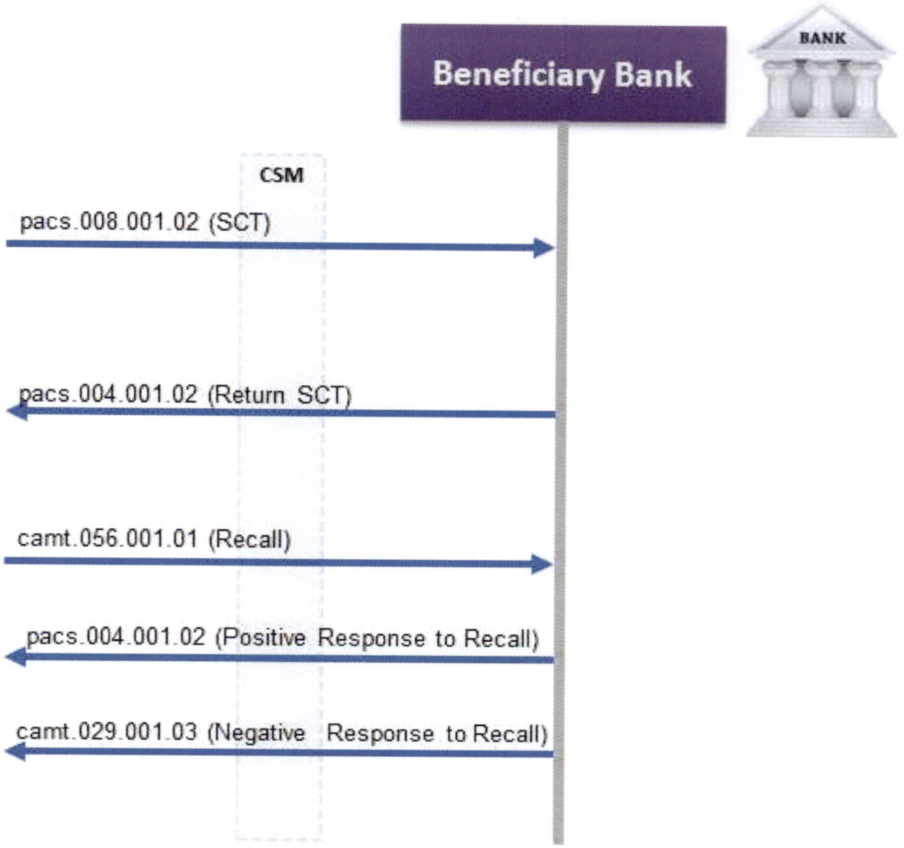

Figure 1.16: Beneficiary bank incoming and outgoing mandatory messages

So as a beneficiary bank, it is not sufficient just to receive the credit transfer. The beneficiary bank must be able to send and receive all the other messages, which are mandatory in the interbank space. A beneficiary bank that can only receive credit transfers, but not send payment returns is not SEPA compliant and cannot adhere to the Scheme. What will happen if such a bank receives a credit transfer that cannot be credited on a customer account because the account is close for instance? Keeping the money is not acceptable and sending the money back through another credit transfer is not what the Scheme expects. A return message must be sent back to the originator bank. Handling the exceptions is a must to become participant to the Scheme.

Another interesting thing to note when we look at the interbank space is the symmetry of messages exchanges between originator bank and beneficiary bank. All messages sent by the originator bank are received by the beneficiary bank and vice versa. The debtor bank does exactly the opposite of what the creditor bank is supposed to do.

The debtor bank and only the debtor bank sends the pacs.008. It never receives it. But the beneficiary bank does. The debtor bank and only the debtor bank sends the camt.056. it never receives it. But the creditor bank does. The beneficiary bank and only the beneficiary bank sends the pacs.004. It never receives it. I am insisting on this to help you grasp a very important point in SCT and SEPA payment in general: *The roles of debtor bank and beneficiary bank can be completely decoupled in the implementation, since they don't do the same thing.*

It is possible to process the debtor bank's messages in one IT application and to have another completely different application handle the beneficiary bank's messages. If you see the same application sending and receiving credit transfers at the same time (and the messages for exceptions handling of course), then it means that the application is handling both debtor bank and beneficiary bank messages. Many CSM see participants as Debtor and Creditor bank at the same time. When a CSM bulks pacs.008 and pacs.004 in the same file and delivers it to a direct participant, the direct participant handles the received pacs.008 as beneficiary bank, but the received pacs.004 as debtor bank.

If everything is not clear for you, don't worry. We will come back to this later when we will look at the payments value chain applied to the SEPA Credit Transfers and how it is generally implemented in a bank's IT system.

Review Questions

1. Draw the two models that payments systems operate with. What are their advantages and drawbacks? Is it possible to combine these two models?
2. List and describe the different types of end parties in the four corner model of the SCT. What are their needs? How can banks respond to them?
3. Explain the concept of clearing and illustrate with examples the differences between bilateral and multilateral clearing.
4. Explain the concept of settlement. What is the difference between Gross settlement and Net Settlement?
5. Define direct participant and indirect participant. Illustrate the relationship between the two in a figure.
6. List the messages exchanged in the SEPA credit transfer scheme. Which ones are used in the Customer-to-Bank space? And which ones are used in the Interbank space?

Discussion Questions

1. Many industry leaders predicted that the number of clearing systems will fall down with the time. Have these predictions proven to be true? What do think? What does the future hold?

2. The volumes of Intrabank and interbank group transactions is growing in many countries and geographies. What are the reasons behind? Can we expect a different tendency in the future?

3. The SCT scheme rules are stricter in the Interbank space than in the customer-to-bank space. Do you agree with this sentence? Justify your response in any case.

Chapter 2 The standard ISO 20022 and the SCT implementations guidelines

LEARNING OBJECTIVES

After reading this chapter, you will be able to answer the following questions:

1. What is the standard ISO 20022?
2. What are the differences between the standard ISO 20022 and the SEPA implementations guidelines?
3. What are additional optional services in SEPA?
4. What are the structures of the different messages formats exchanged in the SCT scheme?

The SEPA messages formats (pain.001, pacs.008, camt.056, and so on) are based on the global ISO 20022 standard. To get along with the structure and content of SEPA messages, we must first understand what the standard ISO 20022 is and how SEPA messages are related to it. This chapter therefore begins with a brief presentation of the ISO 20022. After that, we will look at the differences between the SCT implementations guidelines and the standard ISO 20022. The next logical step will be to consider the so-called AOS (Additional Optional Services) in SEPA. In the final part, a thorough analysis of each SCT Scheme message will be carried out.

2.1 *Introduction to the standard ISO 20022*

A standard is a widely accepted, agreed upon, or established definition of what something should be. According to the British Standards Institution, a standard is “a published specification that establishes a *common language*, and contains a technical specification or other precise criteria and is designed to be used consistently, as a rule, a guideline, or a definition.” The standard ISO 20022 is a Financial Messaging standard, a *common language* that financial institutions can use for the exchanges of financial information with their customers and among themselves.

Like a common language for people, the ISO 20022 standard provides the great advantage of facilitating and improving communication in the financial industry. Nowadays computers are used to process information including financial messages. The ISO 20022 standard allows not only the exchange of structured information, but it is also possible to rely entirely on computers to process it.

The ISO 20022 covers five financial business domains: Payments, Securities, Trade services, Cards, FX (Foreign Exchanges). The payments domain specifies messages supporting payments initiation, clearing and settlement, account and cash management. The ISO 20022 organizes payment message definitions in business areas, which are uniquely identified by four-character codes called business area codes:

- **acmt:** Account Management
- **camt:** Cash Management
- **pacs:** Payments Clearing and Settlement
- **pain:** Payments Initiation

The ISO 20022 message definition consists of two main elements: the syntax and the semantics. The syntax describes the format in which the information in an ISO 20022 message is structured. The syntax used in ISO 20022 is the eXtensible Mark-up Language (XML). The content of a message is put between message elements or XML tag like <FIToFICstmrCdtTrf> for Financial Institution to Financial Institution Customer Credit Transfer. Tag names are defined in such a way that they can be easily understood and remembered by humans. Each tag can itself have sub tags (child tags) and sub sub tags, etc. The tags <Dbtr> and <CdtrAcct> represent respectively the debtor and the creditor account. They are sub sub tags of the <FIToFICstmrCdtTrf> tag. The structure of ISO 20022 XML message documents is described in XSD[5] (XML Schema Definition) documents. The XSD yields many advantages as it allows to describe allowable document content, validate the correctness of data, define data facets (restrictions on data) and define data patterns (data formats).

The semantics is about the meaning of the information provided between tags and how it should be used or interpreted. This is crucial for financial institutions. You can expect a date in a specific tag. But having it is already fine, but not enough. You need to know what you are going to do with it and the impact it will have on the processing of the message. The interbank settlement date does have the same meaning as the creation date and therefore should be interpreted in a completely different way. The standard brings a great benefit. Financial institutions and their customers share the same understanding of the messages content and of the way it should be processed.

After this brief introduction to the concept of standard and to ISO 20022, we will now consider the messages exchanges in SEPA.

2.2 ISO 20022 and SEPA messages

We will begin this paragraph with a close look at one SEPA message: the pacs.008.001.02. What we are about to see is very important to understand the SEPA messages and the implementation guidelines. To get a better understanding of the explanations below, it is strongly recommended to download (and print in color) the pacs.008.001.02 as it is specified in the implementation guidelines and to download the ISO 20022 definition of the same message.

The pacs.008.001.02 specifications in the Implementations Guidelines can be found in the following document EPC115-06 SCT Interbank IG 2017 VX.x.pdf (Take the latest version of the document available when you read this book). To download it, go to the EPC Website - http://www.europeanpaymentscouncil.eu/ and find the SEPA Credit Transfer implementations guidelines. You can make a search directly on google too. Download the PDF document and open it.

Finding the pacs.008.001.02 specifications in the ISO 20022 is a bit trickier. Now I will show you step by step how to get them.

1. Go to the website http://www.iso20022.org/
2. Click on catalogue of messages and under Business domain catalogues, click on Payments
3. Under *List of ISO 20022 payments message definitions per message set,* click on expand all and search for *"pacs.008.001.02"* on the page. (The shortcut CTRL+F is used to search within a Webpage on popular browsers). You will find nothing.
4. Now search for pacs.008.001. When these lines are written, I find pacs.008.001.07 as result. It is the message we are looking for, but not the correct version. ISO 20022's

---

[5] If you want to deep into the topics of XML and XSD, I recommend reading a good book on XML or to go to http://www.w3schools.com.

latest version of the pacs.008 message is 07, but we want the version 02. ISO20022 is five versions ahead than SEPA. What to do now? Just follow the next instructions.

5. Go on top of the page. There is a link called *ISO 20022 Message Archive*. Click on that link.
6. Now search for pacs.008.001.02 again. This time you find it in the table under *Second version of the Payments Clearing and Settlement messages*. On the right of the table, under the column Msg Def Report, download the document **Payments_Maintenance_2009.pdf** and open it.

In the EPC115-06 SCT Interbank IG 2017 VX.x.pdf document, the pacs.008.001.02 specifications are found in chapter 2. In the first chapter, very useful information is provided, that must be considered to understand the specifications: *it is about the message elements available in the Standard ISO 20022 and their usage in SEPA*. Those message elements are shaded in different colors in the specifications depending on how they are to be used in SEPA. In the following, I will show you step by step how to decipher that information.

The Global ISO 20022 XML standard specifies the message elements to use in the different messages. Among these elements,

- Only *a subset of message elements* available in the Global ISO 20022 specifications can be used in SEPA Payments. These message elements are themselves divided in two categories:
    - Message elements that can be used in SEPA CORE Payments. They are denoted by yellow shading in the SEPA Implementations Guidelines. Some of these elements are used exactly with the same rules as in the ISO 20022. But other elements must comply with the SEPA rules, which are more restrictive than the ISO 20022 rules as we will see later.
    - Message elements that can be used in SEPA AOS communities. They are denoted by white shading in the SEPA Implementations Guidelines.
- The other message elements are not available for use in SEPA Payments. They are not supposed to be transmitted neither in SEPA CORE Payments nor in SEPA AOS Communities messages. They are indicated with red shading in the SEPA Implementations Guidelines.

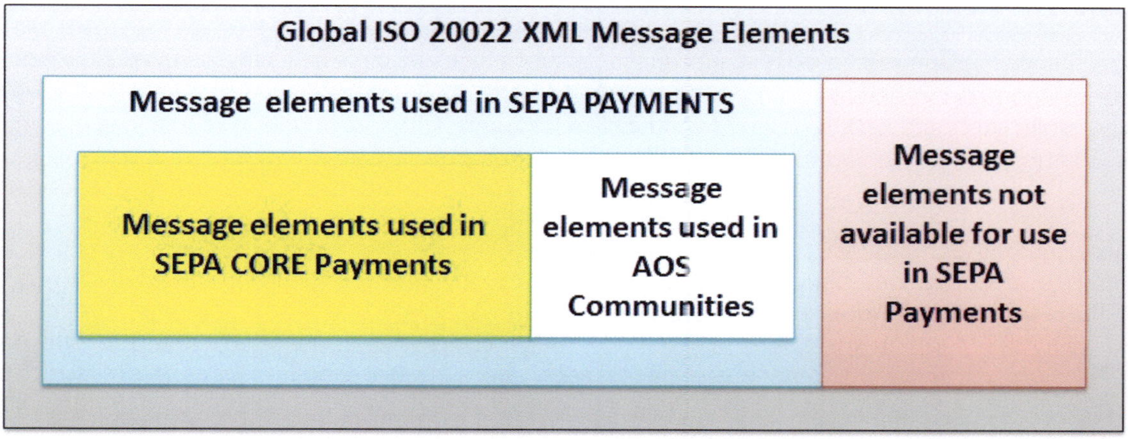

You can now browse through the pacs.008.001.02 message specifications in the implementation guidelines and in the ISO 20022 standard. Can you start to see the differences? We will extensively come back to them later in this chapter. Before that, I will introduce you to AOS communities.

2.3 SEPA CORE Payments and Additional Optional Services

Now you may wonder what the differences between SEPA Core Payments and SEPA Additional Optional Services are. Read the following sentences carefully and study the figure below:

1. Every bank that wants to exchange SEPA Payments **must** adhere to a SEPA scheme, like the SEPA Credit Transfer Scheme, the SEPA Direct Debit Core Scheme or the SEPA Direct Debit Business to Business Scheme. But there is no obligation to adhere to an AOS community.

2. Strictly speaking, in the SEPA CORE PAYMENTS Space, banks can use only message elements denoted in yellow in the SEPA Implementations Guidelines. If a bank uses a message element that is denoted white, it will be rejected in the interbank space.

3. A bank that wants to use message elements denoted in white in the specifications must first adhere to AOS community allowing the usage of those elements. Note that the same bank can belong to multiple AOS communities. There is no limit to the number of AOS communities a bank can adhere to.

4. AOS communities can also use messages that are not specified in SEPA Implementations Guidelines, but they must ensure that these messages do not compromise the interoperability of the Scheme and remain fully compliant with it.

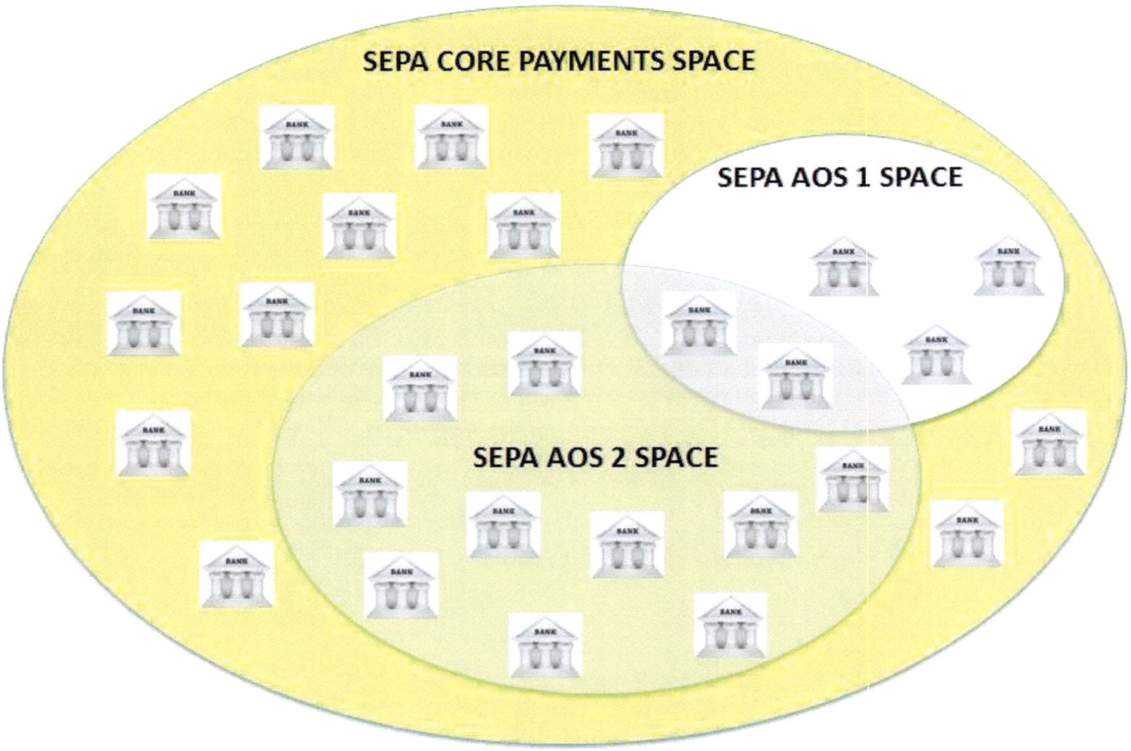

Figure 2.1: SEPA AOS Communities

The picture above depicts what AOS are. They are communities inside the SEPA CORE PAYMENTS Space. A bank cannot become member of an AOS community if it does not first adhere to the SEPA Core Scheme.

Another key point is the fact that a bank must adhere to an AOS community to send or receive message elements allowed in that community. This point is sometimes misunderstood. Many people think that a bank, which is not member of an AOS community, can send the AOS message elements to a bank that belongs to the community. That is not correct. A bank must belong to the community to send those elements. If that is not the case, the message will be rejected in the interbank space.

Now we will have a deeper look at messages used in SEPA Core Payments.

2.4 Message elements used in SEPA CORE Payments

As mentioned above, some of these message elements, denoted by yellow shading in the Implementations Guidelines, are used exactly with the same rules as in the ISO 20022. But other elements must comply with the SEPA rules, which are more restrictive than ISO 20022 rules. To understand this, we need to open both the EPC115-06 SCT Interbank IG 2017 VX.x.pdf (page 9 or 10, *$ 2.1.1*) and the Payments_Maintenance_2009.pdf (page 570) to compare the Implementations guidelines with ISO 20022 specifications.

Let's first look at the similarities between the two specifications. The message elements are indicated in tables. Both tables contain an Index column, a mult. column and a message item or message element column. The indexes denote exactly the same message elements. This indicates that the SEPA Implementations Guidelines are based on the ISO 20022 specifications. To have further explanation on the different columns of the tables, please read the chapter 1.3 Notation Conventions of the interbank implementation guidelines.

One obvious difference is the column SEPA Core Requirements available only in the SEPA Implementations Guidelines. We can see that the yellow cells are sometimes empty and sometimes filled in. Remember that the message elements denoted yellow are those that are allowed to be used in SEPA CORE Payments. When the cell is empty, it means the corresponding message element is to be used according to the ISO 20022 rules. But when it is filled in, it means that the message elements must respect the SEPA rules. Indeed the content of the cell states the SEPA rule that the message element has to comply with. The following table illustrates the differences between SEPA requirements and ISO 20022 requirements. Only few message elements are listed. But it is enough for the comprehension.

Index	Message elements	SEPA Core Requirements	ISO 20022 Requirements
1.2	++ Creation Date Time		Mandatory (mult [1..1]) Date and time at which the message was created
1.4	++ Number Of Transactions		Mandatory (mult [1..1]) Number of individual transactions contained in the message
1.6	++ Total Interbank Settlement Amount	**Mandatory** Usage Rule: Only 'EUR' is allowed. Usage Rule: Amount must be 0.01 or more and 999999999999999.99 or less. Format Rule: The fractional part has a maximum of two digits.	**Not mandatory** (mult [0..1]) Total amount of money moved between the instructing agent and the instructed agent. Any currency is allowed. Number of 18 digits which can have up to 5 decimal digits.

Index	Message elements	SEPA Core Requirements	ISO 20022 Requirements
1.7	++ Interbank Settlement Date	**Mandatory** (AT-42 Settlement Date of the Credit Transfer) AT-42 is the attribute 42 as defined in the SCT Rulebook. See chapter *Business Requirements for Attributes* in the Rulebook.	**Not mandatory** (mult [0..1]) Date on which the amount of money ceases to be available to the agent that owes it and when the amount of money becomes available to the agent to which it is due.
1.9	+++ Settlement Method	Usage Rule: Only CLRG, INGA and INDA are allowed.	CLRG, **COVE**, INGA and INDA are allowed.
1.32	++ Instructing Agent	Usage Rule: Only BIC is allowed.	Not mandatory (mult [0..1]) Agent that instructs the next party in the chain to carry out the (set of) instruction(s). It can be identified as Financial Institution or Branch.
2.49	+++ Name	**Mandatory** (AT-02 Name of the Originator) Usage Rule: **'Name' is limited to 70 characters in length**.	**Not mandatory** (mult [0..1]) Name by which a party is known and which is usually used to identify that party. **Name can have up to 140 characters**.
2.49	++++ Address Line	Usage Rule: **Only two occurrences are allowed.**	Not mandatory (mult [0..7]) **Up to seven occurrences are allowed**.
2.49	++++ Organisation Identification	Usage Rule: Either 'BIC or BEI' or one occurrence of 'Other' is allowed.	Not mandatory (mult [0..1]) Usage Rule: Either 'BIC or BEI' or multiple occurrences of 'Other' are allowed.
2.50	++ Debtor Account	**Mandatory** (AT-01 Account Number of the Originator) Usage Rule: Only IBAN is allowed.	**Not mandatory** (mult [0..1]) Unambiguous identification of the account of the debtor to which a debit entry will be made as a result of the transaction. Can be an IBAN or an other type of account.

Table 2-1 : Differences between SEPA CORE and ISO 20022 Requirements

Useful hint: Since the ISO 20022 rules are not in the table with message elements, you may ask yourself where I got the rules. In the ISO 20022 document, all the indexes are hyperlinks to the places where the definitions are available. So just click on the index on the left to get there.

When we consider the examples listed in the above table, we can summarize the main differences between SEPA rules and ISO rules.

- Many message elements not mandatory in the ISO 20022, are mandatory in SEPA.
- In SEPA the names are limited to only 70 characters, while ISO 20022 allows up to 140 characters.
- SEPA limits the number of address line occurrences to 2, while ISO 20022 allows up to 7 occurrences.
- Accounts are identified only with IBAN in SEPA, while the ISO 20022 allows other types of account.

- Instructing and Instructed Agents are identified by BIC, while the ISO 20022 allows other types of agent identifications.
- And so on.

Now is the time to look at the description of the messages themselves. If you are working on a payment project currently or are planning to start one in the future, you will probably pronounce the word pain.001, pacs.008, pacs.004 and so forth, thousands of times. Unfortunately if those messages have never been introduced to you, you may have some misconceptions about them. If you want to know what you are talking about and what those messages are all about, then this paragraph will be helpful. The goal here is not to list all the message elements available in each message. The list of message elements is in general too long and all of them are not very interesting. Therefore it is better to focus only on the structure of the message and some of its key elements. After reading this, it will be much easier for you to understand the rationale behind each of the messages and what they are used for.

2.4.1 A general introduction to ISO 20022 messages

Simply defined, a payment message is a piece of information exchanged in electronic files between two or more parties with the objective to move funds or provide reporting about the payment execution. The structure and content of the information exchanged must comply with the definition of the standard. XML is the syntax used in the ISO 20022. So payment messages in SEPA are all in XML. Message Definition Reports of all ISO 20022 messages can be downloaded from the ISO 20022 website.

At first glance, messages can seem completely different since they refer to many business areas like Cash Management (camt), Payments Initiation (pain) or Payments Clearing and Settlement (pacs). It is just an impression though, because ISO 20022 messages have quite many things in common.

A payment message consists of several building blocks:

- The message level block, where information about the message itself is found. Message level block or equivalent is mandatory and present only one time in the message.
- The order level block, where information about an order of the message is found. Since a message can be composed of many orders or equivalent, the order level block can be present many times in the message. Depending of the type of message, this block can be mandatory or optional.
- The transaction level block, where information about a transaction of an order or a transaction of a message is found. Transaction level block or equivalent can be present multiple times or not at all.

Remark: Information found at order level in one message can be at transaction level in another message. So it is important to understand where the information is in a specific message.

In addition to the structure, payment messages can have a file in common. Many payments messages can share the same file. The messages appear in a sequential order and the receiver has to split and process each message individually.

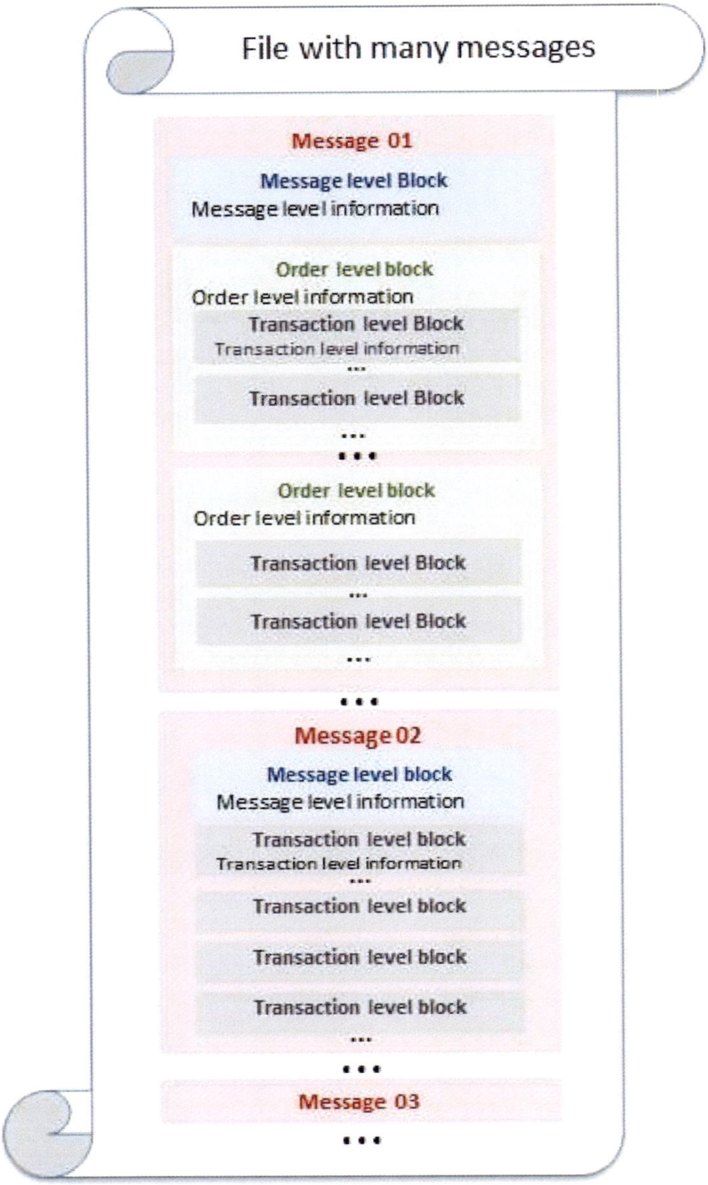

Figure 2.2: File with multiple messages

As depicted in the picture above, messages of different types and structures can be transported in the same file. Although not presented in the picture, note that the file itself may have a header block where you find file specific information like the file identification, creation date, number of messages in the file, and so on. The file header content is generally not part of the standard ISO 20022. It is defined according to CSM and bank communities' needs and shared with all sending and receiving parties.

Things are different for the messages in the file since their structures and contents are defined in the standard ISO 20022. A payment message always has message level information, but it may have either order level information or transaction level information or both. Most of the SEPA messages contain message and transaction level blocks, but no order level block. When a message element is found at message level, it applies to all the sub blocks, order and transaction level blocks, which exist in the message. However, if a message element is found at order level, then it applies to all transactions of that order and to the order itself, but not to the other orders of the message. Message elements found at transaction level apply only to that specific transaction.

After this introduction, we are now going to study the message found in the EPC Implementation guidelines for the SCT. Those messages are described in detail in the ISO 20022 standard. Again the goal here is not to replicate the specifications, but to provide an overview of the messages and then highlight some key message elements that are critical for their understanding.

2.4.2 The Customer Credit Transfer Initiation message (Pain.001.001.03)

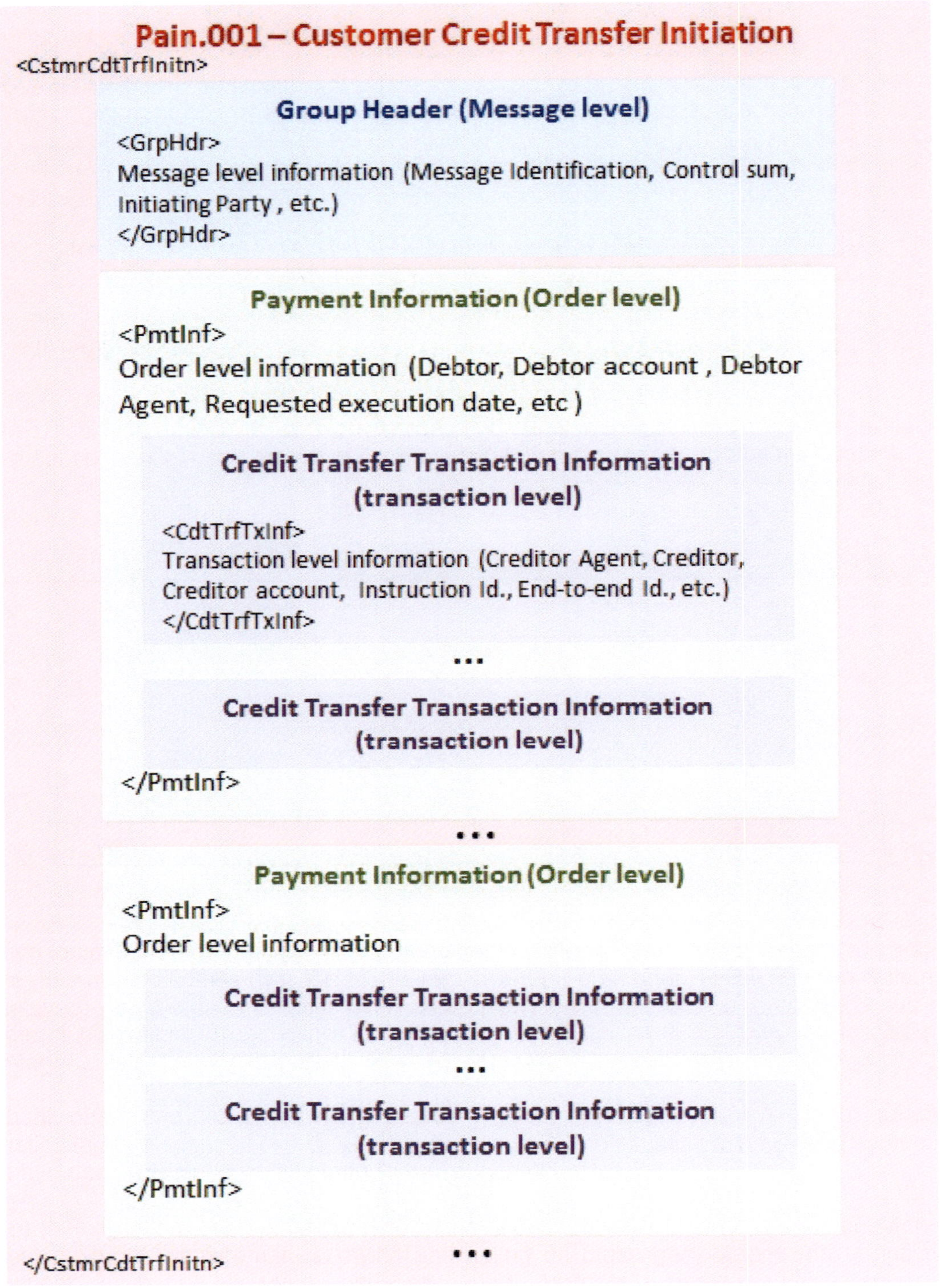

Figure 2.3: Pain.001.001.03 Message Structure

Used by corporations to send credit transfers orders to their Banks, the pain.001.001.03 message is composed of two main blocks: the *Group Header* and the *Payment Information.*

The Payment Information block contains itself one or several *Credit Transfer Transaction Information* blocks:

- The Group header is mandatory and only one occurrence can be present. It contains message level information like the Message Identification used to unambiguously identify the message, the creation date time which indicates when the message was created or the number of transactions which indicates the total number of individual transactions contained in the message. The message element *initiating party* of the Group Header can either be the debtor or the party that initiates the credit transfer on behalf of the debtor. So the initiating party can be different from the debtor.

- One Payment information block constitutes one customer payment order. It is mandatory and repetitive, which means that it must be present at least one time in the message and can be repeated as many times as needed. As depicted in the picture, this block contains order level information which is seen as debit side of all the transactions of the order. The debtor is the originator of the payment order with potentially multiple beneficiaries. This explains why order level information is the same for all transactions. To illustrate this, let's come back to our corporate customers. For the transfer of salaries, they use payment order with many beneficiaries for the debit of their account and credit all accounts of the employees. Interesting message elements in this block are for example Batch Booking, Requested execution date, instruction priority, category purpose, Debtor account and others. The table below lists some key message elements of this level.

- *Credit Transfer Transaction Information* Blocks are fully indented in Payment Information block as depicted in the above picture. Since a transaction requires a debit and a credit side, this block must be present at least once, but can be repeated as many times as needed. Specific transaction information like Instruction Identification, End to End Identification, Creditor, Creditor Account and remittance information is found here.

Remark: The word Instruction is to be used with extreme care. In this message, it is sometimes used to designate the order (See instruction priority at order level) or to designate the transaction (See instruction identification at transaction level). I am using *order* instead of *instruction* in the book because I want to avoid that confusion in my readers' mind.

The table below lists some key message elements of the pain.001.001.03 message.

Mult	Pain.001.001.03 - some key message elements	Definitions / Remarks
[1..1]	+ Group Header (Message level)	
[1..1]	++ Message Identification	Unique reference, created by the instructing party, and sent to the next party in the chain to unambiguously identify the message.
[1..1]	++ Number Of Transactions	Total number of individual transactions contained in the message
[0..1]	++ Control Sum	Total amount of all transactions of all the orders included in the message.
[1..1]	++ Initiating Party	The debtor or a party that initiates the credit transfer on behalf of the debtor
[1..n]	+ Payment Information (Order level)	

Mult	Pain.001.001.03 - some key message elements	Definitions / Remarks
[0..1]	++ Batch Booking	Information used for the order accounting. If batch booking is true, the customer account will be debited one time for the total amount of transactions in the order. If batch booking is false, the customer account will be debited as many time as there are transactions in the order.
[0..1]	++ Number Of Transactions	Total number of individual transactions contained in the order
[0..1]	++ Control Sum	
[0..1]	++ Payment Type Information	
[0..1]	+++ Instruction Priority	Indicates the priority of the order. Can take two values HIGH or NORM. HIGH means that the order is urgent and is to be executed as fast as possible even before NORM orders transmitted before the HIGH one. If not present, the order is considered NORM.
[0..1]	+++ Category Purpose	List of allowed category purposes can be found here: *https://www.iso20022.org/external_code_list.page* Download the External Code Sets spreadsheet and go to the sheet 4-CategoryPurpose. Not all applies to SCT. Depending on the value of this field, orders can be processed and booked differently according to customer to bank agreements
[1..1]	++ Requested Execution Date	Date at which the order will be processed and the customer account debited. If received before the order will be warehoused until the Requested Execution date.
[1..1]	++ Debtor	Debtor, Creditor, Ultimate Debtor and Ultimate creditor are composed of the same message elements in SEPA. They can be either an organization or a private person.
[0..1]	+++ Identification	
[1..1]	++ Debtor Account	Only IBAN is allowed in SEPA Payments. Account can be in EUR or in another currency, but must be held by a bank located in the SEPA zone.
[1..1]	++ Debtor Agent	BIC of the debtor Bank

Mult	Pain.001.001.03 - some key message elements	Definitions / Remarks
[0..1]	++ Ultimate Debtor	This field is used when the debtor does not owe money to the creditor and is paying on behalf of the Ultimate debtor. Example : If your sister asked you to transfer money to your old father, you will be the debtor and she will be the ultimate debtor.
[0..1]	++ Charge Bearer	SLEV is the only code allowed here. It means that charges are to be applied following the rules agreed in the service level and/or scheme. Charges are shared in SEPA.
[1..n]	++ Credit Transfer Transaction Information (Transaction level)	
[0..1]	++++ Instruction Identification	Unique identification created by an instructing party for an instructed party to unambiguously identify the instruction. Since it is at transaction level, it is used to identify a transaction unequivocally. This can change while the transaction goes from one instructing party to another instructing party. Each one can generate its own identification.
[1..1]	++++ End to End Identification	Unique identification assigned by the initiating party, the debtor in general, to unambiguously identify the transaction. It is passed on, **unchanged**, throughout the entire end-to-end chain. It is transmitted in R-transactions and used for reconciliation by the initiating party.
[0..1]	++++ Category Purpose	In general, it is used at the order level and not here.
[1..1]	++++ Instructed Amount	Amount of the Credit Transfer in Euro
[0..1]	+++ Charge Bearer	See description at order level above
[0..1]	+++ Ultimate Debtor	See description at order level above. If used here and not at order level, it means that each transaction of the order may potentially have a different ultimate debtor.
[0..1]	+++ Payment Type Information	In general, it is used at the order level and not here.
[0..1]	+++ Creditor Agent	BIC of the creditor Bank
[0..1]	+++ Creditor	Debtor, Creditor, Ultimate Debtor and Ultimate creditor are composed of the same message elements in SEPA. They can be either an organisation or a private person.

Mult	Pain.001.001.03 - some key message elements	Definitions / Remarks
[0..1]	+++ Creditor Account	Only IBAN is allowed in SEPA Payments. Account can be in EUR or in another currency, but must be held by a bank located in the SEPA zone.
[0..1]	+++ Ultimate Creditor	This field is used when the creditor is not the real beneficiary of the money and is receiving it on behalf of the Ultimate Creditor. Example: If you transfer money to your sister for your old father, your sister is the creditor and your old father, the ultimate creditor.
[0..1]	+++ Purpose	List of allowed purposes codes can be found here: *https://www.iso20022.org/external_code_list.page* Download the External Code Sets spreadsheet and go to the sheet 11-Purpose. Not all applies to SCT.
[0..1]	+++ Remittance Information	Information supplied by the debtor to the creditor to enable matching of an entry with the items that the transfer is intended to settle. It can be unstructured or structured and cannot exceed 140 characters in SEPA.

Table 2-2 : Definitions of some key message elements of the Pain.001.001.03

Differences between pain.001.001.02 and Pain.001.001.03

The pain.001.001.03 (version 3) was released in June 2009 almost 3 years after the release of the pain.001.001.02 (version 2) which occurred in September 2006. Although the latest version recommended in SEPA is version 3, many companies still use Pain.001.001.02. The summary of the main differences is provided in the table below.

Main differences between the version 2 and 3 of the pain messages	
Pain.001.001.02	Pain.001.001.03
Group header bloc	
Element Batch Booking present	Element Batch Booking removed
Element Grouping present	Element Grouping removed
Payment Information bloc	
Element Payment Identification is optional	Element Payment Identification becomes mandatory
Element Batch Booking not present	Element Batch Booking added
Element Number Of Transactions not present	Element Number of Transactions added
Element Control Sum not present	Element Control Sum added
Element Clearing Channel (under Payment Type Information) present	Element Clearing Channel removed
Element Category Purpose (under Payment Type Information) present and list of codes available in the Message Definition Report Document	Codes allowed in Category Purpose have been externalized (*https://www.iso20022.org/external_code_list.page*)
Transaction Information bloc	
Element Creditor Reference under Remittance information present.	Element Creditor Reference under Remittance information present, but the structure is different.

Table 2-3 : Main differences between Pain.001.001.02 and Pain.001.001.03

In addition to the above main differences, many message element types have been changed between version 2 and version 3. The below table contains the list of message elements whose types are different in pain.001 version 2 and version 3. Please consult the message definition reports document to see composition of the types.

In the table below, 'sub' stands for sub element. Payment Type Information is a sub element of Payment Information. 'Subsub' stands for sub sub element. Service Level is a sub element of Payment Type Information and a sub sub element of Payment Information.

Message elements	Type in pain.001.001.02	Type in pain.001.001.03
Autorisation	Max128Text	Authorisation1Choice
Grouping	Grouping1Code	Not existent since element removed
Payment Information	PaymentInstructionInformation1	PaymentInstructionInformation3
Sub: Payment Type Information	PaymentTypeInformation1	PaymentTypeInformation19
Subsub: Service Level	ServiceLevel2Choice	ServiceLevel8Choice
Subsub: Local Instrument	LocalInstrument1Choice	LocalInstrument2Choice
Subsub: Category Purpose	PaymentCategoryPurpose1Code	CategoryPurpose1Choice
Sub: Debtor	PartyIdentification8	PartyIdentification32
Sub: Debtor Account	CashAccount7	CashAccount16
Subsub: Identification	AccountIdentification3Choice	AccountIdentification4Choice
Subsubsub: IBAN	IBANIdentifier	IBAN2007Identifier
Subsubsub: BBAN	BBANIdentifier	BBAN type removed
Subsubsub: UPIC	UPICIdentifier	UPIC type removed
Subsubsub: Proprietary Account	SimpleIdentificationInformation2	Proprietary Account type removed
Subsubsub: Other	Not defined since Other not present	GenericAccountIdentification1
Subsub: Currency	CurrencyCode	ActiveOrHistoricCurrencyCode
Sub: Debtor Agent	BranchAndFinancialInstitutionIdentification3	BranchAndFinancialInstitutionIdentification4
Sub: Debtor Agent Account	CashAccount7	CashAccount16
Sub: Ultimate Debtor	PartyIdentification8	PartyIdentification32
Sub: Charges Account	CashAccount7	CashAccount16
Sub: Charges Account Agent	BranchAndFinancialInstitutionIdentification3	BranchAndFinancialInstitutionIdentification4
Sub: Credit Transfer Transaction Information	CreditTransferTransactionInformation1	CreditTransferTransactionInformation10
Subsub: Payment Type Information	PaymentTypeInformation1	PaymentTypeInformation19
Subsub: Amount	AmountType2Choice	AmountType3Choice
Subsub: Cheque Instruction	Cheque5	Cheque6
Subsub: Ultimate Debtor	PartyIdentification8	PartyIdentification32
Subsub: Intermediary Agent1	BranchAndFinancialInstitutionIdentification3	BranchAndFinancialInstitutionIdentification4
Subsub: Intermediary Agent1 Account	CashAccount7	CashAccount16
Subsub: Intermediary Agent2	BranchAndFinancialInstitutionIdentification3	BranchAndFinancialInstitutionIdentification4
Subsub: Intermediary Agent2 Account	CashAccount7	CashAccount16
Subsub: Intermediary Agent3	BranchAndFinancialInstitutionIdentification3	BranchAndFinancialInstitutionIdentification4
Subsub: Intermediary Agent3 Account	CashAccount7	CashAccount16
Subsub: Creditor Agent	BranchAndFinancialInstitutionIdentification3	BranchAndFinancialInstitutionIdentification4

Message elements	Type in pain.001.001.02	Type in pain.001.001.03
Subsub: Creditor Agent Account	CashAccount7	CashAccount16
Subsub: Creditor	PartyIdentification8	PartyIdentification32
Subsub: Creditor Account	CashAccount7	CashAccount16
Subsub: Ultimate Creditor	PartyIdentification8	PartyIdentification32
Subsub: Purpose	Purpose1Choice	Purpose2Choice
Subsub: Regulatory Reporting	RegulatoryReporting2	RegulatoryReporting3
Subsub: TaxInformation2	TaxInformation2	TaxInformation3
Subsub: Related Remittance Information	RemittanceLocation1	RemittanceLocation2
Subsub: Remittance Information	RemittanceInformation1	RemittanceInformation2
Subsub: Structured Remittance Information	StructuredRemittanceInformation6	StructuredRemittanceInformation7
Subsubsub: Referred Document Information	ReferredDocumentInformation1	ReferredDocumentInformation3
Subsubsub: Referred Document Related Date	ISODate	Not existent since element was removed
Subsubsub: Referred Document Amount	ReferredDocumentAmount1Choice	RemittanceAmount1
Subsubsub: Creditor Reference Amount	CreditorReferenceInformation1	CreditorReferenceInformation2
Subsubsub: Invoicer	PartyIdentification8	PartyIdentification32
Subsubsub: Invoicee	PartyIdentification8	PartyIdentification32

Table 2-4 : Types of message elements in pain.001.001.02 and pain.001.001.03

2.4.3 The FI to FI Customer Credit Transfer message (Pacs.008.001.02)

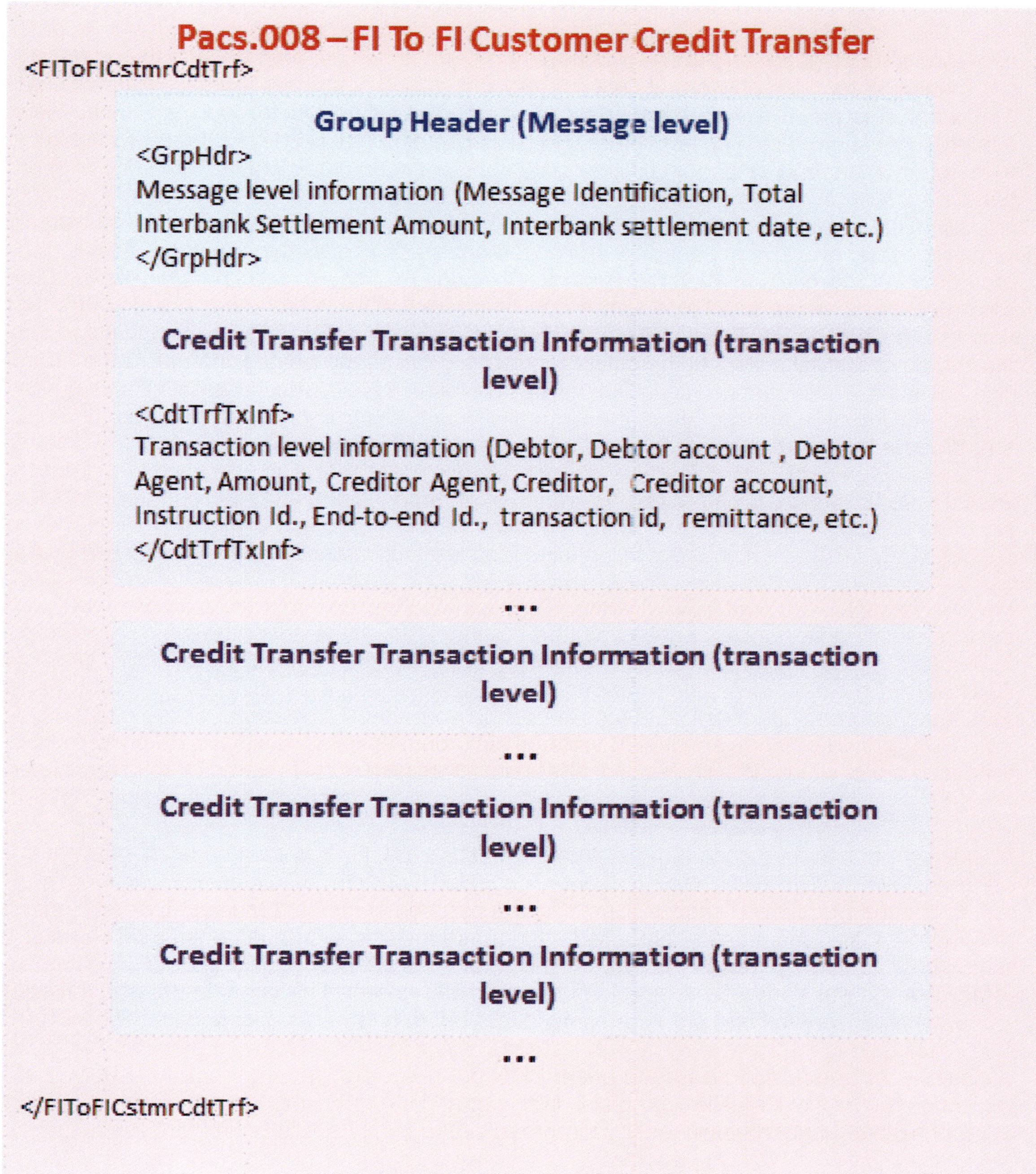

Figure 2.4: Pacs.008.001.02 Message Structure

Used to move funds from debtor account to creditor account, the pain.008.001.02 message is composed of two main blocks: *Group Header* and the *Credit Transfer Transaction Information* block.

- The Group header is mandatory and only one occurrence can be present. It contains message level information like the Message Identification which identifies the message unambiguously; creation date time which indicates when the message was created; the number of transactions which indicates the total number of individual transactions contained in the message. Settlement information (Method and clearing system) is also provided here.

- *The Credit Transfer Transaction Information* block is mandatory and repetitive. At least one should be present in the message and there is no limit up. Unlike in the pain.001, where it contains only credit side information, here it contains elements related to the debit and credit side of the transaction such as Debtor, Debtor Account, Instruction Identification, End to End Identification, Creditor, Creditor Account, remittance information, and so on.

Comparing the structure of pain.001 and pacs.001 leads us to an interesting observation. There is no order level in the pacs.008 and all the debit side information are put directly in the *Credit Transfer Transaction Information* block. The content of the *Credit Transfer Transaction Information block* varies according to the type of the message. The debtor side information found in the order level of pain.001 must be replicated in each of its transaction for the construction of the pacs.008. In the customer-to-bank space, the processing unit is the order which contains debtor information. But in the interbank space, the processing unit is the transaction. Debtor information is at the same level as creditor information and this allows a faster processing and routing of the transaction to the destination.

The table below lists some key message elements of the pacs.008.001.02 message.

Mult	Pacs.008.001.02 - some key message elements	Definitions / Remarks
[1..1]	+ Group Header (Message Level)	
[1..1]	++ Message Identification	Unique reference, created by the instructing party and sent to the next party in the chain to unambiguously identify the message.
[1..1]	++ Number Of Transactions	Total number of individual transactions contained in the message
[0..1]	++ Total Interbank Settlement Amount	Total amount of all transactions included in the message
[0..1]	++ Interbank Settlement Date	
[1..1]	+++ Settlement Method	Only CLRG, INGA and INDA are allowed in SEPA. CLRG if Settlement is done through a clearing system. INGA if Settlement is done through the instructing Agent. INDA if Settlement is done through the instructed Agent.
[0..1]	++ Payment Type Information	In general not present in the Group header, but at transaction level below because it is complicated to handle element like category purpose at interbank level.
[0..1]	+++ Category Purpose	Almost never used in SEPA even if it is allowed. See the definition in the pain.001 message.

Mult	Pacs.008.001.02 - some key message elements	Definitions / Remarks
[0..1]	++ Instructing Agent	BIC of the instructing Agent. Used here if common for all transactions of the message. If a Direct Participant sends the message to the CSM, its BIC will be here. Please note that Debtor Agent's BIC may be different if the DP is submitting transactions for Indirect Participants for example. If the instructing Agent is different for two or more transactions, it will be used at transaction level.
[0..1]	++ Instructed Agent	BIC of the instructed Agent. Used here if common for all transactions of the message.
[1..n]	++ Credit Transfer Transaction Information (Transaction level)	
[0..1]	+++ Instruction Identification	Unique identification created by an instructing party for an instructed party to unambiguously identify the instruction. Since it is at transaction level, it is used to identify a transaction unequivocally. This can change while the transaction goes from one instructing party to another instructing party. Each one can generate its own identification.
[1..1]	+++ End to End Identification	Unique identification created by the initiating party, the debtor in general, to unambiguously identify the transaction. It is passed on, **unchanged**, throughout the entire end-to-end chain. It is transmitted in R-transactions and used for reconciliation by the initiating party.
[1..1]	+++ Transaction Identification	Unique identification created by the first instructing agent, the debtor bank, to unambiguously identify the transaction that is passed on, **unchanged**, throughout the entire interbank chain. It is transmitted in R-transactions and used for reconciliation by the Debtor Bank and Creditor Bank.
[0..1]	++ Payment Type Information	In General present here and only one message element, the service level is indicated, because it is mandatory in SEPA.
[0..1]	+++ Category Purpose	Almost never used in SEPA even if it is allowed. See the definition in the pain.001 message.
[1..1]	++ Interbank Settlement Amount	The Amount of the Credit Transfer
[1..1]	++ Charge Bearer	SLEV is the only code allowed here. It means that charges are to be applied following the rules agreed in the service level and/or scheme. Charges are shared in SEPA. Note that it is mandatory here, but was not mandatory in the pain.001.

Mult	Pacs.008.001.02 - some key message elements	Definitions / Remarks
[0..1]	++ Instructing Agent	BIC of the instructing Agent is used if not common for all transactions of the message.
[0..1]	++ Instructed Agent	BIC of the instructed Agent is used if not common for all transactions of the message.
[0..1]	++ Ultimate Debtor	This element is present here at transaction level. If it is transmitted in the pain.001 at order level, then the bank must replicate that information to all transactions of the order in the interbank pacs.002 message.
[1..1]	++ Debtor	Debtor, Creditor, Ultimate Debtor and Ultimate creditor are composed of the same message elements in SEPA. They can be either an organization or a private person.
[0..1]	++ Debtor Account	Only IBAN is allowed in SEPA Payments. Account can be in EUR or in another currency, but must be held by a bank located in the SEPA zone.
[1..1]	++ Debtor Agent	BIC of the debtor Bank
[0..1]	++ Creditor Agent	BIC of the creditor Bank
[0..1]	++ Creditor	Debtor, Creditor, Ultimate Debtor and Ultimate creditor are composed of the same message elements in SEPA. They can be either an organization or a private person.
[0..1]	++ Creditor Account	Only IBAN is allowed in SEPA Payments. Account can be in EUR or in another currency, but must be held by a bank located in the SEPA zone.
[0..1]	++ Ultimate Creditor	See the definition in pain.001 message
[0..1]	++ Purpose	List of allowed purposes codes can be found here: *https://www.iso20022.org/external_code_list.page* Download the External Code Sets spreadsheet and go to the sheet 11-Purpose. Not all applies to SCT.
[0..1]	++ Remittance Information	Information supplied by the debtor to the creditor to enable the matching of an entry with the items that the transfer is intended to settle. It can be unstructured or structured and cannot exceed 140 characters in SEPA.

Table 2-5 : Definition of some key message elements of the Pacs.008.001.02

2.4.4 The Payment Return message (Pacs.004.001.02)

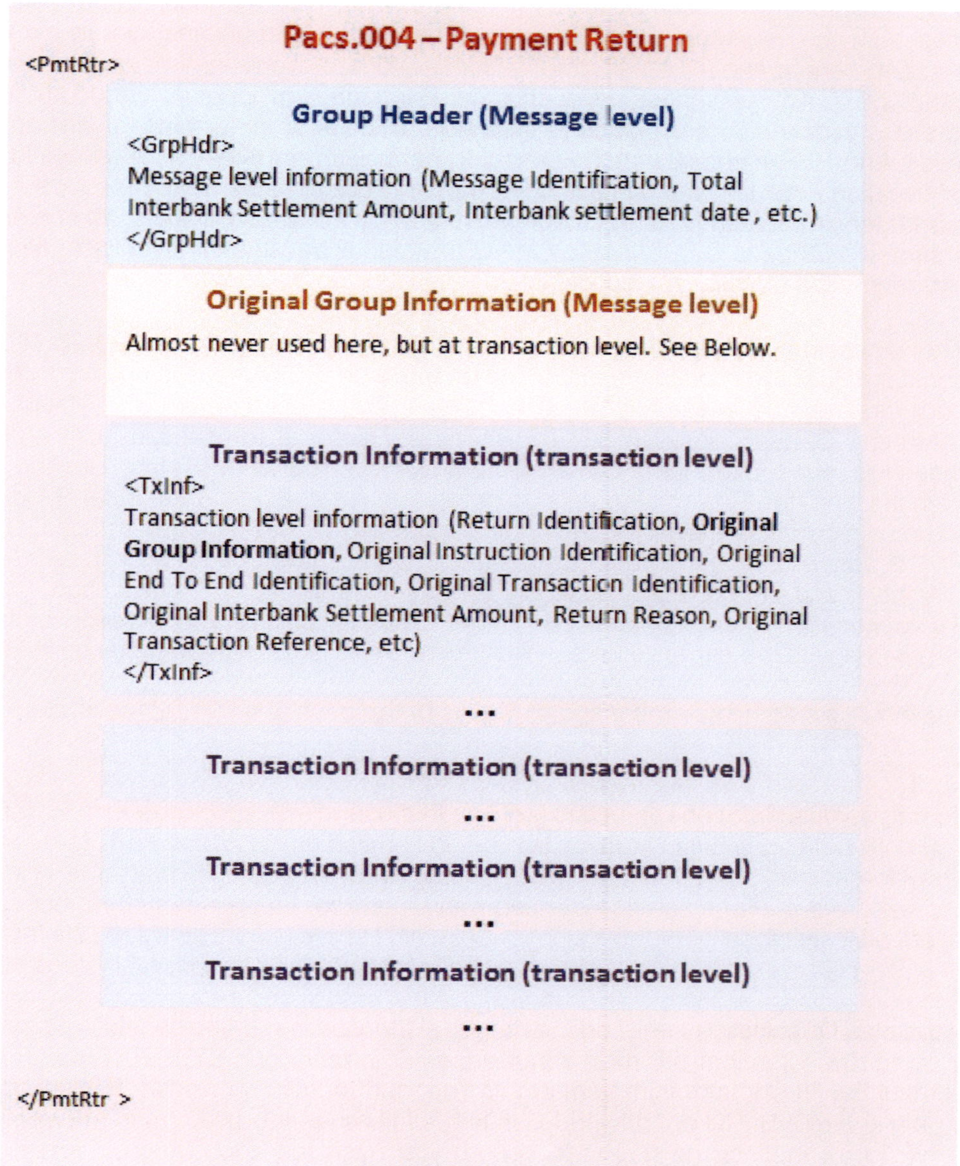

Figure 2.5: Pacs.004.001.02 Message Structure

Used to return funds from creditor bank to debtor bank, the Payment Return message is composed of three building blocks: Group Header, the Original Group Information and the Transaction Information.

- The Group header is mandatory and present once. It contains among others the Message Identification which allows instructing and instructed parties to unambiguously identify the message, and the Total Returned Interbank Settlement Amount which is the total amount of money moved from the creditor bank to debtor bank in the return message. Another interesting message element found here is the settlement method providing the information about how the return is settled.

- The Original Group Information is optional and can be present once according to the ISO 20002. It is a message level block because the information found here applies to all transaction information blocks coming after. It gives information about the original message (the message identification and the name). The Original Group Information present *here* means that all transactions returned were in the original pacs.008 message, which is almost never the case. Indeed, the Original Group Information appears in two different places in the return message: either here or at transaction level. And SEPA requires that element to be present in either here ('Original Group Information') or in 'Transaction Information'. This makes this message element mandatory in the complete pacs.004 message. And because of the reason mentioned above, the Original Group Information is present at transaction level in the very clear majority of the cases.

- The Transaction Information block is optional and repetitive in the ISO 20022, which considers that a complete message can be returned. SEPA sees things a bit differently and requires the presence of at least one Transaction Information block in the message. Consequently, in SEPA, returns are done at transaction level and not at message level. This block contains elements specific to the return like the Return Identification, the Return reason code or the return settlement date. In this block, there are also elements referencing the original pacs.008 at message and transaction levels (for example *Original Group Information*, Original Interbank Settlement Amount, Original end-to-end identification Original transaction identification, Original Transaction Reference and so on.). The Original Transaction Reference must be populated with the same value as the message elements of the original transaction.

The table below lists some key message elements of the pacs.004.001.02 message.

Mult	Pacs.004.001.02 - some key message elements	Definitions / Remarks
[1..1]	+ Group Header (Message Level)	
[1..1]	++ Message Identification	Unique reference, created by the instructing party, and sent to the next party in the chain to unambiguously identify the message.
[1..1]	++ Number Of Transactions	Total number of individual transactions contained in the message
[0..1]	++ Total Returned Interbank Settlement Amount	Total amount of money returned by the instructing agent to the instructed agent
[0..1]	++ Interbank Settlement Date	Date on which the funds are moved from the instructing agent to the instructed agent
[1..1]	+++ Settlement Method	Only CLRG, INGA and INDA are allowed in SEPA. CLRG if Settlement is done through a clearing system. INGA if Settlement is done through the instructing Agent. INDA if Settlement is done through the instructed Agent.
[0..1]	++ Instructing Agent	BIC of the instructing Agent is used if common for all transactions of the message.
[0..1]	++ Instructed Agent	BIC of the instructed Agent is used if common for all transactions of the message.

Mult	Pacs.004.001.02 - some key message elements	Definitions / Remarks
[0..1]	+ Original Group Information	Almost never used here, but at transaction level below. The Original Group Information presence here would mean that all transactions that were in the same Original message are returned. And this is almost never the case.
[1..1]	++ Original Message Identification	
[1..1]	++ Original Message Name Identification	
[0..n]	++ Transaction Information (Transaction level)	
[0..1]	++ Return Identification	Unique identification created by an instructing party for an instructed party, to unambiguously identify the returned transaction. Equivalent of instruction identification in the pacs.008
[0..1]	++ Original Group Information	
[1..1]	+++ Original Message Identification	Message Identification of the pacs.008.001.02 which contained the transaction that is being returned. The message identification is present at Group level in the pacs.008.
[1..1]	+++ Original Message Name Identification	Takes the value pacs.008.001.02 or simply pacs.008 in SEPA
[0..1]	++ Original Instruction Identification	In SEPA, this field is mandatory if provided in the original instruction. Most of the time it is not present in the pacs.004 even if provided in the original pacs.008. There is no check neither in the CSM nor in the bank. And since It can change when you move from one instructing party to another, it can't be used for reconciliation.
[0..1]	++ Original End To End Identification	This field is the End to End Identification of the original transaction that is being returned. This tag is always present. Banks send it back to the customer in various reporting. It is mandatory in SEPA.
[0..1]	++ Original Transaction Identification	This field, mandatory in SEPA, is the transaction Identification of the original transaction that is being returned. Debtor bank uses it to reconcile pacs.004 with pacs.008 during the processing.
[0..1]	++ Original Interbank Settlement Amount	It is the amount of the original credit transfer.

Mult	Pacs.004.001.02 - some key message elements	Definitions / Remarks
[1..1]	++ Returned Interbank Settlement Amount	For the normal return, this amount is equal to the Original Interbank Settlement Amount. For the return as positive answer to a Recall (ie, Reason Code is 'FOCR'), this amount is equal to the 'Original Interbank Settlement Amount' less the 'Amount' under 'Charges Information'.
[0..1]	++ Returned Instructed Amount	Take the same value as OrgnlIntrBkSttlmAmt. In SEPA, it is allowed only in the case of return as positive answer to a Recall (ie, Reason Code is 'FOCR')
[0..n]	++ Charges Information	Allowed in SEPA only in case of a return as positive answer to a Recall (ie, Reason Code is 'FOCR'). Only one occurrence is allowed.
	+++ Amount	Charges or Fee for the positive answer to the Recall.
[0..1]	++ Instructing Agent	BIC of the instructing Agent. Used here if not common for all transactions of the message.
[0..1]	++ Instructed Agent	BIC of the instructed Agent. Used here if not common for all transactions of the message.
[0..n]	++ Return Reason Information	
[0..1]	+++ Originator	It is the Identification of the type of party initiating the R-message. Limited to BIC for an Agent or 'Name' for a non-financial institution. Only BICs are used in SEPA since only banks can send pacs.004.
[0..1]	+++ Reason	The Reason Code for Non-Acceptance of the credit transfer is indicated here. For a positive answer to a Recall, only 'FOCR' is allowed. The complete list of allowed codes in SEPA can be found in the Implementation Guidelines. The list of allowed codes in the ISO 20022 can be found here: *https://www.iso20022.org/external_code_list.page* Download the External Code Sets spreadsheet and go to the sheet 13-ReturnReason.
{Or	++++ Code	See above
[0..n]	+++ Additional Information	This is a Specific Reference of the bank initiating the recall. Only allowed in SEPA for a positive answer to a Recal. In this case, it is mandatory and only one occurrence is allowed.
[0..1]	++ Original Transaction Reference	An exact copy of all attributes present in the original pacs.008 which is being returned. The original attributes that can be present in the pacs.004 are listed below.
[0..1]	+++ Interbank Settlement Date	See Original Transaction Reference above
[0..1]	+++ Payment Type Information	See Original Transaction Reference above

Mult	Pacs.004.001.02 - some key message elements	Definitions / Remarks
[0..1]	+++ Remittance Information	See Original Transaction Reference above
[0..1]	+++ Ultimate Debtor	See Original Transaction Reference above
[0..1]	+++ Debtor	See Original Transaction Reference above
[0..1]	+++ Debtor Account	See Original Transaction Reference above
[0..1]	+++ Debtor Agent	See Original Transaction Reference above
[0..1]	+++ Creditor Agent	See Original Transaction Reference above
[0..1]	+++ Creditor	See Original Transaction Reference above
[0..1]	+++ Creditor Account	See Original Transaction Reference above
[0..1]	+++ Ultimate Creditor	See Original Transaction Reference above

Table 2-6 : Definitions of some key message elements of the Pacs.004.001.02

2.4.5 The FI-to-FI Payment Cancellation Request message (Camt.056.001.01)

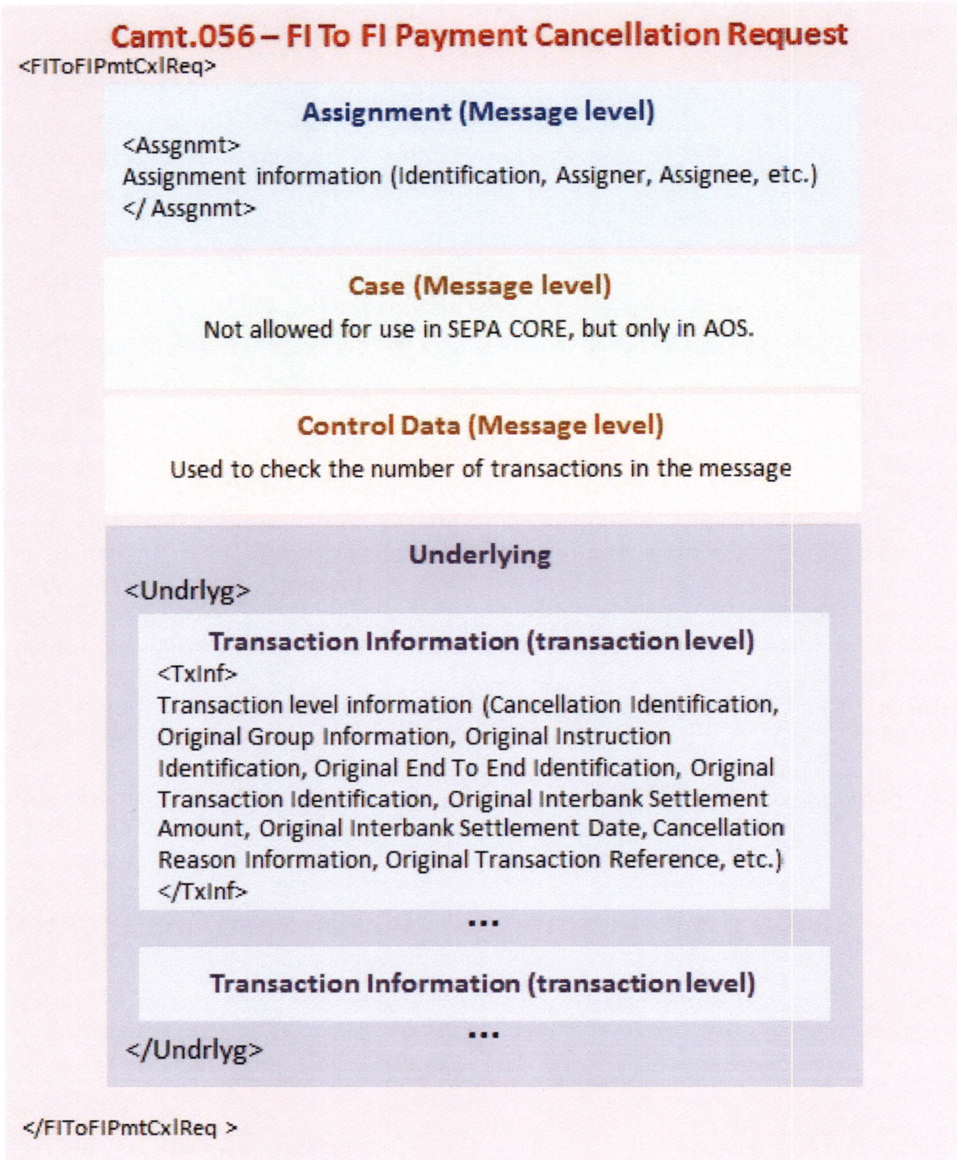

Figure 2.6: Camt.056.001.01 Message Structure

Used to request the cancellation of an original payment previously sent, the Payment Cancellation Request message is composed of four building blocks: Case Assignment, Case, Control Data and Underlying.

- The Case Assignment is mandatory and present exactly once. It contains the unique identification of the case assignment, the BICs of instructing party (Assigner) and instructed party (Assignee).

- The Case block is optional and not allowed in the Core SEPA. It can be used in AOS however. It also appears in two message elements (Original Group Information and Cancellation and Transaction Information) of the underlying block presented below.

- The Control Data Block contains the total number of transactions present in the message. During the processing, this number can be compared with the actual number of transactions found in the message.

- The Underlying block is mandatory and can be present multiple times. However, this block is generally present only once in SEPA messages. It contains transaction information block which is optional and repetitive in ISO 20022, but mandatory in SEPA. This block contains elements specific to the cancellation request like Cancellation Identification and Cancellation Reason Information. In this block, there are also elements referencing the original pacs.008 at message and transaction levels (for example Original Group Information, Original Interbank Settlement Amount, Original end-to-end identification Original transaction identification, Original Transaction Reference and so on.). The Original Transaction Reference must be populated with the same values as the message elements of the original transaction.

The table below lists some key message elements of the camt.056.001.01 message.

Mult	Camt.056.001.01 - some key message elements	Definitions / Remarks
[1..1]	+ Assignment (Message Level)	
[1..1]	++ Identification	Reference that uniquely identifies the case assignment. It can be seen as the message identification.
[1..1]	++ Assigner	Instructing Party. BIC of the sending Bank.
[1..1]	++ Assignee	Instructed Party. BIC of the receiving Bank.
[0..1]	+ Case	Not allowed for use in SEPA CORE. But only in AOS.
[0..1]	+ Control Data (Message level)	It allows to verify that the total number of transaction in the message is correct
[1..1]	++ Number Of Transactions	Total number of individual transactions contained in the message
[1..n]	+ Underlying (Message level)	Even if many occurrences are allowed, you will have only one most of the time in the camt.056.
[0..n]	++ Transaction Information (transaction level)	
[0..1]	+++ Cancellation Identification	Specific reference created by the bank initiating the Recall. This element must be transported up to the Creditor Agent. It is equivalent to instruction identification in the pacs.008
[0..1]	+++ Original Group Information	
[1..1]	++++ Original Message Identification	Message Identification of the pacs.008.001.02 which contained the transaction which is requested to be cancelled. The message identification is present at Group level in the pacs.008.

Mult	Camt.056.001.01 - some key message elements	Definitions / Remarks
[1..1]	++++ Original Message Name Identification	In SEPA only 'pacs.008.001.02' is allowed.
[0..1]	+++ Original Instruction Identification	Contrary to the pacs.004, it is not mandatory and does not have to be provided even if it was in the original pacs.008.
[0..1]	+++ Original End To End Identification	This field is the End to End Identification of the original transaction which is requested to be cancelled. This tag is always present. Banks send it back to the customer in various reporting. It is mandatory in SEPA.
[0..1]	+++ Original Transaction Identification	This field, mandatory in SEPA, is the transaction Identification of the original transaction which is requested to be cancelled. Creditor bank uses it to reconcile camt.056 with pacs.008 during the processing.
[0..1]	+++ Original Interbank Settlement Amount	It is the Amount of the original credit transfer
[0..1]	+++ Original Interbank Settlement Date	Interbank settlement date of the credit transfer that is to be cancelled.
[0..n]	+++ Cancellation Reason Information	Only one occurrence is allowed.
[0..1]	++++ Originator	It is the Identification of the type of party initiating the R-message. Limited to BIC for an Agent or 'Name' for a non-financial institution. Only BICs are used in SEPA since only banks can send camt.056.
[0..1]	++++ Reason	Reason in coded from : DUPL for Duplicate Sending Reasons in Proprietary form : TECH for Technical problems resulting in erroneous SCTs and FRAD for Fraudulent originated credit transfer
{Or	+++++ Code	See above

Mult	Camt.056.001.01 - some key message elements	Definitions / Remarks
[0..n]	++++ Additional Information	Additional Information to the Recall reason code. Only allowed when 'FRAD' is used as a Recall reason code. Only one occurrence is allowed in SEPA and it is not mandatory.
[0..1]	++ Original Transaction Reference	An exact copy of all attributes present in the original pacs.008 which is requested to be cancelled. The original attributes that can be present in the camt.056 are listed below.
[0..1]	++++ Settlement Information	See Original Transaction Reference above
[0..1]	+++ Payment Type Information	See Original Transaction Reference above
[0..1]	+++ Remittance Information	See Original Transaction Reference above
[0..1]	+++ Ultimate Debtor	See Original Transaction Reference above
[0..1]	+++ Debtor	See Original Transaction Reference above
[0..1]	+++ Debtor Account	See Original Transaction Reference above
[0..1]	+++ Debtor Agent	See Original Transaction Reference above
[0..1]	+++ Creditor Agent	See Original Transaction Reference above
[0..1]	+++ Creditor	See Original Transaction Reference above
[0..1]	+++ Creditor Account	See Original Transaction Reference above
[0..1]	+++ Ultimate Creditor	See Original Transaction Reference above

Table 2-7 : Definitions of some key message elements of the Camt.056.001.01

2.4.6 The Resolution of Investigation message (Camt.029.001.03)

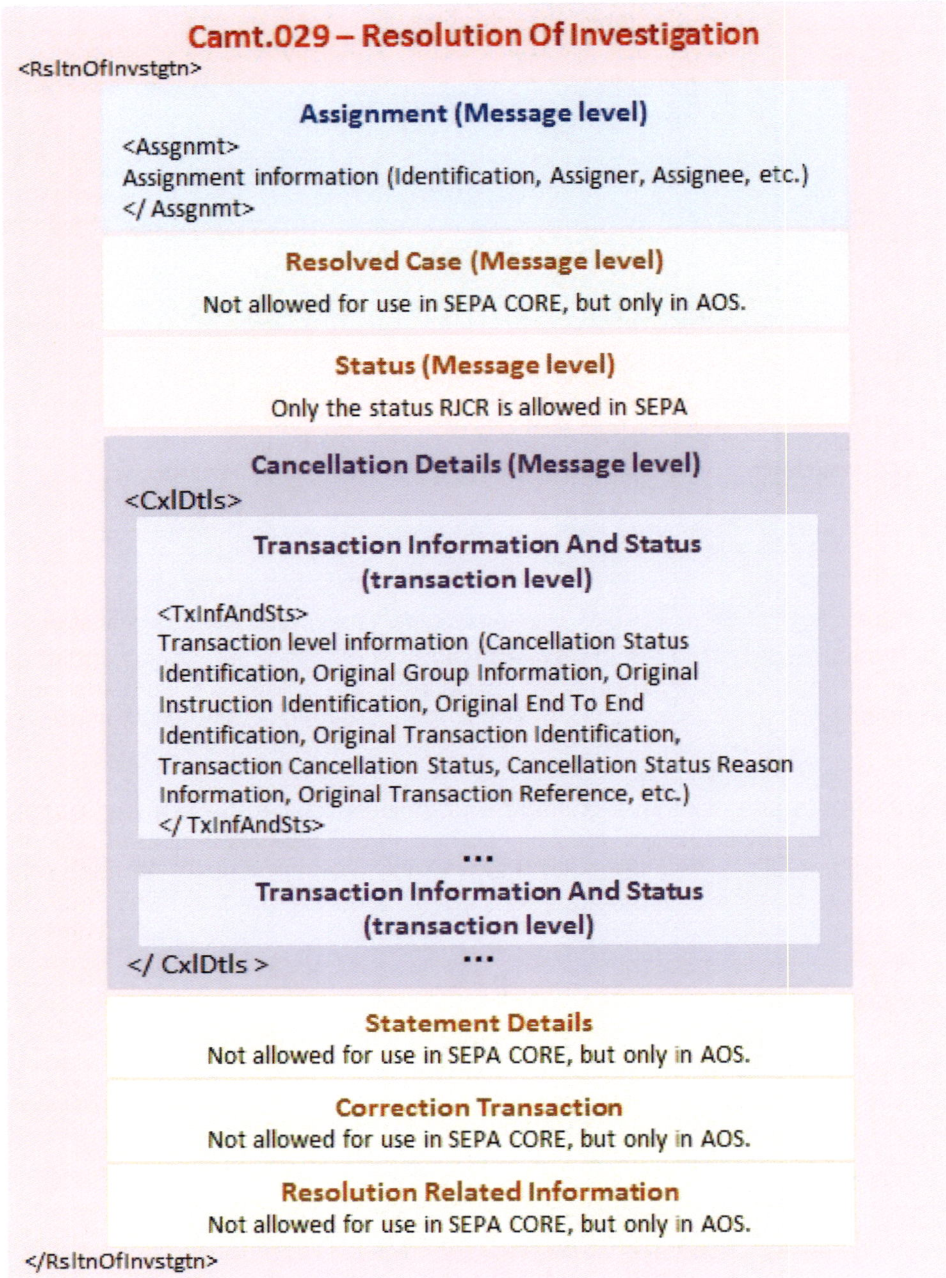

Figure 2.7: Camt.029.001.03 Message Structure

Used in SEPA to provide a negative response to a cancellation request (By the way, it is very limited in SEPA compare to the ISO 20022), the Resolution of investigation message is composed of seven building blocks: Case Assignment, Resolved Case, Status, Cancellation Details, Statement Details, Correction Transaction and Resolution Related Information.

- The Case Assignment is mandatory and present exactly once. It contains the unique identification of the case assignment, the BICs of instructing party (Assigner) and instructed party (Assignee). It is identical to the block with the same name found in the camt.056. But here, the creditor bank is the instructing party and the debtor bank the instructed party.

- The Resolved Case block is optional and not allowed in the Core SEPA. It can be used in AOS however.

- The Status block is mandatory and indicates the status of the investigation. In SEPA, only the status RJCR (Rejected Cancellation Request) is allowed since this message is used for a negative response to a cancellation request. Status RJCR in this block means also that all transactions can take only that status.

- The Cancellation Details block is optional in ISO 20022, but mandatory in SEPA. It must have at least one Transaction Information And Status block which contains critical transaction level information for the processing. As usual, there is specific camt.029 information like the Cancellation Status Identification, the Transaction Cancellation Status and the Cancellation Status Reason Information. There is also information referring to the original credit transfer (Original Group Information, Original Instruction Identification, Original End To End Identification, Original Transaction Identification, Original Transaction Reference, etc).

- The three last blocks, Statement Details, Correction Transaction and Resolution Related Information are all optional in ISO 20022 as well as in SEPA. They can be used in AOS only, not in the SEPA Core.

The table below lists some key message elements of the camt.029.001.03 message.

Mult	Camt.029.001.03 - some key message elements	Definitions / Remarks
[1..1]	+ Assignment (Message Level)	
[1..1]	++ Identification	Reference that uniquely identifies the case assignment. It can be seen as the message identification.
[1..1]	++ Assigner	Instructing Party. BIC of the sending Bank.
[1..1]	++ Assignee	Instructed Party. BIC of the receiving Bank.
[0..1]	+ Resolved Case	Not allowed for use in SEPA CORE. But only in AOS.
[1..1]	+ Status	The sub element Confirmation is the only one allowed under status.
{Or	++ Confirmation	Only RJCR is allowed. RJCR stands for RejectedCancellationRequest. Multiple other codes are allowed in the ISO 20022 which does not limit the usage of camt.029 to a negative response to a cancellation request.
[0..n]	+ Cancellation Details (Message level)	
[0..n]	++ Transaction Information And Status (transaction level)	
[0..1]	+++ Cancellation Status Identification	Unique and unambiguous identifier of a cancellation request status created by the bank answering to the recall.

Mult	Camt.029.001.03 - some key message elements	Definitions / Remarks
[0..1]	+++ Original Group Information	One could believe that information about the received camt.056 is to find here. No True. The camt.029 refers to the pacs.008 as seen below.
[1..1]	++++ Original Message Identification	Message Identification of the pacs.008.001.02 which contained the transaction which was requested to be cancelled. The message identification is present at Group level in the pacs.008.
[1..1]	++++ Original Message Name Identification	Takes the value 'pacs.008.001.02'.
[0..1]	+++ Original Instruction Identification	Contrary to the pacs.004, it is not mandatory and does not have to be provided even if it was in the original pacs.008.
[0..1]	+++ Original End To End Identification	This field is the End to End Identification of the original transaction which has not been cancelled. This tag is always present. Banks send it back to the customer in various reporting. It is mandatory in SEPA.
[0..1]	+++ Original Transaction Identification	This field, mandatory in SEPA, is the transaction Identification of the original transaction which has not been cancelled. Creditor bank uses it to reconcile camt.056 with pacs.008 during the processing.
[0..1]	+++ Transaction Cancellation Status	'RJCR' is the only value allowed. It stands for RejectedCancellationRequest. Two other codes are allowed in the ISO 20022 which does not limit the usage of camt.029 to a negative response to a cancellation request.
[0..n]	+++ Cancellation Status Reason Information	At least one occurrence must be provided.
[0..1]	++++ Originator	It is the Identification of the type of party initiating the R-message. Limited to BIC for an Agent or 'Name' for a non-financial institution. Only BICs are used in SEPA since only banks can send camt.029.
[0..1]	++++ Reason	Reason in coded from : CUST for Beneficiary's refusal and LEGL for legal reason. Reasons in Proprietary form : ARDT for The transaction has already been returned, AC04 for Account closed, AM04 for Insufficient funds on the account, NOAS for No response from beneficiary and NOOR for Original Credit Transfer never received
{Or	+++++ Code	See above
[0..n]	++++ Additional Information	This is used only when code is 'LEGL' in order to precise the reason. Only two occurrences are allowed in SEPA and it is not mandatory.
[0..1]	+++ Original Transaction Reference	An exact copy of all attributes present in the original pacs.008 which was not cancelled. The original attributes that can be present in the camt.029 are listed below.
[0..1]	++++ Interbank Settlement Amount	See Original Transaction Reference above
[0..1]	++++ Interbank Settlement Date	See Original Transaction Reference above

Mult	Camt.029.001.03 - some key message elements	Definitions / Remarks
[0..1]	++++ Settlement Information	See Original Transaction Reference above
[0..1]	++++ Payment Type Information	See Original Transaction Reference above
[0..1]	++++ Remittance Information	See Original Transaction Reference above
[0..1]	++++ Ultimate Debtor	See Original Transaction Reference above
[0..1]	++++ Debtor	See Original Transaction Reference above
[0..1]	++++ Debtor Account	See Original Transaction Reference above
[0..1]	++++ Debtor Agent	See Original Transaction Reference above
[0..1]	++++ Creditor Agent	See Original Transaction Reference above
[0..1]	++++ Creditor	See Original Transaction Reference above
[0..1]	++++ Creditor Account	See Original Transaction Reference above
[0..1]	++++ Ultimate Creditor	See Original Transaction Reference above
[0..1]	+ Statement Details	Not allowed for use in SEPA CORE. But only in AOS.
[0..1]	+ Correction Transaction	Not allowed for use in SEPA CORE. But only in AOS.
[0..n]	+ Resolution Related Information	Not allowed for use in SEPA CORE. But only in AOS.

Table 2-8 : Definitions of some key message elements of the Camt.029.001.03

2.4.7 The Interbank Payment Status Report message (Pacs.002.001.03)

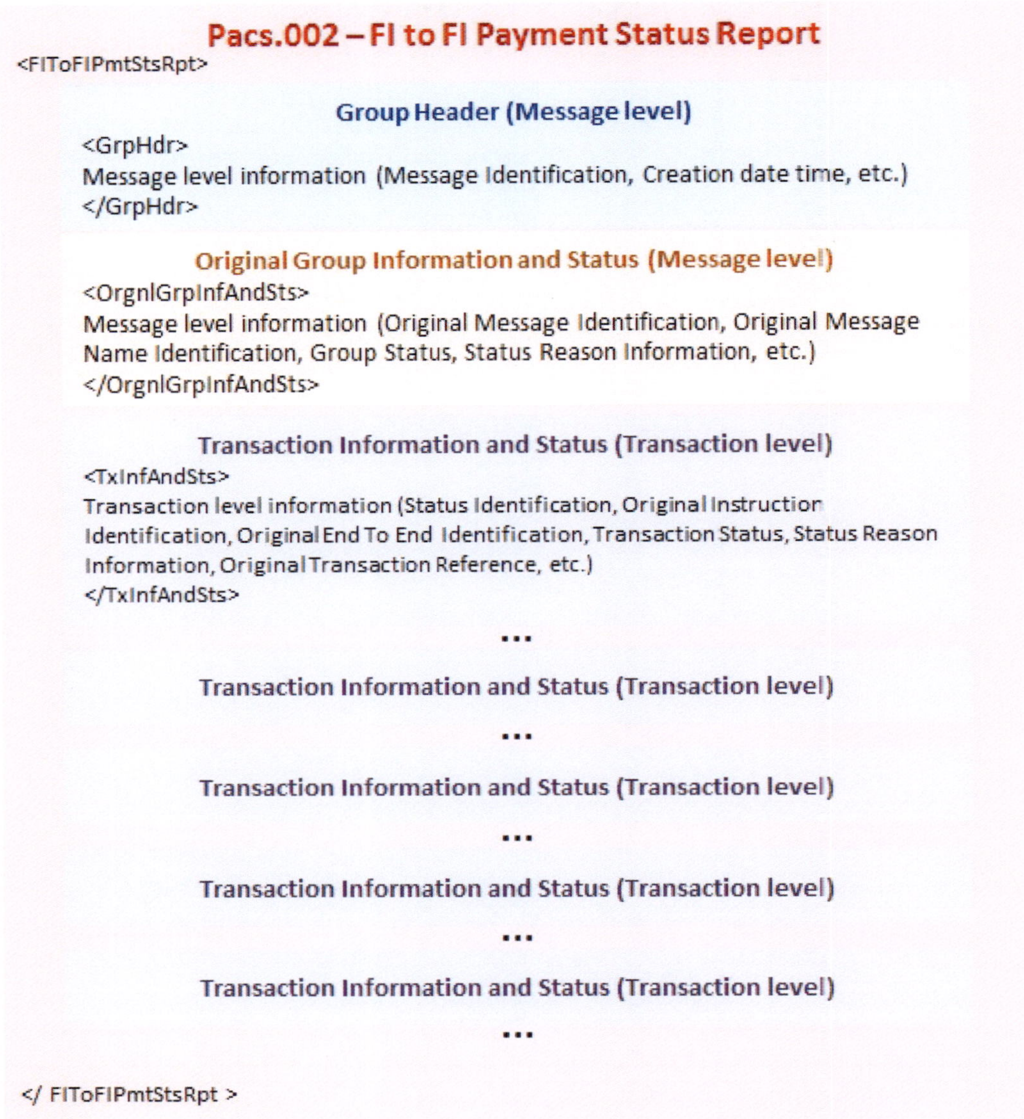

Figure 2.8: Pacs.002.001.03 Message Structure

Used to inform originator banks about the status of pacs.008 they sent. the pacs.002.001.03 message is composed of three blocks: the Group Header, the Original Group Information and Status and the Transaction Information and Status. The pacs.002 can be exchanged between CSMs and banks or between banks directly.

- The Group header is mandatory and present once. It contains among other the Message Identification which allows instructing and instructed parties to unambiguously identify the message. The message Identification is generated by the instructing party and must be unique over a period of time.

- The Original Group Information and Status is also mandatory and present once. It gives information about the original message (the message identification and the name) and why it was rejected. A message can be rejected either partially or totally. It is indicated in the Group Status element respectively with the codes PART or RJCT. Since only

those two codes are allowed in SEPA, a question directly arises. What happens if the original message is completely accepted? In that case, the Group status element which is not mandatory will not be present in the pacs.002 since the codes PART and RJCT cannot be used. So the pacs.002 message will not be transmitted at all according to SEPA at least But in reality, Banks want to have a status acknowledging that the message has been totally accepted. This explains why CSM has defined some variations of the pacs.002 message allowing them to send status of totally accepted messages to Banks.
Another interesting message element in this block is the **status reason information** that must be present either in *Original Group Information And Status* or in *Transaction Information and Status* as required in SEPA. When it is used in this element *Original Group Information And Status,* it is about original message. But when it is used in the element *Transaction Information and Status,* it is about a specific transaction of the original message. It can be used in *Original Group Information And Status* only if the complete message was rejected for a specific reason or if the all the transactions of the original message were rejected for the same reason. If many transactions of the original message are rejected for different reasons, then the status reason information will be used at transaction level, so in each transaction. The reason for rejection of the original message is indicated under status reason information/Reason/Code (Code FF01 is used for instance if the original message was rejected for Invalid File Format). A very limited set of codes is used in SEPA. To see the list of all possible codes allowed in the ISO 20022, go to the page https://www.iso20022.org/external_code_list.page and download the External Code Sets spreadsheet. Go the Sheet **16-StatusReason** to see the list of the codes. Those codes were not introduced at the same time and some of them cannot be used for SEPA Credit Transfers.

- The Transaction Information and Status is optional, but can appear many times in the pacs.002 if needed. If a complete message is rejected, there is no need to have this block since all the information will be available in Original Group Information and Status. Each Transaction Information and Status element contains the detail of a transaction that was rejected and information like Original Instruction Identification, Original End To End Identification, Original Transaction Identification allowing the sending bank to reconcile it with the original transaction. In the transaction status, only RJCT is allowed. This means that only rejected transactions are mentioned in this element. Accepted transactions do not appear at all.

Some key message elements of the pacs.002.001.03 are listed in the table below.

Mult	Pacs.002.001.03 - some key message elements	Definitions / Remarks
[1..1]	+ Group Header (Message Level)	
[1..1]	++ Message Identification	Unique reference, created by the instructing party, and sent to the next party in the chain to unambiguously identify the message.
[0..1]	++ Instructing Agent	BIC of the instructing Agent. Used here if common for all transactions of the message.
[0..1]	++ Instructed Agent	BIC of the instructed Agent. Used here if common for all transactions of the message.

Mult	Pacs.002.001.03 - some key message elements	Definitions / Remarks
[1..1]	+ Original Group Information and Status (Message level)	
[1..1]	++ Original Message Identification	Message Identification of the pacs.008.001.02 for which the pacs.002 is sent. The message identification is present at Group level in the pacs.008.
[1..1]	++ Original Message Name Identification	'pacs.008.001.02' is the only value allowed here.
[0..1]	++ Group Status	Only 'RJCT' and 'PART' are allowed, RJCT for Rejected and PART for Partially Accepted.
[0..n]	++ Status Reason Information	'Status Reason Information' must be present either in 'Original Group Information and Status' or in 'Transaction Information and Status'. Only one occurrence is allowed in SEPA.
[0..1]	+++ Originator	It is the Identification of the type of party initiating the R-message. Limited to BIC for an Agent or 'Name' for a non-financial institution. Only BICs are used in SEPA since banks and CSM that send pacs.002 are identified by BICs.
[0..1]	+++ Reason	Reason Code for Non-Acceptance. Since the reason is provided only for Non-Acceptance, it means that it can be used in SEPA only if the GroupStatus is RJCT. Here are the code allowed in SEPA. AC01, AG02, FF01, AM05, MS03, RC01, RR01, RR02, RR03, RR04, TM01, DNOR and CNOR.
{Or	++++ Code	See cell above.
[0..n]	++ Transaction Information and Status (Transaction level)	
[0..1]	++ Status Identification	Unique reference created by the bank or the CSM that initiated the pacs.002.
[0..1]	++ Original Instruction Identification	It is not mandatory, but has to be provided if it was in the original pacs.008.
[0..1]	++ Original End To End Identification	This field is the End to End Identification of the original transaction which has been rejected. It is mandatory in SEPA and used by Corporate customers for reconciliation.

Mult	Pacs.002.001.03 - some key message elements	Definitions / Remarks
[0..1]	++ Original Transaction Identification	This field, mandatory in SEPA, is the transaction Identification of the original transaction that is being returned. Debtor bank uses it to reconcile pacs.002 with pacs.008 during the processing.
[0..1]	++ Transaction Status	'RJCT' is the only value allowed here. It means we get information only about the rejected transactions, nothing about accepted transactions.
[0..n]	++ Status Reason Information	'Status Reason Information' must be present either in 'Original Group Information and Status' or in 'Transaction Information and Status'. Only one occurrence is allowed in SEPA.
[0..1]	+++ Originator	It is the Identification of the type of party initiating the R-message. Limited to BIC for an Agent or 'Name' for a non-financial institution. Only BICs are used in SEPA since banks and CSM that send pacs.002 are identified by BICs.
[0..1]	+++ Reason	Reason Code for Non-Acceptance. Since the reason is provided only for Non-Acceptance, it means that it can be used in SEPA only if the GroupStatus is RJCT. Here are the code allowed in SEPA. AC01, AG02, FF01, AM05, MS03, RC01, RR01, RR02, RR03, RR04, TM01, DNOR and CNOR.
{Or	++++ Code	See above.
[0..1]	++ Instructing Agent	BIC of the instructing Agent. Used here if not common for all transactions of the message.
[0..1]	++ Instructed Agent	BIC of the instructed Agent. Used here if not common for all transactions of the message.
[0..1]	++ Original Transaction Reference	An exact copy of all attributes present in the original pacs.008 for which a pacs.002 is sent.
[0..1]	+++ Interbank Settlement Amount	See Original Transaction Reference above
[0..1]	+++ Interbank Settlement Date	See Original Transaction Reference above
[0..1]	+++ Settlement Information	See Original Transaction Reference above
[0..1]	+++ Payment Type Information	See Original Transaction Reference above
[0..1]	+++ Remittance Information	See Original Transaction Reference above
[0..1]	+++ Ultimate Debtor	See Original Transaction Reference above
[0..1]	+++ Debtor	See Original Transaction Reference above
[0..1]	+++ Debtor Account	See Original Transaction Reference above
[0..1]	+++ Debtor Agent	See Original Transaction Reference above
[0..1]	+++ Creditor Agent	See Original Transaction Reference above
[0..1]	+++ Creditor	See Original Transaction Reference above
[0..1]	+++ Creditor Account	See Original Transaction Reference above
[0..1]	+++ Ultimate Creditor	See Original Transaction Reference above

Table 2-9 : Definitions of some key message elements of the Pacs.002.001.03

2.4.8 The Payment Status Report message from Bank-to-Customer (Pain.002.001.03)

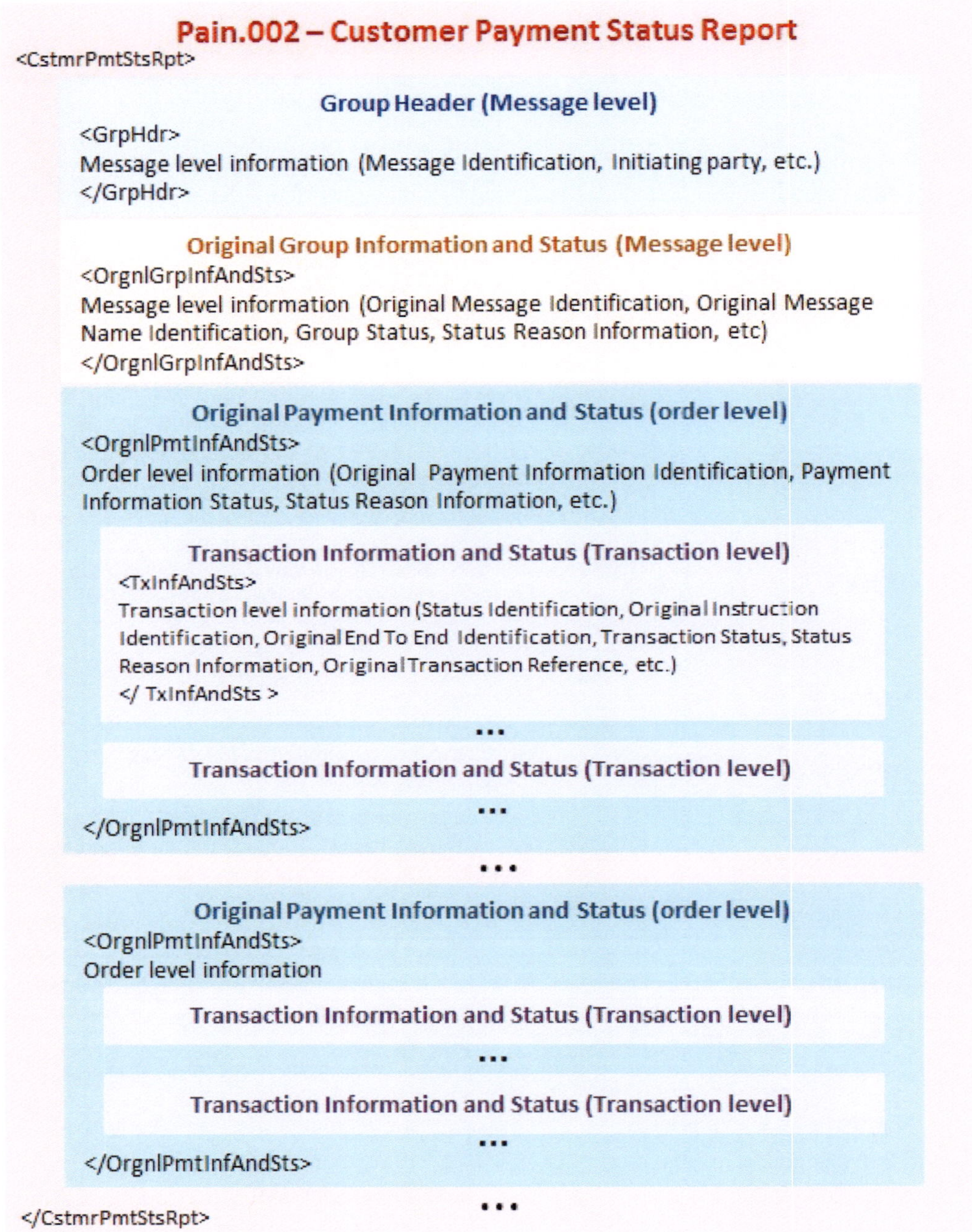

Figure 2.9: Pain.002.001.03 Message Structure

In the standard ISO 20022, the pain.002.001.03 message is presented as having three blocks: The Group Header, the Original Group Information and Status and the Original Payment Information and Status. Considering the Transaction Information and Status as a fourth block, even if it is part of the Original Payment Information and Status, is helpful to understand this message. There are many similarities between pain.002 and pacs.002 messages. The difference resides mainly in the Original Payment Information and Status which is not present in pacs.002. The reason is simple. Remember the composition of the pacs.008. It consists of two building blocks: The Group Header (message level) and the Credit Transfer Transaction Information (Transaction level). So, there is no payment information (order level) and therefore no Original Payment Information and Status can be provided in pacs.002. Let's us look at the blocks of the pain.002 message:

- The Group header is mandatory and present once. It contains among other the Message Identification which allows customer and bank to unambiguously identify the message. The message Id is generated by the Bank.

- The Original Group Information and Status is also mandatory and present once. It gives information about the original message (the message identification and the name) and why it was rejected. The following requirement is made in SEPA implementation guidelines about the Group Status element found in this block: "Group Status, Payment Information Status or Transaction Status must be present with the code 'RJCT'". It looks like the assumption in SEPA is that the pain.002 should be sent only if something wrong happens during the processing of the pain.001 message. But corporate customers demand to receive a pain.002 even if everything is OK. So, banks and customers should go beyond SEPA to close this gap. Coming back to the Group Status, if present here, it means that the complete message was rejected since RJCT is the only code allowed.

- The Original Payment Information and Status is optional and repetitive. A message can contain several Payment Information blocks. If a message is rejected, then all Payments Information are also rejected. And the Original Payment Information and Status does not need to be present in the pain.002. If one or several payments information of the message are rejected (and not the complete message), then Original Payment Information and Status needs be present in the pain.002 for each payment information. A payment information can itself be partially or totally rejected. The Payment Information Status is set to RJCT only if the payment information has been totally rejected. In case of partial rejection, the next block comes into play.

- The Transaction Information and Status is also optional and repetitive. It is completely embedded in the Original Payment Information and Status. If a Payment Information has been partially rejected, then the transaction status will be present for each rejected transaction (Remember that only RJCT is allowed). Group Status and Payment Information Status elements do not have to be present, since the rejection is neither at message level, nor at order level, but only at transaction level. Each Transaction Information and Status element contains the detail of a transaction that was rejected and information like Original Instruction Identification and Original End to End Identification allowing corporate customers to reconcile it with the original transaction sent. Note that there is no transaction identification which is generated and used by the Debtor Bank.

The reason for rejection of the original message / payment information / transaction is indicated under the tag Reason/Code of the corresponding elements. A very limited set of codes is used in SEPA. To see the list of all possible codes allowed in the ISO 20022, go to the page https://www.iso20022.org/external_code_list.page and download the External Code Set spreadsheet. Go the Sheet **16-StatusReason** to see the list of the codes. Those codes were not introduced at the same time and some of them cannot be used for SEPA Credit Transfers.

The table below lists some key message elements of the pain.002.001.03 message.

Mult	Pain.002.001.03 - some key message elements	Definitions / Remarks
[1..1]	+ Group Header (Message Level)	
[1..1]	++ Message Identification	Unique reference, created by the instructing party, and sent to the next party in the chain to unambiguously identify the message.
[0..1]	++ Debtor Agent	BIC of the debtor Bank
[1..1]	+ Original Group Information and Status (Message level)	
[1..1]	++ Original Message Identification	Message Identification of the pain.001 message received by the debtor Bank and for which the pain.002 is sent.
[1..1]	++ Original Message Name Identification	pain.001.001.02 / pain.001.001.03
[0..1]	++ Group Status	'Group Status', 'Payment Information Status' or 'Transaction Status' must be present with the code 'RJCT'. It looks like SEPA limited the usage of pain.002 to inform a customer only about rejects. *If present here, it means that the whole pain.001 message has been rejected by the Debtor Bank.*
[0..n]	++ Status Reason Information	'Status Reason Information' can be present in 'Original Group Information And Status' or 'Original Payment Information and Status' or 'Transaction Information and Status'.
[0..1]	+++ Originator	It is the Identification of the type of party initiating the R-message. Limited to BIC for an Agent or 'Name' for a non-financial institution. Only BICs are used in SEPA since only banks can send pain.002.
[0..1]	+++ Reason	The Reason Code for Non-Acceptance of the Pain.001 messages is indicated here. The list of allowed codes in the ISO 20022 can be found here: https://www.iso20022.org/external_code_list.page Download the External Code Sets spreadsheet and go to the sheet 16-StatusReason.
	++++ Code	See above
[0..n]	+ Original Payment Information and Status (order level)	
[1..1]	++ Original Payment Information Identification	Payment Information Identification of the order received in the pain.001 by the debtor Bank and for which the pain.002 is sent.

Mult	Pain.002.001.03 - some key message elements	Definitions / Remarks
[0..1]	++ Payment Information Status	'Group Status', 'Payment Information Status' or 'Transaction Status' must be present with the code 'RJCT'. We see that SEPA limits the usage of pain.002 to inform a customer only about rejects. *If present here, it means that the whole order has been rejected by the Debtor Bank.*
[0..n]	++ Status Reason Information	'Status Reason Information' can be present in 'Original Group Information and Status' or 'Original Payment Information and Status' or 'Transaction Information and Status'.
[0..1]	+++ Originator	It is the Identification of the type of party initiating the R-message. Limited to BIC for an Agent or 'Name' for a non-financial institution. Only BICs are used in SEPA since only banks can send pain.002.
[0..1]	+++ Reason	The Reason Code for Non-Acceptance of the Pain.001 messages is indicated here. The list of allowed codes in the ISO 20022 can be found here: https://www.iso20022.org/external_code_list.page Download the External Code Sets spreadsheet and go to the sheet 16-StatusReason.
{Or	++++ Code	See above
[0..n]	++ Transaction Information and Status (Transaction level)	
[0..1]	+++ Status Identification	Unique reference created by the debtor bank that initiated the reject.
[0..1]	+++ Original Instruction Identification	It is not mandatory and does not have to be provided even if it was in the original pain.001.
[0..1]	+++ Original End To End Identification	This field is the End to End Identification of the original transaction which has been rejected. Even if it is not mandatory in SEPA, it is present almost all the time. Corporate customers use it for reconciliation.
[0..1]	+++ Transaction Status	'Group Status', 'Payment Information Status' or 'Transaction Status' must be present with the code 'RJCT'. As stated earlier, SEPA limits the usage of pain.002 to inform a customer only about rejects.

Mult	Pain.002.001.03 - some key message elements	Definitions / Remarks
[0..n]	+++ Status Reason Information	'Status Reason Information' may be present in 'Original Group Information and Status', 'Original Payment Information Status' or 'Transaction Information and Status'.
[0..1]	++++ Originator	It is the Identification of the type of party initiating the R-message. Limited to BIC for an Agent or 'Name' for a non-financial institution. Only BICs are used in SEPA since only banks can send pain.002.
[0..1]	++++ Reason	The Reason Code for Non-Acceptance of the Pain.001 messages are indicated here. The list of allowed codes in the ISO 20022 can be found here: https://www.iso20022.org/external_code_list.page Download the External Code Sets spreadsheet and go to the sheet 16-StatusReason.
{Or	+++++ Code	See above
[0..1]	+++ Original Transaction Reference	An exact copy of all attributes present in the original pain.001 for which the pain.002 is sent.
[0..1]	++++ Amount	See Original Transaction Reference above
[0..1]	++++ Requested Execution Date	See Original Transaction Reference above
[0..1]	++++ Payment Type Information	See Original Transaction Reference above
[0..1]	++++ Payment Method	See Original Transaction Reference above
[0..1]	++++ Remittance Information	See Original Transaction Reference above
[0..1]	++++ Ultimate Debtor	See Original Transaction Reference above
[0..1]	++++ Debtor	See Original Transaction Reference above
[0..1]	++++ Debtor Account	See Original Transaction Reference above
[0..1]	++++ Debtor Agent	See Original Transaction Reference above
[0..1]	++++ Creditor Agent	See Original Transaction Reference above
[0..1]	++++ Creditor	See Original Transaction Reference above
[0..1]	++++ Creditor Account	See Original Transaction Reference above
[0..1]	++++ Ultimate Creditor	See Original Transaction Reference above

Table 2-10 : Definitions of some key message elements of the Pain.002.001.03

Now that we are done with the presentation with the SEPA, it is time to share an important note with you about the message elements.

In the Payments_Maintenance_2009.pdf and Enl_Maintenance_2009.pdf documents, there is section called *Message Item Types*. When going through the messages described in those documents, you will notice that many message elements refer to the same message Item type no matter in which message they are used. For instance, the message elements Debtor, Creditor, Ultimate debtor and Ultimate Creditor refer all to the Message Item type *PartyIdentification32* used in the pain.001.001.03, pacs.008.001.02, camt.056.001.01, camt.029.001.03, pacs.002.001.03, pain.002.001.03. Similarly, the message elements Debtor Account or Creditor Account refer all to the Message Item type *CashAccount16.*
The definitions of these message elements are the same, no matter in which message they are used. That is a powerful feature of the standard. It enables you to learn the standard pretty fast and eases the reusability of code in computer programs. Take time to go through the

message elements used in the SEPA message, and you will get acquainted fast with all of them.

We will end this chapter by answering to the following question: **What are the differences between Instruction Identification, End to End Identification and Transaction Identification?**

Before we talk about the differences, let's see what they have in common. Those three message elements are all present in the Credit Transfer Transaction Information. It means that the instruction identification is also transaction level information. Many people think that instruction identification is an instruction or order level information because of the word **instruction**. It is not correct. Instruction identification has nothing to do with the Payment Information (Order level) that we have in the pain.003 for instance. It is called instruction identification because it is used between one **instructing** party and one **instructed** party to identify a transaction

The table below gives a summary of the main differences between these three message elements and their usage.

Instruction Identification	End to End Identification	Transaction Identification
Not mandatory. A message can be sent without it.	Mandatory. Messages without it are not SEPA compliant and will be rejected.	Mandatory. Messages without it are not SEPA compliant and will be rejected.
It is generated by the instructing party for an instructed party to unambiguously identify the instruction. Instructing and instructed parties can be banks or corporations.	It is generated by initiating party (corporation initiating the message), to unambiguously identify the transaction.	It is generated by the first instructing agent (Debtor bank), to unambiguously identify the transaction.
It can be changed by each instructing party in the end-to-end chain.	This identification is passed on, unchanged, throughout the entire end-to-end chain. So, it will not be changed in the whole processing chain.	This identification is passed on, unchanged, throughout the entire end-to-end chain. So, it will not be changed in the whole processing chain.
It should never be used for reconciliation with r-transactions.	It is used for reconciliation with r-transactions by corporations.	It is used for reconciliation with r-transactions by Banks

Table 2-11 : Identification message elements and how they are used

Review Questions

1. Define the standard ISO 20022. List the financial business domains covered by the standard ISO 20022. List the business area codes of the payment domain.
2. The message definition in ISO 20022 consists of two main elements. List them and explain their differences.
3. Describe in one sentence the relationship between SEPA and ISO 20022 XML message elements
4. Illustrate the differences between SEPA Core and Additional Optional Services message elements
5. How are ISO 20022 SEPA messages structured? List and describe their main building blocks.

Discussion Questions

1. SEPA messages are based on the ISO 20022 standard but with additional rules. Why could SEPA not fully adopt the rules of the ISO 20022 standard?
2. Why are some of the blocks in R-messages not used in SEPA CORE messages? Do you think the standardization body can come back on his decision and recommend using it in the future?

Chapter 3 The different Additional Optional Services of the SCT

LEARNING OBJECTIVES

After reading this chapter, you will be able to answer the following questions:

1. What are the different Additional Optional Services in SEPA?
2. What are the characteristics of the Additional Optional Services (AOS)?
3. How can AOS be grouped?
4. What is SEPAmail and what makes it truly unique?

Additional Optional Services (AOS) were introduced in the previous chapter (See paragraph 2.3). AOS are additional because they come in addition the basic SCT Scheme. They are designated in the rulebook as "complementary services based on the Scheme so as to meet further specific customer expectations". To become participants to an AOS, banks or communities of banks must first adhere to the basic SCT scheme. AOS are also optional. It means that it is not mandatory for Banks to become member of AOS communities. There many AOS available on the SEPA Credit Transfer. The list can be found on the EPC website under this link: https://www.europeanpaymentscouncil.eu/what-we-do/sepa-credit-transfer/sepa-credit-transfer-additional-optional-services

The Additional Optional Services can be grouped in many categories:

- OAS to extend the character set in specific communities.
- OAS to use message elements that are shaded white in the SEPA Implementation Guidelines
- OAS to modify the SEPA Core requirements specified for message elements indicated in yellow in the SEPA Implementation Guidelines
- AOS based on messages used by the EPC
- AOS based on messages not used by the EPC

As we will see in this chapter some communities did not really have the choice than to implement AOS. The decision to introduce AOS in other communities was driven by keeping the services that existed before the arrival of the SEPA. These communities did not want to see the end of their existing and sometimes quite useful services. Some AOS initially created in a specific country, have been adopted by other banks outside that country borders. And the adoption can be done quite fast due to the ISO 20022 as common ground.

Banking communities and CSMs are observing each other and there is more cooperation between then as never before. Nevertheless the AOS remain confined at the level of countries. Other banking communities have not massively adopted AOS developed and used by another community. And there is no evidence that this is going to change in the future. The PE-ACH STEP2 has implemented AOS to which Banks located in any SEPA country can adhere. A couple of big banks have chosen to become members of some these AOS communities.

This chapter is entirely devoted to presenting and explaining the different AOS related to the SEPA Credit Transfer.

3.1 AOS to extend character set

The Implementation Guidelines of the basic SCT Scheme restricts the use of characters to the following Latin character set:

a b c d e f g h i j k l m n o p q r s t u v w x y z
A B C D E F G H I J K L M N O P Q R S T U V W X Y Z
0 1 2 3 4 5 6 7 8 9
/ - ? : ( ) . , ' +
Space

This set of characters is not enough for countries like Finland or Greece which use other characters in their local alphabet. Banking communities in these countries have put AOS in place in order to use specific national characters in SEPA messages exchanged among themselves.

The Greek banking community can use the following set of characters in addition to the Latin character set:

α ά β γ δ ε έ ζ η ή θ ι ί ϊ ΐ κ λ μ ν ξ ο ό π ρ ς σ τ υ ύ ϋ ΰ φ χ ψ ω ώ
Α ¶ Β Γ Δ Ε Έ Ζ Η Ή Θ Ι Ί Ϊ Κ Λ Μ Ν Ξ Ο Ό Π Ρ Σ Τ Υ Ύ Ϋ Φ Χ Ψ Ω Ώ
= ! % * ; # _ $ \ { } [ ]

The Finnish banking community has made arrangements corresponding to the special characteristics of Finnish payment transfer. These arrangements, which include the use of local Finnish characters, have been incorporated into the CSM STEP2.

Important to note is that the character set used in a specific community impacts the character encoding that it will use for the SEPA messages. At the beginning of each XML file, you find an XML declaration that looks like one the following:

```
<?xml version='1.0' encoding='ISO-8859-1' ?>
<?xml version='1.0' encoding='UTF-8' ?>
<?xml version='1.0' encoding='ISO-10646-UCS-2' ?>
```

In the first example, encoding='ISO-8859-1' means that the character encoding used for the document content is 'ISO-8859-1'. However, the number of characters allowed in the ISO-8859-1 is limited compared to 'UTF-8' for instance and the ISO-8859-1 does not support the Greek language. The character encoding used in the Greek community must at least support all Latin characters and specific local characters. For Greece, the second and third examples should work because the character encoding UTF-8 and ISO-10646-UCS-2 all support the Latin and Greek characters.

The Baltic countries (Estonia, Latvia and Lithuania) and many others in SEPA have made agreements at country level and/or with EBA STEP2 to support their specific domestic characters. This is not mention on the EPC Website; but you can find that out quite rapidly by making a search on the Internet.

A key take-away from this paragraph: almost all countries with specific local characters have implemented AOS to use them in SEPA.

3.2 AOS to use white message elements

Message elements that are shaded white or not shaded at all (it depends on the eyes of the beholder ☺) in the SEPA Implementations Guidelines, are not allowed to be used in SEPA core payments, but can be used in AOS communities. There are many of such "white" message elements in the implementations guidelines. Some banking communities have chosen to use one or several of them and thus have put AOS in place. We will consider examples from the Finnish, Greek and Italian Banking communities. In the last two examples, yellow messages elements are considered as well because they are part of the AOS. But a more thorough analysis of the yellow messages elements is done in the next paragraph.

Remark: In all the tables mentioned below, do not rely on indexes as they may not match with the ones we have in the latest implementations guidelines. Use the message elements to find the corresponding elements in the latest implementations guidelines.

3.2.1 AOS 1 Acceptance date in Finland

In Finland, it is business practice that a payment is considered paid when the originator has initiated the payment (and not when the beneficiary has received it). This information is provided in the Acceptance date field of the pacs.008.001.002. In the table below, you see how this message element is defined in the Implementation Guidelines. It is a white field. That is the reason why the Finnish Banking community created an AOS in order to use it in SEPA message.

Index	SEPA Mult	Message Element	SEPA Core Requirements
2.29	0..1	++Acceptance Date Time	**ISO Definition**: Point in time when the payment order from the initiating party meets the processing conditions of the account servicing agent. This means that the account servicing agent has received the payment order and has applied checks such as authorization, availability of funds.

Banks in other SEPA countries (Belgium, Sweden, ...) have joined the community of AOS1 Banks through the CSM STEP2.

3.2.2 SCT AOS in Greece

The Greek banking community has created an AOS to use the following white message elements in the pacs.008.001.02 message. You can check on their website: https://www.dias.com.gr/default.aspx?pid=37&mid=1&sid=54. As already said, indexes are different in the latest implementations guidelines. Use the messages elements for your own studies and verifications. They are more reliable.

Index	SEPA Mult	Message Element	ISO Definitions / SEPA Core Requirements
2.29	[0..1]	++Acceptance Date Time	Point in time when the payment order from the initiating party meets the processing conditions of the account servicing agent. This means that the account servicing agent has received the payment order and has applied checks such as authorisation, availability of funds.
2.31	[0..1]	++ Instructed Amount	Amount of money to be moved between the debtor and creditor, before deduction of charges, expressed in the currency as ordered by the initiating party.
2.32	[0..1]	++ Exchange Rate	Factor used to convert an amount from one currency into another. This reflects the price at which one currency was bought with another currency.
2.34	[0..n]	++ Charges Information	Provides information on the charges to be paid by the charge bearer(s) related to the payment transaction.

Index	SEPA Mult	Message Element	ISO Definitions / SEPA Core Requirements
2.35	[0..1]	+++ Amount	Transaction charges to be paid by the charge bearer.
2.36	[0..1]	+++ Party	Party that takes the transaction charges or to which the transaction charges are due.
2.51	[1..1]	++ Debtor Agent/Branch Identification	(AT-06 BIC of the Originator Bank) Usage Rule: Only BIC is allowed. AOS Rule: Branch Identification also allowed.
2.53	[1..1]	++ Creditor Agent/Branch Identification	(AT-23 BIC of the Beneficiary Bank) Core SEPA Rule: Only BIC is allowed. AOS Rule: Branch Identification also allowed.
2.66	[0..1]	Purpose/Proprietary	AOS allows to use the sub tag proprietary under the message element Purpose. In the Core SEPA, only the code is allowed under Purpose.

Table 3-1 : White message elements used in the Greek Banking community

There are two fields that are shaded yellow in the list. You may wonder why the Greek community included them in their AOS. The explanation is simple. The field Debtor Agent (<DbtrAgt>) and Creditor Agent <CdtrAgt> in the ISO 20022 is composed of two sub tags Financial Institution Identification (<FinInstnId>) and Branch Identification (<BrnchId>). In the SEPA core payments, only the first tag <FinInstnId> is allowed. The second one is not allowed and can be considered as a white field. An AOS is therefore required to use the Branch Identification tag.

3.2.3 AOS SCT Routing data in Italy

This AOS was created to continue the previous "Transferability" service which facilitates customer mobility between Italian Banks.

In many (SEPA) countries, when a customer leaves his bank for a new bank, the former bank would close his account and return all the credit transfers received on the former account with the reason code AC04 (Closed account number). In Italy, things are different. The creditor bank does not return the funds, but resends the SCT to the new account held at the new bank. This procedure is enforced only if the customer asks his new bank which holds the new account to switch automatically to his new account all the national payment orders where he is ordering or receiving party on the former account held with the former bank.

In general, the customer initiates new credit transfers from the new account. So the ordering part can be moved very quickly to the new bank. The receiving part is more problematic because it does not depend on the customer, but on the ordering parties. They continue to send credit transfers to the former account until they get the new account information and take it into account. But in the meantime, when the former bank receives a credit transfer on the former account, it forwards the credit transfer to the new account. Most of the time, this happens on the same business day or one business day later. In the new credit transfer initiated by the former bank, which is now debtor agent, some information should be provided to the new bank to make it clear that the SCT has been transferred.

The yellow and white fields indicated in the table below have to be filled as required by the AOS. When the new bank receives it, it has the information about the initial Debtor bank, the initial interbank settlement date and the initial Originator Bank's Reference.

Index	SEPA Mult	Message Element	AOS SCT Routing Requirements
2.12	[0..1]	+++ Local Instrument	*Usage Rule*: Only used if bilaterally agreed between the Debtor Bank and the Creditor Bank.
2.13	{Or	++++ Code	*AOS Rule:* Only '**RTE**' is allowed to indicate that the transaction is a routing SCT.
2.19	[0..1]	++ Interbank Settlement Date	*AOS Rule:* Must contain the Interbank settlement date of the original SCT. It is the message element with index 1.7 (AT-42 Settlement Date of the Credit Transfer) of the original pacs.008 message
2.37	[0..1]	++ Previous Instructing Agent	*AOS Rule:* Must contain the BIC of the original debtor Agent. It is the message element with index 2.51 (AT-06 BIC of the Originator Bank) of the original SCT
2.58	[0..n]	++ Instruction for Creditor Agent	
2.60	[0..1]	+++ Instruction Information	*AOS Rule:* Must contain the transaction identification of the original SCT. It is the message element with index 2.4 (AT-43 Originator Bank's Reference) of the original SCT.

Table 3-2 : White message elements used in the Italian Banking community

The last question to answer is the following: How does the former bank get the new account information? When the customer asks his new bank to switch transfers automatically to his new account, the new bank sends message with new account information to the former banks. After reception of the message, former banks will keep the information and transfer received credit transfers during one year.

Since almost all banks in Italy are member of the AOS SCT Routing, the usage of this service has become a standard in the Italian banking market. Therefore the Italian banking community absolutely wanted to have a SEPA like service after the migration to SEPA.

3.3 *AOS to modify yellow fields requirements*

Message elements to use in SEPA are denoted by yellow shading in the SEPA Implementations Guidelines. The rules that must be followed when using these fields are indicated in the SEPA Core requirements. However, these requirements are different from rules that some banking communities have been applying for years. These communities did not have the choice than to create AOS in order to "modify" the SEPA rules. That is the subject in this sub chapter. We will consider examples of AOS where communities have changed the yellow field requirements to make them better suit their specific needs. The first example is the AOS SCT in Slovakia which was created to support the continuity of the Slovakian specific symbols for payment identification. The second one is the AOS OGM-VCS in Belgium which was put in place to support the continuity of the Belgian structured communication standard for national credit transfers. The last one is the Finnish AOS2 to extend remittance information which has very limited occurrences in the SEPA Core requirements.

3.3.1 AOS SCT in Slovakia

The Additional Optional Service applied in Slovakia to SEPA Credit Transfer is about the field End to End Identification. In SEPA, the related message element can contain up to 35 alphanumeric characters without specific structure and syntax. But this was not OK for the banking community in Slovakia since it has been using specific syntax for End to End Identification for years.

Slovakian specific symbols are created for payment identification. These symbols are used for the reconciliation of payments and must follow the following syntax "/VS[N10]/SS[N10]/KS[N4]"

- /VS[N10] - Variable Symbol indicated by /VS and followed by up to ten digits. It carries payment reference information.
- /SS[N10] - Specific Symbol indicated /SS and followed by up to ten digits. It is used by some institutions for further classification of incoming payments.
- /KS[N4] - Constant Symbol indicated by /KS and followed by up to four digits. It carries payment purpose information.

The SEPA Core and AOS requirements for the End to End Identification message element are summarized in the table below.

Index	SEPA Mult	Message Element	SEPA Core and AOS Requirements
2.3	[1..1]	+++ End to End Identification	(AT-41 Originator's Reference to the Credit Transfer) *Usage Rule*: A customer reference that must be passed on in the end-to-end chain. In the event that no reference was given, 'NOTPROVIDED' must be used. ***AOS Rule*:** When provided the syntax has to be as follow **/VS[N10]/SS[N10]/KS[N4]**

Table 3-3 : AOS rule on yellow message element for the Slovakian Banking community

Some examples of symbols generated according to the above rules lock like this:

- All symbols used: <EndToEndId>/VS657368/SS6338/KS862</EndToEndId>
- SS not used: <EndToEndId>/VS743459/SS/KS7268</EndToEndId>
- SS and KS not used: <EndToEndId>/VS278548/SS/KS</EndToEndId>
- Not provided: <EndToEndId>NOTPROVIDED</EndToEndId>

If two AOS banks in Slovakia exchanged a pacs.008 message, this field must have either 'NOTPROVIDED' or a reference which follows the syntax "/VS[N10]/SS[N10]/KS[N4]". Otherwise, the transaction will be rejected for not complying with the AOS Rule. So the AOS Rule in this case is more restrictive that SEPA Rule, for which the reference can be up to 35 characters and does not have to keep a specific syntax.

3.3.2 AOS OGM-VCS in Belgium

The second example is about the Structured Remittance Information « OGM-VCS » in the Belgian banking community. That standard was in used in that community long before the SEPA. The community wanted to support the continuity of that national standard from legacy payments to SEPA payments and therefore had to create an AOS. Two message elements are concerned by this AOS which is referred to as AOS 1 in the Belgian banking community. The SEPA Core and AOS rules for the yellow field elements are summarized in the following table:

Index	SEPA Mult	Message Element	SEPA Core and AOS Requirements
2.102	[0..1]	+++++ Issuer	***AOS Rule*:** Only 'BBA' is allowed. BBA stands for the **B**elgian **B**ankers' and Stockbroking Firms' **A**ssociation

Index	SEPA Mult	Message Element	SEPA Core and AOS Requirements
2.103	[0..1]	+++++ Reference	*Usage Rule*: If a Creditor Reference contains a check digit, the receiving bank is not required to validate this. *Usage Rule*: If the receiving bank validates the check digit and if this validation fails, the bank may continue its processing and send the transaction to the next party in the chain *Usage Rule*: RF Creditor Reference may be used (ISO 11649) ***AOS Rule:*** Reference must be a 12 digits format number; the last 2 digits are check digits (modulo 97) of the first 10 digits, but if the result is 0, then the check digits are 97.

Table 3-4 : White message elements used in the Belgian Banking community

An example of reference is 111553282236. 36 are check digits for 1115532822 which is the real reference.

SEPA recommends using the RF creditor reference, which can contain up to 25 characters (The reference itself can have up to 35 characters according to the ISO 20022 Rule), but it is not mandatory. SEPA also recommends validating the check digits, but it is not mandatory either. In Belgium, AOS banks expect to have a reference that is structured according to the AOS rule. They validate the check digits. If the validation fails, the transaction is rejected because it does not comply with OGM-VCS standard and therefore not with the AOS. The field issuer remains optional. But if it is filled, it must have the value BBA. Another value will cause the transaction to be rejected.

3.3.3 OAS to extend remittance information with limited occurrences

The AOS, which is subject of study in this paragraph, is a Finnish creation. It is the *AOS2 Bundling several invoices and credit notes to one payment.* To achieve that, the restrictions imposed by SEPA on the remittance information had to be removed. SEPA Core requirements had to be changed and this could only be fulfilled with an AOS. Let us first consider the requirements that we find in the SEPA Implementations Guidelines on the Remittance Information.

Index	SEPA Mult	Message Element	SEPA Core Requirements
2.75	[0..1]	++ Remittance Information	(AT-05 Remittance Information) Usage Rule: Either 'Structured' or 'Unstructured' may be present.
2.76	[0..n]	+++ Unstructured	*Usage Rule*: 'Unstructured' may carry structured remittance information, as agreed between the Originator and the Beneficiary. *Usage Rule*: Only one occurrence of 'Unstructured' is allowed.
2.77	[0..n]	+++ Structured	*Format Rule*: 'Structured' can be used, provided the tags and the data within the 'Structured' element **do not exceed 140 characters in length.**

			Usage Rule: **Only one occurrence of 'Structured' is allowed.**

Table 3-5 : SEPA Core rules on remittance information

Both unstructured and structured remittance information cannot be used at the same time. And only one occurrence is allowed for the one or the other remittance information. And both cannot exceed 140 characters.

The Finnish banking community created the AOS2 to meet three main objectives:

1. the ability to indicate both unstructured and structured remittance information at the same time. Only one occurrence of unstructured remittance information is allowed as in SEPA.
2. the ability to provide up to 9 occurrences of structured remittance information.
3. the ability to extend the length of each occurrence of structured remittance information to 280 characters.

These new rules would be very appreciated by corporate customers and provide a great service to them. They can initiate a payment including one occurrence of unstructured remittance information and several (max 9) occurrences of structured remittance information. After April 2016, AOS2 banks will have the option to support up to 999 occurrences of structured remittance information instead of the former 9 occurrences. This will make this AOS even more powerful. The other requirements remain unchanged.

The rules for the AOS2 are summarized in the table below:

Index	SEPA Mult	Message Element	SEPA AOS Requirements
2.75	[0..1]	++ Remittance Information	(AT-05 Remittance Information) *Usage Rule AOS:* Both 'Structured' and 'Unstructured' can be present.
2.76	[0..n]	+++ Unstructured	*Usage Rule AOS*: 'Unstructured' may carry structured remittance information, as agreed between the Originator and the Beneficiary. *Usage Rule AOS*: Only one occurrence of 'Unstructured' is allowed. **Remark: AOS and Core rules are exactly the same.**
2.77	[0..n]	+++ Structured	Format Rule: 'Structured' can be used, provided the tags and the data within the 'Structured' element **do not exceed 280 characters in length**. *Usage Rule AOS*: **Up to 999 occurrences of 'Structured' are allowed**.

Table 3-6 : Rules added on yellow message elements for the AOS2

Banks in other SEPA countries (like Denmark, Germany, Luxembourg ...) have joined the community of AOS2 Banks through the CSM STEP2.

3.4 AOS based on messages used by the EPC (French SCTR)

When the SEPA arrived, the French Banking community had been using a service for many years to cancel credit transfers that are wrongly settled. That service was called Cancellation of Accounting Transactions wrongly Cleared (In French Annulations d'Opérations comptables Compensées à Tort [AOCT]). There is no equivalent in the SCT core scheme. As a consequence, the migration to the SEPA Credit Transfer meant the end of that service.

One can argue that there is a possibility to cancel a credit transfer in the SEPA Core Scheme. The banks can use it if they want to cancel transfers. This is true, but there is a fundamental difference between the cancellation requests in the SEPA Scheme and the cancellation service of the French Banking communities. As we saw in the previous chapters, the cancellation request in the SEPA core scheme is just a question. It is not a booking transaction and does not move funds. The money is paid back only if the beneficiary bank responds with a positive response. But the scheme allows the deduction of charges from the amount of the original SCT by the beneficiary bank.

After the launch of the SEPA, the French Banking Community realized that it was difficult to recover the money after cancelling (trying to cancel) the transactions with the camt.056. Furthermore, charges were sometimes deducted from the SCT amount. And the total amount deducted was not negligible and grew with the number of transactions to cancel. Quite logically, the community decided to implement the SEPA Credit Transfer Reversal AOS to address all these problems and get back to the old days before the SEPA.

The SEPA Credit Transfer Reversal AOS allows to reverse wrongly SCT transactions sent by Banks, not by customers. The types of errors allowed in the SCTR AOS are strictly limited to duplicate sending and technical problem resulting in erroneous bank coordinates of the beneficiaries (BIC or IBAN) or erroneous amounts. The number of duplicate or erroneous transactions should be high enough to justify the use of the SCTR service and the bank initiating the SCTR has to declare an incident at interbank level.

Unfortunately sometimes banks wrongly issue hundreds of thousands of transactions. Duplicate sending is by far the main reason why banks want to cancel the transactions. It has happened in the past and it will happen in the future despite all precautions to avoid them. Banks appreciate having the AOS SCTR to handle that. Documentation about the SCTR AOS can be downloaded freely from the CFONB Website.

The French community could rely on messages available in the documents that the EPC has published (Implementations Guidelines for SCT / SDD and recommendations). It is easier to understand and implement them because people are already acquitted with similar messages and can even reuse some of the code created in the pass to handle the SCTR messages. And finally interoperability with the SEPA Core Scheme can be easily verified. The next figure shows the messages exchanged in this SCTR AOS.

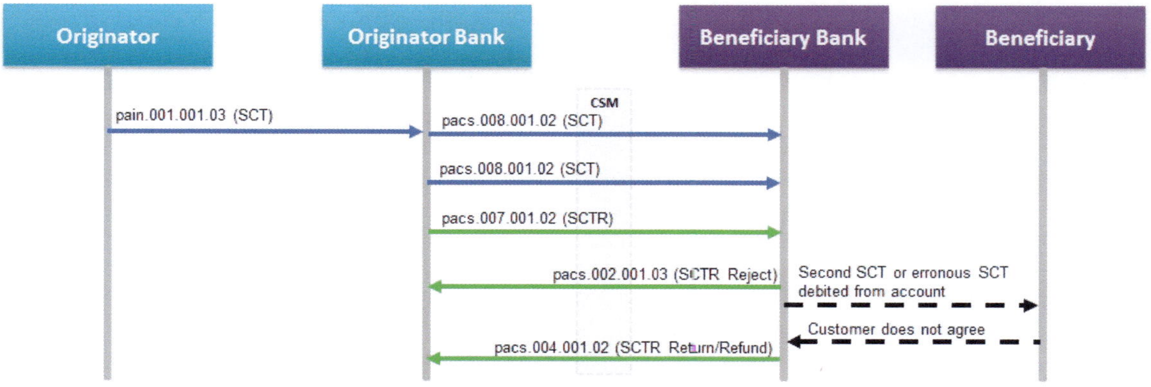

Figure 3.1: AOS SCTR Messages

The messages exchanged in the SCTR AOS are in green color: the pacs.007.001.02 (Payment Reversal or SCTR), pacs.002.001.03 (Reject of the Payment Reversal or SCTR Reject), pacs.004.001.02 (Return / Refund of the Payment Reversal or SCTR Return / Refund). We are familiar with all the messages except the pacs.007.001.02.

The pacs.007.001.02 is an R-transaction of the pacs.008.001.02. But the two others transactions pacs.002.001.03 and pacs.004.001.02 are R-transactions of the pacs.007.001.02. This difference is crucial to process them correctly as we will see below.

The assumption made in the figure above is that the SCTR is sent because of a duplicate SCT. That is why you see two pacs.008.001.02. The pacs.007.01.02 SCTR is sent to cancel the second SCT. In contrary to the camt.056, the pacs.007 is a booking transaction and implies moving the money. No confirmation or reply is expected from the beneficiary bank. The money will be moved at settlement date from the beneficiary bank to the originator bank. The amount of the Reversal is strictly identical to the amount of the original transaction. No charges are allowed and the originator bank can have all the money back.

When the beneficiary bank gets the pacs.007, it performs some checks before accepting it and debiting the customer. Many exceptions can occur during the processing. The beneficiary account can be closed. The original SCT could have never been received. Funds may not be available on the beneficiary account. And so on. The list of all possible reasons can be found in the SCTR Implementations Guidelines published by the CFONB.

In case of exceptions, the beneficiary bank will reject the SCTR. If this happens before settlement, it will send an SCTR Reject. If it is after settlement, it will send and SCTR Return. In practice, banks send SCTR Return. SCTR are always received after settlement. And the banks must transmit SCTR Returns within ten Banking Business Days after the Settlement. Both pacs.002.001.03 and pacs.004.001.02 are booking transactions. They reverse the booking done by the pacs.007.01.02. This means that the funds will be debited from the originator bank and credited to the beneficiary bank at interbank level. And the beneficiary will get his money back.

The pacs.004.001.02 can also be used as Refund of the Payment Reversal. In which case does this apply? The SCTR Refund is initiated by the bank at the demand of the beneficiary who claims for reimbursement of the Reversal amount debited from his account without his consent. The SCTR Refund can be sent up to 13 months after the debit of the SCTR as required by the Payment Service Directive. The beneficiary will then have the final word provided he is right of course.

I will finish this paragraph by answering two questions about messages that people asked me regularly when I worked on a SCTR implementation project.

Question 1: The same pacs.004.001.02 is used to for SCTR Return and SCTR Refund. How to know for which message the pacs.004.001.02 is sent? The answer is provided in the AOS Implementations Guidelines which states (something like the following): *If the 'Return Originator' contains a 'Name', it means that the message is being used as a Refund. However, if the 'Return Originator' contains a BIC, then it means that the message is being used as a Return.*

Index	Mult	Message Element	SCTR AOS Requirements
X.xx	[0..1]	+++ Originator	Mandatory (Identification of the type of party initiating the SCTR R-transaction) *Usage Rule*: Limited to BIC for an Agent (Return) or 'Name' for a non-financial institution (Refund). *Usage Rule*: 'Name' is limited to 70 characters in length.

Question 2: The same pacs.004.001.02 message is used to return either a credit transfer or a payment reversal. How to know when a pacs.004.001.02 should return a SCT or a SCTR? The answer is found in the Implementation Guidelines for the message element Original Message Name Identification. If a pacs.004.001.02 is used to return a SCT, then 'pacs.008.001.02' should be indicated as Original Message Name Identification. But if a pacs.004.001.02 is used to return a SCTR, then the Original Message Name Identification will be 'pacs.007.001.02'.

Index	Mult	Message Element	SEPA Core / SCTR AOS Requirements
X.xx	[1..1]	+++ Original Message Name Identification	'pacs.008.001.02' if the message is used as SCT Return. 'pacs.007.001.02' if the message is used as SCTR Return / Refund

The SCTR AOS has been implemented by the French STET and is used exclusively in the French banking community at the moment.

3.5 AOS based on messages not used by the EPC

3.5.1 The French Change of Account Information (CAI)

CAI stands for Change of Account Information. It is a service to inform the originator bank that the beneficiary account has changed and provide the new account information at the same time. An equivalent service (DCD for Demande de Correction de Domiciliation in French) was used by the French Banking community. The community decided to implement the CAI AOS in order to have an equivalent service after the national Credit Transfer migrated to SEPA.

The account information of a customer can change for various reasons:

- The customer is moving for personal or professional reasons to another city and his account has to be attached to another branch of the bank.
- A Bank is implementing a new core banking system and cannot keep the customer account structure as it is.
- Two banks are merging to create a new Bank. The Bank code must change and this will impact the customer account information.
- And so on.

Generally many end parties send credit transfers and direct debits to a customer account. So when the account number changes, those end parties need to be informed, so that they can update the customer account information. But this requires some time and the bank does not want to reject credit transfers or direct debit sent to the former account. To avoid rejecting incoming transactions, banks put in place lookup tables with the connection between the old account and the new account. So every time a payment is received with old account information, the old IBAN is automatically replaced by the new IBAN and the funds credited on the new account.

This solution is limited in time and the customer can forget to notify all debtors and creditors about the change of his account number. His bank wants to make sure the originators update the account information and start sending payments with new account information before it is too late. In case both originator and beneficiary banks are members of the CAI AOS community, the beneficiary bank will send the CAI message to the originator Bank. The originator bank can inform its customer, the originator, by forwarding a copy of the CAI message to him if it is possible or by sending him an e-mail for instance. The originator is then supposed to update the beneficiary account information in his own systems.

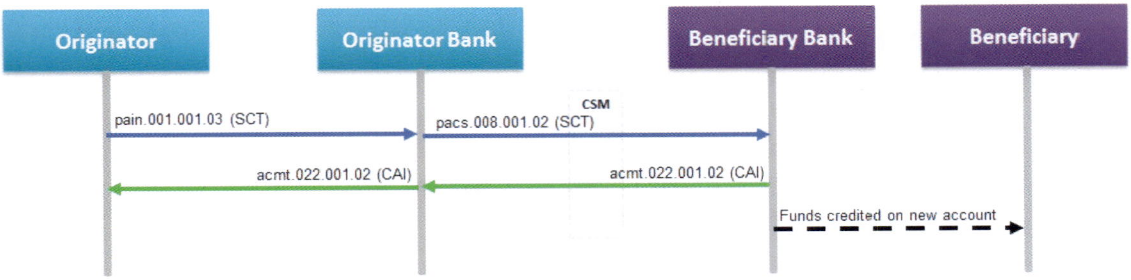

Figure 3.2: CAI AOS Messages

The message exchanged for the CAI is the acmt.022.001.02 (Identification Modification Advice V02) as shown in the above figure. It is the version 2 of acmt.022 message. When these lines are written, the acmt.022.001.02 is the last version available. It can be downloaded from the ISO 20022 Payments messages page and not from ISO 20022 Message Archive as for the other messages we have seen up to now. By the way, you can read on the ISO20022 Website that the submitting organization for this message is the GUF. GUF stands for **G**roupement des **U**tilisateurs de S.W.I.F.T. en **F**rance (SWIFT Users' Group in France).

It is interesting to notice that the CAI is an *account* management message (acmt). That is logical indeed when we consider that the message is used to inform about the change of *account* information. You do not find the acmt.022.001.0x in any EPC document. But fortunately that message is quite simple to understand and therefore to implement.

EBA STEP2 has been offering the CAI AOS since November 2012. But at the moment, there is no interoperability[6] between the CAI AOS offered by STET (CSM of France), and the CAI AOS offered by EBA CLEARING. The French banks using the CAI service of STET cannot use the CAI service of EBA CLEARING; and vice versa. Even without interoperability, we can see that EBA STEP2 saw an interest in implementing this service. And since it is a PE-ACH, all banks in the SEPA area can adhere to the CAI AOS if they want.

3.5.2 AOS SEPAmail

All the AOS that were presented so far have been put in place by banking communities either to extend character set or to make services that were already present in their communities available in SEPA. The AOS SEPAmail is different. It has no root in the past. This time a banking community really looked for ways to create and provide unique services above SEPA. SEPAmail is probably the most innovative Additional Optional Service created up to now. Launched in 2008 by five banking groups in France (BNP Paribas, Banque Populaire Caisse d'Epargne, Crédit Agricole, Crédit Mutuel-CIC and Société Générale), SEPAmail clearly has the ambition to be adopted and used throughout the SEPA area.

---

6 The details are provided in the following document https://www.abe-eba.eu/media/azure/production/1376/smart_local-practices-products-and-requirements-in-post-migration-sepa.pdf

In the subsequent paragraphs, we will first look at the definition of SEPAmail. Then a brief overview of some SEPAmail applications (or services) will be given. If you are really interested in this topic, you can go to the website http://www.sepamail.eu/en/

3.5.2.1 What is SEPAmail?

SEPAmail is the concatenation of two words: SEPA and mail. The first word SEPA refers to the SEPA area and particularly the means of payments used in that area like the SCT and the SDD. The word mail probably makes you think of e-mail and more generally of messages exchange. Simply put, SEPAmail is about exchanging information and documents related to SEPA (and also other national) payments in a *secure and reliable way* among banks themselves and between banks and customers. It can be about asking someone to pay a bill, verifying the reliability of bank identifiers, requesting a customer to sign a SDD mandate, and so on. The end parties, individuals or companies, exchange the information through their banks as you can see on the following figure. Bank A and Bank B are both either senders or receivers of SEPAmail messages on behalf of their customers.

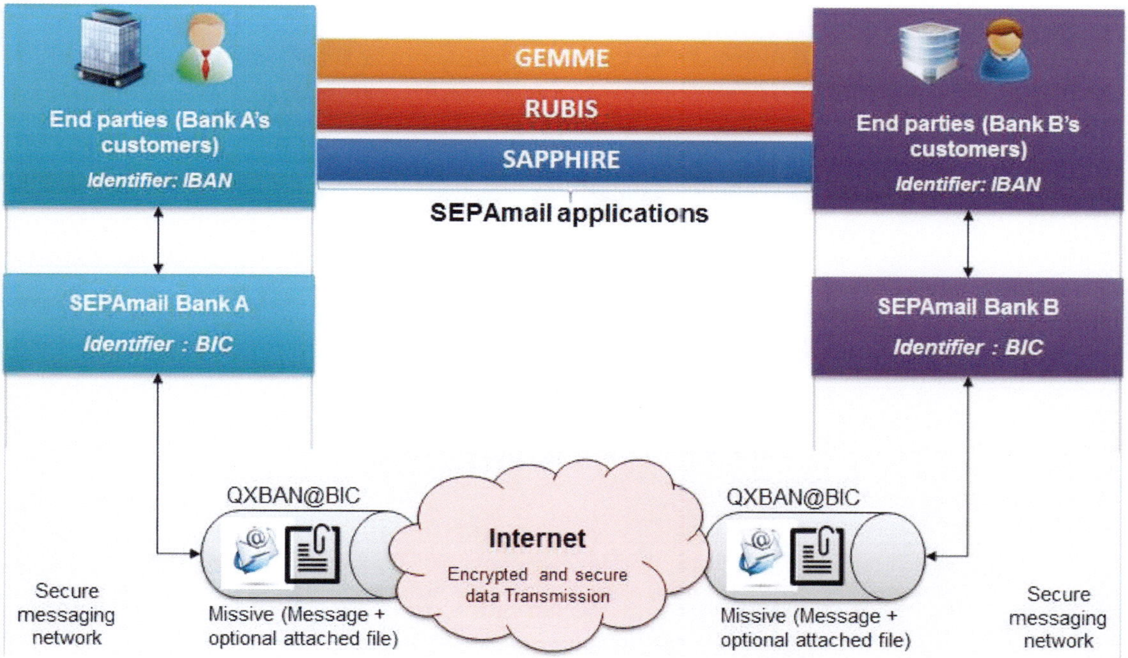

Figure 3.3: The Four Corner Model of SEPAmail

The customers access the SEPAmail messages through their bank secure websites using Personal Computers, smartphones or similar devices. But exchanging data over the network requires a SEPAmail address. It has the following pattern: IBAN@BIC. The IBAN can be compared to the name or user identification in an e-mail address (*IBAN*@BIC is similar *userid*@domain). The BIC is similar to the domain. BIC and IBAN are SEPAmail reference identifiers. An IBAN unambiguously identifies an account and therefore the account holder. The BIC designates a bank. SEPAmail banks act as routing relays of the messages. You are probably wondering why you see QXBAN@BIC (and not IBAN@BIC) on the picture above.

The IBAN is a sensitive data that criminals can use it to carry out fraudulent transactions. Banks did not want to disclose real customers IBAN in SEPAmail communications and therefore created the QXBAN. The QXBAN is an alias or alternate name of the IBAN. It is generated by SEPAmail member banks and consists of exactly 34 characters:

- QX (2 characters) for the "country code" assigned by the iso 3166-2 for private uses
- The control key (2 characters) calculated like the IBAN control key
- The BIC11 code (11 characters) of the bank that generates the QXBAN. In case the BIC contains only 8 characters, it is completed with XXX.
- An internal Bank identifier (19 characters) which is randomly selected and linked to the customer account number.

QXBAN can be considered as an encrypted IBAN. The member banks should keep secret the correspondence between the IBAN and the QXBAN. One IBAN is linked to exactly one QXBAN. At reception, the bank "decrypts" the QXBAN to identify the IBAN and account holder.

SEPAmail data are called missives. A missive is composed of a message structured in XML and binary files that can be attached like invoices in PDF format. XML messages allow the coexistence of the ISO standards with non ISO specific data. This provides some flexibility in the organization and processing of flows between the different parties. SEPAmail relies on the Internet and many standards like W3C and of course the ISO 13616 (IBAN) and the ISO 9362 (BIC).

SEPAmail is a messaging network on top of which many applications have been and will be built. Comparison between SEPAmail network and SWIFTNet is interesting and ease the understanding for those who know SWIFT. SWIFTNet is a secure network on top of which protocols and services are built and made available to participants. Likewise there are applications above the SEPAmail network that can be used by the members and participants. What are they? And for which purpose are they used? Read on to get the answers to these questions.

3.5.2.2 SEPAmail applications

The real value of SEPAmail lies in the applications built on top of the messaging network. An application can be seen as a service with a set of functionalities and messages provided to the end users. Here SEPAmail really stands out from all the other AOS as the number of services that can be created above is theoretically infinite. SEPAmail is not an AOS, but a family of AOS.

SEPAmail designers managed to name all the applications after gems (Great poets and artists!): AGATE, DIAMOND, GEMME, IOLITE, JADE, JASPE, RUBIS and SAPPHIRE. According to the latest news available on the SEPAmail website, the applications GEMME, RUBIS, SAPPHIRE have been deployed and are currently available on the french market. The JADE project is still ongoing and is currently in the specifications phase. The remaining applications are still under discussion among the participating banking groups.

GEMME

Acronym for **G**lobal **E**uropean **M**andate **M**anagement & **E**xchange, this application enables to exchange messages in relation to the management of SEPA Direct Debits and the associated mandates for both creditor and debtor.

A creditor can send a mandate to a debtor and ask for acceptance (signature). A debtor can update a mandate with a new IBAN and inform the creditor about it. The debtor bank can request a copy of the mandate to the creditor. Etc. GEMME allows a paperless mandate process which reduces human error and increases efficiency.

RUBIS

French word for ruby, RUBIS stands for "**R**èglement **U**niversel **B**ancaire **I**mmédiat & **S**EPA", in English "Immediate & SEPA Banking Universal Settlement". This application enables a supplier (creditor) to generate claims with attachments and send them to their customers (debtors). A debtor, on receipt of the message, responds and initiates a SEPA Credit Transfer to pay the bill. He can choose the day that suits him best (before the due date). This is done quickly and easily with few clicks. Besides that, the SCT transports the references for automatic reconciliation with the invoice at creditor's side.

SAPPHIRE

SAPPHIRE stands for **S**ecurity, **A**uthentication, **P**rivacy, **P**ublic Key Infrastructure, **H**ighly Innovative, **I**nteroperable, **R**eliable & **E**xchange. It is a protocol for authentication and signature that can be used with multiple devices and with various softwares. A user can authenticate himself on a SEPAmail plug or any other bank or partner system. SAPPHIRE can also be used to sign SEPAmail messages at several levels before sending it to the bank. It relies on X509 certificates.

JADE

JADE (**J**oint **A**dditional **D**ata & **E**xchange) is the application to send a notification of a credit transfer and at the same time provide an explanatory document to the beneficiary. The credit transfer itself can be initiated immediately or after getting an answer on the notification.

JADE therefore enables a payor to notify and inform a payee before performing a credit transfer. The payee has the option to refuse the transfer before initiation in case he is not the right beneficiary or for some another reason.

Following are a couple of examples where the JADE application is used. An employer sends the pay slips to its employees and initiates the credit transfers. No need to wait for an answer as it is their salaries. A health insurance funds sends a reimbursement notification to an insurant. The money is transferred 5 days later in case of absence of refusal. The insurant may refuse in case he is not supposed to receive the reimbursement.

DIAMOND

Sometimes a debtor or a creditor wants to know if an account exists and if it is open in the name of the person who claims to have it. The SEPAmail application DIAMOND (**D**irect **I**dentity control for **A**ccount **M**anagement **ON** **D**emand) provides a solution for that. It enables to ensure the reliability of an IBAN.

The requester sends a verification request to the bank holding the account being subject to the verification. The verification request is based on acmt.023.001.01 message of the ISO 20022 standards to which specific data is added. The account holding bank replies with a verification report based on the acmt.024.001.01 message of the ISO 20022 standards. Based on the response, the requester now knows if he can initiate a credit transfer or a direct debit towards that account.

IOLITE

IOLITE simply stands for **I**nv**O**incing **LITE**. It is an application used for the transmission of any type of invoices with or without intermediary between companies and customers. Invoicing dematerialization is encouraged and made accessible to companies of small and medium sizes.

AGATE

The description of AGATE (**A** **G**eneric **AT**tachment **E**xchange) makes one think of tweets. This application allows sending one or many short messages of 140 characters and an attachment.

JASPE

JASPE is the acronym for **J**ointed **A**ttached **S**igned **P**DF & **E**xchange. This application enables multiple people to sign a document (pdf format) according to a defined path. A defined path simply means that there are many options to sign the document: 1) one signatory, 2) one signatory and a counter signatory or 3) several signatories. In case of many signatories the order in which they have to sign might be imposed.

I find it fascinating that all SEPAmail applications are named after gems. What about you?

Last interesting point: SEPAmail applications can be used in combination with others. They are not mutually exclusive. End parties have multiple options to send attachments for example. Based on the context and needs, they may choose to use one application or another one.

In conclusion, the majority of the Additional Optional Services were put in place in many countries either to extend the character set or to maintain services that were available before the SEPA. The AOS SEPAmail really stands out because it is not inherited for the past.

Review Questions

1. What is an Additional Optional Service (AOS)?
2. List and describe the different groups of Additional Optional Services.
3. Describe the main features of each AOS group.
4. What is SEPAmail? And what makes the SEPAmail AOS truly unique?
5. Cite and describe few services available in SEPAmail.

Discussion Questions

1. What makes AOS interesting?
2. The possibilities to create AOS are infinite. Do you agree with this sentence? Give your arguments.
3. Why have communities implemented Additional Optional Services?
4. Do you think some AOS might have been integrated in the CORE SEPA scheme? If yes, why did it not happen?
5. Why is the use of many AOS restricted to one community?

Chapter 4 The payment processing value chain

LEARNING OBJECTIVES

After reading this chapter, you will be able to answer the following questions:

1. What is the payment processing value chain?
2. What is Payment acquisition? What is Payment reporting?
3. What is Payment order management?
4. What is Payment exchange?
5. What are the main functionalities needed in each step of the value chain?
6. What are payment status reports? When are they generated during the payment processing?

As introduction to this chapter on the payment processing value chain, let us first define what a value chain is as it is a key concept to understand this chapter. Below is a list of definitions that are often encountered in the literature:

- A value chain is the whole series of activities that create and build value at every step.
- A value chain is a set of activities that a firm operating in a specific industry performs in order to deliver a valuable product or service for the market.
- Interlinked value-adding activities that convert inputs into outputs which, in turn, add to the bottom line and help create competitive advantage.
- And so on

A value chain is a set of interlinked activities. Each activity in the chain creates value by transforming inputs to outputs. All the activities taken together deliver a valuable product or service to the customer. In payments, we mainly talk about services even though the term payment product is widely used in the industry.

The payment processing value chain is the set of activities required to successfully process payments and deliver the service expected by the customers. It consists of three main processes which are payment acquisition and reporting, payment order management and payment exchange.

Figure 4.1: Payment processing value chain

Please note that this chapter is not about the *payment value chain* which is much broader and include activities like payment innovation or marketing. Only the payment processing value chain will be considered. Furthermore, it will be analyzed from the bank's perspective and not from the corporations' perspective or CSM's perspective. The Bank is a critical player in the payment processing. If you remember the open loop model presented in the outset of this book, banks play the roles of intermediaries between end parties and payment systems. Therefore looking at what is happening inside the bank will be helpful in understanding the payment processing.

In the remainder of this chapter, the three main processes of the payment value chain will be analyzed in detail. Each process is itself composed of many activities that will be presented. It is not possible to present an exhaustive list of all activities. Each bank is unique and banks do not perform activities in the same way or in the same order. The idea here is to study the major activities and their purpose. I strongly encourage you to take the time to read this chapter several times until you are able to explain it to the others.

4.1 The Payment Acquisition and Reporting

Simply stated, acquisition is the process of getting orders and instructions from customers and other parties for execution. It is the first process in the processing value chain since the bank must acquire the payment orders before managing and exchanging them.

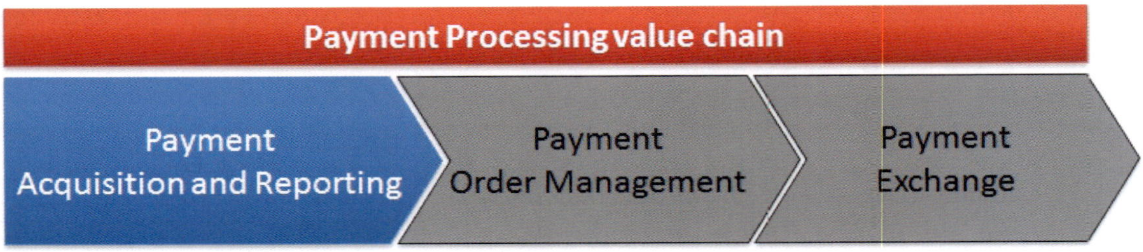

Figure 4.2: Payment acquisition and reporting sub process

A Bank provides many acquisition channels to its customers. In general, the customers get the reporting through the same channels. When information (messages or files) flows from customer to bank, it is considered as acquisition. The other way around, when information flows from bank to customer, the bank considers it as reporting. Generally, banks use the same platform for acquisition and reporting. The customer can then connect to the same platform to send and receive files. But note that they are two distinct topics. While the acquisition takes place at the beginning of the payment processing, the reporting is transverse across the whole process. The payment processing value chain could have been presented like this.

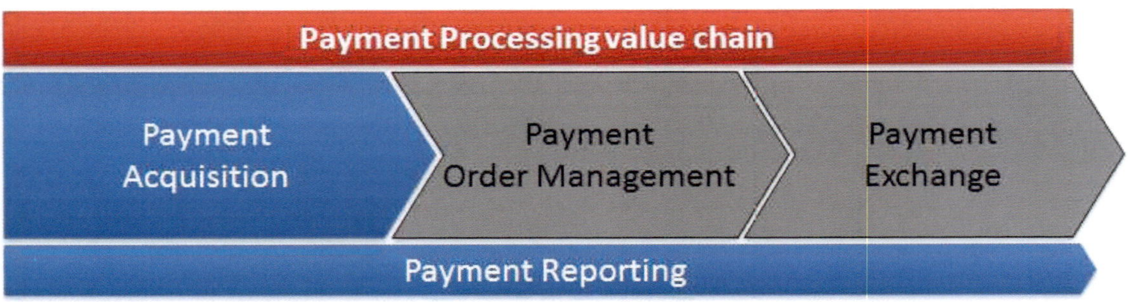

Figure 4.3: Payment reporting - a transverse process

Reporting is about the payment status. Was the payment accepted fully or partially? Was it rejected? Was it successfully booked? Was it exchanged? It tells the customer how far the payment has gone in the process and what is its final status. Payment Order Manager and Payment Exchange Solutions must therefore send information to the reporting platform for the customer to get the latest information. I finally chose the first option (Figure 4.2: Payment acquisition and reporting sub process) to emphasize that acquisition and reporting is usually done on the same platform. But the second option (Figure 4.3: Payment reporting - a transverse process) is also valid.

The picture below depicts the usual acquisition channels through which payments get to the bank.

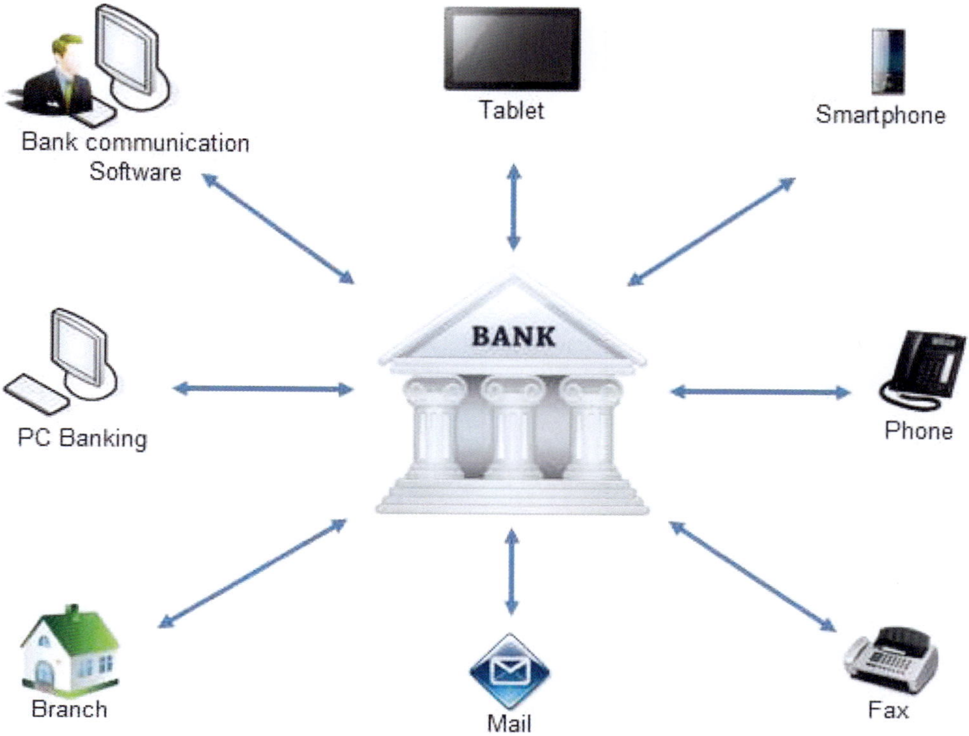

Figure 4.4: Bank Acquisition / Reporting channels

Channels can be grouped in three main categories: manual channels, clever channels and smart channels.

- Manual channels are channels from which the bank receives orders which have to be input manually in payment processing applications. Among such channels, we have the mail, the branch and the fax. There is no automatic control in the channels themselves. That is why they are called manual channels. First controls must be performed manually by bank employees who may ask for additional information if the order is not complete (Missing signature, wrong date, incorrect IBAN, asn.). And after the first controls, someone still needs to input the order in a payment application. Since there is a lot of manual operation involved, manual channels increase the operational risk.

- Clever channels are channels where the customer can input directly the orders himself like Internet, Phones, Smartphones and Tablets. Many controls are integrated into these channels and the customer gets an information almost in real-time if the order cannot be accepted for any reason (Invalid IBAN, Missing beneficiary name, date too far in the future, etc.). The customer can validate the order only if it is complete and all the controls are successful. After the validation, the order is generally processed STP. No human intervention is needed. And this increases the operational efficiency while reducing the operational risk at the same time. The bank just provides the channel and the customer does the rest due to the “cleverness” of the channels.

- Smart channels are channels where the bank will get orders in batch files from their customers or from themselves. The files containing the orders must be received in a secure manner and with the expected format. Many services are implemented in these channels and the bank generally creates an acquisition contract to manage customer conditions and expectations. That is why they can really be seen as smart. In case something goes wrong, the bank will inform the customer immediately through reporting files sent back to him. All this will be analyzed in detail later.

No matter what channel is used, security remains an important topic. There are channels that are more secure than others. And the bank must define procedures to manage the security risks properly and adequately in each of the channels.

Now let us look at the different channels and how banks use them to receive orders from their customers or to send reporting to them. We will analyze them in the same order as they were presented in the categories above.

4.1.1 Manual channels

Mail: Some people still use the mail to send payment orders to their banks. They write a letter to the bank in which they give instruction to execute an order. At reception, the bank verifies the completeness of the order. But how to be sure that the letter really comes from the client? In general, handwritten signature verification is done (So the letter must be signed). If needed, the bank may call the customer to get his confirmation. This is a typical case showing that many channels can be combined to better serve the customer.

Fax: Like the mail, the fax is used to send orders to the bank. Here the handwritten signature is also important and helps verify that the order really comes from the customer. When appropriate, the bank calls the customer for confirmation. If everything is fine, the order will be manually input by a clerk in a bank application.

Branch: The branch is probably the most known bank channel to many people. Customers can go to the branch for any matter to handle with their bank. Some services can be provided only through the branch and not other channels. If for example, a customer wants the bank to execute an order with an important amount (100 000 Euros for example), he will have no choice but to go to his branch. In the branch the customer may fill in a form with the order information and then gives it to a clerk. The bank clerk verifies the customer identity and the order completeness and then proceeds with a manual entry of the order in a payment application. Another possibility to serve the customer in a branch is to welcome him directly and verify his identity. After that the customer gives the information orally to the employee who inputs them directly into the payment application. When the order is complete, it is printed and handed to the customer for verification and signature. After that the order is validated and ready to be executed.

The common point to all three channels above is that an employee of the bank has to enter the payment order manually. And there is a cost related to that. Time (which is money) has to be allocated to that activity. The bank should provide the proper training to the employee, so that he can perform his job well.

4.1.2 Clever channels

Phone: The phone is one of the long-established channels banks use to interact with their customers. For the credit transfer, the customer calls the bank in order to give the instruction to move money from one of this account to a beneficiary account. In the past, a clerk in the bank would answer the customer call and ask him some questions to verify that the customer and not someone else is behind the phone. Only after that the customer would be asked to provide information about the order like the account to debit, the amount of money to transfer, the beneficiary account and the date of execution and so on. But this belongs to history. Things are more sophisticated nowadays.

Today, the customer calls an Interactive voice response, provides a login and a password for authentication and then gives the order information. Most of the times, the customer interacts completely with the Interactive Voice Response (IVR) and does not speak to anybody even though it is always possible to route the call to an employee in a call center. After the order details are given, the order is executed in case no issue is found.

In summary, customer can interacts directly and automatically through the phone to give payment orders. Or he can talk to someone who is going to input the order manually. In that sense, the phone is a hybrid channel. But my choice to put it in the clever channel category is because the IVR is the standard way of serving the customers today.

Smartphone: The Smartphone has become very popular during the last years. Every bank has a mobile application that each customer can download from an app store and install on his Smartphone. The application allows to see the accounts' status and the latest operations and to initiate transfers of funds, in general up to a certain limit. Customers give a login and a password to connect to the mobile application, thus authenticating themselves to access to the services. The customer has to confirm orders by inputting a code or his password again. In case there is an issue with the order, the customer will be informed directly and will correct the order so that it becomes accepted. With a Smartphone, the customer has more autonomy and he can create his orders and manage them directly.

Since a Smartphone is also a phone, customer can also call his bank from his Smartphone. In that case, what was presented above applies

Tablet: Tablets and Smartphones have many things in common. Customers download the bank application from an app store and install it on the tablet. They then have to provide a login and a password to get access to banking services. The differences reside mainly in the displays of tablets which are much bigger than those of a Smartphone. More information can therefore be displayed on a tablet and help enhance the customer experience. Banks do not handle tablets and Smartphones the same way.

PC Banking: It is, as you can see on the picture, a customer using a Personal Computer (PC) to access and use banking services through the Internet. It does not have to be his own PC. He can connect from every PC provided it has an Internet connection. The customer can see all his accounts and get the latest information about debit and credit operations. For security reasons, a login and a password are required to access customer information. The customer authenticates himself by providing them. Security plays a major role in payment orders initiation as well. For the payment orders, many banks require the customer to provide beneficiary details and account and then to wait 24 to 48 hours until the beneficiary is activated. And only after that the debtor can send funds to the beneficiary. Other banks allow sending money to a new beneficiary right away but the customer must authenticate himself again to validate the order. In case a debtor is negligent and does not lock his PC for example, it should prevent bad intentioned people from initiating a payment order.

Except the phones, the three other channels are used over Internet. When you hear or read the term online banking, it is generally about using the banking services through these three channels that allow a customer to interact easily at any time with his bank. Indeed many customers do not really see the need to go to a branch or to call their banks anymore since they can do almost everything including payments initiation through the online Banking. And a customer payment is processed almost always without the need that a bank employee reviews it or performs an action on it. That is called Straight Through Processing (STP). A STP is a processing performed end-to-end without human intervention. The percentage of STP transactions is a Key Performance Indicator for payment managers. The higher it is, the better it is, because the cost to process one transaction is getting less and less. And the bank can allocate its resources to more value added services and become more competitive.

4.1.3 Smart channels and Banking communication software

Banking communication software: Corporations use banking communication software solutions to send files to banks and receive files from them. They send batch files of payment order(s) with one debtor and many beneficiaries. The number of beneficiaries can amount to multiple thousands. The bank receives the files and processes them automatically, in some cases in STP mode, so without any human intervention.

Achieving this can be done only by automatically applying all the controls required for the processing of payments in the Bank IT systems. Bank and corporate customers have to discuss in detail what their respective expectations are in order to avoid bad surprises and disappointments. There are many questions to answer:

- What kind of file formats can be exchanged between the bank and his customer?
- Which protocols can be used for the exchanged of files?
- How can the bank make sure that the company sending the file is really the one it is pretending to be?
- How to be sure that file integrity has not been violated?
- Furthermore, the company sending the files may want the bank to process the orders only if certain specific conditions are fulfilled regarding amounts, speed or signatures among others. How to meet customer expectations in this regard also?

Smart channels are channels used by banks to receive batch files from their customers and to send files to them. They are sometimes called by the names of the underlying protocols like EBICS or SWIFTNet. In all the channels presented before, either the customer goes to the bank or he connects to a system provided by his bank to give his order. Here the orders are input and generated in a system outside the bank IT system. *The customer and the bank must make two different systems communicate in a secured manner and work together.* And this brings challenges that are partly outlined in the questions above.

We will examine each of the questions in the rest of this paragraph.

4.1.3.1 File formats exchanged between the bank and his customer

What kind of file formats can be exchanged between the bank and his customer? This is a key question. Having the list of file formats that the corporate will send to the bank or receive from the bank is the starting point to understand its needs. The EPC make recommendations to use specific files formats in the C2B space (pain.001, pain.002, camt.052, camt.053 and camt.054). It is important to know which version(s) of the pain.001 the corporate is going to send. It can be the pain.001.001.02 or pain.001.001.03. Many companies still send the version 02 even if the EPC is recommending the version 03 in the latest implementations guidelines. Same thing applies for the file format that the bank will send to the company. The version must be indicated clearly. Some services provided by the bank depend on the version of files. That is why it is crucial to clarify this point.

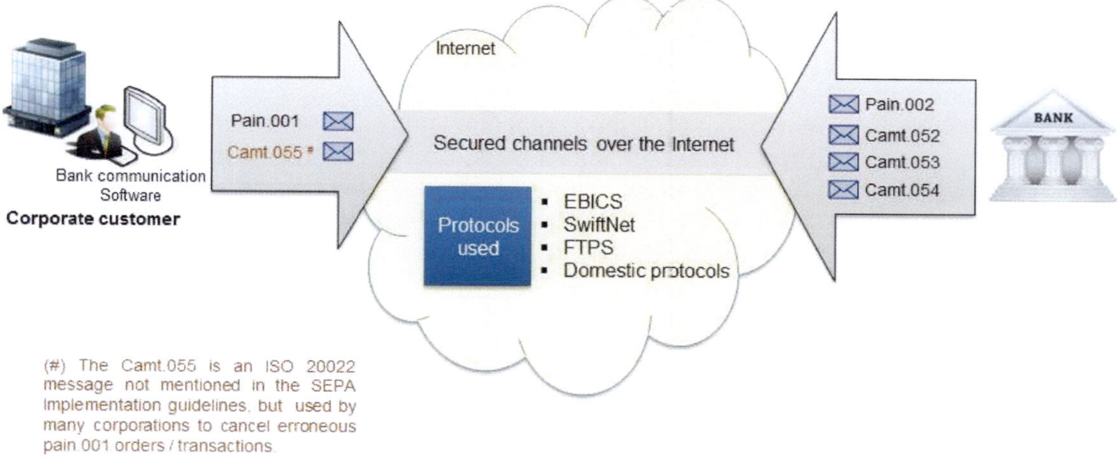

Figure 4.5: Messages exchanged in the C2B space over secured channels

The figure 5.2 shows the type of files that a corporate customer exchanged with its bank(s). All of them are known to you (if you read the previous chapter) except the Camt.055. A corporation may want to send other file formats to the bank, like the camt.055 for example which is not mentioned in the EPC Implementations guidelines. The ISO 20022 camt.055 message is used to cancel orders or transactions. If the customer is able to send it, the bank must be able to receive and process it correctly. They are many other ISO 20022 messages that a corporate may want to send to its bank even if they are not recommended by the EPC. A bank can differentiate itself by providing services to process that type of files.

As we see the answer to this question is not trivial. It really depends on the customer needs and bank offerings. Bank and customer have to agree on the file formats to exchange. Any doubt can lead to a lot of frustration. Corporate customers (and similar) do have very specific concerns that banks must address.

Figure 5.2 shows that the files are exchanged through secured channels over the internet. The channels use protocols and you are probably wondering yourself what a protocol is. Let us discuss that now.

4.1.3.2 Protocols for the secure exchanged of files

Which protocols can be used for the secure exchanged of files? Before answering the question, let me recall the definition of a communication protocol. Here is an excellent definition found in the Encyclopedia Britannica: "In computer science, *a set of rules or procedures for transmitting data between electronic devices*, such as computers. In order for computers to exchange information, there must be a pre-existing agreement as to *how the information will be structured and how each side will send and receive it*. Without a protocol, a transmitting computer, for example, could be sending its data in 8-bit packets while the receiving computer might expect the data in 16-bit packets."

A communication protocol is a set of rules that defines the syntax and semantics of messages that can be exchanged between two computer systems. If both are not using the same protocol, a converter should be put in place to make the communication possible.
Let us illustrate this with an example. If two people speak two different languages, they need a translator who understands and can speak both in order to communicate. If they speak the same language without keeping the syntax (putting the verb always at the beginning of the sentence or putting article always after the noun), they may still understand each other thanks to the great capacities of the human brain. But in the computer-to-computer world, communication is impossible without keeping the syntax

Over the years, different protocols have been developed in many countries worldwide for the secured exchange of files in the Customer to Bank space. Along with the SEPA implementation, some protocols like X.25 had to be replaced because they were based on analog networks and could not transport XML files. Furthermore they were quite expensive to operate and maintain. Today, almost all the protocols used in the C2B space operate over a secure IP Network for two main reasons: Internet Protocol (IP) has become the standard for corporate networks and it is quite chip to operate those protocols compared to former ones.

Among the usual suspects, we have the following protocols: EBICS, SWIFTNet FileAct, FTPS and country specific protocols.

- EBICS stands for Electronic Banking Internet Communication Standard
- SWIFTNet is the secure IP Network of SWIFT. The protocol for file transfer is SWIFTNet FileAct.
- FTPS stands for File Transfer Protocol Secure
- SFTP stands for Secure File Transfer Protocol
- Country specific protocols like CBI (Customer to Business Interaction) in Italy, ISABEL in Belgium, and so on.

Big companies are most of the time customer of many banks. That multibank relationship brings some challenges. If each bank uses a different protocol, the company will have to implement each of them or many translators (Remember that a protocol is like a language. Syntax and semantics must be strictly respected. Otherwise the communication is not possible). As direct consequences, the complexity of its IT infrastructure as well as the operational and maintenance costs will increase.

A standard protocol used across the whole industry greatly simplifies the things for all the players. Corporations can easily address each bank since they use the same protocol or speak the same language. Banks and companies can rapidly handle technical matters pertaining to setting up the link and focus on business subjects that are more important.

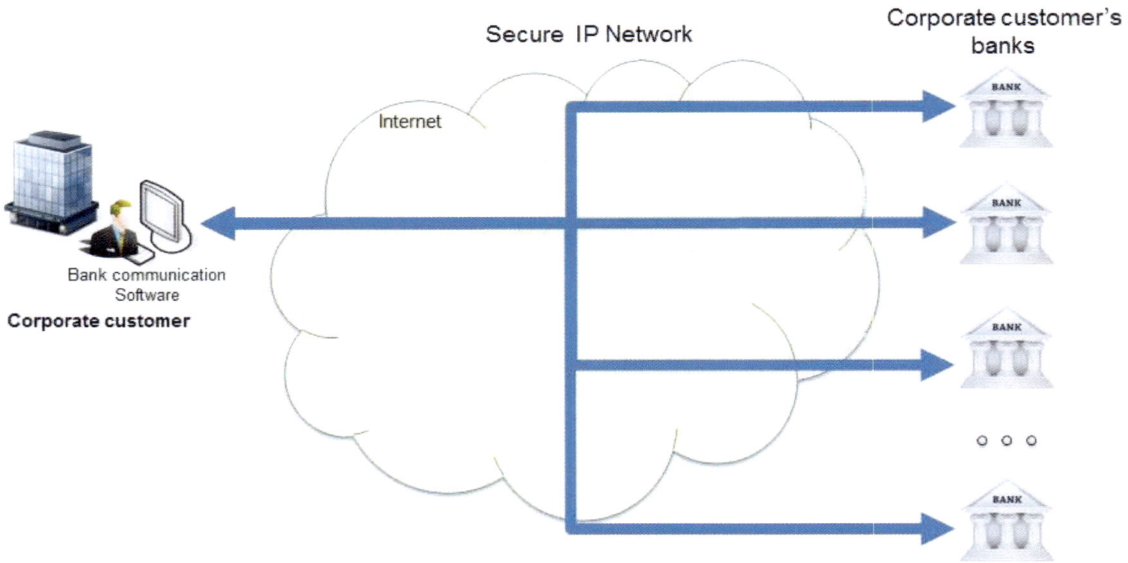

Figure 4.6: Multi-Bank Relationship

Protocols used for Customer-to-Bank communication must meet strict requirements and specifications, particularly in the domain of security. Security is the subject of the next paragraph.

4.1.3.3 Security in the customer-to-bank space

How can the bank make sure that the company sending the file is really the one it is pretending to be? And how to be sure that file integrity has not been violated during the transport from customer to bank? To understand how important these questions are, imagine an attacker that interrupts a file between a customer and his bank, then modifies the content of the order by replacing amounts and beneficiary accounts by his own information![7].

The questions addressed here are about **security**. I briefly mentioned security issues when the manual and clever channels were presented. Smart channels are no exception. And security standards are must even be higher here. The purpose of security for the channels is to guarantee confidentiality, authentication, integrity and non-repudiation among others. Quite many concepts! They are important and we will take a closer look at each of them.

- Confidentiality is a set of rules that limits access to information. According to the International Organization for Standardization (ISO), confidentiality "is the property, that information is not made available or disclosed to unauthorized individuals, entities, or processes". In the financial world, highly sensitive information is carried in messages and unauthorized access to such information would undermine the confidence of users in the network.

- Authentication is the verification of users' identity. It is the process of determining whether someone or something is, in fact, who or what it is claiming to be. Is the user who wants to connect to a terminal and access IT resources, really the one he claims to be? It is not enough to rely on the identity that the person or the resource claims to have. It should be possible to verify that identity and ensure that it is really the case. Using a login and a password is not sufficient as they can easily be stolen and used by ill-intentioned people.

- Integrity is about ensuring that the information is consistent, trustworthy and accurate. In other words, data cannot be modified in an unauthorized or undetected manner. In case data is changed during transport, it will be detected and discarded by the recipient. Data modification is not possible without access to it. By taking steps to ensure that data cannot be accessed by unauthorized people, both confidentiality and integrity are addressed simultaneously.

- To repudiate means to deny. Non-repudiation is thus the assurance that someone cannot deny something. Non-repudiation refers to the ability to ensure that a party to a communication cannot deny the sending of a message that it originated or the receiving of a message that was sent to him. The bank must be able to prove that a specific person sends payment orders that it executes. If an individual working for a corporate could just send payment orders and then denies not having sent them, the door would be open for embezzlements and frauds.

To achieve these security goals, banks and corporations make use of symmetric and asymmetric encryption mechanisms and algorithms to ensure that the communication is secure and reliable. Both algorithms rely on keys used by the sender to encrypt messages and make them non-readable to third parties as well as by the recipient to decrypt and read them. You have probably realized that the subject here is cryptography, the science of using mathematics and computer science to encrypt and decrypt data. It is a very broad subject. In

---

[7] Google man-in-the-middle attack and read related articles if you want to understand more about this topic.

the following I will limit myself to the very basics of encryption mechanisms. If you want to deepen it, I encourage you to read books dedicated to the topic.

Encryption mechanisms combine the use of keys and hash functions to make the data unreadable when it is sent and to do the opposite when it is received. A key can be a word, a number, a string of random letters or a combination of these elements. A hash function is a function that takes input data and creates a corresponding hash value. This happens in such a way that it is practically impossible to invert, that is, to recreate the input data from its hash value alone. For that reason, there are called one-way hash functions. The input data is called the message and the output data is called the message digest or simply the digest. Output data is also referred to as the hash value or simply the hash. Whereas keys are used to keep the data secrets, hash functions are more used as checksums to detect accidental data corruption.

Symmetric encryption mechanisms

Symmetric key mechanisms use the same cryptographic keys for both encryption of plaintext and decryption of cipher text. The key is shared between the two parties. The sender applies the key to the message to encrypt it. The receiver does exactly the opposite. It uses the key to decrypt the message at reception.

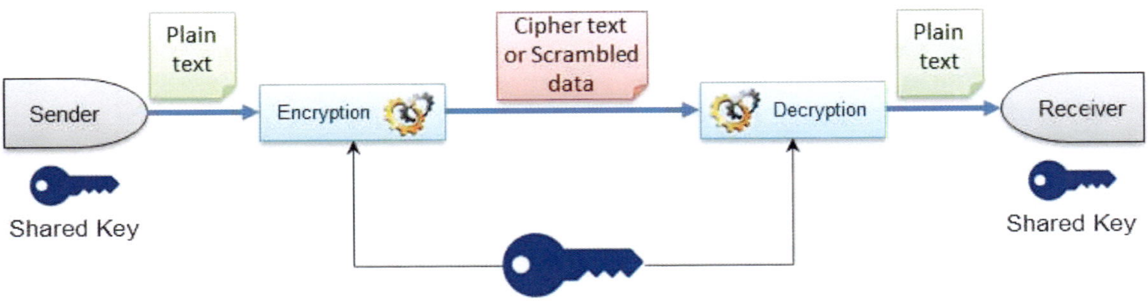

Figure 4.7: Symmetric encryptions

The data is transported as cipher text between sender's and receiver's systems. In case an attacker interrupts it along the way, he will not be able to decrypt the message. This supposes that the key should be impossible to break and to guess. It should remain secret for the sender and receiver only. However, the fact that both parties have access to the secret key is one of the main drawbacks of symmetric encryption mechanisms. In addition, parties involved in the communication have to keep as many keys as they have counterparties to communicate with. It is mathematically proven that for n users, the number of keys needed for pairwise secure communication is n*(n – 1)/2.

Asymmetric encryption mechanisms

Asymmetric key mechanisms use pairs of keys for data encryption and decryption. A pair of keys consists of a public key and a private key. The public key can be shared with any counterparty. That is why it is called public. The private key is known only to the owner. Asymmetric key mechanisms are also referred to as public key cryptography.

In asymmetric encryption system, any sender can encrypt a message using the public key of the receiver, but such a message can be decrypted only with the receiver's private key. As other alternative, the sender can encrypt a message with his private key. But such a message can be decrypted only with the sender's public key. The two figures below illustrate the two encrypting possibilities. In the first one, the sender uses the receiver's public key. And in the second one, the sender uses his private key.

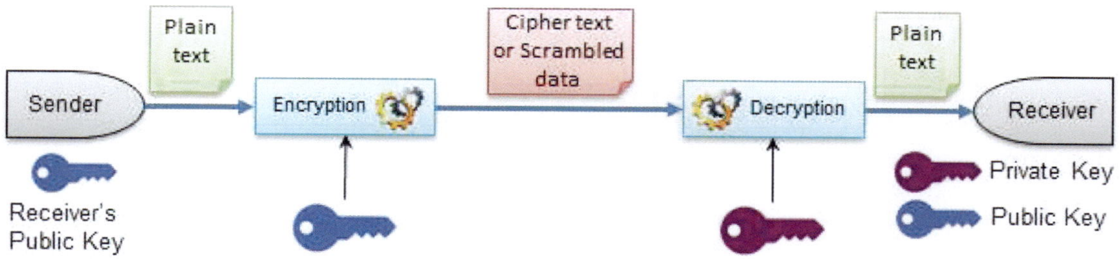

Figure 4.8: Asymmetric mechanisms - Sender encrypts with the receiver's public key

In the first case depicted on the figure above, the sender encrypts the plain text with the receiver's public key. The public key can be known to anyone. So the sender can get it and use it. Now *only* the receiver can read the message, for it can be decrypted by using the receiver's private key. Since that key is unique, no one else but the receiver can read the message. If the message was interrupted during transit, the attacker could not read the content because he does not have the receiver's private key. So if a sender wants to keep a message secret and confidential, he has to use the recipient's public key to encrypt the message. If two parties want to keep their communication confidential, each party will use the public key of the other party to encrypt the messages and will decrypt the messages with his own private key. In this first case, what really matters is the ability to keep the messages confidential. As we will see now, the sender has another possibility if authentication is more important.

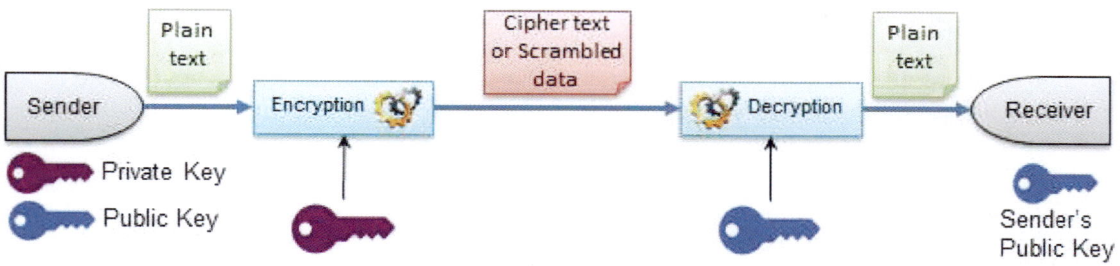

Figure 4.9: Asymmetric mechanisms - Sender encrypts with his private key

Here the sender uses his private key to encrypt the message. Any party having access to the sender's public key can use it to decrypt the message. And we know that almost everyone can see the message since the public key is shared with the world. A sender would therefore consider this alternative if he is to be identified as the only sender of the message. This is authentication. Since the private key is known only by him, he cannot deny having sent the message. This is non repudiation. If confidentiality as well as authentication is to be achieved, then encryption has to be performed with both private key and receiver's public key.

For asymmetric mechanisms to work, a public and private key-pair must be generated and linked together to be used for encryption and decryption. More important, it should be extremely difficult (or impossible) even with high computing power to determine a private key from its corresponding public key. When that condition is met, keeping the private key private is enough for security and the public key can be published without compromising security. RSA is the most famous asymmetric cryptosystem. RSA is composed of the initial letters of the surnames of Ron **R**ivest, Adi **S**hamir, and Leonard **A**dleman, who invented the RSA algorithms.

As announced at the outset of this paragraph, hash functions are also used in the encryption mechanisms. Although they can also make the data unreadable, that is not the main purpose for which they are used. Hash functions are used predominantly for data integrity, to ensure that data has not been modified during the transport. The next figure illustrates how hash functions work. Let us take a closer look at it.

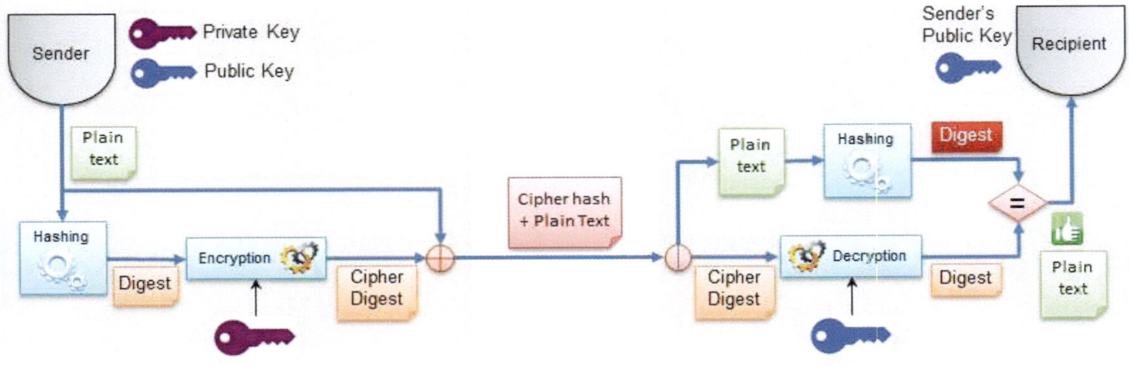

Figure 4.10: Usage of hash functions

The sender first computes the hash value of the message (plain text on the picture) with a cryptographic hash function. The result is the digest. Now the sender uses his private key to encrypt the digest and gets the cipher digest or encrypted digest. As last step, the encrypted digest and the plain test are concatenated and then transported over the network. On the receiver's side, the first operation is to split the plain text from the cipher digest. As next steps, the receiver performs two operations: 1) The cipher digest is decrypted with the sender's public key. The result of the decryption is the digest. 2) The receiver computes the hash value of the message (plain text on the picture) with a cryptographic hash function. The result is the digest or should be the digest. So he has to know the hash algorithm used by the sender.
The next step for the receiver is to compare the digest (decrypted from the cipher digest) with the computed digest. If both are equal, the receiver accepts the plain text and processes it. If both are different, it means that the message was modified in transit. The receiver will discard it. You see that hashing ensures integrity of data. If the data is modified in transit, the computed digest will be different from the decrypted digest.

There are two points I need to come back to:

1) Is the plain text really sent non encrypted over the network? The answer is no. It will be too easy for attackers to view the message. Payment messages should never and are never sent unencrypted over the network. It is obvious. Why then showing you the picture above? To bring you step by step to the reality and help you understand it hopefully.

2) The receiver uses the public key of the sender for decryption. If you remember well, the public key can be known to anybody and potentially to attackers. There is a confidentiality issue as not allowed people can decrypt the message.

To overcome these drawbacks, things are a bit more complex in reality. Please take a close look at the figure below. Only the operations performed by the sender are presented for simplification purpose.

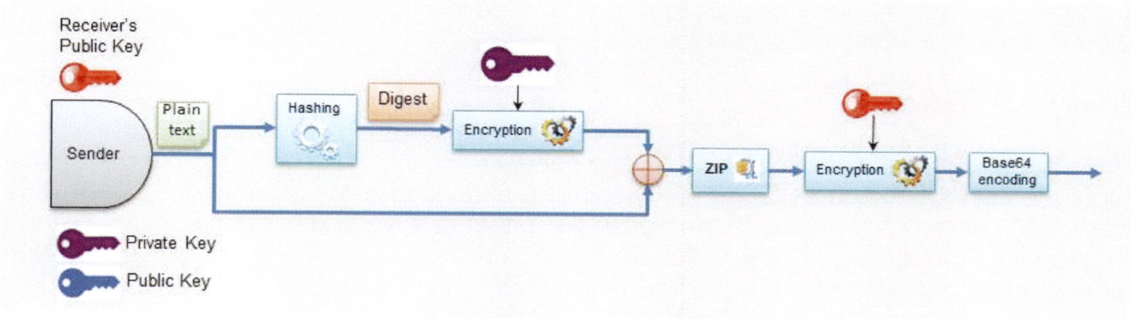

Figure 4.11: Message encryption steps in reality

It starts like in the previous picture. The sender computes the hash value of the message (plain text) with a cryptographic hash function and gets the digest. Then he uses his private key to encrypt the digest and gets the cipher digest or encrypted digest as a result. As next step, the encrypted digest and the plain test are concatenated. Then the whole is ZIP-compressed (compressed files take up less storage space and can be transferred more quickly than uncompressed files). After that the sender encrypts the zip message with the receiver's public key. And finally the encrypted zip message is Base64 encoded and transmitted over the network. Since the receiver's public key is used, only the receiver can decrypt the message. Later he will use the sender's public key to decrypt the cipher digest. As result, authentication, non-repudiation, confidentiality and integrity are guarantee with this method.

Base64 is an encoding and decoding technique used to convert binary data to an ASCII text format, and vice versa. The conversion allows the data transfer over a medium that only supports ASCII formats, such as email messages on Multipurpose Internet Mail Extension (MIME) and Extensible Markup Language (XML) data.

Quite a lot of things! That is the price to pay for security. Fortunately computers can perform all those actions in seconds. Developing all the operations can be difficult, but once it is done and it is working, the computers will take care. But we have not reached the end of our journey yet.

Asymmetric encryption/decryption is quite complex and requires a lot of processing power. Symmetric mechanisms require the sender and receiver to share a common secret. How to avoid these drawbacks? The answer is **hybrid encryption**, a mode of encryption that incorporates a combination of asymmetric and symmetric encryptions to benefit from the strengths of each form of encryption. These strengths are speed provided by symmetric encryption and security provided by asymmetric encryption.

Now look at the figure 5.8 again. If the plain text is a shared key to use in the rest of the communication, the receiver can be sure that it comes from the sender and that only both of them know it. They can continue their communication with the shared key. A new shared key (or session key) is generated and used for every new communication. This increases the security level and the confidence of the users in hybrid encryption.

Now let us conclude on encryption mechanisms based on keys and hash functions. Symmetric encryption mechanisms provide confidentiality and integrity, but do not provide authentication and non-repudiation because the key is shared. Since sender and receiver use the same key, the message can be kept secret and data integrity can be ensured as well. Asymmetric encryption mechanisms ensure confidentiality and integrity as well as authentication and non-repudiation. It is possible because the private key is not shared. Therefore it is possible to identify with certainty which person or resource has performed a specific action. Asymmetric encryption and symmetric encryption can be combined in hybrid encryption to take advantage of their respective strengths: security and speed.

Electronic certificates

There are still a couple of questions to answer about encryption mechanisms and particularly about the keys. Who can generate the keys used in the encryption algorithms? Can anyone do that by himself? On the basis of what can users trust keys and the parties who claim to possess it? To understand how important these questions are, how would you consider a country where each citizen can issue his identity card? How would you know if an identity card is authentic and trustable?

Just like an identity card or a passport, a digital certificate must provide identifying information and has to be forgery resistant. It should also be easily verifiable because it was issued by an official, trusted authority. In cryptography it is called a certificate authority or certification authority (CA). Digital certificates are electronic identity cards of persons or entities issued by CA. They generally contain the following information:

- Serial number: It is used to uniquely identify the certificate
- Signature algorithm: The algorithm used to create the signature of the CA
- Signature of the Certification Authority: The actual signature to verify that it came from the issuer.
- Name of the issuing Certification Authority (CA): The entity that verified the information and issued the certificate.
- Name of the holder: The person or entity who owns the certificate
- Valid-From date: The date at which the certificate is first valid.
- Valid-To date: The date at which the certificate will expire.
- Holder's public key: The public key of the person or entity who owns the certificate.
- Authorized usages: What the public key can be used for (e.g. signature, certificate signing, encipherment, and so on.)
- Thumbprint Algorithm: The algorithm used to hash the public key certificate.
- Thumbprint (also known as fingerprint): The hash itself, used as an abbreviated form of the public key certificate

A certificate is itself digitally signed by a root certificate belonging to a trusted certificate authority which guarantees and controls the certification chain. This provides evidence that a certificate is genuine and valid. And anyone having doubt can verify the certificate genuineness with the trusted certificate authority. Operating systems and browsers keep lists of trusted CA root certificates so they can easily verify certificates that the CAs have issued and signed.

What about the private key? The elements presented above contain the public key and not the private key. Remember that the private is known only by the owner. So the Certificate Authority should not and doesn't have access to the private key. Private keys are generated on the user level based on the information provided by the CA. This means most of the time that the public key initially transmitted by the CA is updated to match the private key generated at user level.

Finally, certificate management is necessary to keep the information up-to-date and valid. Keys have to be renewed before the expiration or if they are compromised or revoked for any reason. More widely, we read the following about PKI on Wikipedia: "Public Key Infrastructure (PKI) is a set of roles, policies, and procedures needed to create, manage, distribute, use, store, and revoke digital certificates and manage public-key encryption. The purpose of a PKI is to facilitate the secure electronic transfer of information for a range of network activities such as e-commerce, internet banking and confidential email." It is a good summary of what PKI is.

After these introductions to encryption mechanisms and electronic certificates, we are now ready to look at the EBICS and SWIFTNet protocols.

4.1.3.4 The EBICS Protocol

EBICS is a highly secure file transfer protocol used for exchange of payment files in the customer-to-bank space as well as in the interbank space. EBICS is a protocol over IP which allows the use of the standard Hypertext Transfer Protocol with TLS encryption (HTTPS) for the transport of data. TLS stands for Transport Layer Security. It is a cryptographic protocol that provides security in communication over a computer network.

EBICS can transport XML and flat files containing a variety of banking information such as account statements; debit and credit payment orders and related r-transactions. Thus SEPA XML messages and the traditional SWIFT MT messages are logically supported by EBICS. Furthermore, EBICS offers checkpoint/restart capability which enables the file transmission process to resume in the event of interruption (rather than having to start over again).

Created und developed in Germany, EBICS was adopted by the French banking community to replace a former protocol which could not transport XML messages and therefore became obsolete. Two versions of EBICS were initially used in France: EBICS T, to replace ETEBAC3 (Echange TElematique BAnque Clients) and EBICS TS, with signature, to replace ETEBAC5. With EBICS T, the debtor sends payment orders files through the EBICS channel and confirms them through another channel (fax, electronic signature ...). With EBICS TS, the files are signed with a digital certificate before being transmitted to the bank. Consequently, no fax confirmation is required and the payment orders can be executed immediately. EBICS T is less costly to implement but it is less secure and expensive to run and maintain over the long term. The Bank of France has urged banks to abandon the fax confirmation necessary to EBICS T for security and cost management reasons. Many French banks abrogated the use of EBICS T in 2015 and the whole French banking community is aiming to suppress it completely by the end of the year 2016. Others communities will probably follow the French model.

The EBICS protocol is gaining more and more ground in Europe. Many countries like Switzerland and Austria are planning to adopt it as the standard for C2B messages exchanges. Large Banks in many SEPA countries have already implemented it to improve their offerings and respond to the demand of multinational corporations using EBICS.

EBICS is an open standard. Specifications can be downloaded at the following URL: http://www.ebics.org/technical-information/

An EBICS communication is always performed on the customer's initiative, no matter in which direction, from the customer to the bank or from the bank to the customer. Since EBICS allows the transmission of both XML and fixed formats files, SEPA payments and country specific files can be exchanged with the same protocol. Before being transmitted, an order file is zipped, encrypted and encoded. The result is then cut into segments of up to 1 MB, and each segment is inserted into an XML message.

For ciphering mechanisms, EBICS uses cryptographic standards RSA, AES and X.509. RSA relies on asymmetric encryption mechanisms. AES, the Advanced Encryption Standard, is a symmetric encryption algorithm. X.509 is a standard for a public key infrastructure (PKI) to manage digital certificates and public key encryptions. EBICS uses a hybrid encryption mechanism.

Highest security is ensured by allowing the use of three pairs of RSA keys and the corresponding certificates on corporate side and three pairs of RSA keys on bank side as well. Let us first consider the certificates on corporate side:

- The authentication certificate: it is used to sign EBICS XML messages. The bank can identify with certainty the corporate customer who sent the XML message. Please note that the authentication certificate identifies the corporation but not its employees. It is the signature certificate presented below that allows the identification of physical person(s) who approved and submitted the orders.

- The encryption certificate: it is used for transmitting the AES key with which the parties will symmetrically encrypt and decrypt the messages. Here is where the hybrid encryption comes into play. The AES symmetric key is transported once in a secure way using asymmetric encryption. After that, both customer and bank continue the communication with symmetric encryption. This is a good compromise to avoid the drawbacks of asymmetric encryption/decryption: complexity and processing power.

- The signature certificate (for EBICS TS) or the sealing certificate (for EBICS T): it is used to create the electronic signature of payment files or to electronically seal the files. Often compared to wet signature, the signature certificate is linked to a unique employee of the company who cannot deny having given the approval to send the orders to the bank. The file is encrypted with the employee's private key and the bank decrypts with the corresponding public key. Many employees can digitally sign the same file. That is called joint signature.

The French implementation uses X.509 certificates for the management of the three key pairs.

On the bank side, EBICS allows to use three pairs of keys very similar to the ones used on corporation side:

- The authentication certificate is used for identification and authentication of the financial institution by the corporate customer. The bank cannot deny having sent payment orders statuses and other type of information.

- The encryption certificate is used for the decryption of the (symmetrical) transaction key to encrypt bank-technical order data sent by a customer to the bank.

- The signature certificate is used to sign the files that are retrieved by a subscriber from the bank system.

First note an important point here to avoid any misunderstanding. The bank can use the three pairs of keys to communicate with all the customers. That is precisely the advantage of asymmetric encryption. The bank does not need and does not have three pairs of keys per customer. It uses the same three pairs of keys to communicate with all its customers.

In general, banks used two key pairs for authentication and encryption. They are enough as the files sent from the bank to the customer contain payment status and reporting. They are created automatically by bank's applications and provide information to the customer about what happened on his account. Approval of a bank's employee is not as important as for payment orders. Approval processes there would be quite burdensome for the bank and the added value for the customer would be almost zero.

4.1.3.5 SWIFT Protocols and the 3SKey

SWIFT stands for *Society for Worldwide Interbank Financial Telecommunication*. SWIFT has created a global telecommunication network for the exchange of financial messages which is now called SWIFTNet. SWIFTNet connects banks and corporations as well as banks among themselves all over the world. The main protocols used by SWIFT members to communicate over SWIFTNet are InterAct, FileAct and Browse.

- **InterAct supports the exchange of request/response messages.**
- **FileAct supports the exchange of files. SWIFTNet FileAct can be used to transport SEPA messages from the corporate customers to bank.**
- **Browse is a secure web-based protocol (HTTPS) for a client/server communication**

SWIFTNet FIN is not a protocol, but a service over the InterAct protocol which enables financial institutions to exchange structured financial messages in MT and ISO 15022 message formats.

Independent of the type of protocol or service used, high level of security standards must be kept. Like EBICS, SWIFTNet combines hash functions, encryption mechanisms and other technologies to ensure that the network remains highly secure and reliable.

SWIFT has taken many initiatives over the years to improve security and make its services easy to use and implement. In October 2010 SWIFT made a quantum leap with the SWIFT Secure Signature Key (3SKey). For many professionals, there is a before and after 3SKey without any doubt.

Before 3SKey, companies had to use several security devices and passwords to connect with their banks through different networks. Each Bank had its own PKI and issued its own certificates. The result was multiple ways of managing (digital) signatures and the related approval processes. The costs required to train the users and run the processes were quite high and were growing steadily. And then came the 3SKey solution.

After 3SKey, corporate users, particularly those operating in an international environment, can now manage their relationships with various banks more effectively through unique personal signatures. Corporate treasurers can get rid of several security devices and passwords for 3Skey, one single USB token and one password to authenticate and approve transactions with all their banks. Approval processes can be streamlined easily. In addition, there is no need for banks to implement and manage their own PKI. They can outsource their PKI infrastructure to SWIFT. Finally, 3SKey is interoperable globally and can be implemented on any network, not only on SWIFTNet. It can be used on SWIFTNet, on any proprietary bank channels, on domestic networks, with EBICS protocols and on other private channels. It has been coupled successfully with Ebics protocol in France.

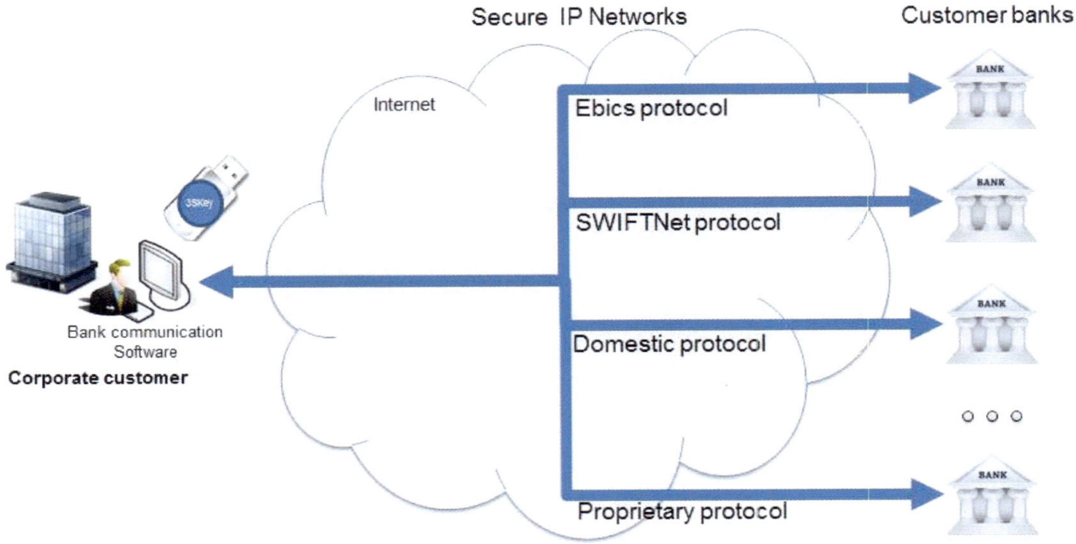

Figure 4.12: 3SKey, the multibank and multi-network personal signature solution

3SKey is a secure solution hosted, operated and maintained by SWIFT. It uses state-of-the-art cryptographic technologies: Public Key Infrastructure, X.509 V3 certificates, RSA keys of 2048 bits, Secure Hash Algorithm 256 digest calculation, Public Key Cryptography Standards (PKCS #7) formatted signatures. 3SKey implements the highest security standards. Banks and corporations can rely on SWIFT instead of building and maintaining their own services. Complexity is reduced and they can focus on their core business.

4.1.3.6 Acquisition and Reporting agreements

Payment acquisition and reporting agreements discussed below are those contracted between bank and customer for the exchange of files over smart channels. The payment order files are sent from the customer to the bank and payment status files are sent from the bank to the customer. Acquisition is about the customer-to-bank files and reporting is about the bank-to-customer files.

A company sending payment order files may want the bank to process the orders only if certain specific conditions are fulfilled. On its side, the bank needs to verify if the customer is keeping to what was agreed or if he goes beyond. Therefore, both parties have to sign a contract, an agreement. Depending on the way how it operates, a bank may have one dedicated contract for acquisition and another one for reporting. But generally, a bank combines both acquisition and reporting in the same contract. Contract information is splitted and shared with the different services and applications needing it for the processing. What kind of services do you generally find in such agreement? How can a bank take into account the specific needs of a corporate customer related to the files acquisition and reporting?

In the following, typical information and services found in banks' offerings will be provided and explained. In general, agreements, users and colleges of signatories are linked to each other as presented in the next figure. An agreement is linked to at least one user. A user can be linked to one or many agreements. And a user can be part of zero or many colleges of signatories. A college of signatories consists of at least 2 users generally with the same level of authority and who can validate and / or sign orders. What you see below is just an example. There are many possibilities. A bank may choose to link a user to one and only one agreement for instance.

At agreement level, you have information like agreement ID or Partner ID (in EBICS), company name, communication protocols, type of files allowed in acquisition, type of files allowed in reporting, start and end dates, etc.

At user level, you find information like User ID, Partner ID (since a user is always linked to at least one agreement), Type of user : Remitter / Signatory, Amount limits at order level, Amount limits at transaction level, Debtor accounts allowed, Beneficiary accounts allowed, Certificates, etc. Communication protocols, type of files allowed in acquisition, type of files allowed in reporting may be refined at user level as well.

The college of signatories contains information about the users who are part of it, the amount limit at order level and the amount limit at transaction level eventually, etc.

We will now look at the different services offered by the bank and how contract information impacts the payment acquisition.

Communication protocols

Protocols are required for the communication of two computing devices. Customer and Bank have to agree on which protocols are going to be used for sending or receiving of files or both. The usual suspects like EBICS and SWIFTNet FileAct for the exchange of SEPA messages certainly come to your mind. But there exist other protocols that have been developed and are widely used at country level in many SEPA countries. They can be used as well.

There are many options. A customer can choose to use several protocols to send and receive payment files. It is also possible to send payment orders with one protocol and receive them with another protocol. Another option is to send specific files through one protocol and other files through another protocol. And this applies also for receiving. You will seldom see the last option in practice but it can be implemented.

For security reasons, the bank has to clearly identify which customer devices / applications can connect to the bank through which protocols. If the customer would request sending or receiving a file through the wrong protocol, the bank would reject it immediately. If a bank mentions only file formats in an agreement and allows customers to send them with any protocol, we would call this permissiveness. This could open doors for attackers. For security reasons, file formats and protocol(s) must be linked.

Type of files allowed in acquisition (customer-to-bank)

The customer-to-bank files for the SEPA Credit Transfer are the pain.001.001.02, pain.001.001.03 and camt.055.001.01. Customers may choose to send only the version 2 of the pain.001 or only the version 3. Others may choose to send both of them.

The camt.055.001.01 does not belong to the mandatory Customer-to-bank files (It is not mentioned in the SCT customer-to-bank implementation guidelines), but a bank can acquire it as well if their customers want and are able to send the file. This is a typical additional service that banks offer to their customers. Not to mix up with SEPA AOS which are implemented in the interbank space. It is an additional service in the sense that it comes in addition to what SEPA requires or recommends in the rulebooks and Implementation guidelines.

In any case, when a bank receives a file from a customer, it will accept and process it only if the customer agreement clearly specifies that file as allowed.

Type of files allowed in reporting (bank-to-customer)

The bank-to-customer files for the SEPA Credit Transfer are the pain.002.001.03, camt.052.001.02, camt.053.001.02 and camt.054.001.02. Practice has shown that the pain.002.001.03 as specified in the SEPA is not sufficient for customers. Banks do send other types of status reports to their customers. These “additional services” are necessary. We will come back to that later on.

Customers may choose to receive all the reporting files or only certain files among them. The bank should ensure the customer gets only what the bank has agreed to provide. If customers receive files that they have never asked for, it is a bad signal and detrimental for the image of the bank.

Digital signatures control

Digital signatures control is a key feature in payment orders acquisition. Many customers see it as true value-added service. In many corporations, procedures require that one or many people (or group of people) sign a file before it is released and sent to the bank. And these companies appreciate if the bank can verify that the file has been signed by the correct people before accepting and processing it.

Simply stated, the main purpose of signatures control performed by the bank is to verify if the user(s) who signed the payment orders are the right ones. There are basically two types of signatures: single signatures and joint signatures.

For single signature, it is enough that one person signs the file, but that person may have to fulfill other criteria like belonging to a specific unit inside the company. Joint signatures require the signatures of at least two persons. Depending on company’s policies, these two persons can work in the same or in different departments. A joint signature may be mandatory or optional.

You may wonder how the bank can know to which unit a signatory belongs. In practice, banks create users who can sign files and group them together in units called colleges or bodies. A college of signatories represents a group of people with specific rights. The bank advises the company after thorough discussions which employees to assign to which college of signatories. The bodies can be established to reflect the organization of the company’s treasury department. But they can also be a mix of people with various responsibilities from different departments. What really matters here is that the bodies can be used to control the signatures as the customer wants. In some case, it can be enough to let one employee from one unit sign the file. In other cases a joint signature may be required. And the two signatories may be part of two distinct colleges of signatories or not. And so on. As we see below, there are many cases to possibly take into account:

- Case 1: Payment orders where one and only one signature is required. And the signatory must be member of a specific college.
- Case 2: Payment orders where joint signature is required. And the signatories must be members of the same college.
- Case 3: Payment orders where joint signature is required. But the signatories can be members of the same college or of different colleges.
- Case 4: Payment orders where joint signature is optional. Two signatures are allowed, but one is enough.

* etc.

Signatory bodies can be used as a powerful tool to provide high quality services to corporate customers. This brief introduction should help you understand the different cases you can encounter in the practice.

Amount limits at order and/or transaction levels

This service applies only for acquisition. The idea behind it is pretty simple. Users are allowed to sign orders and transactions up to a limit amount. The limit amount can apply at order level or at transaction level.

Let us consider an example to make things clearer. In a treasury unit, you may have:

* Employees that can sign payment orders up to 100 K€ but single transactions in an order should not exceed 10 K€.
* Employees that can sign payment orders up to 500 K€ but single transactions in an order should not exceed 100 K€.
* Employees that can sign payment orders up to 1000 K€ no matter what the amount of the single transactions inside the order.
* Few users (one or two) have unlimited amount rights.

When the bank receives a payment order, the amount limits are controlled at order and transaction levels. If there is a mismatch, the order is rejected and the customer is notified.

Debtor accounts control

With debtor account controls, the bank can check if the debtor account indicated in a payment order received from a user belongs to the list of the accounts he is authorized to use. Based on the information provided by the company, the bank associates a list of debtor accounts to users. If a user transmits an order with a debtor account that is not on his list, the bank cannot carry out the order.

Beneficiary accounts control

It is the same service as debtor account controls, but applied on beneficiary accounts. There is a list of beneficiary accounts associated with a user. That user cannot send transactions to other beneficiaries that those on his list. In case the bank receives a payment order with transactions where the beneficiary account is not on the list, it will be rejected.

We terminate on the typical services offered by banks for Payment acquisition and reporting. We went through couple of important services and we can see that they are quite rich. Because the agreements play such a key role, smart channels require more attention and a careful management. Industry leaders do think there is still space for innovation and value added services in the acquisition and reporting particularly.

In conclusion, payment acquisition plays a key role in the payment processing value chain, particularly for corporate customers using smart channels. It is not just about getting the file in the correct format. It is also about offering specific and differentiated services to these customers. Dummy channels acquisition is quite expensive and risky because it requires employees to review the orders and manually input them to a bank application. Clever channels allow customers to input their orders by themselves while checking their correctness and completeness, so that they can be processed immediately.

4.2 The Payment Order Management

After the successful acquisition comes the Payment Order Management, the next sub-process in the payment processing value chain.

Figure 4.13: Payment Order Management Subprocess

Payment orders come from various players and channels: corporates, private customers, other PSP (smaller banks for example), the bank itself ...and the list is not exhaustive. The orders are acquired through multiple platforms. Having a single platform for acquisition (and reporting) would be ideal. In reality, many platforms are in place to address all the constraints and requirements (protocols, payment messages formats, checks and controls) related to acquisition and reporting.

The Payment Order Manager receives payment files from acquisition platform(s) in various standards and formats. It enables (should enable) the bank to get a single view of all payment orders for the same customer, no matter what the type and the format of the payment. This is again an ideal. The reality is that a bank usually has many Payment Order Managers (POMs) to handle different types of payments. Many payment software providers in the industry are offering solutions to reach that target. But we are not there yet, and experience shows that it is not going be an easy thing to do. Ensuring that the same POM can process the volumes of all payment types on time without degrading the customer services is though. Furthermore, "putting all the eggs in one basket" is seen as a risky strategy and should be considered very carefully.

So today most of the banks still use many POMs with the inconvenience of siloed view of payment orders. End users must access different systems to get the full view for a specific customer, which is inefficient and time consuming. I am still waiting to see a POM which will handle credit transfers, direct debits, checks and other types of payments. What I have seen so far are POMs for various types of credit transfers. POM of direct debits are always implemented separately as well as POM for check payments.

The Payment Order Manager for credit transfers receives them in various formats. After processing the credit transfers, the Payment Order Manager forwards the payment transactions to the suitable Payment Exchange Platform for interbank exchanges, clearing and settlement. SEPA Credit transfers transactions may be forwarded to:

- local CSM, EBA STEP2 if they are in XML format.
- TARGET2 if they are in SWIFT MT format. In these case, the beneficiary bank is not reachable through local CSM/STEP2 or the payment is urgent.

A Payment Order Manager may receive one order and forward some transactions to the SCT exchange platform and other SWIFT exchange platform. After performing reachability check, each exchange platform decides to which ACH the payment must be sent.

The following figure depicts the POMS and how it is linked to the other payment processing solutions in the value chain.

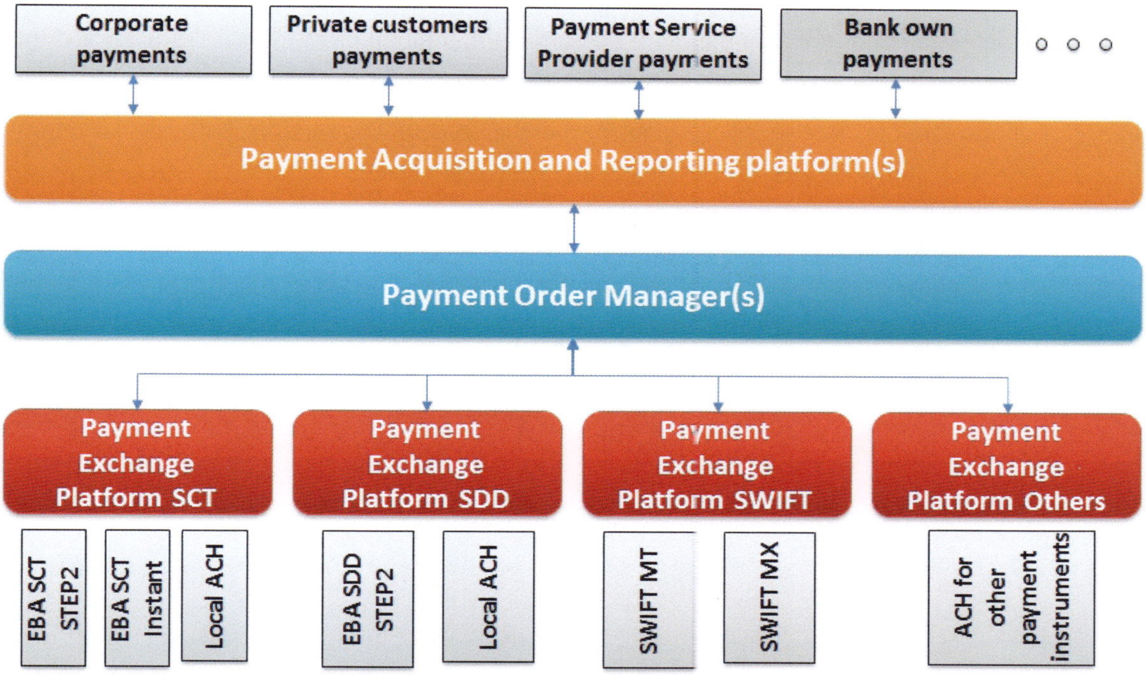

Figure 4.14: Payment Order Manager(s) in the Payment processing value chain

In the remaining part of this paragraph we will focus on POM for SCT only. The payment order management for SCT is about viewing, updating, creating and processing payment orders according to SEPA rules, regulatory requirements, services agreed with the customer and bank's specific requirements. For that, order management relies on many features and services like **payment parsing and validation, IBANs validation and verification, dates and the related controls, duplicate checks, processing agreements, pending order management, balance check, routing and issuing**. The services listed here are not exhaustive. And do not consider that the services are executed in the order indicated above. Depending on the project and organization, several other services may apply and they may be implemented in a different order.

Before examining each service in detail, let us first briefly recall the different types of orders and the customers who use them the most. The payment orders reach the bank through the different channels that were introduced in the previous chapter. There are essentially two types of orders: single-beneficiary payment order and multi-beneficiary payment order.

- *A single-beneficiary payment order* is an order with one unique beneficiary. The debtor can indicate only one beneficiary. Private customers use almost exclusively this type of order. The bank acquires single-beneficiary orders through the channels, then collects them one or several times a day and sends them to the order management system. All the orders that have been successfully acquired are collected and bulked at the next collection time. The order may also be processed in real time. In that case, it will not wait for the next collection time and be transmitted immediately to the Order Management System.

- *A multi-beneficiary payment order* is an order with more than one beneficiary. The debtor therefore indicates several beneficiaries. Corporate customers use multi-beneficiary orders very much. But they also use single-beneficiary orders. The processing of multi-beneficiary orders is obviously more complex than for single-beneficiary orders. What happens for example if one or more transactions in the order is erroneous? Is there a maximum number of beneficiaries an order can have for the correct processing? When should a customer transmit an order with a great number of transactions so that the bank can process it on time? The answers to these questions are essential because there is a direct impact to the customer service. And as we will also see below, the processing agreement is crucial for multi-beneficiary payment orders.

During the acquisition (for corporate customers specifically), the focus was the envelope of the message (protocols, type of files, signatures.). From now on, the center of interest is the content of the message. Remember that Pain.001 messages can contain one or multiple orders and an order can have one or multiple transactions.

The services performed for the processing of the payment will now be considered.

4.2.1 Payment parsing and validation

Parsing and validating that the payment messages and orders are syntactically and semantically correct is the first step. SEPA messages are transported in XML documents that must be well formed and valid. An XML document with correct syntax is called *Well Formed*. An XML document validated against a XSD (XML Schema Definition) document is both *Well Formed* and *Valid*.

Syntax validation is more about structure of the messages. All XML message elements have an opening tag and a close tag. If an opening or a close tag is missing, the message is not well formed and will be rejected. The message elements should appear in a strict order. If the order is not respected, the message will be rejected. Furthermore, some message elements are mandatory and must be present in the message at least one time. If a mandatory message element is missing, the message is not well formed and will be rejected.

Semantic validation means checking that the content inside a message element is correct. Let us consider a couple of examples:

- The lengths of some message elements are limited in SEPA compared to the ISO 20022. The creditor name for example should not exceed 70 characters in a SEPA message. If it contains 80 characters, the message is invalid and will be rejected.

- If an amount is expected in a message element, a name or a date will not be accepted. If specific values (HIGH / NORM for instruction priority for example) are expected in a message element, nothing else than these values should be put there. Otherwise the message will be rejected.

- A BIC consists of 8 or 11 characters formed according to a pattern that is specified in the XSD file. A BIC that does not follow the pattern is invalid and will lead to the file rejection. In the XSD file, the following regular expression is defined for the BIC identifier: <xs:pattern value="[A-Z]{6,6}[A-Z2-9][A-NP-Z0-9]([A-Z0-9]{3,3}){0,1}"/>.

    - [A-Z]{6,6} – The pattern [A-Z] represents an upper case alphabetic character. {6,6} means the string must match at least 6 occurrences, but no more than 6 occurrences, of pattern [A-Z]. In summary, the first 6 characters must be upper case alphabetic characters.
    - [A-Z2-9] - Then follows one alphanumeric upper case character which can take any value except 0 and 1 according to the pattern [A-Z2-9].
    - [A-NP-Z0-9] - After that follows another alphanumeric upper case character which can take any value except the upper character O.

- ([A-Z0-9]{3,3}){0,1} - The last three characters must be upper case alphanumeric characters. {0,1} means that ([A-Z0-9]{3,3}) can be present 0 or 1 time. In summary, the last three characters of the BIC are not mandatory, but must all be upper case alphanumeric characters if they are present.

For those who are very interested in the topics of syntax and semantics in XML, please go this website http://www.w3schools.com/xml/default.asp or download the book XML for dummies.

4.2.2 IBANs validation and verification

Debtor and creditor accounts must be indicated in SEPA payments as IBAN (International Bank Account Numbers). Every time the word account is used in the rest of the book, it refers to the IBAN unless there is another precision. The bank performs essentially two kinds of checks on an IBAN: IBAN validation and IBAN verification. IBAN validation can be carried out by any bank. IBAN verification can be performed only by the bank which is account holder.

IBAN validation consists in checking if the indicated IBAN is a valid IBAN. This is achieved through a quite complex algorithm because IBAN lengths and inherent structures are different in the SEPA countries. The IBAN consists of up to 34 alphanumeric characters, structured as follows:

- 2 alphabetic characters for the **country code** using ISO 3166-1 alpha-2
- 2 numeric characters for the **check digits**, which enable sanity check of the bank account number to confirm its integrity before processing a transaction. Check digits are calculated with an algorithm specified in the standard ISO/IEC 7064:2003.
- And up to 30 alphanumeric characters for the **Basic Bank Account Number (BBAN)**. The number of characters used in the BBAN is country-specific.

So an IBAN always begins with a country code followed by check digits. But the BBAN length varies. A Belgian IBAN is composed of 16 characters (first 4 for country code and check digits, last 12 for BBAN). A German IBAN is composed of 22 characters (first 4 for country code and check digits, last 16 for BBAN). A French IBAN is composed of 27 characters (first 4 for country code and check digits, last 23 for BBAN). A Malta IBAN is composed of 31 characters (first 4 for country code and check digits, last 27 for BBAN) and so on.

In some countries, (additional) check digits are present in the BBAN itself to ensure that the BBAN is correct. The last digit of the Finnish BBAN is a check digit. The last two digits of a French BBAN are check digits. These checks can be performed by banks in all SEPA countries since they are based on public algorithms. But in general only banks of the IBAN country perform the checks.

Another validation at IBAN level consists in verifying that bank and branch codes indicated in the BBAN are correct. Let us consider the following French IBAN: FR76 **30004 01400 62791687632 36** (BBAN is bold). This IBAN is well formed and all the check digits are correct. You can easily verify that at http://www.ibancalculator.com But there is a problem. The Bank code 30004 is for BNP PARIBAS and there exists no branch with the code 01400 for that Bank. The IBAN Plus directory provided by SWIFT contains the bank and branch code of all banks in SEPA. While checking the IBAN, the bank and branch codes **3000401400** are extracted and their existence is validated towards the IBAN Plus directory. Since the codes cannot be found inside, the IBAN is not valid and the payment cannot be processed.

A valid IBAN does not necessarily mean that the payment will be processed successfully. That is where IBAN verification comes into play. An account with a valid number can be blocked, closed or even non-existent. So the status of the account is important for the result of the payment processing and has to be taken into account.

If a payment is received on a closed account for example, the funds will be returned to the sender in most of the cases. But in some cases, the decision to close the account has been taken by the bank itself as a result of a merger for instance. The account has been migrated to another one with a new number. In this case, the closed account will be linked to the new one and the money will have to be redirected automatically to the new account. That kind of situation is encountered quite often today because of projects pertaining to mergers and acquisitions. If an account has been migrated to another one, the verifications must be performed on the migrated account to ensure that it is open and funds can be debited from or credited to it.

4.2.3 BIC / IBAN coherence check

Both the BIC and IBAN have to be valid, but it is not enough. They must be coherent as well. The BIC / IBAN coherence control ensures that a BIC and an IBAN belong to each other. If a payment contains an IBAN of Finland and a Spanish BIC for the beneficiary, then something is obviously wrong. Same thing if the IBAN is of Nordea Finland and the BIC of Danske Bank Finland.

Banks rely on the IBAN Plus directory to perform this control. That directory is provided by SWIFT (https://swiftref.swift.com/iban-plus). It contains all corresponding BIC that can be used with a valid IBAN. If the BIC is not associated to the IBAN in this directory, the BIC / IBAN coherence check will fail.

This BIC of Deutsche Bank Germany DEUTDEFF cannot be linked to the French IBAN FR76 3000 4008 4178 2563 1263 751. Neither can the BIC NORDSESS (Nordea Sweden) nor SOGEFRPP (Société Générale) be associated to that IBAN which belongs to BNP PARIBAS. In each case, the BIC / IBAN coherence check fails. Société Générale is a French Bank and an Iban of Société Générale starts with FR as well. So the BIC/IBAN coherence check considers other parameters like the Bank Code (30004) and the Branch code (00841) to ensure that an Iban is linked to a BIC. The Bank code of Société Générale is 30003. The coherence check of the above IBAN with SOGEFRPP would fail because 30004 does not belong to Société Générale.

4.2.4 Dates and the related controls

Dates play a very important role in payments. Many dates are necessary for the payment processing. And it is important to understand the different dates and for which purpose they are used. That is what this paragraph is about. Let us start by listing the type of dates often used in payments:

- Reception date and time: the date and time (DD/MM/YYYY HH:MM:SS) when the order was received. The time really matters here because the bank processes high number of orders daily and it is important to know at which time exactly an order was received. This date is filled in by the order management application which processes the payment.
- Requested execution date: the date when the bank *should* execute the order. This date is provided by the customer. It is a *wish* that may differ from the reality if the bank is not able to execute the payment on that date.
- Execution date: the date when the order is really executed. It is the date on which the bank debits the account and sends the correct transactions of the order to CSM or to beneficiary accounts directly. This date is visible in the order management application.
- Settlement date: the date when the transaction is settled. Unlike the previous dates, this date is at transaction level, not at order level. For transactions that are settled

through a CSM, it is the date at which the debtor bank is debited and the creditor bank credited. According to the SEPA Rulebook, the standard SCT is settled one day after the execution. But an SCT can be settled at the execution date as well. It is up to the bank.

- Booking date: the date when the order is booked on the customer account. The booking date is not the execution date. A payment can be executed on Day D and booked only on D+1. Payment booking happens most of the time at the execution date, but can be done the day before or days after. And this should not impact the value date normally.
- Value date: Date on which money is available for use on an account. A bank can receive funds and credit the beneficiary accounts only days later (For instance because of anti-money laundering investigations).

The customer can instruct the bank to execute the order immediately (as soon as possible is more correct as you can see below) or at a future date. The bank will schedule the execution according to customer instructions. The bank cannot execute payment orders and settle the related transactions after a point in time during the day. That time is called the cut-off. So there are two possibilities when the customer wants an immediate execution. Either the order is received by the bank before the cut-off and it will be processed and exchanged on that day or it is received after the cut-off and it will be processed and exchanged only the day after.

In the payment jargon, there are business days and calendar days. The next figure is intended to explain these two concepts. A calendar day starts at 00:00:00 and ends at 23:59:59. The business day goes from one cut-off to the next cut-off. In the figure, the business day starts at 15:20:00 and ends at 15:19:59. The Bank can receive payment orders at anytime. The orders that arrive before the cut-off on calendar day D with a requested execution date of D can be processed at D. The requested execution date and the execution date are the same in this case (Business date = Calendar date = D).

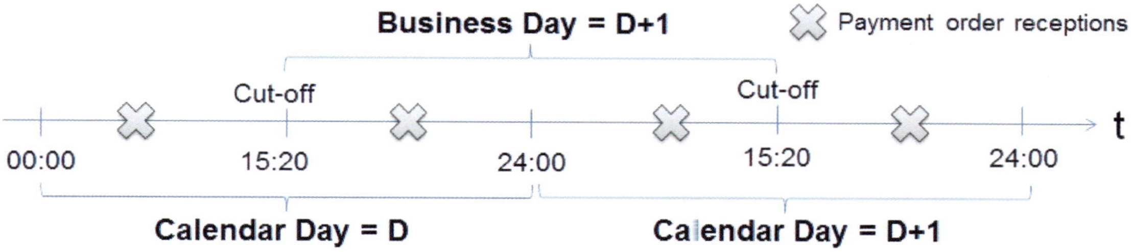

Figure 4.15: Differences between Calendar day and Business day

On the other hand, the orders that reach the bank after the cut-off on calendar day D with a requested execution date of D cannot be processed at D. They can only be processed with an execution date of D+1. In this case the requested execution date is not kept. Requested execution date = D and execution date = D + 1. Note also that Calendar Day = D and Business Day = D+1. The conclusion is that orders are always executed with the current business day as execution date.

Customer can also request the order to be executed many days in the future. Future-dated payments are generally executed early in the morning at the requested execution date. But it does not mean that all the checks are performed on that date. The bank performs first controls (except the balance check) at reception date and rejects the order immediately if it fails the checks. If the controls are successful, the order is stored for execution at the requested date. At execution date which is normally the requested execution date, IBAN verifications are performed again before balance check and execution. The reason is that an account may have been closed or blocked between the reception date and the execution date. For payments that the bank must execute right away, all the controls are done immediately including the balance check.

Coming back to the customer, let us consider the case where he would give a requested execution date which is a public holiday or a weekend day. Payment orders can be executed and/or settled on open business days only. The banks must therefore use their national calendars to determine the payment execution date since they do not want to process and exchange transactions on public holidays. The CSMs have their own calendar which differ from the national calendars. In SEPA, CSMs operate according to the TARGET2 calendar. TARGET2 is closed during the weekends and on specific holidays. The European Central Bank publishes the exact dates on which the TARGET2 system is closed each year. TARGET2 holidays always fall on national holidays. But the contrary is not true since TARGET2 is open on many national holidays. The settlement date must be a TARGET2 open day. So the TARGET2 calendar must be checked during the processing before setting the settlement date.

In summary, to determine the execution and settlement dates, the payment engine has to take into account national and TARGET2 calendars. Payments with a requested execution date which falls on a holiday are automatically postponed to the next open business date. This implies accessing the calendars during the processing and checking that the requested execution date is neither Saturday nor Sunday nor a holiday.

4.2.5 Duplicate checks

A duplicate payment is a payment having identical message elements with another payment while these elements should be different. Duplicate checks are carried out at message, order or transaction level. The purpose is to avoid processing the same message, the same order or the same transaction more than once. The following fields that are naturally used for the duplicate control (Read their definitions in the ISO 20022 documentation and things will be clear):

- Message Identification in the Group header (message level),
- Payment Information Identification in the Payment Information (Order level)
- Instruction Identification, End-To-End Identification, Transaction Identification in the Credit Transfer Transaction Information (transaction level)

Did you notice that the names of all these message elements end with the word **Identification**?

In addition to these elements, the execution date is generally taken into account. The duplicate check is generally performed in a range of dates: current date to few days in the past depending on bank choices.

4.2.6 Processing agreements

Put simply, a processing agreement is a set of processing services that the bank applies for the processing of a customer order. The customer signs an agreement for the services he wants to use. Processing agreements are more related to payments from corporate customers, so payments received in batch files through EBICS, SWIFTNet FileAct or other file exchange protocols.

The debtor bank develops and offers many services. Each service can take different values and one value determines the outcome of the processing. In general the bank has a standard value for each service. But the customer can ask to have non-standard values for one or many of the services. Below is a very simple representation of what a processing agreement looks like.

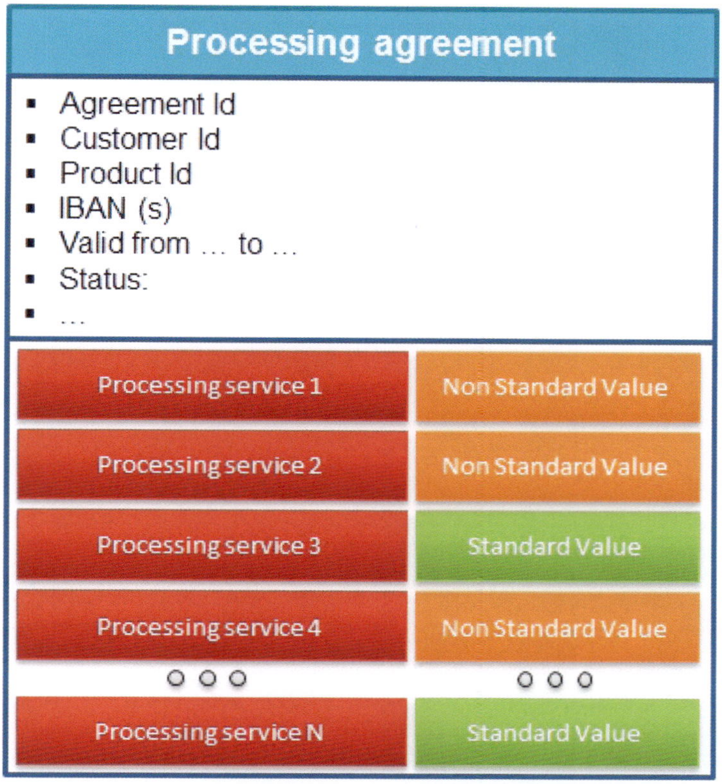

Figure 4.16 : Typical structure of a processing agreement

It is composed of two main parts: the agreement information and the included services. The first part contains information about the agreement like:

- Agreement Id: It is the unique Identification of the agreement
- Customer Id: It is the unique customer identification. The same customer can have multiple processing agreements. This field links one customer to all agreements he may have with the bank.
- Product Id: A payment product created and offered by the bank that is linked to the agreement.
- IBAN (s): The IBAN or the list of IBANs that are linked to the agreement. Each time the bank receives an order, it will check if the debtor IBAN belongs to the list. If that is the case. All the services specified in the contract will be applied for the processing of that order.
- Valid from … to …: Dates from and to which the agreement is valid.

Agreement search and identification are the prerequisites for applying the services. It cannot happen too soon because the payment parsing and validation and IBAN verifications for instance must happen before. It should not happen too late because as we will see some services are required for the processing of the order.

We will now look at the typical services available in agreement. The services presented below give a good overview of the kind of services you can encounter on the market. However the list is not exhaustive. For each service, the name is provided, possible applicable values are given and the usage is explained.

4.2.6.1 Service Execution speed

Values applicable for this service are Normal or High.

- Normal means that the speed will be the one of a normal SEPA Credit Transfer. The order will be executed at D and the transactions to the CSM will be settled at D+1.
- High means that the order will be executed at D and the transactions to the CSM will be settled at D as well.

This service reminds you of the field Instruction Priority <InstrPrty> of the pain.001. If the customer has a contract, it will be apply even if this field is not in the order that he sends.
The customer must send the orders before the cut-off time at execution date D. If not the order will be executed and settled at D+1.

Remark: Sometimes the corporate customer may want the bank to move the speed to High only if the order was received after the cut-off so that the beneficiaries can still be credited on the next business date.

4.2.6.2 Service Requested execution date as Settlement date

Values applicable for this service are No or Yes. It is about how the requested execution date transmitted in the pain.001 should be considered. At the customer's request, it can be considered as the settlement date or as the requested execution date.

- No means that the requested execution date is to be considered as a requested execution date as defined in the pain.001 order.
- Yes means that the requested execution date must be considered as settlement date. So it means that the real execution date is one business day earlier as it is done for the standard SCT.

Remark: For high priority SCTs executed and settled on the same day, this service does not make sense. It is interesting only if the SCT is settled one day after execution.

4.2.6.3 Services Duplicate checks

The duplicate check services enable the client to decide if the duplicate check should be performed, at which level it should happen and finally what should be the outcome, either pending status or rejected status.

A pain.001 message has three levels: message, order and transaction. A corporate customer may want the bank to enable the duplicate check at message level for example and to disable it at order level or at transaction level. The customer may want the duplicate check at order level only or at transaction level only. Furthermore, the duplicate check at order level can concern orders in the same message or all the orders available in the payment engine at processing time. And the duplicate check at transaction level may be either about transactions in the same order or about all the transactions available in the message or even about all transactions available in the payment engine at processing time. There are many options as you can see.

Moreover, a duplicate check may have different outcomes. One outcome can be to put the related message, order or transaction in the pending status. Another alternative is to reject the duplicate immediately. In case of pending status, a user will look at it and take the decision to approve or reject it after contacting the customer if necessary. In case of rejected status, no user action is possible. The bank just informs the customer about the reject.

Now we see that several parameters are required for the duplicate check services management:

- One parameter to specify at which level(s) the duplicate check should happen – message, order or transaction
- Another parameter to indicate the duplicate "depth" (messages in whole database, orders in message, order in whole database, transactions in order, transactions in message, transactions in whole database, etc.). To avoid running the duplicate verification on the whole database, a number of days over which the duplicate check is performed can be given. In case you have 10 business days for example, it means that the duplicates are verified against messages, orders and transactions of the last two weeks.
- Another parameter to indicate what should be the outcome if there is a match – pending status or rejected status

The implementation and processing for the duplicate checks are not straight forward and must be discussed in detail with the customer, so that he makes the choices that best fit his own needs.

4.2.6.4 Service percentage of erroneous (rejected) transactions

The purpose behind this service is to avoid processing an order with too many erroneous or rejected transactions because it can be easier for the corporate customer to regenerate the complete order than to create a new one only with the erroneous transactions.

Let us illustrate that with an example. A large utility company sends an order with 100 000 transactions to its bank. But 25 000 transactions are detected erroneous for multiple reasons during the processing. Two possibilities: Either the bank rejects the 25000 in error and processes the remaining 75 000 correct transactions or the bank rejects all the order because the number of rejected transactions is too high. Which choice is the utility company going to make? It really depends. It may be easy for that company based on the reporting from the bank to identify and correct the problems for the 25000 transactions and resend them again. Or it might be much easier to resend the complete order again.

Offering and managing this service requires putting many parameters in place and each of them can take many values. Think of the following: How many transactions should an order have for this service to be applied? 100, 1000, 10000 transactions? Which percentage of the transactions in error should lead to the full rejection of the order? 20%, 30% or 50%? 25% of 100 transactions is not the same thing as 25% for 100000 transactions. So the number of transactions matters when considering the percentage. Many parameters may therefore be necessary to serve the customers as they want. Setting the standard values is not an easy task here. It is interesting for the bank to analyze the statistic of orders and transactions rejections and the related customer reactions before taking a decision.

4.2.6.5 Service late modification

The objective of this service is to allow the customer to modify or cancel his order as late as possible. The order will be kept in the payment engine until few minutes before the cut-off time. The main advantage for the customer is that he has more time to change his mind about the order. If he does not subscribe to this service, the bank will process the order according to his policies. In general, the order will be executed much earlier.

This service takes two values No and Yes. No simply means that the late modification does not apply. It is the standard value. Yes means that customer is able to modify his orders until very close to the cut-off.

4.2.6.6 Service management of erroneous orders / operations

During the processing of an order, errors can be detected at order or transaction level. If we consider a pain.001, errors at order level can be for instance an incorrect Debtor IBAN, invalid Debtor BIC, wrong number of transactions (Number of all transactions in the order different from the number indicated at order level), wrong control sum (Total amount of all transactions in the order different from amount in the Control Sum), etc. Regarding transactions, problems can be for instance a wrong Creditor IBAN, an incoherent BIC, an invalid amount and so on.

What should happen in the payment engine when the errors are detected? Should the outcome be a reject status or a pending status? It depends on the bank policies and on what the customer wants. A bank can decide never to correct information like debtor IBAN or creditor IBAN in its systems. In those cases, error on IBANs will always have an outcome as reject. But if there is a problem with the control sum or an incoherent beneficiary BIC/IBAN, the bank may accept to put the order or transaction in pending status. The customer will be consulted for the decision whether to accept and process the order or to cancel it. The pending status allows providing a much customized service. Consequently, the non-standard value is usually pending status as outcome and the standard value is rejected status.

4.2.6.7 Service of deferred cut-off

The purpose of this service is to allow the customer to transmit his order at a later time than the official cut-off time. The official cut-off time is the cut-off that the bank communicates to the customers after which no order will be accepted for that day. If the official cut-off time is 11:30 for example, the cut-off for customers subscribing to this service may be 12:00.

This service takes the value Yes or No (Standard value). Naturally, the specific cut-off time for the customer has to be taken into account when processing his orders. The Debtor bank should make sure that orders can really be processed and exchanged on time even if they are received a bit later. If the customer transmits an order with several thousand transactions just a couple minutes before his cut-off time, it will be very difficult to process it on time. Thus the Bank should clearly indicate the conditions under which those late orders can be processed without problem.

4.2.6.8 Service accounting methods for booking entries

Orders and transactions booking is a key feature in payment processing. Interesting for the customer is that Banks can do the bookies entries and present the accounting information in the way that he wants. This service is about the methods that the bank can use to book entries related to the order on the customer account. Note that the total amounts debited or credited from/to the customer account are the same. The difference lies mainly in the methods used to do the accounting.

The accounting methods service provides customers the ability to choose which methods should be applied for the booking entries. To help you understand each method presented below, let us take an example of an order with 10 transactions of 10 € each. 2 transactions of the order have been rejected (for example because creditor IBANs are incorrect) and 8 transactions have been processed successfully. We therefore have the following amounts: Total amount of the order 100 €, Total amount of successfully processed transactions 80€ and Total amount of rejected transactions 20€.

Accounting methods

Gross batchbooking - one debit entry for the total amount of the order and one credit entry for all rejected transactions. For our example, it means the following:

Date	Description	Value Date	Debit	Credit
15/10/2018	Multi-beneficiaries order	15/10/2018	-100	
15/10/2018	Rejected transactions multi-beneficiaries order	15/10/2018		+20

Table 4-1 : Accounting entries for gross batch booking

Net batchbooking - one debit entry for the total amount of successfully processed transactions. For our example, it means the following:

Date	Description	Value Date	Debit	Credit
15/10/2018	Multi-beneficiaries order	15/10/2018	-80	

Table 4-2 : Accounting entries for net batch booking

Hybrid batchbooking method - one debit entry for the total amount of the order and one credit entry for each rejected transactions. You can consider it as Gross Batchbooking for the order and no batchbooking for the rejected transactions. For our example, it means the following:

Date	Description	Value Date	Debit	Credit
15/10/2018	Multi-beneficiaries order	15/10/2018	-100	
15/10/2018	Rejected transaction 1 multi-beneficiaries order	15/10/2018		+10
15/10/2018	Rejected transaction 2 multi-beneficiaries order	15/10/2018		+10

Table 4-3 : Accounting entries for hybrid batch booking

No batchbooking - one accounting entry for each transaction processed successfully. For our example, it means the following:

Date	Description	Value Date	Debit	Credit
15/10/2018	Multi-beneficiaries order - transaction 1	15/10/2018	-10	
15/10/2018	Multi-beneficiaries order - transaction 2	15/10/2018	-10	
15/10/2018	Multi-beneficiaries order - transaction 3	15/10/2018	-10	
15/10/2018	Multi-beneficiaries order - transaction 4	15/10/2018	-10	
15/10/2018	Multi-beneficiaries order - transaction 5	15/10/2018	-10	
15/10/2018	Multi-beneficiaries order - transaction 6	15/10/2018	-10	
15/10/2018	Multi-beneficiaries order - transaction 7	15/10/2018	-10	
15/10/2018	Multi-beneficiaries order - transaction 8	15/10/2018	-10	

Table 4-4 : Accounting entries for no batch booking

The four methods above are those that you will encounter most of time. The names may be different, but they will function as described above. As you see, no matter which method is used, the same amount is debited from the customer account. So the end result is the same. Accounting methods are just used to present the information in different ways.

Here is another thought about the rejected transactions. The rejected transactions considered above have been rejected by the Debtor Bank. It is obvious that some of the processed transactions may be rejected by the beneficiary bank because the beneficiary account does not exist or for some regulatory reasons. The money that was debited from the debtor account has to be credited again to the debtor. The customer can also choose to have batchbooking for all returned transactions on the same day or no batchbooking at all. It depends on his own needs and processing capabilities.

Now you may wonder why a corporate customer would prefer one particular accounting method. It mostly depends on the procedures and the tools used in the company to process the account statement. Individual transactions in an electronic report can easily be reconciled with the sent original transactions and this can be done completely automatically. Sometimes the gross amount in the bank order can be used with other information to reconcile the operation with a previously sent order. These different reasons explain again why it is so important to sit down and discuss with the customer.

4.2.7 Pending order management

During the processing of a transaction many errors may cause it to be put to the pending status. Pending management simply consists of handling transactions in pending status. A manual intervention is in general needed to release the transaction and continue the processing or to reject it.

Who should have access to the pending transactions and what should they be able to do on it? These subjects are related to user rights and the Graphical User Interface. One of the upcoming chapters is dedicated to these two important topics.

The users must understand very well why the message, order or transaction is in pending status and should know what actions to carry out for their management. User training is of foremost importance here. Furthermore, it is good to have a list of all possible situations that lead to a pending status and the related messages and actions. A user can refer to the document, in case he has some doubt about the reason of the pending status. There are errors that occur very often and with much higher frequencies. The users would know how to handle them easily since they are used to them. More difficult to assess and handle are the situations that occur very seldom, once in a year for example. Even if he took a training, the user may have forgotten what the situation is all about. That is why it is important to have the information written down and available, so that the user can refer to it rapidly.

4.2.8 Balance check

The Balance check is probably the most important feature in the payment processing for debtor banks. It is the service that determines if the customer has sufficient funds on his account for the order execution. But having sufficient funds on the account does not always guarantee that the payment will be executed. Banks set daily or weekly limits in online channels because of security reasons essentially. If the total amount of credit transfers for the day or the week exceeds the limits, the bank will not execute it. The customer then has to go to a branch or call the bank.

The balance check takes into account possible credit facilities granted to the customer. The check can be positive even if the balance will become negative after the transfer. In that case, the bank makes a cash advance to his customer as agreed with him. Let us take a simple example of a private customer with 500 € on his account and a line of credit of 1000 €. The total amount available is 1500 € = 500 € (Balance) + 1000 € (Line of credit). The customer can initiate a credit transfer of up to 1500 €. The bank will refuse to execute an order only if the amount is above 1500€. An order with 900 € amount will be executed resulting in a negative balance of – 400 €. The customer may still initiate a 500 € order since he has not totally used funds from his line of credit. The result will be a negative balance of – 1400 €. The example is very simple but is enough to illustrate the logic behind the balance check when credit facilities come into play. The computation of available funds is more complex in reality.

The balance check is ordinarily part of a service performing several other checks mentioned above like:

- checking the validity and existence of account numbers for accounts held by the bank
- verifying the status of the accounts (They should be open and not closed, blocked or frozen).

Checking the balance makes no sense for a creditor bank receiving a credit transfer. The amount of a credit transfer cannot be negative! But the bank must ensure the account is valid and the status is correct.

4.2.9 Routing and issuing

When all the checks have been successfully performed and the customer account has been debited, the next step is to route and issue the payment toward the correct destination. Routing means determining where the payment has to be sent and issuing is the action of sending and delivering that payment to the next party in the chain.

In the bank order management application, transactions can be divided in two groups:

- transactions where sender and receiver is the same bank
- transactions where sender and receiver is not the same bank

The first group, the intrabank transactions, might not need to be sent out. They can directly be "exchanged" inside the bank. I say might not need because I have seen many cases in practice where the application is sending them out before getting them back again. I must admit that it is always difficult to understand the choice.

For the second group, there is no choice. They must be sent out if they have to reach the destination. A message with the outgoing transactions is created and issued to the first but not final destination. For a debtor bank, this means issuing the payment to the exchange platform which will take care of the final delivery.

4.3 The Payment Exchange

The payment exchange is the last step in the payment processing value chain. It comes after acquisition and order management. The main objective in this step is to route and deliver the payment message to the correct destination.

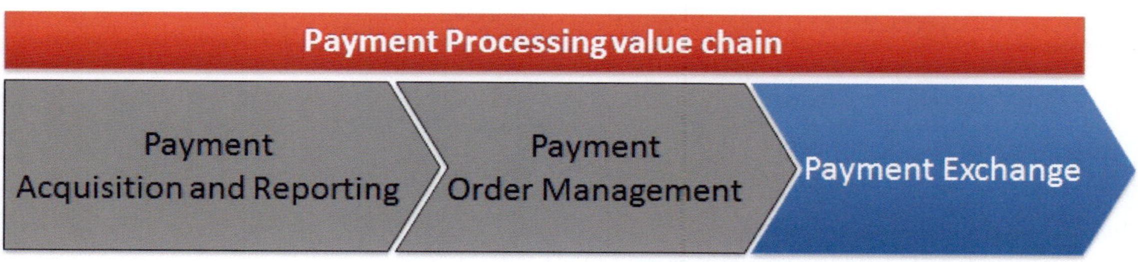

Figure 4.17: Payment Exchange Subprocess

An exchange platform connects many banks of a Bank Group among themselves and connects the Bank Group to the national/regional ACH - when they exist - and to the Pan-European Automated Clearing House (STEP2).

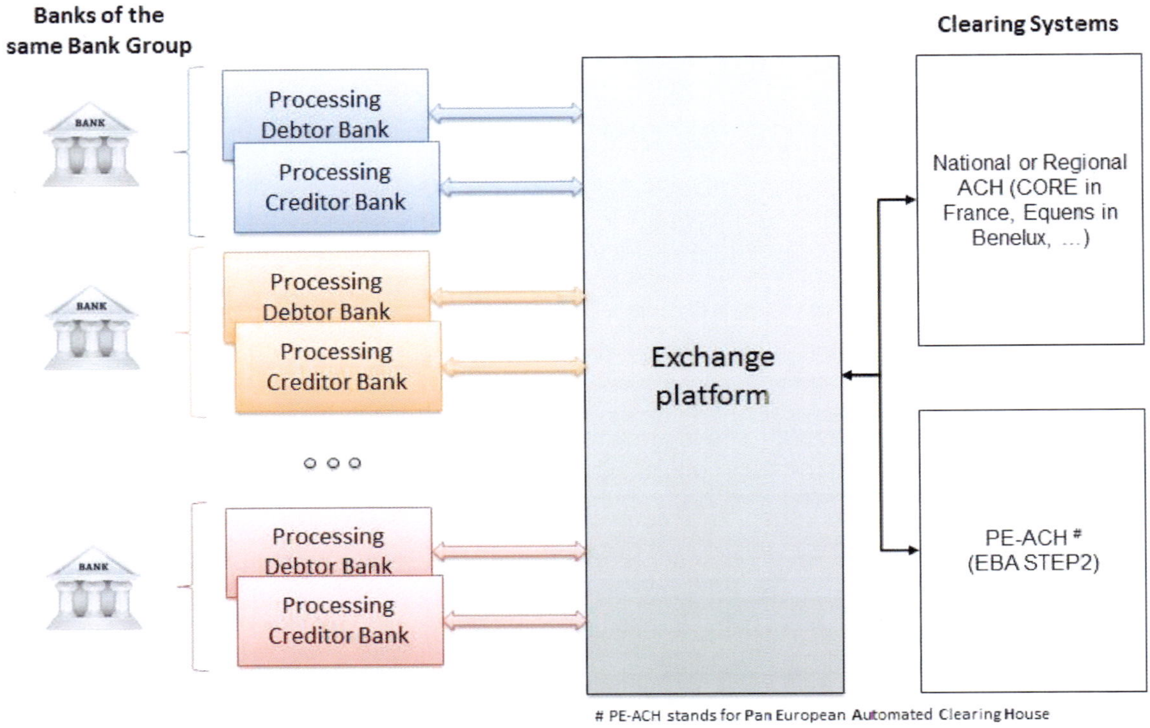

Figure 4.18: Exchange platform

The exchange platform is a focal point for payments from all banks of the Bank Group to other banks of the Group or from / to clearing systems. Generally it receives messages in interbank formats and issues them in interbank formats as well. More concretely, it means that pain.001 and camt.055 messages received from the customer have been transformed during the processing in order management applications (See previous chapter) and issued in pacs.008 and camt.056 formats to the exchange platform. After processing, the platform itself creates and issues messages in pacs.008 and camt.056 formats toward the destinations.

The above figure shows that the platform exchanges payment messages with Debtor Bank and Creditor Bank processing applications of each bank of the Group. I could have called them Bank Order Management applications. But I prefer the term Bank processing applications which is more generic and applicable in any situation. All arrows in the pictures are bi-directional indicating that messages are sent in both directions.

Let us briefly recall the messages exchanged between the platform and the debtor bank. The debtor bank sends pacs.008 and camt.056 messages to the platform and receives pacs.004 (as normal return and as positive response) and camt.029 from the platform. I don't need to explain that the two last messages come from the creditor bank which can be inside or outside the Group. You have become a master now and understand that easily. ☺

The Creditor bank on its side receives pacs.008 and camt.056 messages from the platform and sends pacs.004 (as normal return and as positive response) and camt.029 to the platform. Pacs.008 and camt.056 messages come from a debtor bank inside or outside the group. That debtor bank receives the pacs.004 and camt.029 sent by the creditor bank.

In the subsequent sections, we focus on some of the key features available in an exchange platform. We first take a look at the payment messages validations. Then the routing and the different routing directories are considered and finally the crucial bulking and debulking function is discussed.

4.3.1 Payment messages validations

When the platform receives a message, it carries out some technical validations to make sure it is correctly formatted and some functional checks to validate his content. The platform can then "ensure" to process and send payment messages that are SEPA compliant. Below are list of typical validations made:

- Message format validation
- BIC validation
- IBAN Validation
- BIC / IBAN coherence check
- Duplicate check
- Date and timeline validation
- and so on

Now you might say that many of the checks were already performed in the Order Management applications. Why then doing these verifications again?

One first reason is that the exchange platform cannot rely solely on external applications for these checks. It has to do it itself and ensures that only valid payment messages are accepted.

Another reason is that the platform exchanges payment messages with many processing applications and validations may be performed only partly in some of them. In that case, performing the check in the exchange platform can avoid propagating potential errors.

At last, a change might happen between the time when the checks were made in the processing application and the time when the exchange platform receives the payment. This particularly applies for BIC validation which is based mainly on participation directories that are updated regularly. As a result a BIC that was valid yesterday may not be valid today anymore. This can be detected only if the check is done again before issuing and delivery.

Remarks:

1. In a Service Oriented Architecture, validations are done by services. The same service can be called at different point in the processing value chain. When we say that validations are made again in the exchange platform, it does not mean that they are implemented again. The same validation services can be shared by payment processing modules and exchange platform.
2. If payment processing and exchange platform modules are implemented in one application, some validations may be skipped in the one or the other module. Since it is the same application that performs all the checks, they can be spread throughout the different modules.

4.3.2 Routing and the ACH and SWIFT directories

The main purpose of an exchange platform is to route transactions and deliver messages. Therefore Routing and Issuing play a major role in payment exchange. Routing is based mainly on the BIC (Bank Identifier Code or Business Identifier Code). A BIC contains either 8 characters for the primary office or 11 characters for subsidiaries.
Routing a payment from one bank of a group to another bank of the group is quite simple. Sender's and receiver's BIC are available and well known and the platform knows exactly where to send the messages in order to reach any bank of the group. When it comes to external banks, the bank has to rely on information provided either by CSM or by SWIFT in directories.

A CSM knows all participant banks that are reachable through it. Remember that a bank may be a direct or an indirect participant. The CSM collects all the information related to participant banks and put them together in the so called **participation directories**. A CSM may have one directory for the direct participants and another one for the indirect participants. It may also have a single directory which contains both direct and indirect participants. The directories have to be updated frequently since new participants can join the CSM and old participants may change their status from indirect to direct for example or may end their participation.

CSM Directories have to be uploaded in the exchange platform and updated regularly in order to use the latest information for validation and routing. Outdated information results in routing failure (for new participant) or wrong routing (for old participant whose data has been updated but has not been taken into account yet). Directories are used for routing, but not only. Many directories are also used for validation as we will see in the coming sections.

Remark: Routing directories are different from SEPA Registries. SEPA Registries contains the list of all banks that are participants in SEPA Payment Schemes. On the following EPC page http://epc.cbnet.info/content/adherence_database you can download the list of all banks that have joined the different SEPA Schemes (SCT, SDD Core and SDD B2B). But these registries do not provide enough information to route SEPA Payments.

4.3.2.1 The routing directories

Routing directories are provided by national/regional CSMs, by EBA STEP2 (the PE-ACH) and by SWIFT. Each national/regional CSM as well as EBA STEP2 provides information for their own members that are either direct or indirect participants. If you want to have an overview about all CSMs a bank is connected to, you won't find them in those directories. The SEPA Routing directory of SWIFT is the place to look for all possible routes to reach a particular bank. It contains SEPA payments routing data for all financial institutions operating in the SEPA countries. As a consequence each operational BIC able to process SEPA payments is found there. It is nice to have all the information at one place. But keeping it up-to-date is a big challenge. Indeed, the SEPA Routing directory is not always up-to-date. And it is sometimes updated many weeks after CSMs or EBA directories as the experience on the ground has shown. This has led to routing issues and many banks that were completely relying on it at the beginning of their SEPA journey changed their mind to work with directories provided directly by national CSM or EBA. When these lines are written, SWIFT has the goal to replace the SEPA Routing Directory with the SEPA Plus product. Will the information be updated rapidly and synchronized with the different CSMs? Only the future can tell us.

Let us now list key characteristics of SEPA Routing Directory and EBA STEP2 Directories.

SEPA Routing Directory key features and specificities

- Identification of participants in SEPA Credit Transfer scheme.
- List of the multiple Automated Clearing Houses through which a bank is directly or indirectly reachable for SEPA payments
- Indicates if a bank has a preferred clearing channel
- No information is provided about participants who have joined AOS offered by different CSMs
- Even if it is updated monthly, Information is not always up-to-date and this leads to routing issues from time to time.

EBA STEP2 Directories key features and specificities

- EBA provides directories for each SEPA Scheme: SCT, SDD Core, SDD B2B

- Information about STEP2 direct and indirect participants to SCT are available in two files: one for direct participants and one for indirect participants
- The additional optional services (AOS) of the scheme to which a participant has adhered are also indicated in the files. It is only for AOS implemented by EBA.
- No information is available about any other CSM a Bank is connected to for SCT exchanges.

The EBA STEP2 features and specificities apply also for most of the national/regional CSMs.

Directories are used also for validation or enrichment purpose. SWIFT provides many other directories that can be used to validate IBAN and BIC during the processing of SEPA payments like the BIC Directory, the Bank Directory Plus, IBAN Plus and SEPA Plus. For more details, please refer to the SWIFT page https://swiftref.swift.com/products-services

The IBAN Plus and SEPA Plus are used for validation and enrichment. The IBAN Plus can be used to validate an IBAN and ensures the coherence of the IBAN with a BIC that has been provided (It is called IBAN/BIC coherence check). In case the BIC has not been provided, the payment can be enriched with the corresponding BIC retrieved from the directory. IBAN Plus directory has become crucial since in Customer-to-bank space the BIC became optional in cross-border SEPA Payments in February 2016 (It has been optional in national payments since February 2014). Banks enrich the BIC if it is not provided by relying on that directory. SEPA Plus contains the IBAN Plus and the routing information for all the SEPA Schemes.

How can directories be uploaded to an exchange platform?

Directories are provided in FULL and in DELTA version most of the time. The FULL Version contains all the data of the directory. The DELTA version contains only the records that have been updated *compared to the previous version*. This last information sounds like a detail, but is very important. If you failed to upload two DELTA versions or more, you cannot just take the last DELTA version, upload it to your exchange platform ad claims that all the information is up-to-date. You have to upload all the previous versions until the last one. Otherwise you may have inconsistencies or wrong information in your database.

When uploaded the first time, you have to take the full version. There is no choice. From the second time onward, you can choose either to use the full version or the delta version.
Loading the FULL version takes longer time. The existing records must be cleared before all records are inserted. And this should happen ideally when there is no processing of payments in the platform, so in general quite late in the night, very early in the morning or during the week-end. Otherwise lot of payments may end in pending or rejected status. So the choice to upload the FULL version brings some constraints you must be aware of.

Loading the DELTA version is the other option. The database does not have to be cleaned up. New records are added and existing records are updated. So it takes less time. It is important to make sure that updates are done properly. If you load the Delta version when payments are being processed, processing problems related to (new) data in the Delta file is less likely to happen. So you don't have to "isolate" the platform for that. You can do the upload at a moment when the traffic is very low.

To conclude this paragraph, we will now focus on the routing process itself. As already said, the platform has to rely on information provided by CSMs in directories for the routing. How does that happen? After the validation of the destination BIC, the platform determines if the BIC belongs to one bank of the Group or to one indirect participant. If that is the case, the transaction is routed directly to the destination. If it is not, the platform first checks if the BIC is present in the participation directory of the CSM (STEP2 as well). In case the control is successful, the platform routes the transaction to the CSM. But a bank can be reachable through many CSMs. To know which one to route the transactions too, priorities should be defined. The transaction is then routed to the CSM of higher priority.

Transactions are routed individually but they are not submitted individually toward the destination. In general, many transactions are grouped together in a message that the platform sends to the destination. This takes us to another important feature of an exchange platform: Bulking and Debulking.

4.3.3 Bulking and Debulking

Bulking is the process of grouping many transactions of the same type in a single order or message. Debulking is the reverse process which consists of degrouping or splitting an order or message and extracting all the transactions it is composed of in order to process and route each of them individually.

Debulking is performed for messages that are received and Bulking is done for messages to send. A pacs.008 message received from EBA or a national CSM can contain transactions to various destinations (Entities of the Group and Indirect participants). Each transaction must be routed and delivered to the receiving party. And this requires to debulk the message. On the other side, before the exchange platform sends transactions, it will bulk all transactions to the same destination in a message. In addition to the destination, the settlement date and the type of transaction play a role in bulking and must be taken into account also.

Do you remember how a standard pacs.008 message is formed? It consists of two main parts which are the Group header and the Credit Transfer Transaction Information. A tag right at the beginning of the message indicates his type (pacs.008.001.02). The date is present in the Group Header. As consequence, only transactions of the same date and type can be grouped in the same message. But what about the destination? The platform has to figure out which transactions with same or different beneficiary BICs are going to the same destination, so that it can group them in the same outgoing message. For that, a logic must be implemented in the exchange platform to link a Group of BICs that are related to the same destination. For instance, all BICs belonging to one bank of the group must be grouped in a “specific entity”. When the platform processes the payments and identifies all creditor BICs belonging to the list, it can group all transactions toward that entity in the same message.

Let us consider clearing systems as example. The BICs belonging to banks outside the Bank Group are reachable through a Clearing System. The Clearing System should be defined as an entity to which the exchange platform can send messages. And all BICs outside the Bank Group have to be linked to that entity. This allows the platform to group all the transactions to that destination in one message.

Now an exchange platform can be connected to multiple CSMs and a BIC may be reachable through multiple CSMs as well. How then to know to which CSM the message should be sent (and thus in which outgoing message it should be grouped)? This conflict is solved with routing prioritization. If a transaction can be exchanged through multiple CSMs, then the platforms needs a logic to decide to which CSM it will be sent. In this case, the transaction is delivered to the CSM of higher priority with other transactions grouped altogether in a message.

4.4 Payment application architectures

The Figure 4.18: Exchange platform depicts a logical view of high level functional blocks responsible for the payment processing and exchange. The required sub functionalities can be implemented in many different applications depending on the past and current context of a bank. This paragraph is about the different types of application architectures that support the functions to process and exchange payment messages. Application architectures should help us to find the answers to the following questions:

- Where are the applications/modules responsible for the interbank exchanges?
- Where are the applications/modules responsible for the debtor bank messages processing?
- Where are the applications/modules responsible for the creditor bank messages processing?

In the following subparagraphs, different application architectures will be presented and discussed. If you understand them, you can make the architecture analysis for your own Bank quite easily. Because after going through these examples, you will be able to find out where the different applications and components are in your own project and how they all fit into the big picture. Please take note that Acquisition / Reporting applications have not been included to keep things simple. Let us now look at the first architecture.

4.4.1 Payment Application Architecture example 1

Exchange platform, Debtor Bank and Creditor Bank processing are implemented in one single application

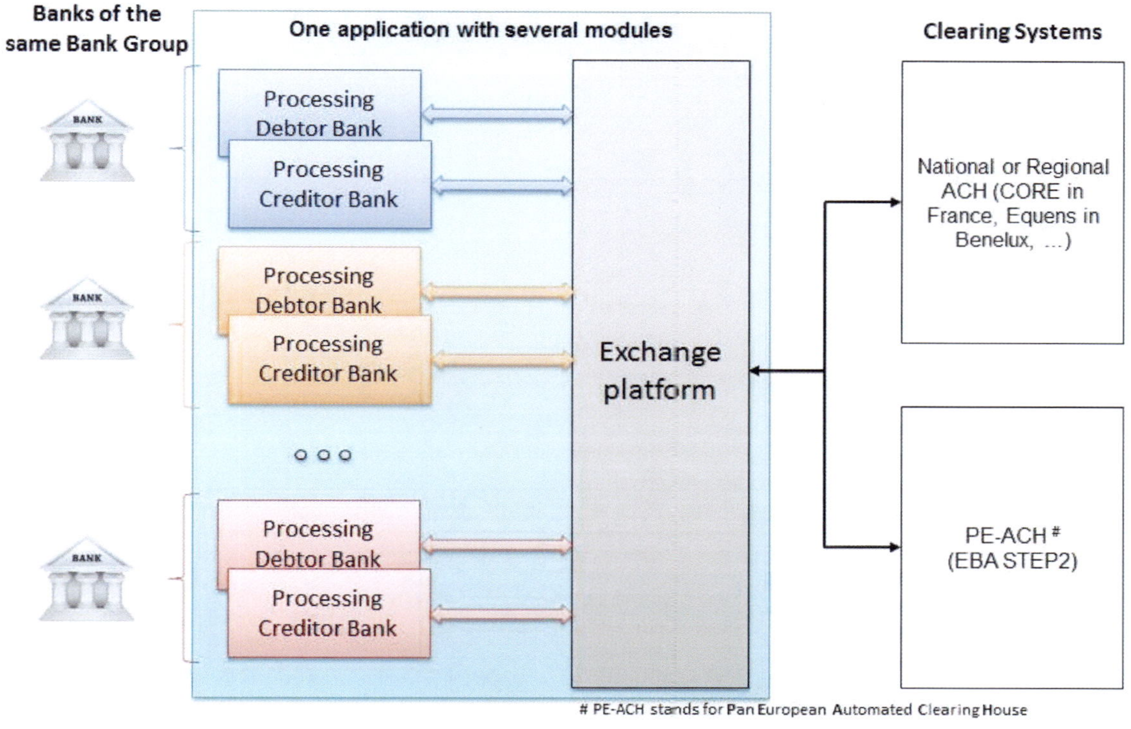

Figure 4.19: One single application for the debtor and creditor banks and exchange platform

This architecture consists of one single application with many modules: one module in charge of the payment exchange and one or more modules responsible for the debtor bank and creditor bank messages processing. Each bank of the bank group has dedicated module(s) for the processing of its payments. The payment exchange module (exchange platform) interconnects all the banks between themselves and connects the whole Bank Group to the market, the clearing system. The payment exchange module is usually operated by the bank which is direct participant to the CSM. The banks operate their own modules including the direct participant (DP). The DP operates its own debtor and creditor bank modules in addition to the exchange platform.

Many payment engine solutions of the market use a Service Oriented Architecture (SOA). SOA enables to build many modules upon a set of standard services, therefore enhancing reusability, flexibility as well as efficiency in the implementation. An SOA based application can provide all the modules necessary for the payment exchange and processing. Many legacy applications in the different banks can be replaced with one single application. Processes and operations can be simplified. In addition, the communication between banks is improved as they used the same application and very probably that same GUI. As we can see, this type of architecture yields some interesting benefits. One drawback is that "all eggs are being put in the same basket" as one application holds all the modules. So the availability, reliability, performance and robustness of the application become even more essential.

A bank may want to use a market solution to replace payment messages processing applications and not the exchange platform. The result is the second architecture.

4.4.2 Payment Application Architecture example 2

Exchange platform implemented in one application. Debtor Bank and Creditor Bank processing implemented in another application

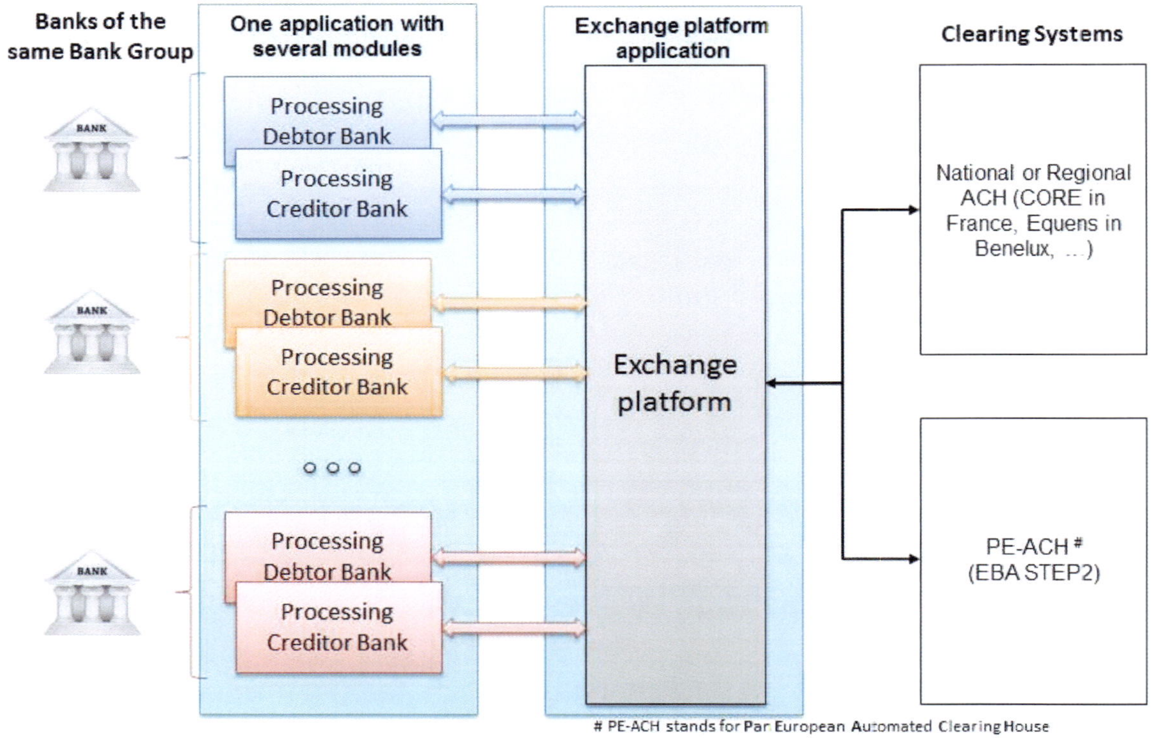

Figure 4.20: One application for debtor and creditor banks and another one for the exchange platform

In this architecture, there are two main applications. The exchange platform is implemented in one dedicated application. The debtor and creditor bank messages processing are implemented in another application. That application is divided in modules for each bank of the Group.

Different reasons may explain why the bank group came to that architecture. It is replacing the legacy payment engines available in the different branches but want to keep the exchange platform because investments were made to enhance or replace it recently and it is performing well. Or maybe there are many specific features in the current exchange platform and after careful studies the decision has been made to keep it as it is. Whatever the case, interfaces must be set up between the two applications for the exchange of the payment messages.

If the bank group consists of many banks, then "quite many eggs are being put in the same basket". The payment processing application has to be very reliable and robust as well. Potential issues may have huge impacts.

We have two independent applications to interface in this architecture. It is a challenge. But the complexity can further increase as we will see next. Let us now look at the third example of application architecture.

4.4.3 Payment Application Architecture example 3

One application for the Exchange platform, one application for Debtor Bank messages processing and one application for Creditor bank messages processing

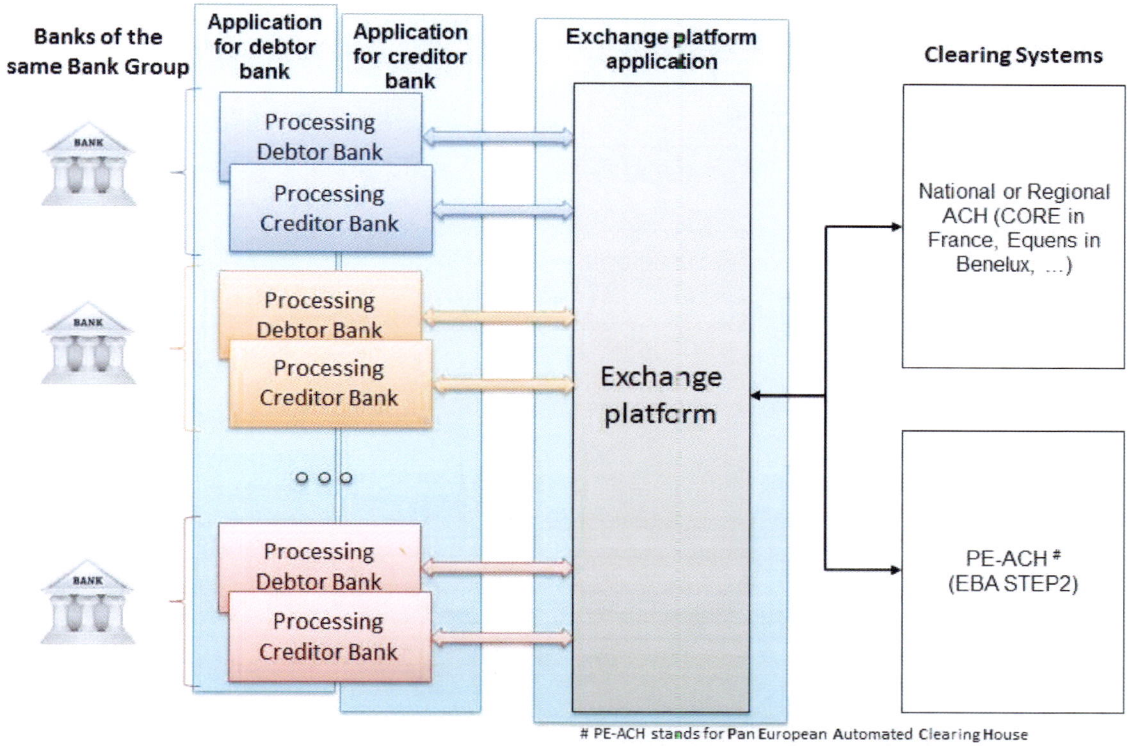

Figure 4.21: One application for debtor banks, another for creditor banks and another application for the exchange platform

This architecture consists of three main applications: one for the exchange platform, one for the Debtor bank processing and one for the Creditor bank processing. It is important to remember that Debtor bank and Creditor bank processing can be implemented in different applications.

Many reasons might explain why debtor bank and creditor bank features are in different applications. But we will consider one typical reason. The bank implemented one application many years ago for both debtor and creditor bank payment processing. The application became old and could not deliver the expected business value anymore. Then the bank made the decision to migrate and improve debtor bank functions in a new application. Creditor bank processing was kept in the old application as it was still fine for the business.

Therefore the bank ends up with three main applications. Interfaces must be built between the Exchange platform and the Debtor bank application on one hand, and between the Exchange platform and the Creditor bank application on the other hand. Implementation is a bit more complex than in the previous example where we had only two main applications. Integration and maintenance of the three applications is more challenging, but we are not yet at end of our journey. The next architecture will take us to another level of complexity.

4.4.4 Payment Application Architecture example 4

One application for the Exchange platform, Debtor Bank messages processing implemented in own specific application(s) and Creditor Bank messages processing implemented in own specific application(s)

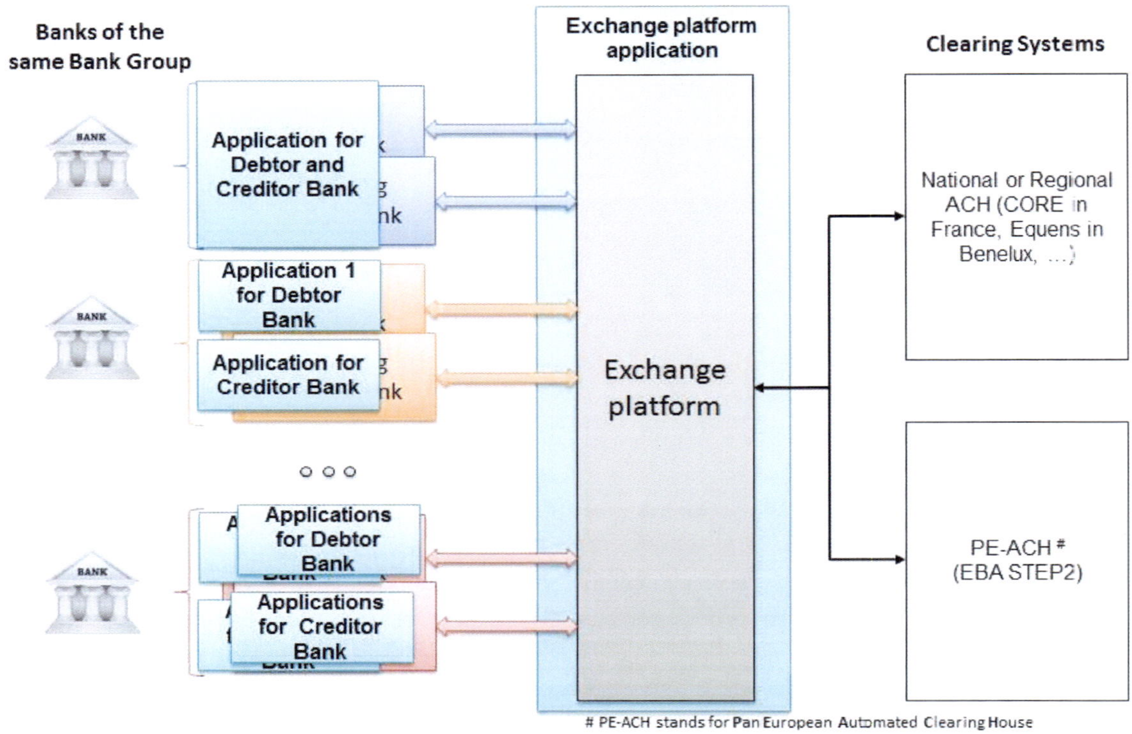

Figure 4.22: Multiple applications for debtor bank and creditor banks and one application for the exchange platform

What we see on the figure above is the result you get when each bank of a Bank Group decides on its own which approach and which applications to use for payment processing. It is very heterogeneous IT landscape. The first bank uses the same application to process Debtor bank messages and well as Creditor bank messages. The second bank uses one application for Debtor Bank messages and another application for Creditor Bank messages processing. The third bank uses many applications for Debtor bank messages processing and many applications for Creditor Bank messages processing as well. Question about the third bank: How does it come the Bank uses that many applications for processing? Answers are history and legacy. The bank had legacy applications that were adapted for SEPA Payments. It ended up receiving and processing pain.001 messages in multiple applications, sending pacs.008

messages from another application and sending camt.056 from again another application and so on.

In practice, you find such architectures in bank groups that expanded through mergers and acquisitions and that did not launch program to implement a common payment platform for the whole bank group. Many of them still have a long way to go before getting where they want to get. Having so many different applications is not the ideal situation. The more applications you have in your architecture, the more money you have to spend for implementation, maintenance and change. That is because the functions are scattered in many applications and you need to set up a lot of interfaces to make the whole work together. As a consequence the complexity increases and the agility lowers.

A rule of thumb in application architecture is therefore the following: *the less applications you have, the better it is.* But do not understand that the first architecture presented above is always the best in any case because there is only one application. Each bank has its specific needs and requirements that have to be taken into account to put in place its "own best" architecture. Sometimes, it may mean having two applications instead of one. For example very big volumes may drive this choice.

As a conclusion, many options exist for application architectures implementation. What we have seen in this chapter can guide you in a better analysis and understanding of application architectures for your own projects. Keep in mind that there is no best architecture because markets, customer expectations and the bank itself are evolving. What was excellent yesterday can become obsolete. And what is good today may not be as relevant tomorrow anymore. So the architecture must take into account not only the current situation and future goals of the bank but also the market trends and evolutions.

4.5 The Payment Status Reports

The customers, and particularly the corporations, are keen to know the status of a payment order that is being processed. They appreciate to have reports about the status all along the processing. Payment Status Reports (PSR) is the solution to address these needs. They give visibility to the customer on his orders and transactions while these are being processed in the different applications of the payment processing value chain.

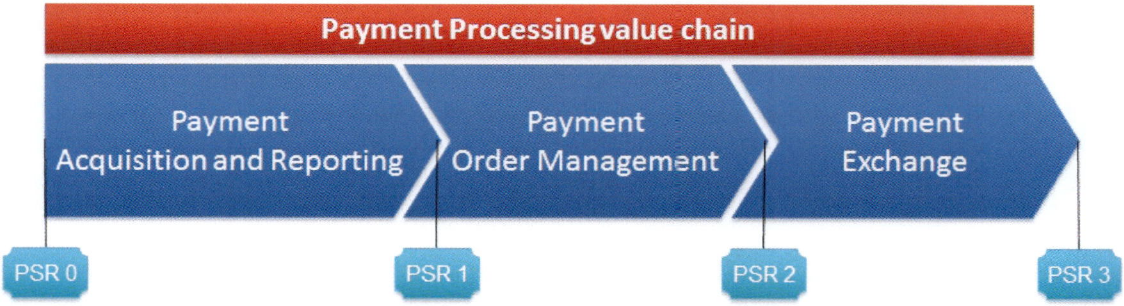

Figure 4.23: Payment Status Reports in the payment processing value chain

Payment status reports are reporting messages sent by the bank to a customer to give him information about the progress of payment orders processing and execution. A PSR can be either positive (fully accepted message or order) or negative (fully rejected message or order) or partially positive (partially accepted message or order – you can also see this as partially negative – I prefer to see the glass half full rather than half empty ☺).

PSRs can be divided into two groups: technical PSRs and functional PSRs. PSR 0 and PSR 1 on the picture are considered of technical nature. PSR 2 and PSR 3 are considered of functional nature.

The above figure shows at which stage the PSRs are created and sent to the customer during the processing. PSR 0 is generated right after the file reception. The PSR 1 is produced at the end of the payment message acquisition. The PSR 2 is created after the reception and controls of the order in the Payment order management application. The PSR 3 is about the exchange of the transactions with CSMs and beneficiary banks. The PSR 3 is generated and sent to the customer after receiving the acknowledgement (ACK or NACK) from the receiving parties. Acknowledgements are received at transaction level and aggregated at order level before delivery to the customer. The customer is interested in the order primarily not in the single transactions. A successful PSR 3 means that the order was acquired, processed and exchanged successfully with the beneficiary banks (The happiness !!!). The subsequent paragraphs handle the different PSRs in detail. To better understand the following, remember that payments are transmitted in a file. A file can contain one or multiple messages. A message can contain one or multiple orders and an order can have one or multiple transactions.

The PSR 0 is a Technical Acknowledgment at protocol level (File exchange). *It is the protocol PSR.* Each protocol has own rules that must be followed by the parties exchanging the file. When the bank establishes a communication with a customer via the protocol EBICS for instance, the controls executed are not the same as for the SWIFTNet protocol. Even if there are many similarities, these two protocols have their specificities (Length of payload, types of messages, etc.). If the exchange does not comply with the protocol rules, the bank cannot accept the files and won't go further.

The PSR 1 is a Technical Acknowledgment at acquisition level (Messages). The exchange of the file using a specific protocol was successful. Now the bank will start looking into the content. If the file contains several messages, it is splitted and each message is controlled. For two messages transmitted in the same file, one may be accepted and the other one rejected. XML messages that are not well formed will be rejected but those that are well formed will be accepted. Depending on the services implemented by the bank, it may go deeper in the content (order or transaction level) during the acquisition and performs controls that are supposed to be executed in the downstream applications. But in general, PSR 1 is about messages acquisition.

The PSR 2 is a functional acknowledgment about the processing of the order and related transactions in the order management application. If there are multiple orders in a message, one PSR 2 will be transmitted for each order. The message has been acquired successfully. It is splitted in individual orders and sent to the payment order management application. The whole message can also be transmitted to the order management application which will then take care of splitting it. Now the functional controls are executed on each order. Typical checks done at this stage are the debtor account verifications, dates, duplicate checks, transactions verifications and so on. Does the account exist? Was the order transmitted on time? Is it a duplicate? Is that type of transactions allowed for the account (it is not a saving account)? Are all the transactions OK and routable? In case controls at order level are negative, the full order is rejected (or goes to pending status) and the information is conveyed to the customer in the PSR 2. In other cases, controls may fail only at transaction level causing them to be rejected immediately or to be put in pending status. The customer finds the detail status in the PSR 2 as well. He can then take the necessary actions to correct the order or transactions and resend them to the bank. A successful PSR 2 means that the message containing the order was acquired without problem and that all the controls on the order and transactions were OK. But it does not mean that everything is fine yet. Even if it is rare, you may still have some bad surprises. That is why the PSR 3 is needed.

The PSR 3 is a functional acknowledgment about the **exchange** of all transactions of a given order. These transactions are sent to beneficiary banks. The beneficiary bank can be the debtor itself (on-us transaction), another bank inside the same group (intragroup transaction) or a bank outside the bank group. Checking the correct reception of an on-us transaction is pretty easy. When the transactions are sent to creditor banks internally or externally, a confirmation (ACK) from the receiving bank indicates if it was accepted. Otherwise it is a NACK. The debtor bank gets positive or negative response from the creditor banks and aggregates them at the order level. Then it produces the PSR 3 to forward the results to the customer. A successful PSR 3 means that the message containing the order was acquired correctly, all the controls on the order and transactions were OK and all transactions were exchanged successfully with beneficiary banks.

The PSR 0 to 3 play a key role in the corporate customer-to-bank relationship. These reporting are consumed and processed automatically by application (s) on customer side. They are linked to previously sent files, messages or orders. Message elements like Payment Information Identification at order level and End To End Identification at transaction level are used for that purpose. Potential discrepancies and issues are displayed on application screens. Employees can see them and take the decision on the next course of actions rapidly. Accuracy of the content of the PSR 0 to 3 is therefore crucial.

Review Questions

Describe the three main components of the Payment processing value chain.

Payment acquisition and reporting

- Describe payment acquisition and payment reporting. What is the main difference between the two?
- Explain the concept of channel
- List the different channels that can be involved in payment acquisition and reporting
- Explain what manual channels are and give some examples
- Explain what clever channels are and give some examples
- Explain what smart channels are and give some examples
- What is a protocol? How are protocols used in payment acquisition and reporting?
- What services do acquisition and reporting agreements contain? Give a brief description of each service.

Payment order management

- Describe payment order management
- List and describe the functionalities needed for payment order management
- Illustrate the difference between IBAN validation and IBAN verification
- Name the dates used in Payment order management. Give a definition for each of them.
- What is the BIC / IBAN coherence check? Illustrate with examples
- What is the balance check? Why does it happen almost at the end of payment processing?
- List and describe the services available in order management processing agreements
- Explain what pending order management consists in
- Define routing and issuing and explain the differences

Payment Exchange

- Describe payment exchange and the main functionalities needed for it
- What is payment routing?
- List SWIFT and ACH directories needed for payment routing

- What is Bulking? And what is Debulking?

What are payment application architectures used for?
Draw the main types of architectures in payment
What are Payment Status Reports used for?
Name the Payment Status Reports and describe briefly what they contain.

Discussion Questions

Payment acquisition and reporting have been grouped in the first step of the payment processing value chain. However, the payment reporting can be seen as a separated step in that value chain. What do you think about that?

What from your point of view is the determining factor for a bank to choose the communication protocol(s) to implement?

Is there a best payment application architecture? Give your arguments.

Chapter 5 What is a SEPA Credit Transfer?

LEARNING OBJECTIVES

After reading this chapter, you will be able to answer the following questions:

1. What are the main features of a SEPA Credit Transfer?
2. What are really the IBAN and BIC used as account and bank identifier in SEPA?
3. What does it mean to have shared fees in SCT?
4. What is a non-urgent Transfer?
5. What is the SCT maximum execution time? When does it begin and end?
6. What are ultimate debtor and ultimate creditor?
7. Through which channels can a SCT be acquired or cleared and settled?

The SEPA Credit Transfer (SCT) is a payment instrument in euros used for the transfer of funds between two payment accounts held by banks located within the SEPA area[8]. In other words, both the sending and receiving accounts must be registered with banks (or bank branches) located in a SEPA country. The SEPA Credit Transfer must follow a common set of rules, practices and message formats defined at European level. The business and technical requirements of the SCT are defined by the European Payments Council (EPC) in a set of documents: the Rulebooks, the Implementation Guidelines and other publications. They all can be downloaded from the EPC website www.europeanpaymentscouncil.eu/ .

As payment professionals, we are interested in knowing what really makes the SCT different from other types of credit transfers. The above definition gives some hints but it is not enough. As we will see in the following paragraphs, the SCT is based on a set of business and functional rules that we must clearly understand. Before we get into detail, find below the summary of the features that set the SCT apart:

- IBAN and BIC are used as account and bank identifiers respectively. In the early days, both had to be provided by the originator. The beneficiary Bank BIC obligation was abolished on 1st Feb 2014 for domestic payments and on 1st Feb 2016 for cross border payments.
- The currency of the instructed amount is EUR. No other currency is allowed.
- The original amount is forwarded without any deduction, and charges are billed separately.
- The originator and the beneficiary share the fees. It is not allowed that only one party, either the originator or the beneficiary, bears the costs.
- The SCT is a non-urgent transfer. However, there is a guaranteed execution time of one business day. The beneficiary account is credited at the latest one business day after the execution the SCT order by the originator bank.
- The SCT can transport up to 140 characters of remittance information.
- Ultimate debtor and Ultimate creditor information can be included in an SCT
- The SCT does not depend on acquisition and clearing channels.

In the rest of the chapter, we will examine each key feature of the SCT listed above.

---

[8] The SEPA area covers the European Economic Area composed of the 28 Member States of the European Union, the 4 Member States of the European Free Trade Association (Iceland, Liechtenstein, Norway and Switzerland) and Monaco and San Marino. The List of SEPA countries is available in annex 1.

5.1 The SCT uses the IBAN as account identifier

The IBAN (International Bank Account Number) serves as the unique identifier for the bank account in SEPA payments. Debtor and Creditor accounts must be provided in IBAN formats.

IBAN is an acronym of **I**nternational **B**ank **A**ccount **N**umber. It was originally developed to facilitate payments within the European Union but the format is flexible enough to be applied globally. The IBAN format is standardized in the ISO 13616. The length of the IBAN is variable depending on the country, but it is fixed in a single country. As examples, the French IBAN contains exactly 27 characters while the German IBAN has a length of exactly 22 characters.

Like an international phone number, the IBAN is used to identify an account internationally. An IBAN is unique in the whole word. You cannot find two different accounts in the same country or in different countries with the same IBAN. It uniquely identifies a bank account regardless of where it is held. The IBAN is used to facilitate automated processing of cross-border payments and therefore to increase the speed and quality of processing.

Since the accounts structures are different between countries and geographical areas, it is not an easy task for businesses and governments to understand the differences between national and cross-border account structures. This leads to incomplete orders of transfers that cause delays in their processing. And the banks have to contact their customers several times to request them to complete the payment orders to foreign countries. The use of IBAN overcomes this major drawback.

The first version of ISO 13616, which specifies the IBAN, was published in 1997. And it has been reviewed 2 times since then, in 2003 and 2007. The establishment of SEPA has contributed to the adoption of this standard by European countries. But the number of countries using IBAN is still quite low. Around 80 when I write these lines. Many people think that the IBAN is already in use in all countries or can be used in International payments to any country. This is wrong. And we still have a long way to go. The list of countries that use the IBAN can be found in the IBAN registry of SWIFT. The number of countries using the IBAN will certainly increase in the coming years, as it yields many advantages.

The IBAN structure consists of maximum 34 characters and is composed of:

- 2 alphabetic characters for the ISO country code of the IBAN. As an example, a Belgian IBAN always starts with BE, the ISO code for Belgium.
- 2 numeric characters for IBAN check digit. This key is used for verifying the validity of an IBAN. The checking algorithm can be found rather quickly by searching on the Internet[9].
- The number of remaining characters varies, but cannot exceed 30 characters. This group of characters is called BBAN (Basic Bank Account Number). Depending on the country, we find alphabetic, numeric or alphanumeric characters in specific positions. In France for example, the BBAN is known as the bank account details (French RIB) and it has 23 alphanumeric characters.

So the BBAN is part of IBAN. In fact we can write the following equality IBAN = [ISO country code] [Check digits] [BBAN].

---

[9] This article of Wikipedia gives quite detail information about the check digit algorithm with a couple of examples https://en.wikipedia.org/wiki/International_Bank_Account_Number#Check_digits

The BBAN structure is different per country but always has the same length in a particular country. I take the example of the French BBAN. It is composed of exactly 23 characters:

- The first 5 characters are numeric and represent the code of the bank where the account is held. It is the bank code which is assigned by the central bank (Bank of France in this case).
- The following 5 characters are numeric also and represent the code of the bank branch. The central bank assigns bank branch code as well.
- Then follow 11 alphanumeric characters. This is the customer account number. The Bank can choose whatever account number it wants as long as it follows some rules defined for the banking community at national level. It is completely at its discretion. Banks usually give a structure to account numbers to identify and handle them easily.
- The last 2 characters are check digits for the BBAN. They are used to check the validity of the French BBAN. If you read the verification algorithm, you will see that these check digits are computed with the 21 characters presented previously. So the first 4 characters of the IBAN are not taken into account.

As already mentioned above, the structure of the BBAN is not the same in different countries. More specifically, the BBAN of many countries[10] does not have check digits. The German BBAN (18 characters) and the dutch BBAN (14 characters) for example do not contain verification digits.

We will conclude this paragraph on the specificities of some IBANs. The French IBAN is the best example to illustrate those specificities. The country code of France is FR. Knowing that, you expect that all French IBANs start with FR. Don't you? But this is not always the case. The country code of a French IBAN does not always begin with FR as one might think.

France has Overseas Departments and Territories (In French départements et territoires d'outre-mer, usually referred to as the DOM-TOM), which can be designated by a specific "country" code in addition to the country code FR. As a consequence, two country codes can be used in the IBAN of a DOM-TOM. In the following table, the list of the DOM-TOM is indicated with the ISO country codes allowed in their IBAN.

DOM-TOM	ISO country codes allowed in the IBAN
Guadeloupe	GP or FR
French Guiana	GF or FR
French Polynesia	PF or FR
Martinique	MQ or FR
Mayotte	YT or FR
Monaco	MC or FR
New Caledonia	NC or FR
Réunion	RE or FR
Saint Pierre and Miquelon	PM or FR
Southern and Antarctic Territories	TF or FR
Wallis and Futuna	WF or FR

Table 5-1 : French Overseas Departments and Territories

10 The structure of BBAN each country is presented on the site http://www.ecbs.org/iban.htm

Note: The IBAN check digits depend on the ISO country code that appear at the beginning of the IBAN. If you consider Guadeloupe for example, the IBAN check digits will be different if you have GP than if you have FR at the beginning of the IBAN.

Now when you see an IBAN starting with FR, concluding that the account is located in Metropolitan France can be wrong. You need to analyze other information like the BIC or the Bank account details to know where the account is really located. These specificities make validity checks of IBAN (length, country, check digits) a little more complex for France.

But the "good news" is that France is far from being an exception. We also find these specificities in IBAN for United Kingdom, Denmark, Norway, Italy ... in short for all countries which have DOM / TOM or similar territories.

Converting BBAN to IBAN

Since SEPA Payments require the IBAN, all national accounts formats (BBAN) are to be converted into IBAN. This is the responsibility of the bank holding the account. The Bank must communicate the IBAN corresponding to the BBAN to his customer. But you don't need to wait for your Bank to know which IBAN corresponds to a specific BBAN. You can do the conversion yourself if you know the conversion algorithm. Even easier, many Internet sites[11] provide BBAN to IBAN convertors.

The BBAN to IBAN conversion works pretty well for the countries where the BBAN is properly structured and contains accurate information about the banks.

But, as can be read on the website of the ECBS (European Committee for Banking Standards), the tools that automatically generate IBANs from domestic account numbers are not guaranteed to give correct IBANs because of the following reasons:

- The BBAN cannot always be automatically derived from the domestic account number.
- The BIC cannot always be derived from the BBAN.

The ECBS therefore concludes that the generation of the IBAN is primarily the responsibility of banks or payment service providers holding the account. They must work with the relevant national and international bodies to ensure that the IBAN generation algorithm is correct. The purpose of the standard is to make the conversion clear and easy for all countries and to automate it as far as possible.

5.2 The SCT uses the BIC as Bank identifier

The BIC is a standardized international identifier (ISO 9362) used in the financial exchanges. The understanding of what the BIC is fundamental in payments.

Firstly we have to learn the meaning of the acronym BIC. Many believe that BIC stands for Bank Identifier Code while others believe that it stands for Business Identifier Code. At the time I am writing these lines, a fight between "Bank Identifier Code" and "Business Identifier Code" on Google Fight[12] appoints the first expression as the outright winner. In view of these results, one would think logically that BIC means Bank Identifier Code. But it's not that simple as we will see.

---

[11] One of the famous website is http://www.ibancalculator.com/

[12] Go to http://www.googlefight.com to learn more about the google fight game.

To find the correct answer, we need to refer to the various versions of the standard ISO 9362 which defines the BIC. In the 1994 version, the BIC is defined as Bank Identifier Code (Bank Identifier Code). That was the vision of the ISO at that time. The BIC would be used exclusively to identify Banks or similar financial institutions. But the ever-growing needs of multinational corporations in financial exchanges had not been anticipated. To simplify and automate the processing financial exchanges with banks, identification of large companies by BICs became necessary.

In the revised version of the standard in 2009, the definition of BIC evolved to take into account large companies' needs. Since then BIC stands for Business Identifier Code. It is used for the identification of financial and non-financial institutions. When assigned to a non-financial institution, the code is also called **Business Entity Identifier or BEI**. It is SWIFT (Society for Worldwide Interbank Financial Telecommunication), that manages the registration of BIC and the BIC repository. This explains why the BIC code is also known as SWIFT-BIC, SWIFT code or SWIFT ID.

The BIC is used to uniquely identify an institution globally. From a BIC, you can derive the company or the bank that it names. Although the identification is important, the BIC is not primarily used for that. The main function of the BIC code is to route financial messages from the issuing institution to the receiving institution. Routing a payment is finding the way to make it reach the beneficiary bank. In SEPA, interbank routing algorithms rely almost exclusively on the BIC code.

The BIC is exactly 8 (BIC8) or exactly 11 (BIC11) characters long and is made up of:

- **Institution code** (4 alphabetic characters) identifies the organization (bank or corporate), or a group of affiliated organizations at a global scale.
- **Country code** (2 alphabetic characters) indicates the country or geographical location where the institution is located. It is codified in the format ISO 3166-1 alpha-2 country code.
- **Location code** (2 alphanumeric characters) specifies the city or region, in which the institution is located within a country or geographical location.
    - When the second character is "0", it is a test BIC as opposed to a BIC used on the live network.
    - When the second character is "1", it is a passive participant in the SWIFT network. Passive participants cannot be contacted directly over the network.
    - When the second character is "2", it indicates a reverse billing BIC, where the recipient pays for the message as opposed to the more usual mode whereby the sender pays for the message.
- **Branch code** (3 alphanumeric characters) is used to indicate a branch or agency of the institution within the same country or geographical location. It is not uncommon to see many bank branches located in the same city. The location code is not enough for their identification. All branches can be identified with branch codes. The branch code is mostly used by banks and less by corporations. Unlike the first 8 characters which are mandatory, the last 3 are optional. 'XXX' is used for primary office.

As examples, the BIC NDEAFIHHNCL specifies Nordea Bank (NDEA) in the country Finland (FI). The location is Helsinki (HH) and it is one specific branch in Helsinki, the one with the branch code NCL. The BIC NDEADEFFDKK specifies Nordea Bank (NDEA) as well, but this time in the country Germany (DE). The location is Frankfurt (FF).and it is one specific branch in Frankfurt, the one with the branch code DKK.

Now you may wonder yourself: How does a bank know to which branch to route the payments, even if there is no branch code in the BIC? The answer lies in the IBAN or more specifically the BBAN. In many countries, the BBAN contains the branch code which, in general, is codified differently as in the BIC. In France for example, the bank branch code composed of 5 numeric characters, is part of the BBAN and can be used to route the payment to the correct branch. In case no branch code is indicated in the BIC of a received transaction, the bank branch code will be extracted from BBAN and used for routing.

In SEPA, the BIC is mandatory in interbank messages within a country and between two countries. However, in the customer-to-bank space, the BIC has been optional for national transactions since 1st February, 2014. It became optional for cross border transactions on 1st February, 2016. Optional BIC means that a customer who sends an order, provides the IBAN, but may not indicate the BIC. The bank has to figure itself what BIC belongs to the IBAN and enrich the payments. We are talking about beneficiary BIC primarily since determining the debtor IBAN is straight forward.

5.3 The SCT allows only shared fees

The costs of a SEPA Credit Transfer are shared between the originator and the beneficiary. It means that the originator pays the service charge to his bank and the beneficiary pays third-party charges including his own bank if applicable.

Basically a transfer may be issued with three types of charges or fees:

- SHAR or SHA - shared fees: the services costs are shared between the originator and the beneficiary. The originator pays charges to his bank for the service, while the beneficiary pays other bank charges (the fees of its bank and any intermediary banks). The beneficiary receives the instructed amount deducted from the charges.
- DEBT or OUR – all charges for the debtor and no charge for the beneficiary: the debtor supports the costs charged by his bank, the beneficiary's bank and any intermediary banks. The beneficiary receives the total amount instructed.
- CRED or BEN - All charges paid by the beneficiary and no charge for the debtor: the beneficiary pays the costs charged by his bank, the originator's bank and any intermediary banks. The beneficiary receives the instructed amount minus the charges.

In SEPA payments, you find the charge information in the message element Charge Bearer <ChrgBr>. And only 'SLEV' is allowed as value. The definition of SLEV is the following: *charges are to be applied following the rules agreed in the service level and/or scheme.* Since in the SEPA scheme, only shared fees are allowed, it is another way to say that costs are shared (SLEV is equivalent to SHAR).

According to the SEPA rules, the charges must be billed separately. Banks should not report only the instructed amount from which charges have been already deducted. They must report the total instructed amount and the charges separately. Let us take an example to illustrate that. A customer goes to a branch and instructs the bank to initiate a credit transfer with 100 EUR. The bank charges 2 EUR for this service. The charges have to be reported separately to the customer.

The customer account statement should not have only one line as you see below,

Date	Description	Value Date	Debit	Credit
16/03/2018	Credit transfer order to beneficiary and charges	15/03/2018	-102	

but it should look like what you see in the following table.

Date	Description	Value Date	Debit	Credit
16/03/2018	Credit transfer order to beneficiary	15/03/2018	-100	
16/03/2018	Charges of Credit transfer order	15/03/2018	-2	

102 EUR is debited from the customer account in each case. However the first report does not comply with the regulation because the customer does not see clearly how much the service costs him.

A transfer with OUR or BEN charges is not a SEPA Credit Transfer. The banks may not handle that transfer in the same way as SCT. In general, the banks do not charge the beneficiary of a SCT even if the scheme allows to do so. Therefore only the debtor pays fees most of the time.

If a bank chooses to charge fees for sending SCT, then it must charge them uniformly to all European Economic Area (EEA) participants, banks or payment institutions located in the same country in another EEA country. As example, a bank cannot charge 3 EUR for sending an SCT to one EEA country and 4 EUR for sending an SCT to another EEA country. It would break the regulation. Now note the following interesting point. Switzerland is member of SEPA, but not member of the European Economic Area. Payment services may therefore be priced differently for Switzerland.

5.4 The SCT is a non-urgent transfer

An urgent transfer is a customer order to be executed by the payer's bank with a high priority. This means that the order is executed before lower priority orders the bank may have received before. The transfer must be exchanged as soon as possible. The beneficiary receives the funds on the day of execution and may in some cases be notified of the receipt of the transfer in less than one or two hours after the execution. This type of transfer is settled in *Real-time* gross settlement (RTGS) systems. In any case, the debit of the payer's account and the credit of beneficiary's account are performed on the same day. In SEPA area, urgent payments are settled in TARGET2, the RTGS system which is maintained and monitored by the European Central Bank.

In contrast to an urgent payment, the SCT does not have to be settled on the same day, but one business day later according to the rulebook. And the settlement happens in retail payment systems (so not in RTGS) like EBA STEP2. The debtor bank debits its customer, keeps the money and makes it available to the beneficiary bank only one business day later. This is called the float, the interval between the day the debtor account is debited and the day that amount is actually paid to the beneficiary bank.

The table below gives a summary of what we discussed above.

Urgent transfer	SEPA Credit Transfer
• Execution at D • **Settlement at D (No float)** • Settled *in real-time* in large-value payment systems (RTGS)	• Execution at D • Settlement at D+1 (Float of 1 Day) • Settled *not in real-time* in low-value / retail payment systems

Table 5-2 : Urgent Transfer vs SEPA Credit Transfer

However, and please keep this important point in mind: *It is not forbidden to settle a SEPA Credit Transfer on the same day.* The rulebook does not prohibit it. The tendency today is to settle credit transfers on the same day without requesting additional charges for the service. This is driven by the market that is pushing more and more toward real-time payments.

But many banks still want to stick to the rulebook and settle the SCT after one business day. In one of my previous project, I saw a payment product called Accelerated SEPA Credit Transfer. The difference from the normal SCT, you guessed it already, is that it is settled on the same day. Business people did not want to call it urgent SCT though because as said before, urgent payments are settled in RTGS systems, which is not the case for the SCT. This is an interesting subtlety to know. Isn't it?

5.5 The SCT execution time is one business day

The maximum execution time of the SCT is one business day for national and cross-border transactions. This period begins after checks and acceptance by the debtor bank to process the transfer and send the funds. If the client gives an incomplete or erroneous order, the transfer cannot be executed and the execution time cannot even start. The Bank informs the customer through a reject statement. In case the bank does not process a correct transfer received on time, it must bear the consequences.

A **business day** is an official working day of the week. Another common used term is **working day**. Typically, these are the days between and including Monday to Friday and do not include public holidays and weekends. In contrary, a **calendar day** is any day of the week, including weekends and holidays. That being said, there is another important difference to grasp between business day and calendar day in payments. A calendar day starts at 00:00 and ends at 24:00 whereas a business day goes from one day cut-off to the next day cut-off. A cut-off is a predetermined time after which a bank can no longer accept orders to process and deliver for settlement on that same day. The cut-off marks the end of one business day and the start of the next business day.

In the picture below, we have considered a business day whose cut-off is at 16:00.

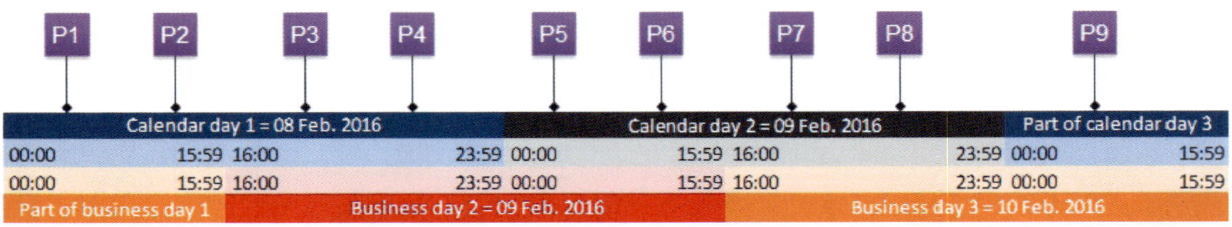

Figure 5.1 : Difference between business day and calendar day

Business day 1 starts at 16:00 and ends 15:59. The same applies for the other business days. The calendar day starts at 00:00 and ends at 23:59. The business date starts while the calendar day is still ongoing. The calendar day is 08 February 2016 and the business day of 09 February 2016 starts already after the cut-off. All orders that reach the bank after 16:00 belong to business day 2.During the calendar days, customers send orders to the bank through the different channels like Internet. The orders may reach the bank at any point in time, during the night, in the morning, late in the afternoon, any time. Let us consider a couple of orders to understand what it really means to execute a SCT in one business day.

The bank gets the orders P1 in the morning and P2 in the afternoon of the calendar day and before the cut-off of day 1. So they are executed on business day 1 and settled on business day 2. As a reminder, execution means debiting the customer account and sending the transactions of the order to beneficiaries directly or through a clearing system. Settlement happens when the money is moved from paying bank to payee bank in Target2. Settlement can happen anytime on business day 2. Most of the time it happens at the start of the business day. But a debtor bank may ask the CSM to settle a transaction at a specific time during the business day. The beneficiaries of the payments get the money on business day 2.

The orders P3 and P4 reach the bank during the calendar day 1 but after the cut-off. So the business day 2 has already started. They will be executed in business day 2 and therefore be settled in business day 3. The execution can happen right after the bank receives the money or later, but it should be performed on business day 2. A bank receives an order at 22:20 in the night. It can execute it right away or waits until 6:00 the next morning. That will still be the business day 2 for the CSM. So P3 and P4 are received on calendar day 1, but on business day 2 on which they are executed and sent to the CSM. The settlement happens on Business day 3. The accounts of beneficiaries are credited on the business day 3 also.

5.6 The SCT allows amounts exclusively in EUR

The amount of a SEPA Credit Transfer order must be in Euros. It is theoretically unlimited. In the implementation guidelines, there is a technical limit of 999 999 999, 99 €. So for amounts over one billion, two transfers must be carried out. But these cases are very seldom in the reality, so that the technical limit covers the vast majority of the cases.

The amount of the SCT cannot be in a currency different from EUR. But this does not apply to the accounts. The originator account or beneficiary account or both can be in another currency than EUR. In that case, banks will provide the forex conversion and charge fees to the customer. This foreign exchange transaction is separate from the SCT execution itself.

As already mentioned, banks are not allowed to make any deduction of the amount transferred. This is a regulatory requirement. The fees must be debited and reported separately.

If the amount of a transfer is in a currency other than the euro, then that transfer is not a SCT even if the payer and payee accounts are held in banks in the SEPA area. This is called international transfer. The processing of USD transfers from one account held in Finland to an account held in another SEPA country is different from the SCT processing in many regards. I don't go into details since it is not the topic of this book.

5.7 The SCT can carry up to 140 characters unstructured or structured Remittance Information

Here is the definition of the remittance information found in the ISO 20022 Payments - Maintenance 2009 / Message Definition Report document: "Information supplied to enable the matching of an entry with the items that the transfer is intended to settle, such as commercial invoices in an accounts' receivable system."

Before SEPA, it was not possible to transmit as many characters in the remittance information in almost all SEPA countries. In France for example, only 31 characters were allowed. With 140 characters, the debtor can provide all the information required by the beneficiary to automatically match the transfer with an invoice and even more. So the remittance information plays a key role for Straight-through Processing (STP). This means that the matching between a payment and an invoice is performed automatically in accounting applications and there is no human intervention.

The actors who use the remittance information are obviously the corporations that process their transactions in accounts receivable systems. The remittance information is transported mostly in payments between corporations or between individuals and corporations. When the beneficiary is a company or a government agency, it tells the debtor which information to provide as remittance data so that the matching can happen automatically. The remittance information is less used in payments between individuals. But in any case, the Beneficiary Bank must deliver the received remittance data in full and without alteration to the Beneficiary.

The remittance information can carry unstructured or structured information. Unstructured Information means that it can contain up to 140 alphanumeric characters or special characters like / - ? : ( ) . , ' + which are allowed in the standard SEPA. In the SCT rulebook, it is said that the unstructured remittance information may carry structured remittance information, as agreed between the Originator and the Beneficiary. In general, this is done by providing several information items separated by slashes (/). Special characters like Less-than sign (<) and Greater-than sign (>) used in XML tags are not allowed. Therefore they cannot be carried in the unstructured remittance.

According to SCT rulebook, the structured remittance information can be allowed, under the conditions that the tags and the data within the 'Structured' element do not exceed 140 characters in length. All message elements specified under the <Strd> tag in the ISO 20022 cannot be used in SEPA. Otherwise the 140 characters would not be sufficient. The AOS 2 was created among other reasons because these banking communities wanted to carry more than 140 characters and exchange more information than allowed in the standard SEPA.

The Creditor Reference Information element under the <Strd> tag contains two important sub elements: the type and the reference.

- Under the type, only the sub element code can be specified and it must have the value 'SCOR'. SCOR stands for **S**tructured **CO**mmunication **R**eference. It indicates a structured communication reference provided by the creditor to identify the referred transaction.

- For the reference, the EPC recommends that beneficiaries adopt the ISO Standard 11649 to compute the creditor reference. The Creditor Reference is an alphanumeric string of maximum 25 characters, with the letters "RF" at the beginning. After the letters are two check digits, to validate that the reference entered is correct. The remaining part of the Creditor Reference (up to 21 alphanumeric characters) is the Reference itself.

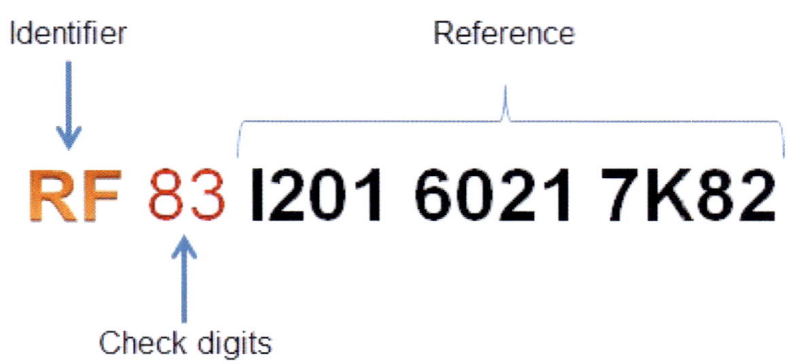

The reference displayed above matches the requirements of the standard ISO 11649. It starts with the Identifier RF. Then follow the check digits "83" in this case. The check digits algorithm is the same as the algorithm used for calculating the check digits for the IBAN[13]. The debtor bank is not obliged to check the correctness of the Creditor Reference provided in the Originator's order. The EPC recommends doing it but it is an obligation. Furthermore, the use of the ISO 11649 method to compute the creditor reference is not mandatory as well. You can have references like 7395M2L47 or T7826H89289298 as content of the <Ref> tag. Unless agreed between the originator and the debtor that only ISO 11649 compatible references are allowed, the transaction should not be rejected.

Now you know better what the remittance information is and what it is used for. Important to keep in mind is that it can contribute to **S**traight **T**rough **P**rocessing. And this brings many benefits in terms of cost reduction and operational efficiency.

In addition to the remittance data, the end-to-end identification is also used to improve the STP rate in processing. Many banks display both fields on their transactional website for the ordering customers to fill them in. And many people wonder themselves what they are. Let us finish this paragraph with a focus on the differences between the remittance information and the End-To-End Identification. The common point is that they are used for automated end to end processing. But as you see in the table below they are some differences.

Remittance Information	End-To-End Identification
Up to 140 characters length	Up to 35 characters length
Generated by the Creditor and communicated to the debtor to put in his payment order. The debtor may also provide it to help the creditor understand to what the transaction relates.	Generated by the Originator to uniquely identify a payment transaction
If no remittance is given, it remains EMPTY.	If no reference is given, 'NOTPROVIDED' must be used.
Used to match payments with customer invoices.	Used to reconcile R-transactions with original transactions. The debtor can see transactions for which an exception was raised and take the necessary actions.

Table 5-3 : Remittance information and End-to-end Identification characteristics

5.8 The SCT can transport ultimate debtor and ultimate creditor Information

Another interesting characteristic of the SEPA Credit Transfer is the ability to transport ultimate debtor and ultimate creditor. In SEPA messages, ultimate debtor and creditor information can be found respectively in the message elements <UltmtDbtr> and <UltmtCdtr>. These message elements are all based on the message element(s) ***PartyIdentification32*** as well as the debtor and creditor information. This puts the light on one characteristic of the ISO 20022: Reusability. The components and elements are reused across messages of the standard. This enables to process and maintain them easily. [14]

---

[13] For those who are interested in the details of the algorithm, please refer to the Wikipedia article on the subject.

[14] If you want to depend this subject, please read the chapter one of the book ISO 20022 for Dummies.

Debtor, Creditor, Ultimate debtor and Ultimate creditor are all either a person or an organization. Therefore the standard uses the same set of elements for their identification. If a programmer writes code to parse and map debtor information to an internal data structure for example, the same code will work to parse Creditor, Ultimate debtor and Ultimate creditor. So he can develop much faster thanks to reusability.

You may still wonder yourself what ultimate debtor and ultimate creditor really are. I will take two examples to illustrate those concepts. The first one is about a corporate group with parent and subsidiary corporations where the supplier payment is centralized in the parent corporation. Therefore payment orders are issued by the parent corporation. To avoid any confusion on the beneficiary side, the parent corporation can indicate the subsidiary as ultimate debtor. When the beneficiary receives the money, he knows that it ultimately comes from the subsidiary. The parent corporation just plays a role of an intermediary in the transaction.
The second example is about sending money to a teenager through one his parent, because the teenager does not have a bank account yet. In this case, the teenager can be clearly designated as Ultimate creditor in the transactions. His parent will receive the money on his behalf.

The picture below shows that debtor and creditor plays the roles of intermediaries between their banks and the Ultimate debtor and Ultimate creditor.

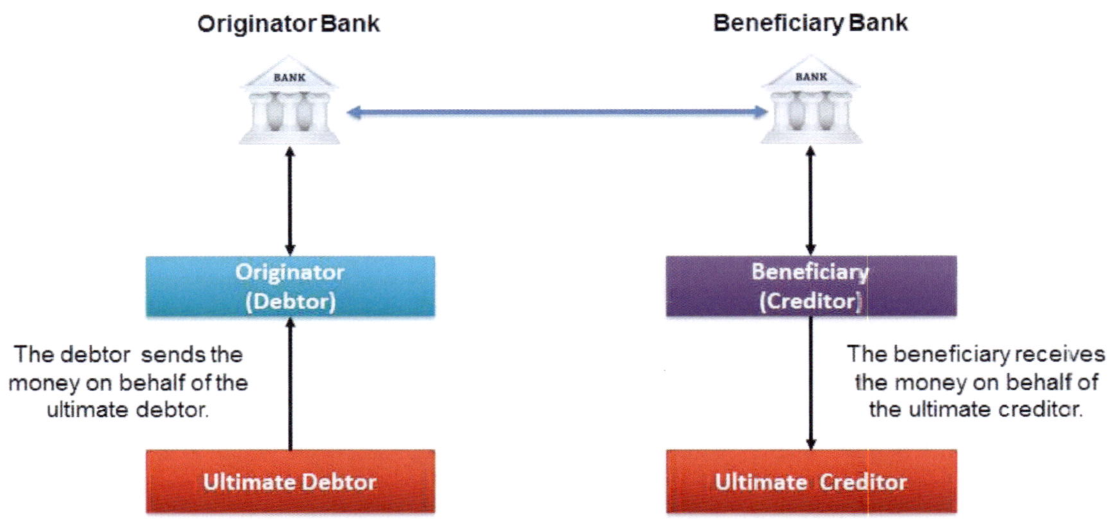

Figure 5.2 : Ultimate debtor and ultimate creditor

To conclude this paragraph, I want to draw your attention to two remarks:

1. In the pain.001.001.03 message, the message element <UltmtDbtr> can be indicated either at Payment Information level (Index 2.23) or at Credit Transfer Transaction Information level (Index 2.70).
2. The message element <UltmtCdtr> is available only at Credit Transfer Transaction Information level (Index 2.81).

The reasons are quite straight forward when you have the knowledge of course. ☺ If the message element <UltmtDbtr> is used at Payment Information level, it means that all transactions in the order have a common ultimate debtor. If it is used at Credit Transfer Transaction Information level, it means that the ultimate debtor is provided for that single transaction.

5.9 The SCT is independent of acquisition and clearing channels

During my years in the payment business, I have seen that many people really struggle with this topic. When you begin in payments, it is not straight forward to understand that the SCT is independent of acquisition and clearing channels. After reading this paragraph, things will be clear for you.

As we saw in the previous chapter (4.1), a bank receives payment orders through a lot of channels including SWIFTNet. Many people believe a SWIFT transfer is anything but a SEPA Credit transfer. It is probably because SWIFT is strongly associated with international transfers. Well, this is not correct. A SWIFT transfer can be a SEPA Credit transfer. If you have a transfer where debtor and beneficiary accounts are located in SEPA, it is not urgent and charges are shared, then it is a SEPA Credit Transfer and has to be executed as such. The SEPA Credit Transfer is independent of the acquisition channel. In the SEPA rulebooks, there is no mention about sending SCT to the Bank through specific channels. So a bank does not take the channel into account when determining the type of transfer. What matters is the content of the received orders. The rulebooks recommend the use of ISO 20022 messages in XML format to transport SEPA orders between customers and banks. It is a recommendation, not an obligation. Banks can receive SEPA payments in SWIFT MT / MX format, EDIFACT format or in other proprietary formats.

The same logic applies for the clearing. A SEPA Credit transfer can be cleared through local clearing systems, the PE-ACH STEP2 and the European RTGS Target 2. So do not think that SCT cannot be cleared and settled on Target 2. A bank can receive a payment order in pain.001 format, process and debulk it, and then send transactions in pacs.008 or SWIFT MT103 / MX pacs.008 formats to the clearing systems. A bank can also receive a payment order in MT format, process and debulk it, and then send transactions in pacs.008 or SWIFT MT103 / MX pacs.008 formats to the clearing systems. A transfer is not an international transfer just because it is exchanged through SWIFT.

The following figure illustrates what is said above. The SEPA Credit Transfer comes from various channels with various formats and goes to various clearing systems with different formats as well. Please let me insist again on this: it is the SEPA Credit Transfer not another type of transfer.

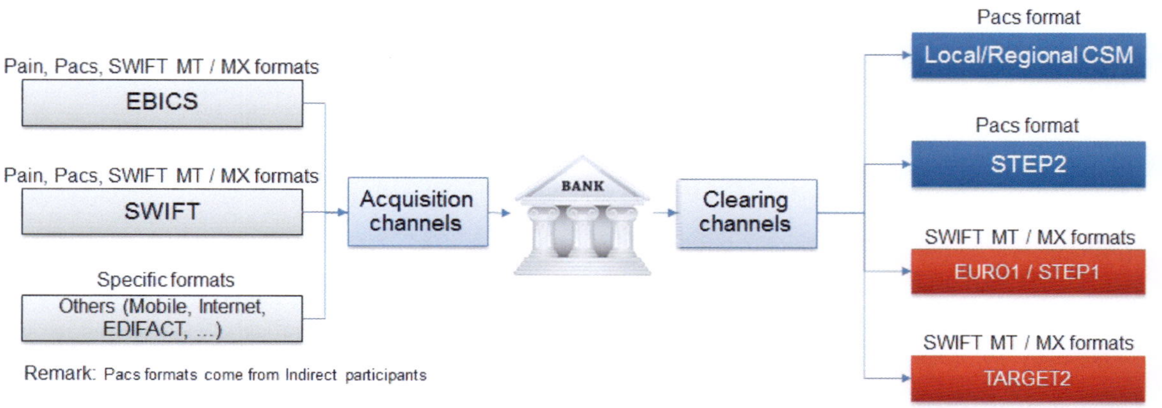

Figure 5.3: Different acquisition and clearing channels of the SCT

It is now clear. The SEPA Credit Transfer is independent of acquisition and clearing channels. SEPA Credit Transfers can be acquired in pain, pacs, MT, MX or specific formats and can be cleared in pacs, SWIFT MT and MX formats.

Review Questions

1. List the main features of the SEPA Credit Transfer
2. The IBAN
   - Is the IBAN used in all countries?
   - Explain the difference between IBAN and BBAN
   - What are IBAN check digits used for?
   - What are specificities of French and English IBAN?
3. The BIC
   - What is the original meaning of the acronym BIC? What does it stand for today?
   - How many characters can a BIC contain? Break down the BIC and explain the different parts
   - What is a test BIC?
4. Explain what a non-urgent transfer is
5. Illustrate the SCT maximum execution time of one business day with a drawing
6. The SCT allows only shared fees. What does it mean? Which other fee option exist?
7. Define and explain what ultimate debtor and ultimate creditor of SCT are
8. acquisition and clearing channels

Discussion Questions

1. Why have SEPA countries adopted the IBAN and BIC standards? Were there other possibilities?
2. Banks in some SEPA countries are settling the SCT on the same day and after one business day. Give some reasons to explain why. Will the settlement on the same day become the market standard everywhere in SEPA?

Chapter 6 Booking and Account balance management

LEARNING OBJECTIVES

After reading this chapter, you will be able to answer the following questions:

1. What is the double entry bookkeeping principle?
2. What are the booking and non-booking transactions in the SCT scheme?
3. What are the accounting schemes of the booking transactions?
4. What are Nostro, Vostro and Loro accounts? Can Vostro and Loro be used interchangeably?
5. What are shadow and mirror accounts?
6. How does account reconciliation work?
7. What is account balance management?
8. What are merged accounts?

Booking constitutes a critical feature in payment processing. At the end of the day, making a payment is moving customer money from one account to another. Banks are responsible for holding customer accounts. They have to make sure that accounts are debited and credited correctly when a customer sends or receives funds.

Booking issues are among the worst that a bank can experience particularly if there is a customer impact. Many people think booking is a very complex subject. My view is that it is not correct to see the things that way. We should not underestimate the subject of course. Booking is grounded on principles. If you understand those principles, things will become much easier for you. And no matter, what the situation, you will know where to start and the right questions to ask.

This chapter starts with the fundamental double entry bookkeeping principle. Then booking transactions and non-booking transactions for the SCT are presented before going into the details on how bookings are performed for the different booking transactions. After that, a focus is made first on Nostro and Vostro accounts and secondly on shadow and mirror accounts. The chapter ends with account balance management.

After reading this chapter, Booking will not be a mystery for you anymore. I strongly recommend you to read this chapter many times until you are able to explain its content to your colleague or someone else.

6.1 The double entry bookkeeping principle

One fundamental concept in booking is the double entry which says that every financial transaction has equal and opposite effects in at least two different accounts. *For payment processing, the principle states that for every accounting event there are two effects – one debit effect and one credit effect.* Accounting events are generated by payment engines during the processing of payment transactions. An accounting event contains information to send to the accounting systems to debit and credit accounts. In general, the events created by the payment engines are not readable by the accounting systems. They have to be transformed in the format expected by accounting systems before delivery.

An accounting event creates two or more entries on different accounts. *The total amount of debit entries must be equal to the total amount of credit entries.* That is the principle of double entry expressed in other words. One also says that the booking is balanced. If it is not clear for you what an accounting event is, don't bother about it now. We will extensively come back to that later. Let us illustrate the double entry principle with a couple of examples.

Example 1: An accounting event which generates two booking entries on two different accounts as you can see on the following table.

Debit		Credit
ACNT1 - Amount		ACNT2 + Amount
Total Debit (amount)	=	Total Credit (amount)

The debit entry is done on one account (ACNT 1) and the credit entry is done on another account (ACNT 2). The amount debited is equal to the amount credited. This is by far the most common case. The same amount is debited from one account and credited to another account.

Example 2: An accounting event which generates four booking entries on four different accounts as you can see below.

Debit		Credit
ACNT1 - Amount 1		ACNT2 + Amount 2
		ACNT3 + Amount 3
		ACNT4 + Amount 4
Total Debit (amount)	=	Total Credit (amount)

One debit entry is done on one account (ACNT 1) and three credit entries are done on three different accounts (ACNT 2, ACNT 3 and ACNT 4). The total amount of debits is equal the total amount of credits (Amount 1 = Amount 2 + Amount 3 + Amount 4), so that it complies with the double entry principle.

Example 3: An accounting event which generates four booking entries on four different accounts as you can see below.

Debit		Credit
ACNT1 - Amount 1		ACNT3 + Amount 3
ACNT2 - Amount 2		ACNT4 + Amount 4
Total Debit (amount)	=	Total Credit (amount)

Two debit entries are done on two accounts (ACNT 1 and ACNT 2) and two credit entries are done on two other accounts (ACNT 3 and ACNT 4). The total amount of debits is equal the total amount of credits (Amount 1 + Amount 2 = Amount 3 + Amount 4), so that it complies with the double entry principle.

As you can now see, there are multiple possibilities. An accounting event can debit one or more accounts and credit one or more accounts. But at the end of the day, the total amount of debits must equal the total amount of credits, so that the accounting event is balanced.

In the examples above, we see that each entry is performed an account. For the booking, the bank uses many kinds of accounts that can be grouped in two main categories: customer accounts and internal accounts. Customer accounts and internal accounts themselves can be of several types. Typical customer accounts are current accounts, loan accounts, saving accounts and so on. Typical internal bank accounts are application accounts, pending accounts, Profit/Loss accounts, shadow accounts and so on. We will see below in which cases the different types of accounts are used. Before that, we have to understand the differences between booking and non-booking transactions.

6.2 Booking transactions and non-booking transactions

Booking transactions and non-booking transactions are used in the SCT scheme. A booking transaction is a transaction that will result in moving funds from one bank to another bank. Accounting events must be generated by the payment engine during the processing of booking transactions and corresponding orders. Accounting events must then be sent to booking systems where they are transformed and used to make debit and credit entries on accounts.

Booking and non-booking transactions are visible in the figure below.

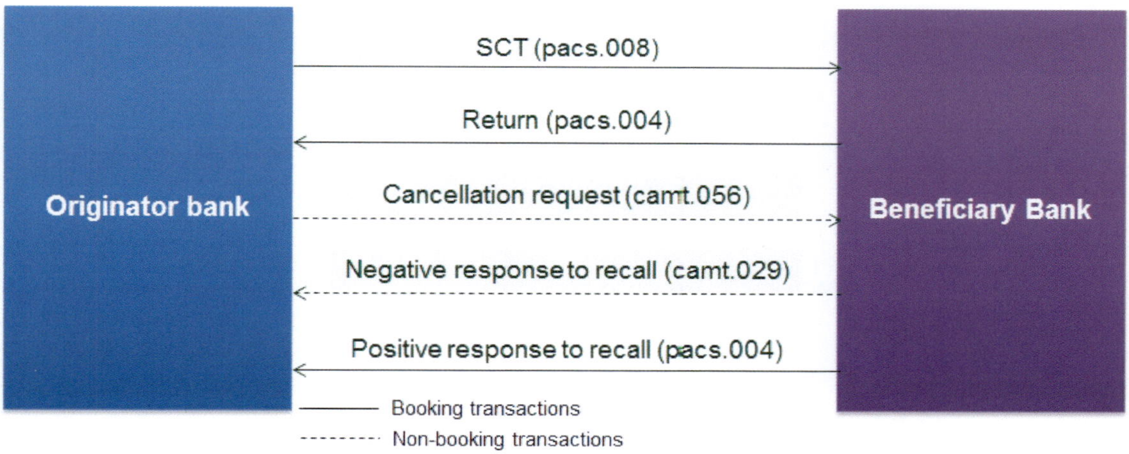

Figure 6.1: Booking and non-booking transactions of the SCT Scheme

Credit transfer (pacs.008), Return and positive response to cancellation request (pacs.004) are booking transactions. When CSM process them correctly, funds are moved between banks.

Cancellation request (camt.056) and negative response to cancellation request (camt.029) are non-booking transactions. Their successful processing by CSM does not result in transfer of funds between banks. But as we will see later, some accounting event can still be generated when these transactions are processed in the bank, but never in the CSM.

So Clearing systems move funds after the successful processing of booking transactions. For the pacs.008.001.02 for example, the result of the processing will be to debit funds from the debtor bank account and credit funds to the creditor bank account at settlement date. Debtor bank on its side takes the money from the ordering customer account and creditor bank has to credit its beneficiary customer account. Do you see the booking chain coming up? Funds are moved from the beginning (debtor bank customer) to the end of the chain (creditor bank customer) through the clearing system. In the subsequent paragraphs, we will analyze the booking of the different messages inside the bank. Creditor bank will be considered first and then we will look at the debtor bank case. This order makes things easier to understand.

6.3 Creditor bank credit transfer (pacs.008.001.02) booking

The creditor bank receives the credit transfer and credits the beneficiary account. The credit transfer may arrive through the CSM or from another bank of the group. But it can also be from a debtor of the same bank in case of intra bank transfers. Below we assume that the credit transfer comes from a CSM. In that case, it first reaches the exchange platform (PE Application) and then it is forwarded to the Payment Processing Engine (PP Application) of the creditor bank. Accounting events must be generated during the processing of the credit transfer since the bank is receiving funds. In the following figure, you have an illustration of accounting events generated during the processing.

When the exchange platform receives and processes the credit transfer, it generates an accounting event (ACC EVT 1) that will result in:

- Debiting the CSM shadow account and
- Crediting the PE Application Account

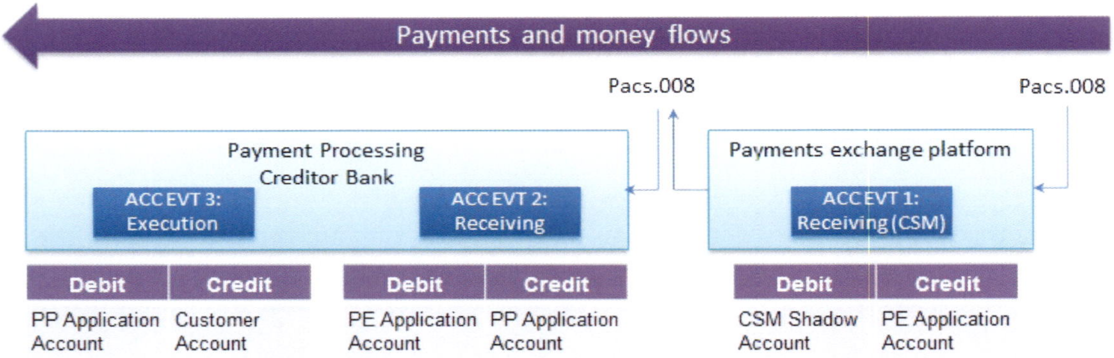

Figure 6.2: Accounting events for the correct reception of a credit transfer from a CSM

The first event (ACC EVT1 - payment receiving from CSM) materializes the fact that the bank has received money from the CSM. That is why the bank takes money from the CSM account and put money on the application account. Money is now in the Payments Exchange Module or Application (PE Application). But we know that it cannot stay there. It is not the final destination. Money has to move further. This happens when the exchange platform sends the transfer to the Payment Processing Application (PP Application). After the successful receipt of the transfer, the Payment Processing Application takes money from the Payment Exchange Platform and puts it on its own account (ACC EVT2 - payment receiving from PE Application). Money is now in the Payments Processing Application. But it cannot stay there either. The money is still not on the beneficiary account.

As next step, the Payment Processing Application checks the beneficiary account for its existence and status (Open/Closed/Blocked/etc.) before crediting the money on it. If everything goes well, which means that the account is open and there is no restriction, then the customer account is credited (ACC EVT3 - payment execution to credit beneficiary). Funds must be debited from the PP Application account which has been credited before. And that is the end. Money is now on the beneficiary account, the final destination. ☺. Ins't it easy?

Let us take a close look at the two applications accounts (Payments Processing Application and Payments Exchange Application) mentioned above. Have you noticed something about them? Money comes and goes. It never stays on these accounts. The two accounts are credited and debited every time. So at the end of the day, the total amount credited should equal the total amount debited. They are just used to verify that the funds are moved correctly. Their balances should be zero if all payments are processed and moved without issue.

Let us go back to the execution of the credit transfer (ACC EVT3), when money is moved to the beneficiary account. If something goes wrong during the checks (Account does not exist or is closed for instance), the funds cannot be credited on the account. Nevertheless the bank cannot keep them for itself. That would be legally and ethically not correct. But the money is there, it has been received. What to do with it? That is where pending accounts come into play. Bank will put the money on a pending account. And the result of accounting event 3 will look like in the figure below.

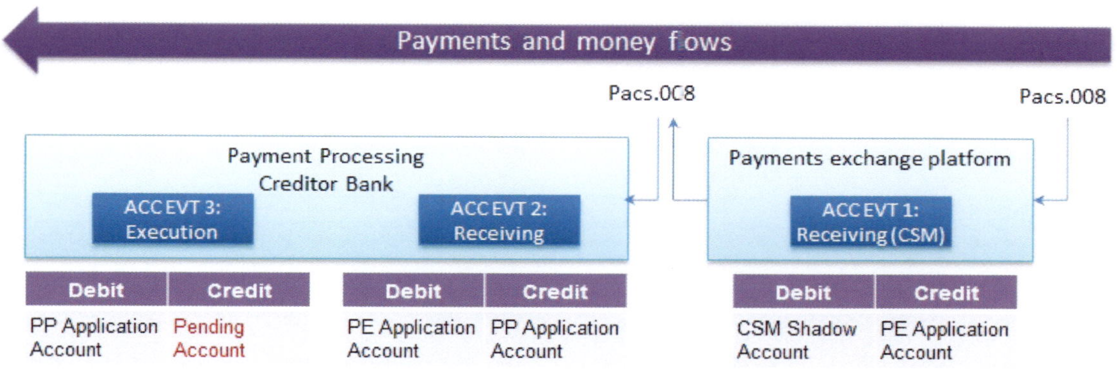

Figure 6.3: Accounting events at the reception of a credit transfer for which beneficiary account cannot be credited

If a credit transfer is stuck in an intermediary status in the Payment processing application, because of any reason (a technical problem for example), funds may also be credited on a pending account. And after the successful completion of the processing, funds will be moved from the pending account.

Pending accounts are used to keep the money for a "short" period of time until the processing carries on or until a decision is taken on what to do with it. Money is not supposed to remain on those accounts. It just comes and goes. In case the beneficiary account does not exist and the customer is not known at all by the bank, there is no other choice than to return the money. This brings us to the next paragraph.

6.4 Creditor bank Return (pacs.004.001.02) booking

The creditor bank receives the funds and cannot credit the beneficiary account for multiple reasons (Reasons for an interbank return are available in the SCT INTER-BANK IMPLEMENTATION GUIDELINES). The bank must return the funds to the debtor.
The bank put the funds on a pending account when the credit transfer was received. Logically funds have to be debited from that account for the return. That is the result of the first accounting event (ACC EVT 1) below after the generation of the credit transfer Return. Funds are debited from the pending account and credited to the Payment Processing Application Account.

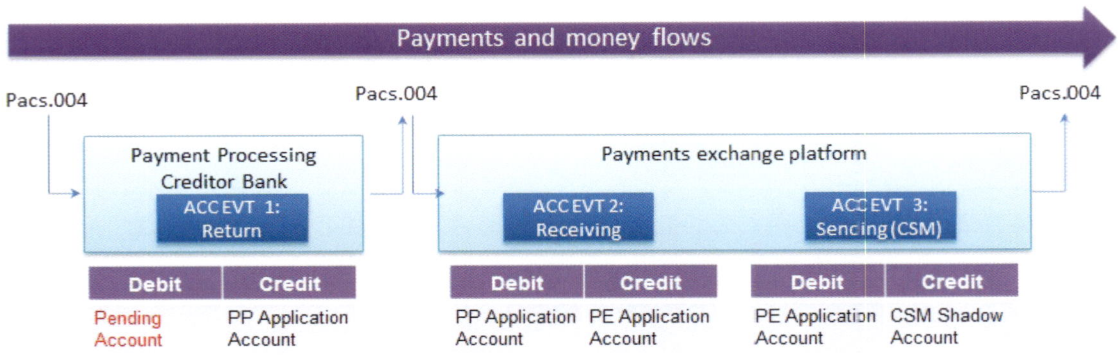

Figure 6.4: Accounting events for the booking of the return

Next step is to send the payment Return to the exchange platform. After receiving the return, the platform takes funds from the Payment Processing Engine and puts them on its own account (ACC EVT 2). Last logical step is to send the return to the Clearing System. As a consequence, the accounting event 3 is generated. The outcome is the debit of the Payment Exchange Application account and the credit of the CSM shadow account. The CSM shadow account must be credited since the money is "given" to the CSM. The CSM shadow account is usually called CSM account for simplification purpose. In paragraph 6.10, we will see what shadow accounts are.

When credit transfer was received from the CSM, funds were debited from the CSM account. Now that the payment is returned, funds must be given back to the CSM. That is why the CSM account is now credited. It makes sense. Doesn't it?
The pacs.004 can also be sent for a positive request to a cancellation request. The booking is different from the normal return as we will see in the next paragraph.

6.5 Creditor bank pacs.004.001.02 (Positive response of a camt.056) booking

The positive response to a cancellation request is used to return funds that were already credited on the beneficiary account. The SCT Scheme allows the creditor bank not to return the funds totally. The bank can charge that operation and return the money only partially. Please note that nothing is charged to the creditor, the beneficiary of the received SCT that is being returned. Charges are taken from the amount to be returned. It will become clear when we will look at the accounting events.
Before that, let us briefly recall the message elements used in the positive response to a cancellation request.

Mult	Pacs.004.001.02 message elements	Definitions / Remarks
[1..1]	++ Returned Interbank Settlement Amount	For the normal return, this amount is equal to the Original Interbank Settlement Amount. For the return as positive answer to a Recall (ie, Reason Code is 'FOCR'), **this amount is equal to the 'Original Interbank Settlement Amount' less the 'Amount' under 'Charges Information'**.

Mult	Pacs.004.001.02 message elements	Definitions / Remarks
[0..1]	++ Returned Instructed Amount	Take the same value as OrgnlIntrBkSttlmAmt. In SEPA, it is allowed only in the case of return as positive answer to a Recall (ie, Reason Code is 'FOCR')
[0..n]	++ Charges Information	Allowed in SEPA only in case of a return as positive answer to a Recall (ie, Reason Code is 'FOCR'). Only one occurrence is allowed.
	+++ Amount	Charges or Fee for the positive answer to the Recall.

Table 6-1 : Amounts in the return as positive response for a cancellation request

The amount returned is less than the original SCT amount if fees are charged. The Creditor Bank keeps the fees for itself. It is an income. So fees are credited to a Profit & Loss Account. The figure below shows generated accounting events for the positive response to a cancellation request.

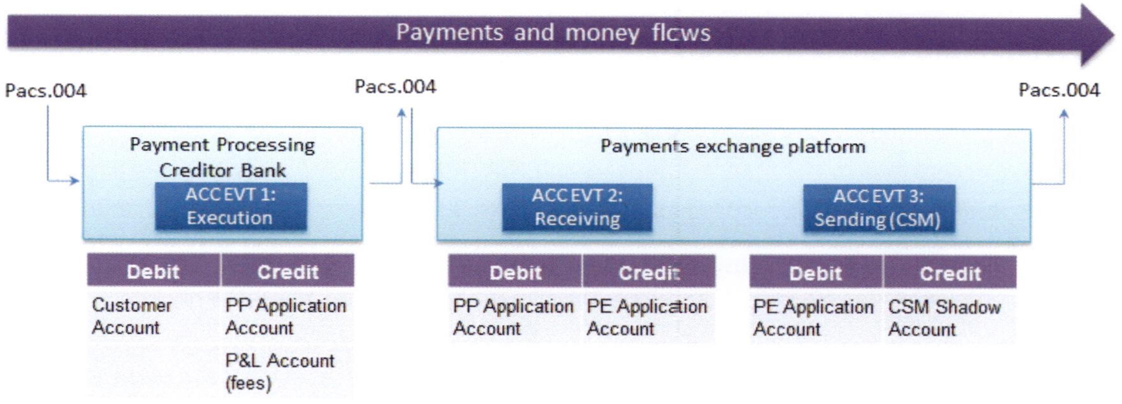

Figure 6.5: Accounting events for the booking of a pacs.004 FOCR

The accounting event 1 is generated after confirmation that funds are available on the customer account and thus can be returned. If funds are not sufficient on the beneficiary account, the bank will send a negative response to the cancellation request. We assume that money is there. The accounting event 1 will have the following results:

- Debit of the beneficiary account from the original amount of the credit transfer
- Credit of the Payment Processing application account with the returned amount (original amount of the credit transfer minus the charged fees)
- Credit of the Profit & Loss Account of the Bank with the charged fees

The total amount debited equals the total amount credited. The accounting event is balanced.

The two next steps are the same as for the normal payment return. The transaction is sent to the payment exchange platform which forwards it to the CSM. The corresponding accounting events are generated when the exchange platform receives and forwards the pacs.004 FOCR.

Now let us consider the transactions and orders bookings for the debtor bank.

6.6 Debtor bank credit transfer (pain.001 and pacs.008) booking

Now that we are used to the figures with payments and money flows, I will start this paragraph with the outline for credit transfer booking. Let us consider the interesting case of a corporate customer sending payment orders to the debtor bank in pain.001 message format. The pain.001 format is kept while the message goes through the Acquisition platform. The payment processing application receives the pain.001 format and converts it to pacs.008 format before sending it to the exchange platform.

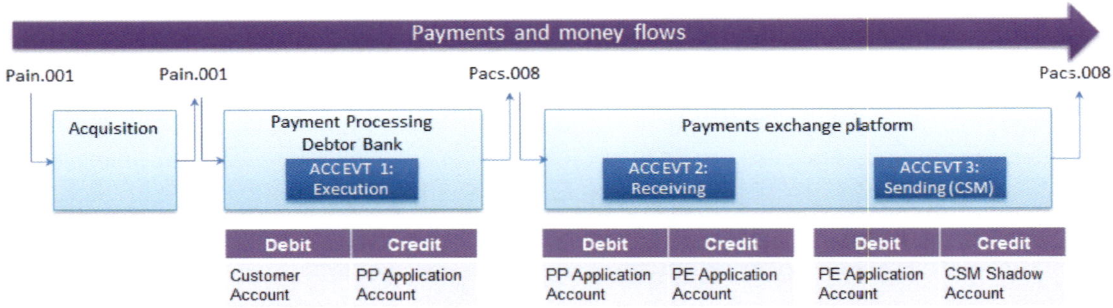

Figure 6.6: Booking of credit transfers orders and transactions by the Debtor Bank

6.6.1 Payment order with one instruction and one transaction

To keep things simple, let us first look at the case where the order received contains only one instruction which itself contains one transaction for a beneficiary outside the bank group. To be more concrete, we will take an example of an order with one instruction and one transaction of 50 k€.

In the figure, we see on the left side that no booking event is generated in the acquisition platform. The reason is simple. The order has not been executed yet. So the debtor account cannot be debited. If you send an order to your bank and its rejects it, nothing will happen on your account. The bank will just inform you that your order has been rejected. Same thing happens here.

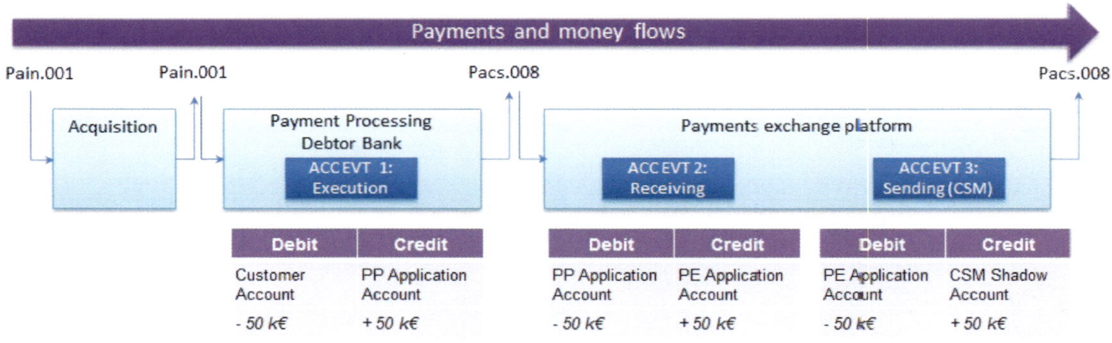

Figure 6.7: Accounting events for the booking of a single transaction order of 50 k€

Thus the booking starts only when the order is accepted and executed – ACC EVT 1 for execution of payment order - it means when money has been reserved for the transfer (Remark: Please note that an executed order remains in the bank for some time before it is transmitted to the CSM.) Right after execution, the bank takes the money from the debtor account. The beneficiary account (held by an outside the Bank) cannot be credited right after debiting the debtor. So the funds have to be put on an internal account. In general, the bank will use an internal account which is linked to the processing application as we saw in the

Creditor bank part. The Debtor Bank processing application has its own internal account. If there are many applications in a bank group fulfilling that role, each of them will generally have its own account to make a logical separation.

When the internal account of the processing application is credited, it now "owns" the money. But it is not the final destination and funds have to move again. And this happens when the payment is sent from the processing application to the exchange platform. The money is then moved from the processing application to the exchange platform. An accounting event (ACC EVT 2 – payment receiving by the PE application) is generated to debit the internal account of the processing application and credit the internal account of the exchange platform.

The exchange platform account has been credited after receiving the transaction from the processing application. The funds cannot stay there either. It is not the final destination. So they must be forwarded again. And this happens when the transaction is sent to the clearing system. Exchange platform internal account is then debited and clearing system shadow account is credited. The money is now in the clearing system and the bank has fulfilled his mission. It is now up to the clearing system to move that money to the beneficiary bank.

Do you see how money flows? It is debited from the debtor account and moved up to the CSM account. The application accounts are just transit accounts. Money comes and goes and is supposed to stay there. So if money stays there, it means that something has gone wrong.

We do know that the CSM is not the final destination of the funds. The funds are intended for the beneficiary. To close the loop and see how the money gets to the beneficiary account, please refer to the paragraph 6.3 above. Now we can easily see what happens inside the CSM. The CSM does two things to process this payment:

1. Debit of the debtor's bank shadow account and credit of CSM application account (when the transaction is received)
2. Debit of the CSM account and credit of beneficiary's bank shadow account (when the transaction is forwarded)

This is done to compute interim positions and better assess the risk. Do not forget that funds really move between banks after clearing and settlement.

6.6.2 Payment order with one order and many transactions

We now consider that the debtor bank has received a pain.001 message with one order which contains 10 transactions with the following characteristics:

- 2 intra bank transactions: Debtor and beneficiary are customers of the same bank. The transactions will not be sent to the exchange platform. They will remain in the Payment Processing Application.
- 3 intra group transactions: Debtor bank and beneficiary bank belong to the same Group and are connected through the exchange platform. Therefore those transactions won't be sent to the CSM.
- 5 CSM transactions: Debtor Bank and beneficiary bank does not belong to the same Group. Thus these transactions must be sent to the CSM.

Trx 1	Debtor Bank (Bank 1)	Creditor Bank (same Bank 1)	10 k€
Trx 2	Debtor Bank (Bank 1)	Creditor Bank (same Bank 1)	10 k€
Trx 3	Debtor Bank (Bank 1)	Creditor Bank (Bank 2 inside Group)	10 k€
Trx 4	Debtor Bank (Bank 1)	Creditor Bank (Bank 2 inside Group)	10 k€
Trx 5	Debtor Bank (Bank 1)	Creditor Bank (Bank 2 inside Group)	10 k€

Trx 6	Debtor Bank (Bank 1)	Creditor Bank (Bank 3 outside Group)	10 k€
Trx 7	Debtor Bank (Bank 1)	Creditor Bank (Bank 3 outside Group)	10 k€
Trx 8	Debtor Bank (Bank 1)	Creditor Bank (Bank 4 outside Group)	10 k€
Trx 9	Debtor Bank (Bank 1)	Creditor Bank (Bank 4 outside Group)	10 k€
Trx 10	Debtor Bank (Bank 1)	Creditor Bank (Bank 4 outside Group)	10 k€

Two important remarks before moving forward:

1. What is said above about the transactions may be different from what you will see in your particular project. Cases exist where PP Application sends intra bank transactions to the exchange platform and receives it again, or where those transactions are even sent to CSM and received again. Some banks of the Group may not be connected to the exchange platform and transactions to those banks will have to go through the CSM. So there are multiple possibilities and configurations that you can encounter. What I present here is one possibility. But the good news is that if you understand it well, you won't have problem to understand the other ones.
2. We have also considered that there is only one order being processed in the payments applications. In reality many orders are processed simultaneously. This may lead that the PP Application bulks many transactions coming from different orders to the same message and forward it to the processing platform. The exchange platform can also bulk many transactions from different messages which have the same destinations.

Now think about this question: Will different destinations have an impact on the booking? The answer is Yes, of course.☺ Please read the explanations provided below carefully.

In the following figure, you can see the accounting events generated and how the money moves from the debtor account to the various destinations.

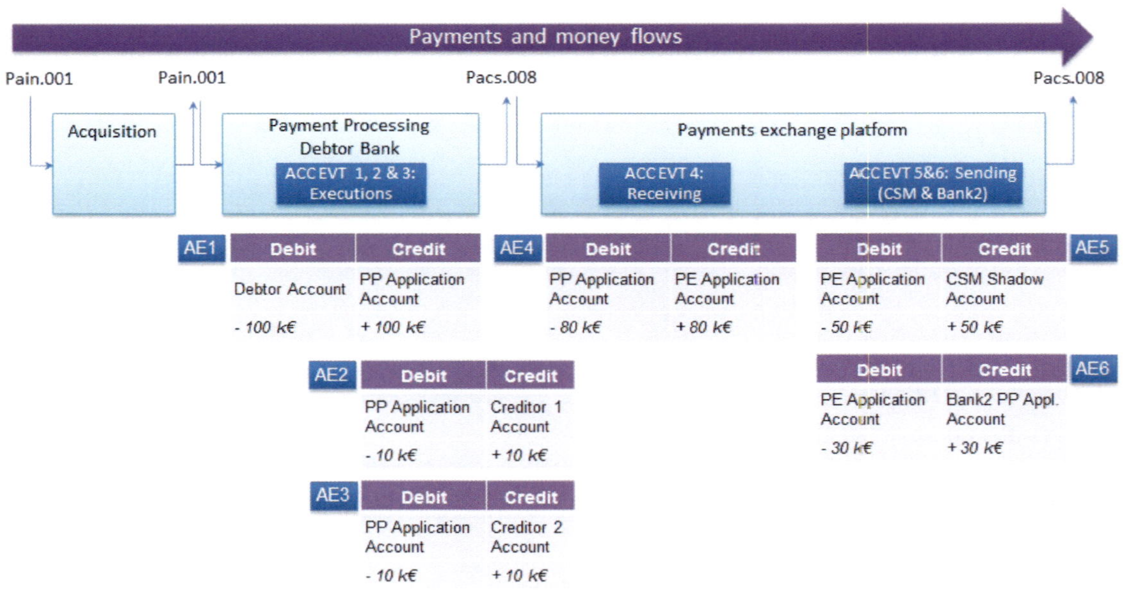

Figure 6.8: Accounting events for the booking of a multiple transactions order

The Acquisition platform receives, processes the pain.001 message and forwards it to the debtor bank processing application. No accounting event is generated in the Acquisition platform as already explained above.

All checks are done successfully and after the balance check, money is debited from the debtor account and credited to the PP Application Account (AE1 or Accounting Event 1). Since the order has multiple transactions, the number of entries made and displayed on the account statement of the debtor depends on the processing agreement (See chapter 4.2.6 for more details). To simplify, we assume that a single entry with the total amount of processed transactions is made on the debtor account.

Transactions can now be sent to their destination. 2 out of 10 transactions will remain in the PP Application because beneficiaries are customer of the same bank. 8 out of 10 transactions will be bulked in a pacs.008 message and forwarded to the exchange platform, which itself will bulk 3 transactions in one pacs.008 message and send them to the Bank 2, and 5 transactions in another pacs.008 message and send them to the Clearing System.

The credit sides of the two intra bank transactions can be executed immediately (if beneficiary accounts exist and there is no restriction on them) and the beneficiaries credited. The funds are debited from the PP internal account for that purpose as you can see in Accounting Events 2 and 3 (AE2 and AE3).

The 8 transactions to other Banks reach the exchange platform and are correctly received. The sum of amounts of the 8 transactions is debited from the Processing application and credited to the exchange platform (AE4). Booking entry for each single transaction on internal accounts would lead to a very high number of entries. And this is not really required because at the end of the day what is really important is that the accounts are balanced meaning that total sum of debit equals total sum of credits. This explains why most of the time we have a unique booking entry with 80 k€ instead of eight entries of 10 k€ each.

The exchange platform routes the transactions according to their destinations. 5 transactions are sent to the CSM and 3 transactions are sent to Bank 2. For the 5 CSM transactions, the account of the exchange platform is debited and the CSM account is credited respectively by the amount of 50 k€ (AE5). The 3 transactions sent to Bank 2 leads to the debit of the internal account to the credit of the Bank 2 application account (AE6).
Remark: The Accounting Event 6 can be generated when the PP Application of the Bank 2 receives the transactions. In that case, there is no need to generate it in the exchange platform.

If you consider the movements on each internal account (PP Application or exchange platform), you will see that the total amount of money credited is equal the total amount of money debited. And that is how it should be. They are transitory accounts and consequently are not supposed to keep any money.

To connect the dots, let us now answer the following question: **What will the clearing system do?** Remember that it is not debiting and crediting the bank account every time it receives the money (See 1.3). Recall also that payments are sent to and received from the clearing system at the same time.
After clearing, the net positions are computed. If the bank's net position is negative, its account in TARGET2 will be debited and the account of the clearing system will be credited with the amount corresponding to the net position. If the bank's net position is positive, its account in TARGET2 will be credited and the account of the clearing system will be debited accordingly. So on its TARGET2 account the bank will never see the multiple amounts (booked on CSM shadow account) of specific messages that were sent from the exchange application to the Clearing System. But it does not matter. The important thing for the bank is to make sure that

the total amount of money debited or credited from/to its TARGET2 account after settlement reflects what is on the clearing system shadow account in the bank general ledger.

For a net debit position after clearing, the net amount of entries performed on the shadow account must be positive and equal the amount that the clearing system will debit from the TARGET2 account of the bank. When the bank credits the clearing system shadow account, it is "giving money" to the clearing system. So the clearing system has to take that money from the TARGET2 account which is then debited accordingly.

The opposite applies of course. For a net credit position after clearing, the net amount of entries performed on the shadow account must be negative and equal the amount that the clearing system will credit to the TARGET2 account of the bank. When the bank debits the clearing system shadow account, it is taking money from the clearing system. So the clearing system has to give that money by crediting the TARGET2 account of the bank accordingly.

Clearing systems send reports to banks with total numbers of transactions sent and received and corresponding amounts in debit and in credit. For credit transfers sent, the amounts will be in debit since the bank has to pay the clearing system. But for credit transfers received, the amounts will be in credit since the clearing system has to give money to the bank. The same applies for returns. For returns sent, the amounts will be in credit since the bank has to pay the clearing system. But for returns received, the amounts will be in credit since the clearing system has to give money the bank.

If the clearing system claims that the bank has sent or received more transactions than it actually did, then you have a problem. Just trusting the CSM is not the right approach. It might also fail to execute its processes correctly. So Banks and CSM should try to understand what really happened and undertake the corrective actions.

After this analysis of CSM bookings, we will now consider the booking of pacs.004 transactions. A Pacs.004 can be a normal return or a positive answer to a cancellation request.

6.7 Debtor bank pacs.004.001.02 (normal return) booking

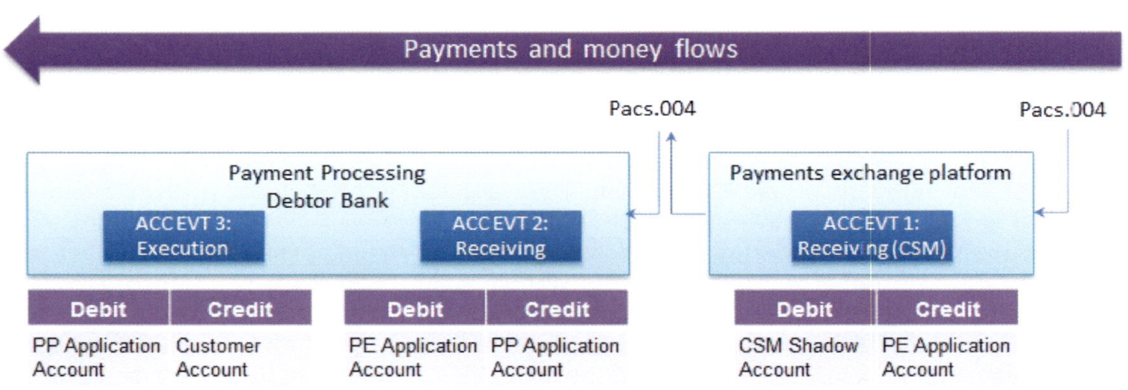

Figure 6.9: Accounting events for the booking of return in the debtor bank

When the debtor bank receives a return, it means that the creditor bank is returning the funds to the debtor. So receiving a return is receiving money. The debtor bank TARGET2 account will be credited at settlement date no matter if the return is accepted or rejected by the debtor bank after processing. Let us first take the case where the return is accepted and processed correctly.

The return sent by the clearing system is first received by the exchange platform. Therefore the money has to move from the clearing system to the exchange platform. The bank debits the clearing system shadow account and credits the internal account of the exchange platform. As next step the return is sent from exchange platform to the processing application. The funds are then moved from the internal account of the exchange platform to the internal account of the processing application. But you will easily agree with me that is not the final destination. We need another step to give the money back to the customer. Thus the internal account of the processing application must be debited and the customer account credited.

We see something interesting here. Transaction is not sent out of the processing application to another customer application. It remains inside. During the processing, some checks are performed to see if the money can be booked on the customer account or not. If the customer account is closed or does not exist for example, money cannot be credited on it. If the checks are successful, the processing application can generate an accounting event based on the outcome to debit its internal account and put the money to the customer account for instance.

What happens if the customer account does not exist or is close? In that case, the money has to be put somewhere else, on another internal account in general a pending account.

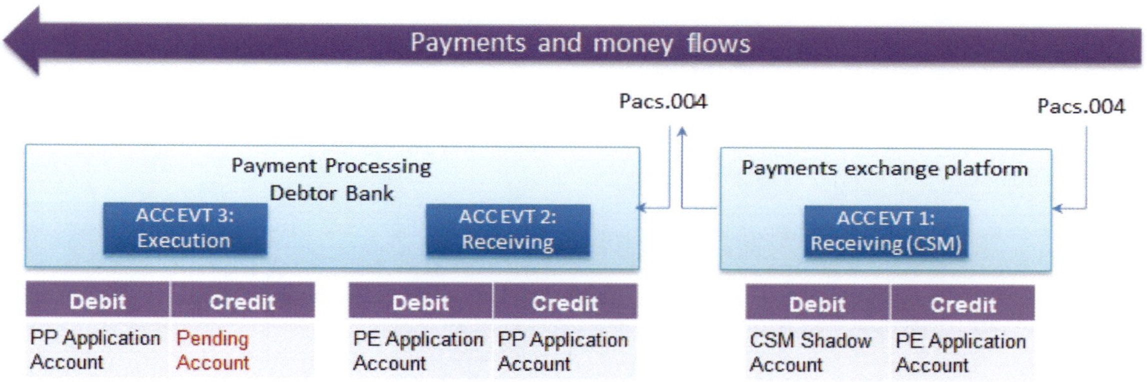

Figure 6.10: Accounting events for the booking of return in the debtor bank (Debtor account issue)

Pending accounts are transitory accounts. Funds are not supposed to stay there. The bank has many possibilities to handle return that cannot be credited on the debtor account. Few of them will be mentioned below.

- Possibility 1: The bank has never sent the original transaction for that return. You are surprised. Aren't you? I guarantee you that it has happened many times and will happen again. A bank receives a return for which it has never sent a credit transfer. The bank may call the creditor bank and find a way to send the money back.
- Possibility 2: The bank did send the original transaction. But that customer account has been closed meanwhile. The bank can put the money on another account of that customer provided he has other accounts of course. If the customer left the bank, the bank can contact him and transfer the funds to his account outside the bank. If the bank cannot find the customer and give him the money, money should be kept on a specific account. It is the customer's money.

On the CSM side, the clearing system will not debit creditor bank account and credit debtor bank account immediately. This will happen after the settlement process. Please refer to the chapter on Clearing and Settlement Mechanisms where you find more details about this topic. Let us move to the pacs.004 as positive response to a cancellation request.

6.8 *Debtor bank pacs.004.001.02 (Positive response to a camt.056) booking*

The positive response to a cancellation request is exchanged in the same message format as the normal return: the pacs.004.001.02. Most of the booking entries are similar as for the normal return except what will happen on the customer account.
There an important point to consider when booking the positive response to a cancellation request. Who made the mistake of sending an erroneous credit transfer? It can be the customer itself or the bank. The one who made the mistake has to pay the cost. We will consider the two options in the following and see how it impacts the booking.

6.8.1 Option 1: The customer made the mistake of sending the erroneous credit transfer

As you can see, the only difference between following picture and former one is what happens on the customer account (See ACC EVT 3).

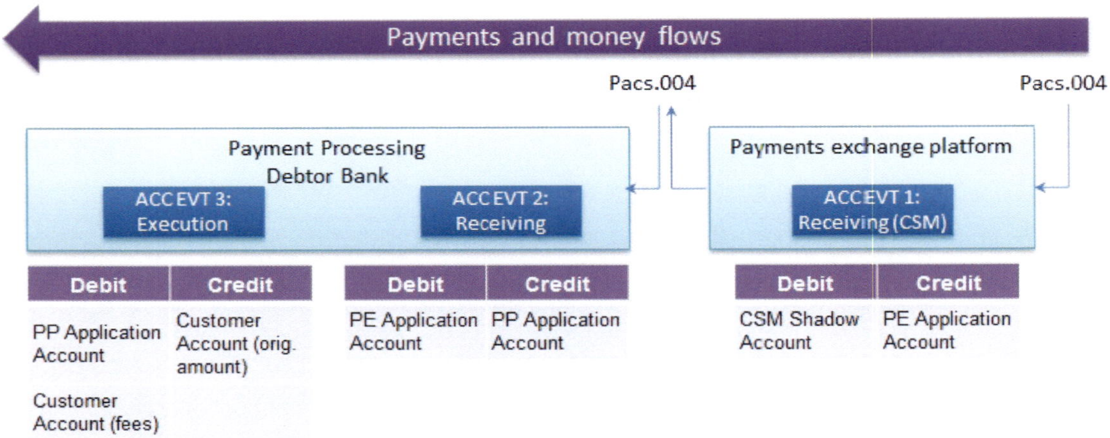

Figure 6.11: Accounting events to book a pacs.004 FOCR for a recall due to customer mistake

Two entries are made on the customer account. Recall that the creditor bank can keep a part of amounts as fees. The Returned Interbank Settlement Amount is equal to the 'Original Interbank Settlement Amount' less the fees. *The fees are taken from the amount to return and not from the beneficiary.* This means that only the Returned Interbank Settlement Amount is credited by the CSM to the bank TARGET2 account. That is the amount that will move from shadow account to PE and PP accounts.

If fees were taken, the debtor bank cannot credit the Original Interbank Settlement Amount to its customer. It will credit only the Returned Interbank Settlement Amount. But at the same time, the bank wants the customer to make the link with the transaction that has been recalled. So it will credit the debtor account with Original Interbank Settlement Amount and debit it with the fees. It is exactly the same as crediting the account with Returned Interbank Settlement Amount. But the customer can easily understand what happened. If the information on the customer account statement is comprehensive enough so that the customer can make the link with the recalled SCT, the bank may decide just to credit the account with Returned Interbank Settlement Amount.

In case of negative response sent by the creditor bank, the customer will lose all the money. His account was debited when the credit transfer was sent and he will not have the money back unless he uses other means. Things are different when the bank recalls a credit transfer which was sent because of its own mistake. Let us look at that case now.

6.8.2 Option 2: The Debtor Bank made the mistake of sending the erroneous credit transfer

The bank has to pay for the error this time and not the customer.

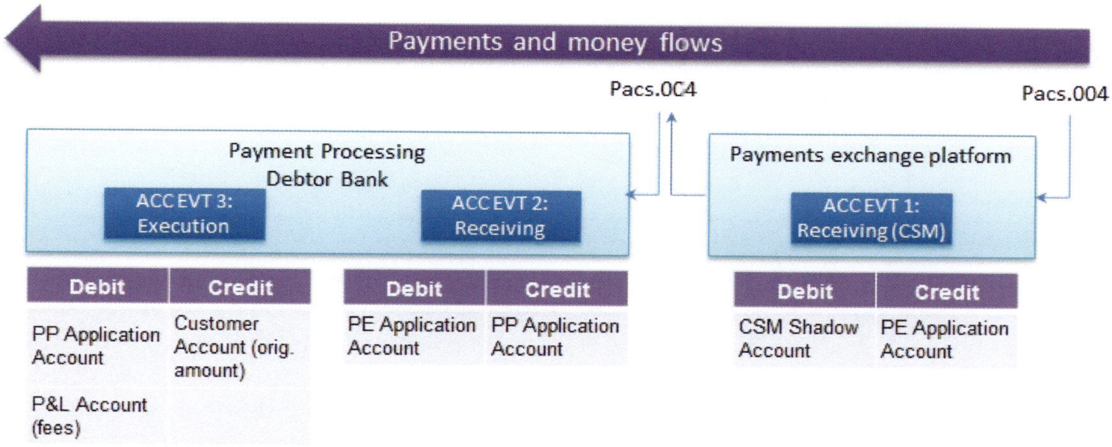

Figure 6.12: Accounting events to book a pacs.004 FOCR for a recall due to debtor bank mistake

Only one entry is made on the customer account. It is the credit of the **original amount** that was sent in the erroneous credit transfer. All the money is given back to the customer. But the bank does not receive that original amount. It only receives a part of it, the original amount less the fees to be more precise.

Look at the fees. They are debited from a Profit & Loss Account of the Debtor bank. So the bank pays the fees with its own money. If there is one debit of PP Application account with Returned Interbank Settlement Amount and one credit of customer account with original amount of the credit transfer, the accounting event would be unbalanced. This cannot be. Debiting the fees from P & L account brings everything in order again. And the double entry bookkeeping principle is kept. ☺

In the practice, that is what you will see most of the time: when the bank recalls the erroneous transaction, it credits the customer account immediately with the total amount by debiting its P & L account. So the payment engine generates accounting events while processing the recall which is a non-booking transaction. But note that the CSM does not move any money. Money moves inside the debtor bank from the bank to the customer and will move from the creditor to the debtor bank later if the pacs.004 is received; but the end result will be the same. After the return of the funds partially or totally, the debtor bank credits its P & L account. If the funds are returned partially (fees were taken), the bank will lose only the fees. If the funds are not returned at all (negative response), the bank will lose the total amount. With the knowledge you have now, it should not be a problem to figure out the end-to-end flows of funds in this case.

This concludes the creditor and debtor bank bookings. We have considered quite simple cases to give you an introduction and help you understand the booking principles. In your own project, you will certainly encounter less or more complex situations particularly related to exception handling. For example, how is the booking if the exchange platform rejects directly an incoming transaction without even forwarding it to the Processing Application? And what if an outgoing credit transfer is rejected in the Processing Application while trying to credit the beneficiary account? And the pacs.002, in which cases does it require booking? And so on. Answers are not always trivial and some of them depend on the choices made by the Bank. But the principles presented here can be of great help.

We are not yet the end of our journey on booking. There are still other important topics I will share with you in the subsequent paragraphs.

6.9 Nostro, Vostro and Loro accounts

In the same way that corporations can open accounts with several banks, a bank itself can open accounts with many other banks. Those accounts are called Nostro and Vostro or Loro accounts. The same account can be called Nostro, Vostro or Loro account. It depends on the relationship that a bank has with that account. To help you understand the difference between Nostro account, Vostro account and Loro account, I will take the example of three banks Bank 1, Bank 2 and Bank 3. Let assume that Bank 1 opens an account with Bank 2 as shown below. Both Bank 1 and Bank 2 have an account relationship. Bank 3 is not part of the relationship.

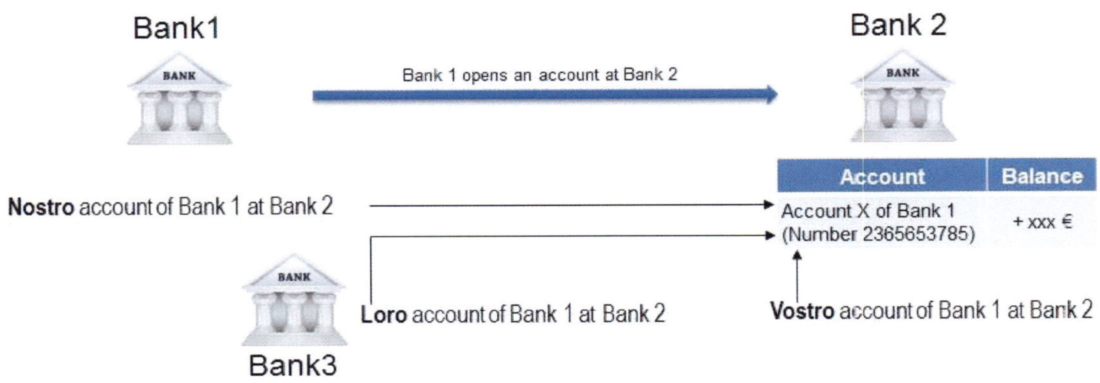

Figure 6.13: Same account is called Nostro, Vostro or Loro account

The Bank 1 will call that account its *Nostro* account and the Bank 2 will call it the *Vostro* account of Bank 1. As you see we don't have two accounts but only one. The same account is called Nostro account by the account-owning Bank and Vostro account by the account-holding Bank. Nostro is the Italian word for "our", Vostro the Italian word for "your" and Loro the Italian word for "their". The account X belongs to Bank 1 since it has opened it. That is why Bank 1 calls it Nostro account (For Bank 1 employees, it is logically *our* account). Bank 2 holds the account of Bank 1. Thus it calls it Vostro account (For Bank 2 employees, it is logically *your* account). Do not forget that Bank 1 and Bank 2 have an account relationship. If we now consider banks that are not part of the account relationship, like Bank 3 for example. Bank 3 calls the account Loro account (For Bank 3 employees, it is logically *their* account with Bank 2). Many people say Loro and mean Vostro. Be aware that Loro should be used by a Bank when it is not part of the relationship.

Confusion may come when Bank 2 also opens an account with Bank 1 as you can see in the following figure. Both banks are now in a bilateral account relationship.

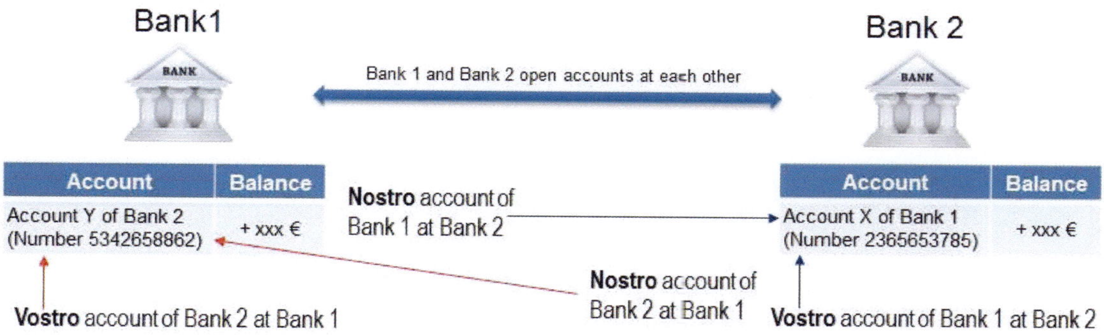

Figure 6.14: Nostro and Vostro accounts between two banks

In that case you have to be very careful when you are taking about Nostro or Vostro account. People tend to mix those two notions and sometimes say Vostro when they should say Nostro and vice versa. As you see in the figure, the accounts are completely different. Each bank holds the account of the other bank. They have different numbers and most of times even different currencies.

To summarize, I will give you few tips to remember easily what a Nostro or a Vostro account is: if you are working for a particular Bank (your Bank), the account of that Bank which is held by another bank is the Nostro account. *That account is not in the books of your Bank.* The account of another bank held by your Bank is the Vostro account. *This account is present in the book of your Bank.* The accounts of other banks that are not present in your books are called Loro accounts.

Now why would a bank open an account at another one? They are multiple reasons for that. One major reason is the setting up of a correspondent network with many banks to settle payments in foreign currencies. Another common reason is to use the services provided by the other bank for the exchange of payments with clearing houses and central bank. If we consider indirect participants and direct participants in SEPA, the indirect participants use services provided by direct participants to access the clearing systems. Since transactions processing involves moving money, it is important to have a clear view of the amounts being credited or debited. An indirect participant opens an account with the direct participant which is debited or credited after the transactions have been processed. Like for any customer account, the indirect participant receives an account statement from the direct participant where all debits and credits are reported. Now comes this interesting question: how can the indirect participant be sure that the content of the account statement is right and accurate? This takes us to the next crucial topic, the mirror accounts and shadow accounts.

6.10 Shadow accounts and mirror accounts

Shadow account or mirror account designates the same thing, the mirror of a real account. Key words here are mirror and shadow. A mirror gives the faithful image of a person or a thing, but it not the real person or thing. Similarly, a mirror account gives the image of an account, but it is not the real account itself. However, if you know what is happening on a mirror account, you can easily deduce what the movements on the real account should be.

When companies or people are in business, every party wants and needs to be sure that the numbers are correct, i.e. it is not cheated by the other☺. There are essentially two options: either you blindly trust the other party or you follow the numbers yourself. The problem with the first option is that one party can do whatever it wants, the other party will just accept it. We all know that this is not correct and professional. Don't we? Money is crucial. And everyone has to know his own numbers. This is particularly true for banks that send and receive important amount of payments every day.

Using a mirror account allows to follow and even control what is happening on the real account. When entries are made on the real account, entries are also made on the mirror account and vice versa. Entries on a mirror account are always of opposite sign to entries on the real account. Thus it is considered that the mirror of plus (+) is minus (-) and the mirror of minus (-) is plus (+).

To illustrate what the mirror account really is, we will take the example of the account relationship between an indirect participant and a direct participant. The second is exchanging payments with a CSM on behalf of the first. The indirect participant opens an account with the direct participant. It is the real account. Every time the direct participant receives or sends booking transactions to the indirect participant, the real account is debited or credited. But the indirect participant wants to see and control what is happening on the real account. For that it creates a mirror account that will give the image of the booking entries on the real account, so that it can now "see" the real account.

The picture below depicts how mirror accounts and real accounts work.

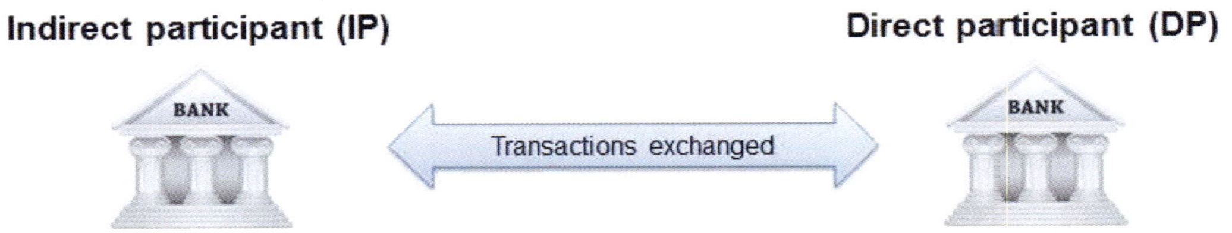

Mirror account		
Transactions	**Debit**	**Credit**
Sends a pacs.008 to DP (150 k€)		+ 150 k
Receives a pacs.008 from DP (70 k€)	- 70 k	
Sends a pacs.004 to DP (75 k€)		+ 75 k
Receives a pacs.004 from DP (100 k€)	- 100 k	
Total balance		55 k

Real account of IP		
Transactions	**Debit**	**Credit**
Receives a pacs.008 from IP to forward to CSM (150 k€)	- 150 k	
Sends a pacs.008 received from the CSM to IP (70 k€)		+ 70 k
Receives a pacs.004 from IP to forward to CSM (75 k€)	- 75 k	
Sends a pacs.004 received from the CSM to IP (100 k€)		+ 100 k
Total Balance	- 55 k	

Figure 6.15: Mirror account vs Real account

Let us have a close look at the two accounts. First take note of the mirror effect: the entries on the two accounts are of same amount with opposite sign. Every time the mirror account is debited, the real account is credited and vice versa. A debit for the Indirect Participant is a credit for the Direct Participant. A credit of the Indirect Participant is a debit for the Direct Participant.

Some questions may arise in your mind:

1. Why is the mirror account credited when a pacs.008 is sent?
2. We are sending money, should we not debit the account?

There are two important things to remember here: *1) Money comes from customer account and 2) accounting events must be balanced.* Since the money comes from IP customer accounts, those accounts must be debited. There is no alternative. After debiting the money, the IP can first credit the payment application account as you can see on the next figure. When the transaction is submitted, the application account is debited and the mirror account is credited. That is how money reaches the mirror account and this explains why it is credited. Crediting the mirror account is like giving money to the DP so that it can use it for the settlement. You see? It fits perfectly!

The (real) account of the Indirect Participant is debited and credited by the Direct Participant. The mirror of that account is credited and debited by the Indirect Participant. The Indirect Participant must ensure that there are sufficient funds on the real account as agreed bilaterally with the Direct Participant. Otherwise the Direct Participant may not process and forward transactions to the CSM. This does not mean that the real account balance cannot be negative. In any case, the Indirect Participant must follow the balance to ensure that it does not go beyond the authorized limits. And obviously the mirror account is of great help to do that.

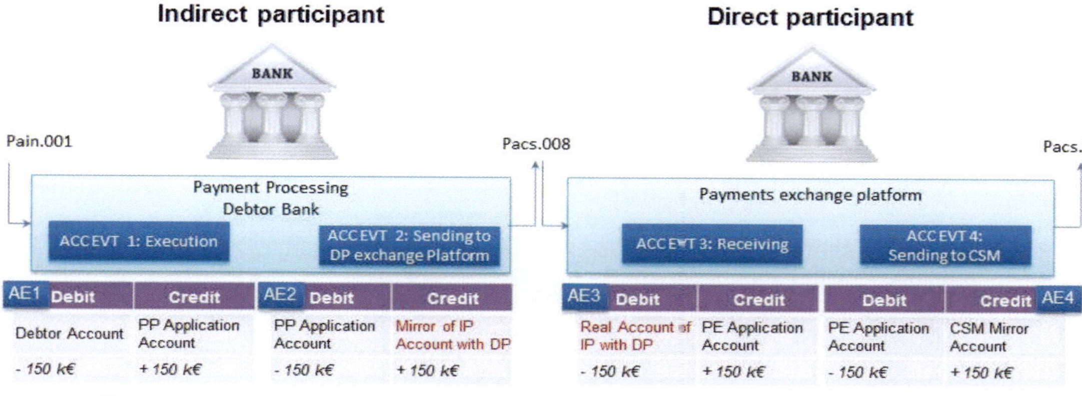

Figure 6.16: Accounting events for the processing of a SCT from an IP to a DP

Let us go back to Figure 6.15: Mirror account vs Real account. The total balance of the mirror account is 55 k€. And therefore the balance of the real account is the opposite which is -55 k€. The Indirect Participant (IP) has a negative balance on its account held by the Direct Participant (DP). It has to credit the account for it to have a positive balance again. If the balance of the real account was positive, the balance of the mirror account would be negative. And the Indirect Participant could take money from the real account.

In our case, the balance of the real account is negative. The Direct Participant has a settlement commitment on TARGET2 and must receive the funds from the Indirect Participant. The IP has to pay the DP. Now how will that happen? Some may think that the IP will just take the "money" from the mirror account to credit its real account with the DP. But that is not correct. First the mirror account does not have any money. It is just an account to follow what is happening on the real account. Second, the settlement between banks normally happens through the European Central Bank (ECB) unless agreed otherwise. So the IP needs to initiate an ECB transfer to credit the DP account with the ECB with the corresponding amount. For the execution of the transfer, the IP ECB account must be debited (if there is sufficient balance of course). After debit confirmation from the ECB, the IP credits its mirror ECB account and debits its mirror account with DP. Furthermore, the DP ECB account is credited. As a consequence, the DP logically debits the mirror of its ECB account and credits the real account of the IP. At the end of this transaction, the balances of IP real account and IP mirror account are zero.

Indirect participant

Debit	Credit
Mirror of IP Account with DP	Mirror of IP ECB account
- 55 k€	*+ 55 k€*

European Central Bank

Debit	Credit
IP ECB account	DP ECB account
- 55 k€	*+ 55 k€*

Direct participant

Debit	Credit
Mirror of DP ECB account	Real Account of IP with DP
- 55 k€	*+ 55 k€*

Figure 6.17: Settlement between Indirect Participant and Direct Participant through the European Central Bank in SEPA

Remark: In real life, the amounts involved are much larger. Furthermore, the IP has the possibility to transfer the funds to its DP account from another account it may have with another bank. That would still go through the ECB.

At this stage, we clearly see the importance of mirror accounts. They are just indispensable in accounting. Now think about this question: what would happen if the balance of the real account is -56 k€ while the balance of the mirror account is 55 k€? The Indirect Participant would see immediately that something wrong happened and would start to investigate with the help of the Direct Participant. Having a mirror account is really of great help to understand what is going on and undertake the necessary actions to fix potential issues.

6.10.1 Reconciliation of real and mirror accounts

Reconciling an account means proving that the account balance is correct. For that, it must be checked that each accounting entry on the account is accurate and justified. In case discrepancies are identified, they must be investigated and actions must be taken to fix underlying issues.

To make the reconciliation process simple, a good practice is to use the same method (batch booking or single booking) to perform entries on both real and mirror accounts. If each party sticks to the rules, the entries should be of same amount with opposite sign. They can then be compared easily on both sides for the reconciliation. How to ensure that two accounting entries, one on the real account and one on the mirror account, refer to the same transaction? Using only the amount to reconcile does not work as many transactions with same amount can be sent or received. The value date can be added as reconciliation criteria, so that the amount as well as the date are used to reconcile the entries. Unfortunately this does work either. Many transactions of same amount can be processed on the same day. Furthermore, one transaction can be processed at D one side and at D+1 on the other side because it is received on the other side after cut-off for instance.

So what to do? We need a unique reference to use on both sides for reconciliation purpose. That reference should allow to identify a transaction uniquely on both sides. Both parties must agree on what to use as reference, if the reference must be created and how it is structured or if an ISO 20022 field can be used. In the standard ISO 20022, it says about the transaction identification, a message element at transaction level of the pacs.008: "Usage: The transaction identification can be used for reconciliation, tracking or to link tasks relating to the transaction on the interbank level. *The instructing agent has to make sure that the transaction identification is unique for a pre-agreed period.*" The requirement to keep the transaction unique for a pre-agreed period is to ensure that two transactions with the same identification are not processed on the same day or even same week. In case the parties want to create a reference, it should be unique for a pre-agreed period.

With the transaction identification as reference, we are *certain* that accounting entries that are reconciled relate to the same transaction. This works for single booking i.e. when an accounting entry is performed for each and every transaction. In case of batch booking, both parties should, as already said, agree on how to group transactions and how to create the unique reference to use for reconciliation. Let us illustrate single and batch booking reconciliation with two examples, one for each booking method.

Example of reconciliation with single booking

Real account entries

Entry text	Value Date	Debit	Credit
Outgoing SCT IND-PART-UNIQUE-TRXID	Settlement Date	- 150 k€	
Incoming SCT DBT-BNK-UNIQUE-TRXID	Settlement Date		+ 60 k€

Mirror account entries

Entry text	Value Date	Debit	Credit
Outgoing SCT IND-PART-UNIQUE-TRXID	Settlement Date		+ 150 k€
Incoming SCT DBT-BNK-UNIQUE-TRXID	Settlement Date	- 60 k€	

As requested in the ISO 20022, the debtor bank generates the transaction identification used for reconciliation. The debtor bank decides what is its structure and over which period it will be unique. The transaction identification is transported end to end.

For the outgoing SCT, the reference IND-PART-UNIQUE-TRXID is the transaction identification generated the indirect participant debtor bank that is sending the SCT.

For the incoming SCT, the reference DBT-BNK-UNIQUE-TRXID is the transaction identification generated by the debtor bank. In this case, it can be a bank located in another country or in the same country that is sending the SCT to the indirect participant.

Example of reconciliation with batch booking

Real account entries

Entry text	Value Date	Debit	Credit
Outgoing SCTs PPR-UNIQUE-REF-ID 4748 TRX	Settlement Date	- 341 k€	
Incoming SCTs PEP-UNIQUE-REF-ID 11207 TRX	Settlement Date		+ 644 k€

Mirror account entries

Entry text	Value Date	Debit	Credit
Outgoing SCTs PPR-UNIQUE-REF-ID 4748 TRX	Settlement Date		+ 341 k€
Incoming SCTs PEP-UNIQUE-REF-ID 11207 TRX	Settlement Date	- 644 k€	

For the batch booking, the structure of entries texts may look like the following examples:

- Entry text example 1 =« Outgoing SCTs + [Generated reference forwarded to the other party] + [Space] + [Number of grouped transactions] + TRX»

- Entry text example 2 =« Incoming SCTs + [Generated reference forwarded to the other party] + [Space] + [Number of grouped transactions] + TRX»

The reference in the first entry text is generated in the payment processing application of the indirect participant debtor bank. It can be forwarded to the direct participant as Message Identification or in another field.

The reference in the second entry text is generated in the payment exchange platform of the direct participant. It can be forwarded to the indirect participant as Message Identification or in another field.

The reconciliation of real and mirror accounts happens automatically in dedicated applications and in general daily, late in the afternoon on the same day or early in the morning for the previous day. Sometimes, it can even happen twice a day, depending on the frequency at which the real account holder delivers the account statements. Important is that each party knows exactly where the references are and how long they can be.

6.11 Account balance management

Account balance management is a crucial topic in payments. It is closely related to subjects like cash management and cash pooling and presents interesting challenges. In this chapter, we will see some of those challenges and outline solutions that banks have put in place to address them.

The goal of account balance management for the bank is very simple: ensuring that the customer is using only the funds that are available to him. If not properly done, the bank may realize only quite late that the customer has used more funds than he is allowed to. And it can even lose money in case the customer disappears ☹. But at the same time, the bank does not want to prevent customers from initiating transactions when funds are available. So it has to take into account possible credit lines also and make sure that when the customer receives credit transfers, the received amount is taken into account as soon as possible. Expectations are particularly high for corporate customers which may debit and credit their accounts quite a lot of times during the day. We will now consider two types of account balance management: Balance management for a single account and balance management for Merge Accounts.

6.11.1 Balance management for a single account

The main challenges are illustrated by two cases that follow:

Case 1: A bank customer has 1500 € of balance on his account and a line of credit of 500 €. In total he can debit 2000 € from his account. The bank does not update the account balance every time the customer initiates a transfer. The bank debits funds for all transactions from the customer account only once in the evening. With the time the customer becomes aware of that fact. So he initiates 4 transactions of 1500 € which makes a total of 6000 €. All transactions are executed during the day and the bank must credit the CSM account at settlement date. In the evening, the bank realizes that the customer did not have sufficient funds available and that the transactions should have never been accepted and executed☹. *To avoid this, the bank has to update the account balance every time the customer initiates a transaction.*

Case 2: A bank customer has 500 € on his account and a line of credit up to 500 €. He is expecting 1500 € to be credited on his account, so that he can initiate a credit transfer of 2000 € to pay a supplier. He wants to pay on the day the money is supposed to be credited on his account to avoid additional fees and interests. The bank receives a credit transfer of 2000 € in the morning. But the funds are credited on his account only in the evening. Therefore he is not able to initiate the transfer to the supplier during the day and is very disappointed ☹. *The bank should improve the service by making the funds available to the customer as soon as possible.*

The two cases bring to light the issues faced by banks. If the bank does not update balances when the transactions are done during the day, this may not only drastically impact the customer service, but also can cause the bank to lose money. Ideally a bank would like to know and update the exact balance a customer has on his account to the minute. It means that every time the customer sends or receives funds, this is taken into account in seconds or minutes. Unfortunately, this is not possible today in many banks because their accounting systems cannot update the customer balance in real-time or nearly real-time.

Many accounting systems still run on batch processing with flat files. And the bookings are performed once or twice a day. How then to follow the customer balance for his sake and the sake of the bank? Many banks have put in place a Balance Management System (BMS) which takes care of updating the balance after each transaction. The BMS is interfaced with the Accounting system for the exchange of balance information.

After the batches of the middle or end of the day, all booking entries are carried out on customer accounts and the latest balances become available. Note that the BMS may not be aware of some movements, debits or credits, performed on an account (some fees debited by the bank for instance). That is why the accounting systems must communicate the latest balance to the BMS. The BMS will then proceed with the latest balance information.

The BMS keeps the *intraday account balance* and updates it every time the customer account is debited or credited by the payment engines. And this is done as soon as possible to have accurate information - critical to make good decisions – for the employees and customers. When the customer initiates a credit transfer, his intraday balance is updated by the BMS *before* his order is executed. This is how the bank reserves the funds from the customer account. When a customer receives funds, his intraday balance is updated by the BMS *after* the execution of the order. This is how funds are made available pretty rapidly to the customer after the execution of the transfer.

The intraday balance kept in the BMS is different from the real account balance available in the accounting systems. The intraday balance is updated very often by the BMS as seen above. The real account balance is updated once or twice a day. The same transaction first creates an intraday entry on the account through the BMS and later the final entry through the accounting systems. The accounting entry texts are in general the same, so that the customer does not see the differences between intraday and final entries. But they are not the same. The intraday balance takes the value of the real balance after the real balance is updated.

It is obvious that the *intraday balance* in the BMS is the one to be considered for a balance check. And since it is updated after each transaction, it is pretty reliable. Now let us reconsider the two cases mentioned at the outset of this paragraph. What would happen in case there is a BMS in place?

Case 1 with BMS: A bank customer has 1500 € of balance on his account and 500 € of line of credit. In total he can debit 2000 € from his account. The bank is updating the account balance through the BMS every time the customer initiates a transfer. So after the first transaction, the intraday balance is 0. When the customer initiates the second transfer, the transaction is blocked because of Non-Sufficient Funds (NSF). He is informed that only 500 € are available on his line of credit. The customer cannot take the Bank money anymore. ☺

Case 2 with BMS: A bank customer has 500 € on his account and 500 € of line of credit. He is expecting 1500 € to be credited on his account, so that he can initiate a credit transfer of

2000 € to pay a supplier. He wants to pay on that day to avoid additional fees and interests. The bank receives the credit transfer of 2000 € in the morning. About 15 minutes after, the credit transfer is executed and the customer intraday balance is updated through the BMS. The customer can pay his supplier on that day and avoid fees. He is very happy. ☺

6.11.2 Balance Management for merge accounts

You are very probably wondering yourself: what are merge accounts? Let us introduce this paragraph with the answer to that question. Merging two or more accounts of a customer is bringing them together or unifying them, so that considered together they act or behave like one single account.

Banks offer the merge accounts service to professional and corporate customers. It is of little interest for individuals. The implementation of that service can be implicit (The bank applies the service to all corporate customers. They are informed in the terms and conditions and no specific subscription is needed) or explicit (the customer must subscribe to the service. Otherwise, he cannot use it). The implementation depends on country regulation and bank policies. There are a lot of options that can be offered in that service. I do not go into details because it is not the topic of this chapter whose aim is to explain how the balance management is done with merge accounts.

We will take an example of a corporate customer who has four accounts he has requested the bank to handle as a merge account. The account balances are visible on the table below.

Accounts	Balances
Account 1	- 10 k€
Account 2	+ 120 k€
Account 3	- 75 k€
Account 4	+ 140 k€
Merge Account	+ 175 k€

The merge account balance is the sum of the balances of the four accounts (-10 + 120 -75 + 140 = 175).

Now the customer wants to initiate a credit transfer of 150 k€ to debit from the account 1. If the balance check takes only the account 1 balance into account, the transaction will be rejected. Same thing applies for account 2, account 3 and account 4 individually. There are not sufficient funds on none of those accounts. But when the merge account balance (175 k€) is considered, the transaction is accepted. The amount is then debited from the account 1. And the balance of the account 1 is updated to -160 k€. The merged account balance becomes 25 k€ after the execution as you can see on the table below.

Accounts	Balances
Account 1	- 160 k€
Account 2	+ 120 k€
Account 3	- 75 k€
Account 4	+ 140 k€
Merge Account	+ 25 k€

The customer can execute the transaction from any of the account. It is fine as long as the "merge account" balance contains sufficient funds.

In case the customer receives a credit transfer of 50 k€ on any of the accounts (let's say account 2 for instance), the balance of that account will be updated. And the balance of the merge account has to be updated also since that account belongs to the merge account. The result is what you see on the following table.

Accounts	Balances
Account 1	- 160 k€
Account 2	+ 170 k€
Account 3	- 75 k€
Account 4	+ 140 k€
Merge Account	+ 75 k€

The above examples bring us to the following conclusion. *If an account belongs to a merge account, a debit or a credit on it results in debiting or crediting the merge account also.* Now a question: Is the merge account a separate account with a specific number or is it just the sum of all accounts belonging to it? I let you ponder over it ☺.

Review Questions

- Explain accounting events and the double entry bookkeeping principle. Give some examples.
- List the booking and non-booking transactions of the SCT scheme
- Booking of ***Creditor Bank*** transactions
  - Describe how the booking is performed for a correctly processed credit transfer. Make a drawing.
  - Describe how the booking is performed for a credit transfer in pending status. Make a drawing.
  - Describe how the booking is performed for the return of credit transfer. Make a drawing.
  - Describe how the booking is performed for the positive response of a cancellation request. Make a drawing.

- Booking of ***Debtor Bank*** orders and transactions
  - Describe how the booking is performed for a correctly processed credit transfer order (The order contains 5 intra bank, 5 intragroup and 5 CSM transactions. Each transaction amount is 100 €). Make a drawing
  - Describe how the booking is performed for a credit transfer order in pending status. Make a drawing.
  - Describe how the booking is performed for the return of credit transfer. Make a drawing.
  - Describe how the booking is performed for the positive response of a cancellation request (Costumer's mistake). Make a drawing.
  - Describe how the booking is performed for the positive response of a cancellation request (Bank's mistake). Make a drawing.

- Define and illustrate with a drawing what Nostro and Vostro accounts are.
- Define and Illustrate with a drawing what shadow accounts (also called mirror accounts) are
- Explain the concept of accounts reconciliation. What is a reconciliation criteria? How to choose it?
- Define Account balance management and explain why it is important
- Explain what merged accounts are. Illustrate with an example.
- Explain the differences between account balance management for single account and for merged accounts. What are the advantages and disadvantages for a customer?

Discussion Questions

- Can booking events be generated for non-booking transactions? Give your arguments
- Mirror accounts and related Loro accounts can be reconciled even if the booking is happening at different levels, the one at transaction level and the other at order level. Is this a correct statement? Give your arguments.
- Imagine a booking system where booking happens on a real-time on customer accounts. Would it still make sense to perform an account balance management?
- How can processing agreements impact Debtor Bank bookings? Give examples

Chapter 7 The Graphical User Interface

LEARNING OBJECTIVES

After reading this chapter, you will be able to answer the following questions:

1. What are navigation menus? What do they contain?
2. What transactions information should be displayed on the screen?
3. How are original transactions and r-transactions inked on the GUI?
4. What are user rights and roles? How are they used to control user actions?
5. What are the worklist items (WLI)?
6. What are 3270 screens?

The Graphical User Interface (GUI) plays a key role in applications in general and payment engines are no exception. The GUI is much more than a display. It is the door that let people see what is happening inside the payment engine. It is the tool that operators use to carry out their work on a daily basis. The GUI must therefore be attractive and easy to use.

You can have the best technology implemented inside your payment engine. Unfortunately the end users do not care that much about it and frankly many of them won't understand if you would try to explain it to them. The users do care about what they do and see. The GUI can consolidate or ruin a product reputation quite rapidly. So this subject of GUI is to be taken very seriously.

Creating an easy-to-use and functional GUI is not an easy task. However, finding the right colors, buttons, layouts, menus, etc. is only a tiny part of what needs to be done. The GUI entails subjects like user rights and roles, application administration and configuration.

Following questions and many others will be answered in this chapter:

- What should be displayed on the GUI?
- Who are the users of the GUI?
- What are they using it for?
- How often are they going to use it? Will they use it sporadically, on a daily basis, weekly basis?
- Which payment engines parameters can be configured through the GUI?
- and so on.

7.1 The navigation menu

The navigation menu is in general located either on the left of the page or on the top of the page as shown in the following figures.

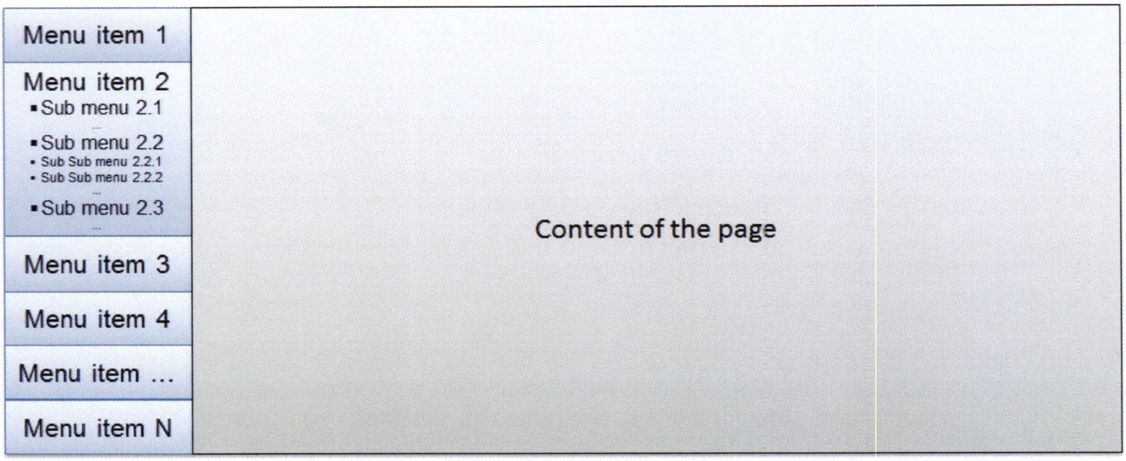

Figure 7.1: Navigation menu on the left of the page

When displayed on the left, all the menu and sub menu items are usually shown permanently. As a consequence, only the rest of the page width can be used to display the content.

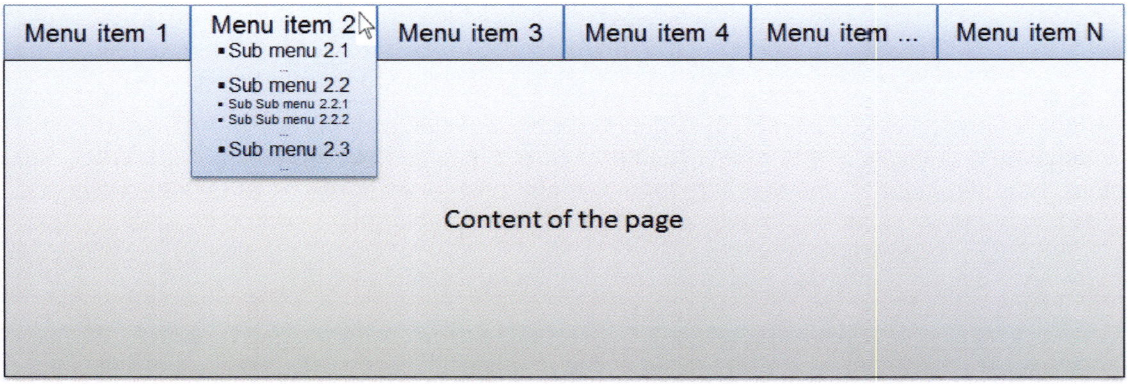

Figure 7.2: Navigation menu on top of the page

When located on top of the page, submenu items under a menu item are displayed generally when the mouse comes over the menu item or after a click on it. These sub menu items are displayed over the page content. They disappear after a user click on one of the sub menu items or elsewhere on the page. Here the entire width of page can be used to display the content.

A bank offers and processes many payment types, not only the SEPA Credit Transfer. In practice the bank can choose either 1) to have one GUI to access each type of payment or 2) to have one GUI to access all / many types of payments.

For the first option, each payment type has a dedicated GUI. The menu/submenu items are about payment management (viewing and acting on messages, orders and transactions), payment exchange (routing and exchange partners), banks administration, user administration, worklist items, parameter settings and other topics. It depends on the payment engine and the bank's needs. Since there is a GUI for each payment type, the users must select the specific GUI required for their work. The link to the GUI for SCT is different from the ones for SDD Core and SDD B2B. Users who are not supposed to work on some payments get an access denied message if they try to connect to the related GUI.

For the second option, the GUI is comparable to a canvas providing access to all types of payments. The top menu items are about the different payment types like SCT, SDD Core, SDD B2B or Cross border Transfers. The submenu items are similar to what we saw above (Payment management, banks administration, and so on). The users have access to the GUI but inside the GUI, they see only the menu items of payments they are supposed to view or act upon. A user working on SCT and SDD Core would see only the menu items related to those payments. SDD B2B or Cross Border Payments will not appear in his menu. The filtering is made according to the user rights and roles. We will come back to that in detail later in this chapter.

Naming and organizing the menu items is highly important. Grouping the submenu items under the menus in a logical way requires excellent knowledge and understanding of Payment processing and configurations of Payment Engines. It is recommended to do this in team and confront different views. In general, involving operational people with good customers and payment knowledge brings excellent results. The menu items should be easily understandable. They should not raise multiple questions in the mind of users. If necessary use multiple words to make things as clear as possible.

I have seen many different navigation menus in my payment projects. There is no best way to organize them and making a recommendation would not be right. The access to the payment GUI and the design of GUI menu items depend on the organizations (people and activities they perform), the software package (Configuration) itself and other factors like applications and security policies. Just take note that the tools are not an end in themselves. The tools are there to support the processes. A keen understanding of the business processes is necessary to take the right decisions. Therefore communication and collaboration between projects and end users are key success factors. Naming and organizing the menu items is a team work.

Let us finish this paragraph with a few words about Breadcrumbs. Breadcrumbs are extremely useful. They allow users to keep track of their locations when they navigate in the Payment Engine GUI. They can see which screens they visited before the one they are viewing. It is a good practice to display breadcrumbs on top of the page content. Even better is to display the breadcrumb items as hyperlinks. The user can then click on one of them to go back to a previous page very easily. It is a better alternative than using browser back buttons which are not always supported by payment engine software vendors.

7.2 The payment messages on the GUI

In chapter 2, we saw that a payment message consists of many levels of information: message level information, order level information and transaction level information. The Pain.001 and Pain.002 messages have three levels of information whereas all the other messages have only two levels of information (message level and transaction level). This paragraph is about how payment messages are captured and displayed on the GUI.

7.2.1 Payment capture

As we saw in chapter 4, banks acquire payment through various channels and means. In this paragraph, the focus is about payment capture or manual input. If a customer fills in a form with order information like Debtor IBAN and name, beneficiary IBAN and names, amount, requested execution date, remittance information, etc. then that order must be manually captured in Bank's payments systems. Payment engines GUI (native or customized) are used for that purpose.

Capturing payment information should be as easy and efficient as possible while preventing the user from entering incorrect information. The number of items to manually input should be as limited as possible. This reduces the number of errors while increasing the operational efficiency since payments can be captured faster. Below is a list of few best practices.

- Check digits in IBAN should be validated and the user informed immediately in case of failed validations.
- The BIC of the Beneficiary Bank should be automatically enriched.
- For the amounts, it is better to foresee two fields on the screen separated by a decimal point or the equivalent. The user can clearly distinguished the units and cents. He does not have to type the decimal point which is taken care internally by the application.
- Requested execution date should be automatically filled in with current date. The user may be able to change it if he wants. This should be done by choosing a date on a calendar and not by manually inputting a date. In that way, you are sure that the date will always be in the expected format. Date formats are different in English and French for example and it is easy to mix months and days. This is avoided easily by the use of a calendar.
- Be careful about the character set used on free text fields like the names, addresses, remittance information. If some special characters are not accepted, the users should not be allowed to enter them. Or they should be immediately converted in allowed characters. For the second solution, you save one error message (This character is not allowed) and avoid user frustration. He might not know what to do if he just reads that a specific character is not allowed.
- At the end of the capture, the full order should be displayed to the user after the first validation. He can recheck all the information input and correct if necessary. If everything is OK, he will revalidate again or confirm the order.

7.2.2 Payment information on the GUI

Many ISO 20022 messages contain many hundreds message elements and, in addition, there are fields generated by the payment engine that must be added to a payment message. Displaying all the fields of a payment message on one screen is neither practical nor user-friendly. A choice must therefore be made about which fields to display on the screens. These fields should be relevant for the end users and provide useful information in case of investigation or customer requests. The decision is pretty easy to make for some of the fields, but can be hard for others. In general, a payment engine GUI contains the fields listed in the table below. For ISO 20022 fields, the XML Tag is indicated in parenthesis. Message level is indicated as M, Order level as O and transaction level as T.

Level	Field	Description
Message	Message key	Unique reference generated by the payment engine and used to identify a single message in the system
Message	Message Identification (<MsgId>)	Message reference created by the sender and forwarded in the SEPA message
Message	Message format	It can take values like pain.001.001.02, pain.001.001.03, pacs.008.001.02, camt.056.001.01, ...
Message	Message status	Status of the message assigned by the payment engine after processing: rejected, processed, pending, on hold ...

Level	Field	Description
Message	Reception date	Date at which the message is received in the payment engine. In search screens, users can enter From and To reception dates
Message	Sending party (<InstgAgt>)	BIC of the sending Bank. It can be different from the debtor Bank
Message	Receiving party (<InstdAgt>)	BIC of the receiving Bank. It can be different from the beneficiary Bank
Message	Payment scheme	Payment processing scheme. It can take values like SCT for SEPA Credit Transfer (or SDD for SEPA Direct Debit)
Order	Order key	Unique reference generated by the payment engine and used to identify a single order in the system
Order	Instruction Priority (<InstrPrty>)	Priority level with which the order should be processed. It can the values H (High) or N (Normal)
Order	Order status	Status of the order assigned by the payment engine after processing rejected, processed, pending, on hold … It depends on the status of the message. An order is automatically rejected if the corresponding message is rejected.
Order	Order Category Purpose (<PmtTpInf> <CtgyPurp>)	It provides information about the purpose of the order and may trigger special processing. So interesting for the end user.
Order	Requested Execution Date (<ReqdExctnDt>)	Date at which the order should be executed as requested by the order
Order	(Real) Execution date	Date at which the order is really executed. Requested and real execution dates are the same most of the time. But where they are different, it is useful information. In search screens, users can enter From and To execution dates.
Order	Payment Information Identification (<PmtInfId>)	Order reference created by the sender and forwarded in the SEPA message
Order	Order amount	Amount of the order. . In search screens, users can enter From and To amounts.
Order / Transaction	Interbank Settlement Date (<IntrBkSttlmDt>)	The date at which the order / transaction is settled. This information is more important at transaction level. In search screens, users may enter From and To settlement dates.
Message / Order	Total Interbank Settlement Amount (<TtlIntrBkSttlmAmt>)	Total amount of transactions contained in the order or message
Order / Transaction	Debtor name (<Dbtr><Nm>)	Name of the debtor. It may be available at order level and / or at transaction level depending of the message type.
Order / Transaction	Debtor Account <DbtrAcct> (Debtor IBAN)	IBAN of the debtor. It may be available at order level and / or at transaction level depending of the message type. This is in general available as search criteria in search screens.
Order / Transaction	Debtor Agent (<DbtrAgt>)	It is the BIC of the debtor bank. It may be available at order level and / or at transaction level depending of the message type.
Transaction	Beneficiary name (<Cdtr><Nm>)	Name of the beneficiary. It is available at transaction level only.
Transaction	Creditor Agent (<CdtrAgt>)	It is the BIC of the beneficiary Bank
Transaction	Creditor Account (<CdtrAcct>)	IBAN of the beneficiary. This is in general available as search criteria in search screens.

Level	Field	Description
Transaction	Transaction key	Unique reference generated by the payment engine and used to identify a single transaction in the system
Transaction	Interbank Settlement Amount (<IntrBkSttlmAmt>)	This is the transaction amount. Good to have as search criteria when an order contains high number of transactions.
Transaction	End To End Identification (<EndToEndId>)	It is generated by initiating party to unambiguously identify the transaction. Good to have as search criteria since users can easily find a transaction with it.
Transaction	Transaction Identification (<TxId>)	It is generated by the Debtor bank, to unambiguously identify the transaction. Good to have as search criteria since users can easily find a transaction with it.
Transaction	Remittance information (<RmtInf>)	It is generated by the creditor and communicated to the debtor to put in his payment order or just indicated by the debtor for the creditor.
Transaction	Transaction status	Status of the transaction assigned by the payment engine after processing: rejected, processed, pending, on hold … It depends on the status of the order. A transaction is automatically rejected if the corresponding order is rejected.
Transaction	Original transaction key	This is available in R-transactions only. It provides for example the transaction key of the original credit transfer related to a return.
…	…	…

Table 7-1 : Fields generally visible on the payment engine GUI

As we see, many fields displayed on the screen do not come from the standard SEPA messages but from the payment engine. The keys (message key, order key and transaction key) generated by the payment engine are used to uniquely identify the message, its orders and transactions. Reception dates and statuses are important to see at what time the payment was received and what happened during its processing. Other fields like requested execution date, creditor accounts, amounts or end to end identification are useful when there is a need to search for a customer order or transaction.

The payment order management and the payment exchange applications support different processes and activities of the payment processing value chain. Even if the fields displayed on the related applications screens are almost the same, there are some slight differences that really matter to end users. In the order management, end users are particularly interested in customer orders. They want to find the relevant information to serve their customers effectively. On the payment exchange side, the interest is more on the exchange of payments with the CSM and other banks. There users do not work with customer orders, but with interbank messages which usually contain transactions from different customer orders. So end users see the same payment information from different angles because payment order management and the payment exchange are different processes. Let us illustrate that with the pain.001 and pacs.008 messages.

The pain.001, which is used in the payment order management, is a three levels message received from corporate customers. The requested execution date field is crucial to customers and should be displayed on the screen. If the requested execution date is changed for any reason, it is important for the bank users to be aware of it. So the (real) execution date should be on the screen as well or provided through other means (History messages for example). There are other fields that customers care a lot about. A customer which sets the instruction priority to high expects the order to be processed with higher priority. The category purpose and amount of an order may impact the way that order is processed. The creditor IBAN and BIC reveal if the beneficiary bank is located in the same country or in another SEPA country.

This information sometimes impacts the way transactions are processed and/or reported to customers. Since end to end identification and remittance information can be used to identify a transaction uniquely, users like to see their values if they are provided by the customer. The transaction settlement dates, even though not included in the standard pain.001, are often set after the successful execution of the order. All the above mentioned fields contain precious information for the customers as well as for the bank users. They are almost always displayed on the order management application screens.

The pacs.008, the vehicle for the interbank exchange of SEPA credit transfers, is a two level message with message and transaction levels. It does not contain the requested execution date field, but the settlement date that end users first look at when they analyze transactions. Another key message element in the pacs.008 is the transaction identification that is generated by debtor banks to uniquely identify each transaction at interbank level. The end users like to see it on the GUI. Debtor BIC and IBAN, amounts and creditor BIC and IBAN contain useful information for the users as well. End to end identification and remittance information may not be displayed on the payment exchange application screens. They are not as important in the payment exchange as in the order management. The BICs are of particular interest. At interbank level, banks examine what other banks do and if they apply the SEPA rules correctly. And this can influence some decisions in regards to the processing of transactions to or from these specific BICs or banks. So end users look at the information in Pain.001 and Pacs.008 messages from different angles because their interests are not the same.

At this stage, we see that knowing what is displayed on the GUI for each message type is essential. Otherwise, it will be very difficult to connect the dots and really get the insight required to diagnose and resolve queries and issues. Things can be confusing when you have a two levels message which is mapped and displayed in three levels on the GUI. I always request people I work with to study the messages handled in their projects and make the link between the ISO 20022 message elements and what is displayed on the GUI screen. In general, they make interesting discoveries and things become clearer. I strongly recommend you, dear reader, to do the same if you want to deepen this topic☺. For that purpose, you need to read the ISO 20022 documentation of the messages and your project GUI specifications. Then prepare and input own data that you have created and can identify without ambiguity and see how and where they are displayed on the screens. It will then become clear which fields at which level in the payment message are mapped into which field in the payment engine.

To conclude this paragraph, let me share one last point from my own experience. It happens that payment operators see only part of the messages / files coming from corporate customers. Customers send pain.001 files. But the complete message with orders and transactions may not be visible by payment operators because it is splitted into orders in the acquisition platform and only individual orders are forwarded to the payment engine. If something goes wrong during the message level processing, the message may remain stuck in the acquisition platform. Payment operators, who often deal with the customers, may not be aware of it. If a customer calls and complains about a particular file he has sent, it is not right to say to him there is nothing in the payment engine so nothing was received. The operators must be able to see what happens before or refer the customer to another service (The first option is better and customer friendly☺). This has to be taken into account when creating work instructions. Things are much easier when payment operators can see file and message level information in the payment engine. They are informed faster and can act quicker if something goes wrong. The GUI is much more than just screens on which information is displayed. It is a tool that should help operators to work efficiently and best serve the bank customers. One interesting topic when we talk about efficiency is how original transactions and R-transactions are displayed on the GUI.

7.2.3 Original transactions and R-transactions on the GUI

Original transactions are credit transfers or r-transactions which can themselves have a related transaction as we see on the following figure.

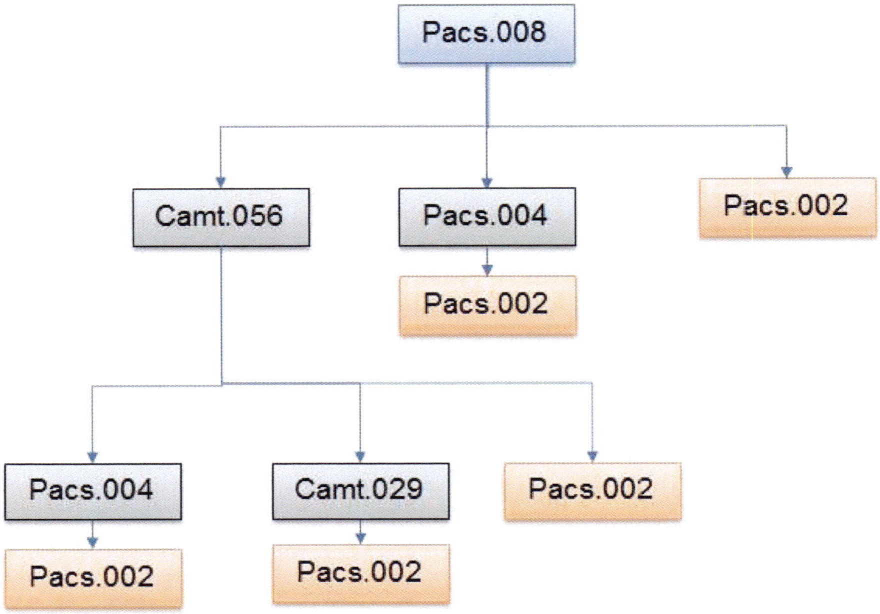

Figure 7.3: Original transactions and related transactions

The pacs.008 stands out. It is the transaction which directly or indirectly "gives birth" to all the other transactions. In contrary to pacs.008, R-transactions cannot exist by themselves. They are initiated or received as result of exception handlings on an original transaction. The camt.056, pacs.004 and camt.029 are R-transactions which can themselves "give birth" to other R-transactions. The response to a camt.056 is either a pacs.004 FOCR or a camt.029. Any transaction (except the pacs.002) can "gives birth" to a pacs.002 if it is rejected for a technical or functional reason.

When an R-transaction is processed, the payment engine tries to reconcile it with the original transaction it relates to. Original transaction information in the r-transaction is used for that purpose. Since the processing of an R-transaction may impact the original transaction status, the users want to easily identify and access related original transactions through the GUI.

If a user has to manually find out which original transaction relates to an r-transaction or vice versa, it will be quite cumbersome. He must first find out what the original transaction information of the r-transaction is. Then he must copy and keep that information somewhere. After that, he has to make a search to find out the transactions in the systems which have it as transaction information. Doesn't that sound pretty lengthy and complicated? This is called manual reconciliation and it is not an option. There is a much easier way to find original transactions and make the users really happy: the hyperlinks.

Hyperlinks can be used to link original transactions and R-transactions. When the payment engine reconciles an R-transaction successfully, it can create hyperlinks from the R-transaction to the original transaction and from the original transaction to the R-transaction. The text to display as hyperlink is the *original transaction key* on the R-transaction screen and the *r-transaction key* on the original transaction screen. The hyperlinks are highlighted on the (r-) transaction screens and a user can easily navigate from an r-transaction screen to an original transaction screen and vice versa. He just needs to click on the hyperlinks. This is very easy to use. Moreover the user can rely with confidence on the reconciliations made by the payment engine and does not have to perform any manual reconciliation. The creation of hyperlinks between transactions drastically simplifies end users' lives.

7.3 The user actions

7.3.1 User rights and user roles

User rights determine which actions a particular user is allowed to perform and are closely related to his role and his duties within the Bank. Actions are performed through the GUI on different type of data (Payment data and configuration or static data). They can be classified in two groups: viewing actions and modification actions.

- Viewing actions consist in accessing the data without making any modification on it. The user is allowed to see the data, but he cannot change it or alter it in any way.

- Modification actions are about updating or deleting an existing data or creating new data. Data is changed during the process and set to a value or moved to a state that the user wants.

User rights are all permissions or authorizations given to users that enable them to access and perform actions through the GUI or not. They can be seen as the set of functions that can be carried out and the data that can be accessed through each function.

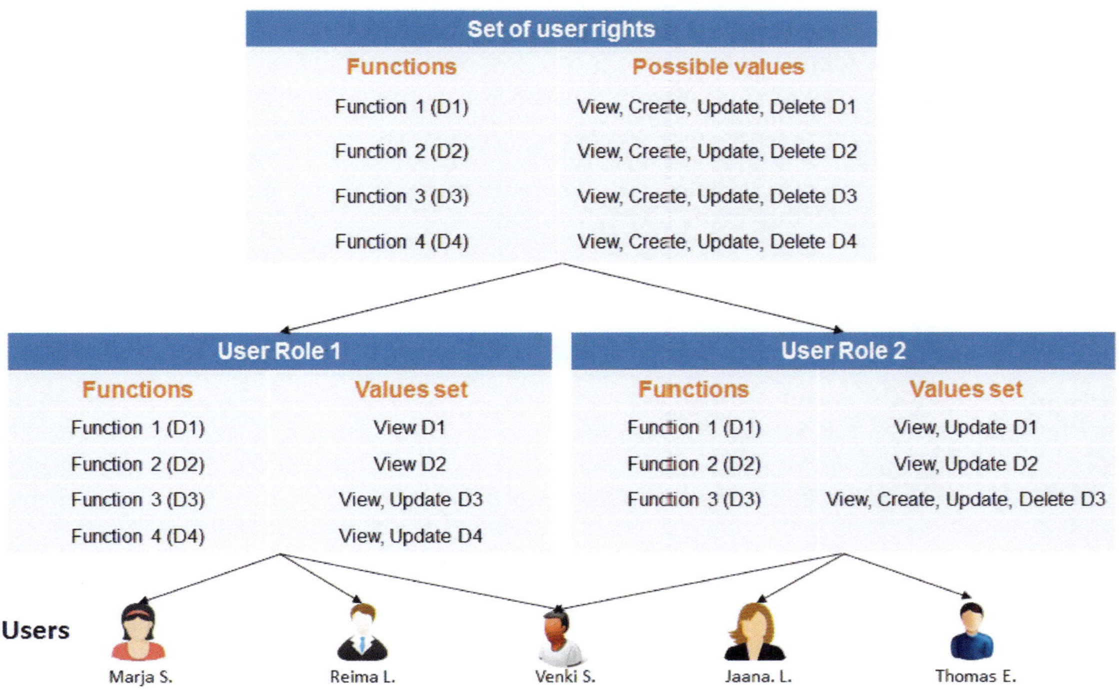

User roles (sometimes called user profiles) are derived from user rights. To create a user role, the functions that the role can perform must be defined as well as the data it can access. At least one user role must be associated to one user. Otherwise, the payment engine would not "know" and control what actions the user is allowed to do. Many user roles can be associated to the same user. She / He must then choose a role to connect to the payment engine GUI if the combination of profiles is not supported. The combination of many profiles allows the user to perform actions that all profiles together can do. If the combination of profiles is not possible, the user will have to logout from a profile and connect with the profile allowing him to do what he would like to do. Finally the same user role can be associated to many users. These users then have the same rights and can do exactly the same actions on the GUI.

User roles and indirectly user rights are the foundation upon which Role-Based Access Control (RBAC) is built. RBAC objective is to restrict system access to authorized users only. The user roles are loaded in the user session, when the user logs into the application. Menu and sub menu items are filtered according to the user role, so that the user sees only the items / functions that he can perform. In this context, a session is an interactive information interchange or dialogue between a computer and user. The session is established when the user logs in to the payment engine GUI, and then torn down at some later point when he logs out. A session is typically stateful, meaning that a party involved in the communication must save information about the session history in order to be able to communicate smoothly, as opposed to stateless communication, where the communication happens with independent requests and responses.

Let's take an example to be more concrete. Let's say a user role indicates that an associated user can access payment data only. When he logs into the system, the menu items related to payment data will be displayed on the GUI. The menu items related to configuration management and other subjects will not be visible under his menu. For payment data, the user role contains specific restriction about what the user can or cannot do like the following:

- Message: no action allowed (no view, no create, no update, no delete)
- Order: view and update action allowed (no create, no delete)
- Transaction: view and update actions allowed (no create, no delete).

Since the user is not allowed to perform any action on messages, the submenu item related to messages is not visible to him. However, the submenu item related to orders is visible since his role allows him to view and update the orders. But the user is not able to create or delete any order. At last, the sub menu item related to transactions is visible to him since his role allows to view transactions. He can also repair transactions or perform actions to update transaction information. But creating or deleting transactions is not possible. The role information is loaded and kept in the session during the communication between user and the Payment Engine through the GUI. It is used to control access to payment information. The same principle applies to configuration data and other type of information.

The structure of the menu items generally impacts the way the user role information is organized and structured. As we saw above, the same application can be used to handle Debtor Bank and Creditor Bank payments. There are two options: 1) the same menu items can be used for both Debtor and Creditor banks. Or 2) you may have specific menu items for Debtor Bank and specific menu items for Creditor Bank. In the first case, viewing a transaction would mean viewing Debtor Bank and Creditor Bank transactions. In the second case, it must be specifically indicated in the role if a user is allowed to see Debtor Bank transactions only or Creditor Bank transactions only or both.

In conclusion, user rights is a crucial subject. Keep in mind that when you talk about GUI, you are implicitly bringing the user rights and roles in the scope of your project. A GUI always implies different categories of users with different profiles that must be implemented and tested accordingly. The impact of user rights on a project is substantial both in terms of cost and quality and therefore that topic must be handled very carefully.

7.3.2 The search

The search is certainly the most used feature on the GUI. It is required to find specific payment messages, orders, transactions or other information among thousands or even millions. For that, the user must input search criteria and launch the search. A search criterion can be any payment information as long as it is stored in table columns, which usually are themselves part of relational databases[15].

If we consider the building blocks of a pain.001 message for example, almost all message elements can be used as search criteria. In the Group Header (Message level), message identification, creation date and time, number of transactions, initiating party, etc. can be used as search criteria. In the Payment Information (Order level), payment information identification, payment method, debtor account, debtor agent, requested execution date, etc. can be used as search criteria. In the Transaction Information (Transaction level), instruction identification, end-to-end identification, amount, Creditor Agent, Creditor account, etc. can also be used as search criteria. In addition, we saw above that payment engines generate internal information like message internal identification and status, order internal identification and status, transaction internal identification and status among others. And they can also be used as search criteria.

Although almost every field can be used as search criteria, it is not effective to use them all. Putting all possible fields on a screen as search criteria is not a good approach. We need to find out the key fields or message elements that really matter for the search and limit the search criteria to them. It is quite easy to identify some of them. Debtor and creditor accounts, debtor and creditor BICs, the requested execution date of the order, the transaction end-to-end identification and the different statuses are the usual suspects. But sometimes, a message element which is not even mandatory in SEPA can play an important role for a bank and has to be used as search criterion. If a bank uses the category purpose code to identify and apply specific services to corporate customers, that field become important and can be used a search criteria. The end users need that information to diagnose and fix potential issues and so they appreciate to be able to search with it.

Finding out the right search criteria requires a good understanding of how the information is used. Therefore the end users from various business units should be involved in the design of search screens.

The picture below depicts the different steps of a search in a payment engine.

---

[15] A relational database is a collection of data items organized as a set of tables with rows and columns from which data can be accessed or reassembled in many different ways without having to reorganize the database tables. It was invented by Edgar Frank Codd at IBM in 1970.

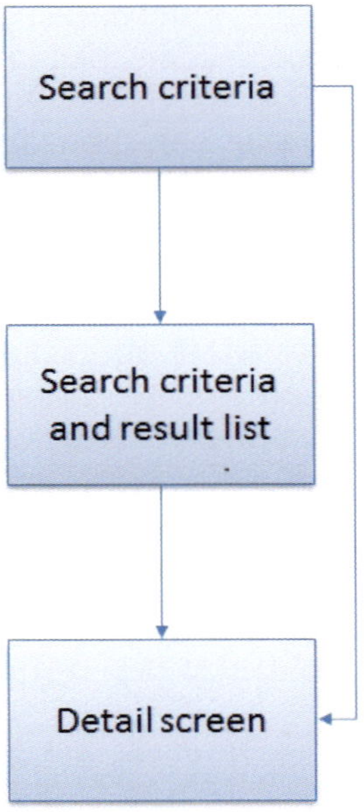

Figure 7.4: Generic search steps

The user inputs search criteria on the search criteria screen. After a search, payment messages, orders or transactions which match the criteria are retrieved from the payment engine database and displayed on the screen generally as a list. The result can also be a detailed screen of a message, order or transaction if it was the unique result of the search. When the search result is a list, it is recommended to display the results below the search criteria. The user can then immediately compare the criteria and the results. And if the search does not work well, it helps to find out what is wrong.

The result list of a search should contain enough information to help the user in his quest. This is very useful when the user does not know precisely what he is looking for. Consider a corporate customer who sends hundreds of transactions daily. He instructs the bank in a branch to send a recall for one specific transaction. He remembers the amount of the transaction and that it was sent seven days ago to a Danish bank. He does not have the transaction details with him. After a first search, multiple transactions with the same amount are displayed for that particular day. Fortunately the BICs are also displayed on the list of search result and there is only on creditor BIC with the country code DK. The operator can find out which transaction should be recalled. This shows that choosing which data to display on a result list is important. When doing this exercise, one should always ask himself which information is more likely to be used by the end user.

Payment engines software are in general equipped with a standard GUI designed by the vendors who decided which search criteria to have on the GUI. Vendors tend to put quite many search criteria on the GUI probably with the rationale that it is good thing to sell their product. The experience shows that some of those search criteria are not really required for particular implementations. They are on the standard GUI because they were designed in other context and for other purposes many years ago. In addition, some search criteria are duplicates of others in the sense that they will lead to the same search results if the one or the other is used. And finally, users will never use some search criteria either because they are not really needed or because they don't know what it means (or it is difficult for them to remember what it means).

As conclusion to this paragraph, here is a list of tips and suggestions about search screens:

- Take the search criteria one by one and make sure you understand what each of them really means.
- If a search criterion is not required for your implementation, ask the vendor to remove it from the screen. End users will not have to ask themselves every time they come over it what it is and how it can be used. Precious time will be saved.
- If a search criterion is a duplicate of the other, it is preferable to remove it from the screen. It will help you to reduce the complexity. Keep things simple.
- If you find out later that a search criterion you requested is not needed, it is preferable to remove it from the screens. Sometimes you will not know upfront if a search criterion is really needed or not. You have to observe how users make searches and if possible measure it. It will then be easier to decide if the criterion should be kept or removed. Remove a criterion every time you can. Keep things simple.
- Make search with many relevant criteria at the same time and ensure yourself that it works. The more criteria you have in a search screen the more complex it becomes. The number of combinations increases exponentially with the number of search criteria. And the experience shows that trying all possible combinations does not really make sense. It is better to focus on combinations that really matters. When you have identified the relevant combinations, you need to be sure that it really works. One way to do that is to make queries 1) directly to the database and 2) through the GUI and then compare the results of both. They should be the same of course.

7.3.3 The worklist items (WLI)

Many exceptions can occur during the payment processing at message, order or transaction level. When an exception occurs, someone must examine it and when possible take some actions to fix the problem. This is where worklist items come into play. They are lists of work items that users have to do on payments with exceptions or issues.

A worklist item, as its name indicates, requires a payment operator to perform an action. That action can be done inside or outside the payment engine. When the action is carried out in the payment engine, it is called an *actionable WLI*. If the action has to be executed outside the payment engine, it is an *informational WLI*. In the second case, the information provided in the WLI is the trigger of a procedure to execute with another tool outside the payment engine. For each WLI, it must be clearly defined what has to be done, by whom, when, with which tool, etc. These are the procedures that the operators should follow to handle the different items on their worklists. In summary, each worklist item, actionable or informational, requires actions to be taken.

Payment engines process millions of payments but end users are not interested in all of them. In fact, the time would not be enough to look at each transaction. Consider a bank group which sends and receives about 1 000 000 transactions a day. If one transaction can be viewed in one second, then around 278 h (=1 000 000 / 3600 s) would be needed for one million transactions. This means around 35 people working 8 hours a day just for viewing the transactions. The cost is huge and not acceptable for such a non-value added task. That is the reason why end users only view the transactions for which an exception was raised during the processing and on which they have to take some actions. Missing even one of those orders or transactions can have serious consequences for the bank and for its customers. The users must see and act on them. Now the question is how do they find those payments? The answer is very simple. The users do not and should not have to look for them. The payment engine itself “finds” them and pushes them to the users.

The worklist items must be pushed to users, so that they don’t need to make any search to get them. Searchs can be made only to refine WLI list but not to see them. WLI are selected by the payment engine itself and displayed to users. That is very practical and convenient. Letting the users search for messages, orders or transactions with exceptions, increases the operational risk. Since search screens are in general specific to messages, orders or transactions, a user will have to go to many places to find all the WLI he is looking for. And someday for sure they will forget to input a search criterion or to make a specific search and some worklist items will be "forgotten". Automatic selection of all WLI by the payment engine and direct push to the users is an excellent way to increase operational efficiency and mitigate the operational risk.

Since worklist items are pushed, it is important during the implementation to ensure yourself that all payments messages, instructions or transactions that have to be in the WLI are really there. Take the time to study their life cycles and understand the types of exception that may occur during their processing. After that, list the cases that from your point of view should be on the WLI. And then compare with what the vendor says should be on the WLI and what is really displayed on the WLI. You may sometimes be quite surprised by the results. Vendors provide worklist items in their own GUI, based on their own view of what should be displayed there. Search criteria for the WLI are therefore built upon the standard implementation. However most of the time, the bank asks vendors to develop specific features and this leads to adding other information and statuses to the Payment engine. Checking that the WLI takes those specificities into account is crucial. Do not just rely only on the vendor to do it. Do it yourself or make sure a skilled and experienced Business Analyst in your team does it.

7.3.3.1 Prioritization of worklist items

Now that we have ensured that all worklist items are displayed on the WLI screen, we need to work on the *prioritization*. Obviously the items on the worklist are processed with different types of actions which have different levels of priorities. Some items have to be handled immediately, some the same day, some in one or multiple days and so on. It depends on many parameters like the type of orders / transactions, the reception time, the requested execution date, the customer agreements, etc.

Let us consider the example of a pain.001 message that the bank receives on a day which is the same as the requested execution date. If one or more orders received in the pain.001 message go to the WLI, the payment operators have to handle them before the cut-off of the day. Otherwise the requested execution date cannot be kept and the customer won't be happy. The bank must take into account the time that might be required to handle potential exceptions when it communicates a cut-off time to a customer. That is why the cut-off time communicated to customers is in general hour(s) ahead of the CSM cut-off time.

Here is another example. This time it is another customer who sends his orders on the same day but with a requested execution date one month in the future. If orders go to the WLI, they don't have to be handled on the same day. An operator can take actions on them one or several days in the future since the requested execution date is in one month. These orders should not appear on top of the list of WLI.

Cancellation requests received by a creditor bank do not need to be handled right away. The Bank has 10 business days to reply. Therefore it is OK if the cancellation requests are not on the top of the list of WLI. If we consider a credit transfer to return by a creditor bank, doing it one day after reception is also fine since the bank has up to three business days to return the funds.

So the above examples illustrate that WLI have different level of priorities. Payment operators appreciate when the WLI are classified according to the priorities. They can see what WLI should be handled first and by what time a particular WLI must be completed. Search criteria on the WLI screens which enable operators to filter the WLI by type, priorities, amounts, time to cut-off, etc. are also very useful.

Payment operators are usually part of a team led by a team manager. For the manager, it is important to have an overview of all WLI at a specific point in time sorted by priorities as well. The team lead can then allocate resources to the most important tasks to perform before a given deadline.

The key take-away is that end users truly care about prioritized Work List Items. But finding the right priority for each WLI is not always a trivial task and regularly depends on the bank's specific needs. That is why the end users must be involved in the prioritization workshops, if you want to make the right things right. ☺

7.3.3.2 Messages on the worklist items

Another key topic for worklist items is the information displayed to users on the screen. The following question should be considered carefully: *Can the user easily understand what the message means and therefore what he is supposed to do?*

Working with the assumption that users have very little time to handle a worklist item is a good approach. Users should not spend more time than necessary to analyze a WLI and decide what to do. The messages that they see should be straight forward to them. When a user starts to think about what a message really means, it is not a good sign. Of course, this is not totally avoidable but couple of actions can be undertaken to prevent it.

Proper and adequate trainings are to be provided to each user. Do not assume that things are easy and the users can manage on their own. People should not discover WLI when they are in work situations. They should be trained on the WLI before. It is not about a mere presentation on Powerpoint. Presentations and documentations are important and should be prepared carefully. But do not neglect the practice. Users should practice, practice and practice. The more they practice, the more they will read and understand about what they do and the more confident they will become.

Since we all tend to forget quite rapidly, it is better to have WLI messages that are as clear as possible and that will not lead end users to (mis)interpretations and wrong decisions. In case they have questions, they should be able to rapidly access the documents where they can find the answers, ideally in less than two minutes when they are in work situations. A best practice is to have the list of all the possible WLI messages available in a specific document, a workbook for example where you can find references to procedures or other resources which contain detailed information about what needs to be done. A user can then easily find a message and the link to related documentation through a search in the workbook. And this can be done in less than one minute.

If users have received adequate trainings, all messages on WLI are as clear as they can possibly be and the work instructions can be found rapidly when needed, then all conditions are met for users to make good decisions and keep the customers and the bank happy.

7.3.4 Audit log or audit trail - Logging of actions

The Payment Engine is behaving in a very strange way. There was no new delivery. Nevertheless, the orders and transactions are not being processed as expected anymore. But everything was fine just an hour ago. What happened? How to find it out? This is where the audit log comes into play. It enables to see which parameter has been modified, what was the previous value, who did it, when it happened and so on.

The audit log is a file or a database table where all user events occurring in the Payment Engine are recorded. Remember that a user can view, modify, delete or create data. All actions performed by users on the GUI are logged into the audit log. This is done for regulatory, operational and security reasons. Keeping the history of what happened on the data is crucial not only to fix potential problems that users may have mistakenly caused, but also more generally to find out what specific actions the users have performed on payment data or static data in the payment engine. In many countries there exists a regulatory requirement to keep the audit logs during a determined period of time.

Payment transactions contain sensitive data like names, addresses, account numbers, amounts and remittance information. The analysis of payment records of a particular customer can tell quite a lot about him: his place of residence, his purchasing habits, his family and so on. If a user takes the illicit habit to view payment data of a customer, the audit log can help to find it out. If a user takes an incorrect decision on an order, the audit log can help to find it out also. The presence of an audit trail can deter ill-intentioned users.

The audit log can be accessible through the Payment Engine GUI directly or the payment engine can feed an external system with audit log information as we will see in the next chapter. In the first case, that feature should be available to users with high privileges. And no need to say that it should not be possible to edit or delete audit log records from the GUI.
In summary, the audit log allows to record and keep user actions on the GUI while complying with regulatory requirements.

7.3.5 Settings and parameters management

Simply put, a payment engine is a computer program that runs with specific settings and parameters. Assigning values to the settings and parameters in such a way that it fits the needs of the Bank operating the payment engine is an important part of any implementation project. Several people in a project can be dedicated only to that activity. While doing it, it is crucial to take into account how settings and parameters will be managed in production. Following questions must be answered:

- Who will (not) have access to which parameters and settings for view?
- Who will (not) have access to which parameters and settings for modification?
- Which parameters and settings can (not) be changed directly through the GUI?

The answers to the first two questions may determine how the parameters are going to be grouped and displayed on the GUI if you are building a custom solution. If the users do not have to move through many menus and pages to see the parameters they are looking for, precious time will be saved in the long run. With regards to the last question, it is sometimes overlooked during projects. And this leads to an unnecessary high dependency toward the payment engine vendor because one realizes quite late that even the tiny change in parameters requires a new delivery from the vendor. By asking yourself these questions early in the project, you can challenge the vendor and ask him to make some parameters editable through the GUI directly, so that no delivery will be needed in case their values must be changed in operating conditions.

The list of settings and parameters is pretty long: Exchange partners, routing rules, calendars, cut-offs, exception handlers, settlement date calculation, etc. Setting the correct values for a bank is a real challenge. This is particularly the case when the values of certain parameters depend on each other. For the implementation, we must ensure that settings and parameters reflect the customer needs. Receiving training from the vendor and reading his documentation to understand the product is essential. And also you have to talk to the Bank's subject matter experts (SMEs) to understand their needs and requirements. But this is only the beginning. Settings and parameters are of multiple types and used for multiple purposes. It is important to distinguish between what is functional and what is technical. Then for each setting or parameter, you must fully grasp the impact any change will have and eventually who is going to make it. At time the definition of technical and functional parameter should be clarified because vendor and customer do not always understand it the same way. Changing a "technical" parameter may have functional impacts and changing a "functional" parameter may have technical impacts.

When implementing a new payment engine, users tend to decide who is going to manage which parameters based on the current processes and what they are used to. This can become quite heavy if users absolutely want to keep their old way of doing things. They can go as far as requiring the vendor to implement new features or adapt existing features to their own processes. Be careful not to fall into that trap. Challenge the users and ask them to explain the reasons behind their choices. It should not be only because that is how they have been doing things. Leveraging the new possibilities and opportunities offered by the payment engine should be considered also. Most of the time, it is less costly to accept the standard implementation of vendor than to modify or add functionalities.

Settings and parameters management is a team work. Bringing vendor experts and functional and technical teams together yield interesting results. The goal should be to keep the things as simple as possible for the teams who are going to run and maintain the payment platform.

7.4 The 3270 screens

Globally, many banks continue to rely on legacy IT systems that were implemented in the 1980s and 1990s. As a consequence, payment engines running on 3270[16] mainframe applications (or similar) are still in use in banks' back offices and front offices. The 3270 screens were invented long before the Web technologies became widespread. Therefore their design is grounded on different principles. They are not as powerful as Web technologies which enable end-users to experience an intuitive navigation and greatly assist them in data entry. Since many banks still run their payment business with the 3270 applications, it is worth looking at the issues and challenges faced by end-users in those contexts. That is the aim of this paragraph.

The 3270 screens pose three main issues that will be analyzed in detail in the rest of this paragraph:

1. The unintuitive navigation between the different menus and pages of the application
2. The limited information that can be displayed on one page screen
3. The most often non-existing or incomplete documentation

Let us now consider the first issue on our list: the unintuitive navigation. Navigation is about moving from one menu item to another or from one page to another in an application. If you have ever used 3270 screens, I am sure it took you some time to get used to it. You have to learn the keyboard commands to move inside the application. Even if you can use the mouse to do few things, you need to combine it with keyboard commands because it does not allow you to do everything. And since there are no hyperlinks available on 3270 screens, the user mostly moves through the pages by going back and forth between the different menu and sub-menu items. This can take some time, particularly for new users. Furthermore, the 3270

---

[16] A 3270 screen is a non-graphical text only monochrome black screen with green/white letters display.

screens flow may constitute a big productivity hurdle when you work on r-transactions. The navigation from an r-transaction to an original transaction or from an r-transaction to another r-transaction can be complex, again because there is no hyperlink. If it is poorly designed, the user may have to find an original transaction reference of the credit transfer, copy it and use it to search all the related r-transactions. Keyboard shortcuts are of great help to move faster. This brings me to make the following suggestion: learning the keyboard shortcuts by heart is a good way to increase your speed and efficiency when you work with 3270 screens. It can be very difficult at the beginning but pays off if you persist. I have seen people who can work faster on 3270 pages than on Web page because they master the shortcuts very well after a lot of practice of course.

The second issue is about the very limited amount of information that is displayed on a 3270 screen compared to a Web page. SEPA payments contain a lot of information and one page of 3270 screen is not sufficient to display them all. Message elements like the remittance information have up to 140 characters, names and address lines up to 70 characters. Ultimate debtor and ultimate creditor information take up much space as well. Therefore what to display and how to organize transactions information on screens must be thought of carefully. If transaction information is displayed on two screens or more, put the most important message elements on the first one. Message elements like debtor name, debtor account, creditor name, creditor account, creditor BIC, execution date, amount and the identifications, are in general sufficient for the operators when they are analyzing a transaction. Those key message elements should be put on the first screen. The users would then not need to navigate between many pages to find important information. Precious time is saved when we consider the number of transactions operators have to handle during a week, a month or a year. The tip here is the following: for the information to display on screens, consider in priority what really matters to operational people and ensure they are easily accessible. For each message element available on the screen, it must be clear why it has been chosen and not another one. Do not display message elements that are not necessary to diagnose and solve potential problems.

The last issue - but not least - is the non-existing or incomplete documentation. 3270 applications have been around for decades. Project teams that worked on their initial implementation are not in the bank anymore. There is no documentation available or the initial documentation is not up-to-date anymore because it was not updated with the evolutions carried out during the years. It is almost impossible to get an overview of the application features and functionalities. Users come and go and work on a piece of the application. They get the training orally and by observing what others do on the screens to handle worklist items for example. In these conditions, the knowledge transfer is a real challenge. And this lack of knowledge leads to many operational mistakes and issues. On 3270 screens, operators usually take decisions with codes like 1, 2, A, B, Y, N, etc. Confirmation messages are not always shown after an action. As a result, users are not always fully aware of the consequences their decisions may have. I will tell you an experience with regards to this.

Once I was consultant for a bank where operators were using a 3270 screen to handle WLI. Two decisions with codes 0 or 1 could be taken on credit transfer that had arrived on a closed, non-existent or incorrect account. The meanings of the decision were the following:

- 0: Correct the creditor account, so that money is credited on the corrected account
- 1: Correct the creditor account, so that money is credited on the corrected account; but in addition inform the debtor that the creditor account has changed by sending him a CAI (CAI is explained in paragraph 3.5.1).

Some of the operators knew that they could use 0 or 1 to correct the creditor account, but very little knew what the difference really was and therefore were using 0 or 1 randomly.

Here are some tips to address the challenges mentioned above: Be extremely careful with the training provided to the end users on 3270 applications. Ensure that they understand each decision taken on the screen and their consequences. Document the training (WORD or PPT document), so that users can consult it again and again when needed. It is also recommended to document the application retroactively whenever possible.

The challenges posed by 3270 screen are many, but can all be overcome. Learning keyboard shortcuts, making application information easily accessible, training the end-users carefully and documenting the application, are recipes that work.

Review Questions

- How are navigation menus structured?
- There is an excellent way to link original transactions and transactions on the GUI. Describe it and explain why it is so practical for the end users
- Describe the typical actions users perform on a GUI. How are user roles and profiles used to control them?
- Explain what Worklist Items are and why they so important.
- Explain what audit trail (also called audit log) is. For what purpose is it used?
- Explain what settings and parameters are used for.
- What makes the use of 3270 screens difficult?

Discussion Questions

- Is there a best way to structure the navigation menu of Payment Engine GUI? Give your arguments
- The search complexity increases with the number of criteria. How to master and manage that complexity?
- Is it possible to implement a payment engine without Worklist Items? Give your arguments
- There are many things happening during the payment processing that are not visible on the GUI. What do you think about this statement?
- The 3270 screen are still pretty widely used. Why? How to deal with the challenges they bring?
- The use of 3270 screens does not have only drawbacks. Could you list some advantages it brings? Explain why you see things like that.

Chapter 8 The payment engines in the Bank IT landscape

LEARNING OBJECTIVES

After reading this chapter, you will be able to answer the following questions:

1. What is an Interface? What different types of interfaces exist?
2. What is the difference between synchronous and asynchronous messaging?
3. What is the difference between batch and transactional modes?
4. What are the typical surrounding systems of a payment processing application?
5. What are the typical surrounding systems of a payment exchange platform?

The Bank IT landscape consists of tens to even hundreds of IT applications and systems. Payments Engines are generally part of a rather complex Bank's IT architecture because payment processing relies on services and functions implemented in many applications other than the payment engine. Calling services implemented in other applications requires building interfaces. File exchanges between a payment engine and a surrounding system happen through interfaces. A payment processing application gets payment messages from the channels, relies on an external system to perform the balance check, the screening or archiving of transactions. Thus interfaces play a crucial role. You may wonder what they are. This chapter first provides a presentation of the different types of interfaces. In the second part, surrounding systems of a payment engine and their interfaces are considered.

8.1 Introduction to interfaces

Interfaces are the means through which either two distinct applications or a human and an application exchange information. The previous chapter was about human-to-application interactions (GUI). This chapter is more about the exchange of information between applications. There are many types of interfaces as we will see later. But they are all used for the same purpose which is the information exchange. When you analyze an interface, it is important to understand which information is exchanged. But apart from that, two questions to answer are:

- Is the interface working in batch or transactional mode?
- Is the interface using synchronous or asynchronous messaging?

The next paragraphs will explain what synchronous and asynchronous messaging are as well as batch and transactional modes.

8.1.1 Synchronous and asynchronous messaging

Synchronous messaging describes information exchange between two applications or systems where both parties work simultaneously in real time. Both applications must be present at the same time for the communication to take place. The sending application (also called client) waits for a reply from the receiving application (also called the server) and cannot initiate a new communication until it gets the reply. If there is message queue between the two applications, then one application places a message in the message queue and then waits for a (message) response from the other application before it continues processing.

A good example to illustrate a synchronous messaging is the classic telephone call with traditional landline telephone system. When you make a phone call, the other party must answer your call for the communication to happen. And while you are calling, your line is busy if someone else is trying to reach you and you cannot initiate a new call. And the same applies to the other party. When it takes your call, nobody else can build a communication with it and it cannot start a new call. You see that both parties must be in the communication at the same time. And both are blocked during the communication. When the caller starts the call, he is blocked until the receiver accepts it and also during the conversation that follows. And when the receiver accepts the call, he is also blocked until the conversation ends.

Synchronous messaging requires both the sender (payment engine) and receiver (surrounding applications) to be available at the same time during the message exchange. After sending a request pertaining to a specific transaction, the processing of that transaction is blocked until the response is received from the surrounding application. Resources are consumed to set up the communication and send the request. They are released only after getting the response.

Synchronous messaging is a two way communication. Sender sends a message to receiver and waits around until it gets a reply. Therefore it is used for example, when it is required to get a reply from a surrounding system *right away* before carrying on with the payment processing.

Now let us look at asynchronous messaging. Asynchronous messaging describes information exchange between two applications or systems where one application places a message in a *message queue* and does not need to wait for a reply from the other application to continue processing. The parties taking part in the message exchange do not have to be present at the same time. The messaging will complete successfully even if the receiving party is not available at all. Unlike synchronous messaging, resources are not blocked, they are consumed just to send/receive messages.

An example to illustrate asynchronous messaging is the e-mail exchange. You can write and send/reply an e-mail at any time. You do not have to wait until the receiver is ready to communicate. Your message is sent to the receiver's mailbox. And he can access it few seconds, minutes, hours or days later and then replies. Both sender and receiver send the e-mail or reply when they choose to do so independently of the other party. So they are not blocked at all during the communication.

For a payment engine, asynchronous messaging is generally implemented through exchange of messages / files with surrounding systems using technologies like MQ Series or SOAP (Simple Object Access Protocol):

- The Payment Engine creates and sends a request to its (request) queue.
- The receiving system reads its (receiving) queue and fetches the request.
- The receiving system processes the request and writes the reply to its (response) queue.
- The Payment Engine reads its (reply) queue and processes the reply.

Asynchronous messaging enable flexibility and offer higher availability. But it introduces few problems too:

a) Many requests can be sent to the same application before getting a reply. How to match a response to the corresponding request in the Payment Engine?
b) Replies may come in different order as requests were sent (If one request is lost and one takes longer time for example). Same question as above: How to match a response to the corresponding request in the Payment Engine?
c) It is more difficult to guarantee that a reply will be received in the expected timeframe because of many reasons: the request may not reach the surrounding application; or the reply may take longer than expected or even get lost. What to do to avoid this?

As solution to the first two problems a) and b), a mechanism must be in place allowing the Payment Engine to correlate a reply with a request. In general, each request is uniquely identified through an identifier, which must be present in both the request and the reply message.

The next main problem c) is solved most of time through a time-out mechanism. The request may be resent one or multiple times again. In case the reply still does not come after a predetermined period of time, an alert will be generated and sent to someone who can investigate why the reply was not received and take the necessary actions.

In conclusion, do not think synchronous messaging is better than asynchronous messaging. They both have their advantages and drawbacks. It really depend on the situations and what should be achieved. In general if immediacy is crucial, probably synchronous messaging will be preferred. In all other cases, asynchronous messaging will be implemented.

Two other important things to understand about the interfaces are the batch and transactional processing modes.

8.1.2 Batch and transactional modes

An interface can run in batch processing or in transactional[17] processing. The main difference between the two lies in the human intervention during processing. Batch processing (executed in a batch job) is done without manual intervention, while transactional processing can be done with it. By abuse of language, an interface used with batch processing is called batch interface. And the one used with transactional processing is called transactional interface.

Batch interfaces are *non-interactive user interfaces*. All the details of the batch job are specified in advance in the batch processing, and the output is produced only after all the processing is done. There is no prompt for further user input after the processing has started. Batch jobs are planned and executed according to a defined frequency. Many batch jobs run during the night. Batch interfaces mostly use asynchronous messaging with replies in seconds or minutes. But they can also use synchronous messaging.

Transactional interfaces are *interactive user interfaces*. The user uses an interface (graphical or not) to key in data as input for the processing. All the inputs of a transactional program are not known in advance. The user can provide input before and after the execution has started. Response time really matters here since the user wants to see the result of his actions as soon as possible, in few seconds generally. To avoid long response times, transactional interfaces are generally used with synchronous messaging or with very little response time if it is asynchronous.

In conclusion, synchronous and asynchronous messaging should not be mixed up with batch and transactional modes. They all relate to interfaces, but are completely different concepts. Both batch and transactional processing can be used each with synchronous and/or asynchronous messaging.

8.2 Surrounding systems of a Payment Engine

Payment Engines (Payment Order Management applications and Payment exchange applications) interact with many surrounding systems in the bank for the successful processing of payment instructions and transactions. In this paragraph, we will lock at these surrounding

[17] Not the same thing as transaction processing which has a total different meaning. This is the definition provided in Wikipedia: transaction processing is information processing that is divided into individual, indivisible operations called transactions. Each transaction must succeed or fail as a complete unit; it can never be only partially complete.

applications and the functions they implement. We will also see how they communicate with payment engines. Please note that the list of applications presented here is not exhaustive. However, a good overview is provided and this can help you to get acquainted with the main applications you will encounter in your own projects.

First we will present the surrounding systems of a Payment Order Management application. And then the systems that surround a Payment Exchange Platform will be considered. We will explain why we may have same surrounding systems for both payment engines and highlight the differences in the way they interact with the surrounding applications.

8.2.1 Surrounding systems of Payment Order Management application

Payment Order Management (POM) applications are responsible for managing payments orders and transactions for the debtor bank or the creditor bank or both. As discussed in the chapter 4, POM applications can be implemented in many different ways. No matter what the implementation, they will be interfaced with many other applications. We will now consider the functions implemented in those applications, how they interact with the Payment Engine and contribute to the overall payment processing. If you are working on a SEPA project or running a SEPA payment platform, it is a good idea to take your application architecture and check if the applications presented below are present on it or not. And most important, ask yourself how they communicate with the POM and which types of interfaces are used. It will help you to get the most out of this chapter.

The figure below shows the different systems that a POM application can be interfaced with.

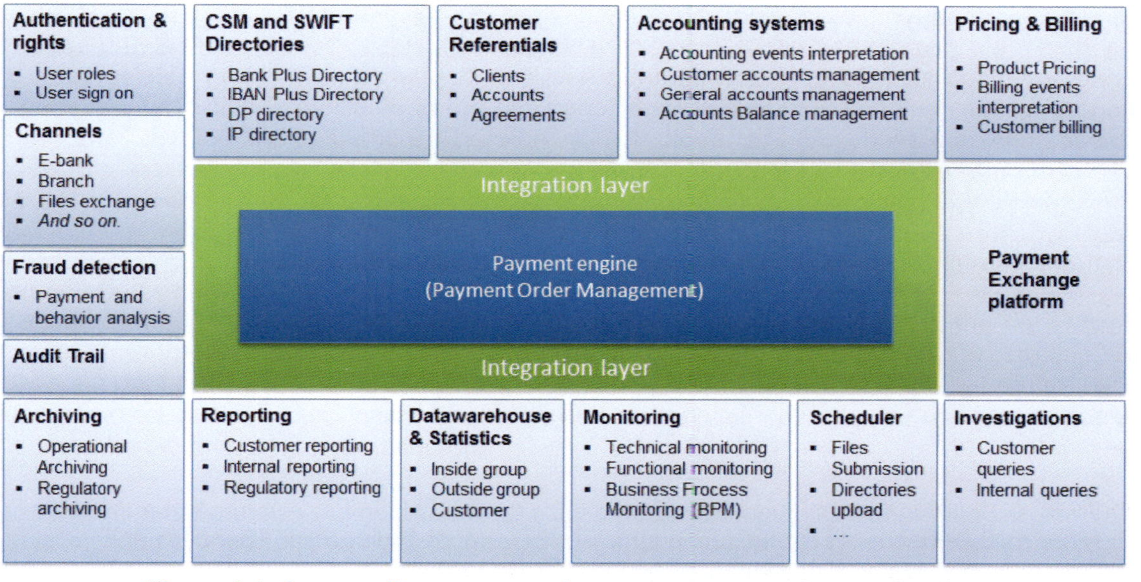

Figure 8.1: Surrounding systems of a payment processing application

The Integration layer plays a crucial role. A good practice is to implement standards across the Bank that all surrounding systems should use to communicate with the payment engine. That specific topic is beyond the scope of this book. Now let us consider each surrounding system.

8.2.1.1 Authentication & rights

Payment engines are equipped with a Graphical User Interface (GUI) which allows users to view payment information and perform other actions. The authentication ensures that the user accessing the GUI is really allowed to do so. The user must be declared and a profile or role must have been linked to her / his account.

The roles are important because users have different needs pertaining to the payment processing. Many users can access the payment engine, but they are not allowed to see the same thing or to perform the same actions. Some users have roles with super power rights like the administrators. They can do almost everything possible on the GUI. And other users have roles with more basic rights like the customer services employees that may only be able to view payments. In between, payment operators have roles allowing them to view and perform actions on payments. The approach consisting of restricting system access to authorized users is known as Role-Based Access Control (RBAC). It is vital in any organization.

In all banks, an employee directory (usually called LDAP) already exists. And as mentioned above, not only the employee must be known and declared, but also the role(s) that he or she uses to access the payment engine must be linked to his identification information. The roles we are talking about are for the payment engine only. But there are many other applications in the Bank with the same needs of rights and authentication. Each application of the bank does not and cannot implement these functions.

Here is the point I want to underscore: Employee directories, applications list and associated user rights are in general centralized and implemented in one or more applications outside the payment engine. And even if some payment engines in the market allow to manage a list of users and associated rights for the payment processing, a bank would generally prefer the payment engine to be interfaced with its own outside applications where those features are centralized. It is the easiest and less costly solution on the long term. Managing the list of users accessing the payment engine in the payment engine itself is not only complex on the long term, but also it makes the payment engine a silo application not integrated with the others. And this is just not acceptable nowadays.

Let us come back to authentication and explain the concept of single sign on. The Authentication process verifies the identity of a person (or a system) and ensures that he is really who he claims to be. Generally a user inputs his login and his password. Sometimes a physical support like a smartcard may be required. A user uses a piece of information (password), a smartcard or a combination of two to authenticate himself. She or he must go through the authentication process before accessing the payment engine or other applications in the bank. In case there is no single sign on, users would have to go through that process every time they need to access a new application. Since a bank has hundreds of applications in the IT landscape, this can be quite cumbersome for the users and a real productivity slowdown.

The Single Sign-On (SSO) is a property of access control of multiple related, but independent software systems. With the SSO a user logs in with a single login and password to gain access to multiple systems with the same username and password. The access to the payment engine with SSO does not happen automatically. A lot of work (configuration and sometimes development) must be done upfront to make it possible. The payment engine must become part of the single sign on in the organization so to speak. And one or more interfaces may be required for that.

After the successful sign in of a user, the payment engine must clearly identify his rights (through his role). The user should be able to do only and only what he is allowed to do. So there must be a logic in the payment engine to control that he is not going beyond his permissions.

8.2.1.2 Channels

The payment orders reach to the bank through the channels. In the chapter 4.1, the different channels used by customers have been presented in detail. If a channel accepts a message or an order, which means that all the controls are successful, the next step is to forward the message or order to the POM application. Thus the Payment Engine must be interfaced with the channels to receive the files coming from them. In general the payment engine sends acknowledgement messages to the channels.

The file exchange happens depending on the technology used for integration:

- A channel creates a file with the payment messages (pain.001 or similar) and put them in a folder where the payment engine consumes it at predefined times, once every two hours for example.
- Or a channel prepares the file with the payment messages and inform the payment engine that it is ready, so that it can fetch it immediately.

This interface is generally implemented with batch jobs using asynchronous messaging.

8.2.1.3 CSM and SWIFT Directories

In the chapter 4.3.2, ACH and SWIFT directories have been presented in detail. I refer you to that section if you want to know more about this topic. The description provided below is at a high level.

SWIFT provides directories[18] with Bank data like BIC Directory or Bank Directory Plus and directories with SEPA data like IBAN Plus and SEPA Plus. The Bank Directory Plus can be used to validate a BIC while the IBAN Plus can be used for IBAN validation, BIC validation and BIC/IBAN coherence checks.

ACH provides directories containing its direct and indirect participants to a SEPA Scheme like the SCT. Payment engines use these directories for routing essentially.

ACH and SWIFT directories are therefore consulted for IBAN and BIC validations and for routing. Uploading them to the payment Engine is logically a prerequisite for the payment processing. Directories are updated by SWIFT and ACH usually with a monthly frequency. The latest versions must be uploaded to the payment engine as soon as possible to avoid issues related to outdated information.

Directories are provided in xml or flat txt files. Batch jobs with asynchronous messaging are executed with the same or higher frequency (than the one at which directories are updated) to upload them to the payment engine. The file is downloaded from SWIFT or ACH and placed in a first directory. We can call it TO PROCESS directory. The payment engine fetches it from the TO PROCESS directory and processes it. After the successful processing, the file is moved to another directory that we can call PROCESSED directory. In some cases, multiple files may be required before the payment engine starts the processing.

8.2.1.4 Customer Referentials

The payment engine accesses customer referentials to perform some checks and enrich the payments. They are mainly three referentials or three groups of referentials (Clients, Accounts and Agreements). The keys to access and retrieve information are the IBANs provided in the payment order and transactions. The IBANs must be accounts hold by the Bank. It can be

---

[18] For those who want to have very detailed information about SWIFT Directories, go the following web sites: https://www.swift.com/our-solutions/compliance-and-shared-services/swiftref

either the debtor or creditor IBAN. Note that other information can be used as keys as well, however it must be possible to derive them from the IBAN or to first retrieve them with the help of the IBAN.

The accounts referential(s) are consulted to check if the account existence and status. An account may exist but be closed or blocked. It is therefore important to retrieve the status.

The client referential(s) are called for the enrichment of customer information like Name, Address, Customer Identification Number, Customer segment or category and so on. They typically provide the Name and Addresses as known by the Bank which might sometimes be different from those present in the payment message. In that case, Name and Addresses will be replaced by the ones retrieved from the referentials.

The Agreements referentials give details about the agreement the customer has signed with the Bank for the processing of his payment orders. All agreement parameters required to process an order must be retrieved. Sometimes the choice is made to retrieve more information so that the payment engine can pass them through the context to other applications after the processing. In chapter 4.2.6 processing agreements services are handled in detail.

Now comes an interesting question. How many interfaces do we need here? Three interfaces, one for each referential or only one for all the three referentials? There is no strict answer to this question. In practice it is common to implement a service which itself rely on other services to retrieve all the information, concatenate it and send it to the payment engine. The service can be called in batch or transactional mode, and asynchronous messaging is used in general. In transactional mode, a short response time is expected.

8.2.1.5 Fraud detection

The fraud detection aims at analyzing the payment and the customer behavior and then decides if it is a fraudulent payment or not. If the customer accesses his accounts in two different countries (let's say Paris France and Dublin Ireland for example) to initiate (high) amounts transactions in 5 minutes, then something is strange. The Bank would rather stop or reject the transactions and then call the customer.

Payment transactions and additional information like dates, hours and IP addresses, are sent to the fraud detection module. It replies after analysis and the order processing is stopped if the payment is identified as fraudulent. Fraud detection solutions rely on multiple techniques to spot fraudulent behaviors: analytics, rule processing and risk scoring among others.

The Fraud detection application is called during the processing of the payment using synchronous or asynchronous messaging. Response should come in a reasonable amount of time as the bank wants to ensure that the payment is not fraudulent before forwarding it to the clearing system or before crediting the beneficiary. In case of a hit (the application claims the transaction is fraudulent), the transaction may be cancelled, rejected or postponed. The transaction will be further investigated by an operator to confirm (true hit) or infirm (false hit) the fraud detection result. Fraud detection algorithms are updated regularly to take into account the latest findings.

8.2.1.6 Accounting systems

Accounting systems must be interfaced with the Payment Engine. Payment processing is about moving funds. And that happens through the accounting systems where booking entries are made on the different accounts.

But booking entries are the result of a multi-step process. First, the payment engine generates the Accounting Events. And then the events are extracted, formatted and forwarded to the Accounting systems. Remember that an accounting event is balanced and results in at least two entries: one debit and one credit entry. Accounting events are interpreted and elementary events created for the individual entries to make on the accounts.

An entry can be made either on a customer account or on a general account. If the entry has to be made on the customer account, it will be forwarded to the Customer accounts management system. If the entry has to be made on a general account, it will be forwarded to the General accounts management system. Both systems may be implemented in the same application. But making an entry on a customer account is not the same thing as making it on a general account. Many controls and checks must be performed before making an entry on a customer account. Some of the controls are regulatory and thus necessary for compliance. In some cases, booking can be made only after many attempts on a customer account. On general accounts, the booking almost never fails and the first attempt always results in a success.

The account balance management system, which plays a key role in payments, is also part of the accounting systems (Or at least many consider it as such). It keeps and manages the intraday balances of customer accounts. When a balance check is performed, the payment engine forward the request to the account management system which itself relies on the account balance management system to reply. Please refer to chapter 6.11 to have detail information about the account balance management.

In summary, at least two interfaces are needed between the payment engine and the accounting systems. The first one is required for customer account verifications (balance checks and other checks) and balance updates when necessary during the processing of the payment. The second interface is used to send accounting events to be interpreted for the creation of accounting entries.

Asynchronous messaging is generally applied here in batch and/or transactional mode. When a user validates an immediate order, the balance check is performed immediately and he is informed in case there is a problem. He may reduce the amount of the order and retry again until the order is accepted. This is a good example which shows how important the response time is in transactional mode. Even if asynchronous messaging is used, the response should be delivered in a reasonably short time.

If we consider the case where the customer gives a future dated order. The balance check is performed at execution date in batch mode. If the response comes 30 minutes later, it does not matter. The customer is not online. The order will be rejected and he will receive a notification.

8.2.1.7 Audit log or Audit Trail

Payment processing is at the heart of financial transactions. Keeping the trace of the different user actions on transactions is vital.

The audit trail shows who has accessed the payment engine GUI and what operations he or she has performed and at what time. It tells the history about what happened on a message, order or transaction and on configuration data. Therefore, it can be used for audit purpose.

Most payment engines in the market include an audit trail component. Actions that can be traced there are limited to those performed in the payment engine. It is already pretty good but not sufficient. This is because in the payment engine you cannot see what happens before the transaction was received or after it was submitted. Dedicated audit trail application connected to the payment engine and other systems are required to get the end-to-end view.

The payment engine is most often interfaced with a dedicated audit trail application. The audit trail content consists essentially of the following information:

- Identification of the user making the action (View, create, update, delete). The user ID must be unique; otherwise it will be difficult or even impossible to trace back to the person who performed the action.

- Identification of the payment on which an action was made: The payment must be uniquely identified. It is the only way to ensure traceability.

- Date and Time Stamp: This is important to construct the story. It says exactly when an action was performed. In case of multiple similar actions. This can help to determine in which sequence the events happened.

- User Action: It provides the action that the user did on the payment. For a modification (create, update, delete), the original values and new values must be kept. They are needed to be able to have a complete history and to be able reconstruct the sequence of events.

Batch mode with asynchronous messaging is generally used for the exchange of information between the payment engine and a dedicated audit trail application. However, the exchange of information may happen almost on real-time or at specific defined times during the day.

8.2.1.8 Pricing & Billing

Pricing is the process whereby a business sets the price at which it will sell its products and services. Billing is the process of generating an invoice to recover sales price from the customer. Although they are highly correlated, pricing and billing are completely different things. Pricing must be done before billing. The billing system cannot do much without the prices. ☺

Regulation imposes banks to price payment products and related services, so that the customer is clearly informed about how much he is going to pay if he uses a product or service. Banks earn very little money on individual customers on SCT. Most of the money they make is in on SCT products and services provided to corporate customers.

Pricing & Billing strategies are multiple and quite complex. An entire book might not be sufficient to handle them. However, when you look at the pricing catalog of banks, you encounter following types of pricing:

- Subscription pricing: the customer must pay it every month or every quarter, no matter how many times he has used the services.

- Pricing per order / transaction: the customer pays when an order is processed globally and for each individual transaction processed in the order

- Pricing for value-added services like increasing the speed of the order, repairing orders or transactions and so on.

After the successful processing of an order, the Payment engine must send information to the Billing system. Many services are required to process a payment order but not all of them are invoiced to the customer. A filtering must happen on billable events either in the payment engine or in the billing system or somewhere else. In general, the billing system receives the information in a file in txt or xml format from the payment engine. The exchange is done in batch mode using asynchronous messaging.

8.2.1.9 Archiving

Data archiving is the process of moving data that is no longer actively used to a separate storage device for long-term retention. Archive data is older data. However, it is still important to the bank and may be needed for future reference. Archive data is also retained for regulatory compliance. In payment, two types or archiving must be distinguished: operational archiving for a duration of 15 to 18 months for SEPA payments and regulatory archiving for a duration of 10 to 15 years.

Operational archiving is about transactions that are a couple of months old. It is called operational archiving because it is primarily intended for payment operators and other people working on payment operations. Sometimes operational archiving happens in the payment engine itself where transactions are kept during 15 to 18 months. But it can be carried out in an external application as well. The Payment Services Directive (PSD) gives the customer the right to ask for an immediate refund up to 13 months after the unauthorized debit. This is probably one of the reasons why the operational archiving period is 15 to 18 months.

Regulatory archiving is performed during a much longer time, 10 to 15 years. It is more intended to the Compliance & Legal departments that may have to refer to the archived data. Unlike operational archiving which can be done in the payment engine itself, regulatory archiving is always implemented in an external system. The amount of data to archive for regulatory reason is huge. Data archives should be indexed and the application must have good search capabilities so that messages, orders and the corresponding transactions are easily located and retrieved when needed.

The payment engine is interfaced with one or more external systems for archiving. At least one interface must be built to the regulatory archiving application where data are kept for years. If operational archiving is done outside the payment engine, other interface(s) must be put in place as well. These interfaces usually run in batch mode with asynchronous messaging.

8.2.1.10 Reporting

Reporting provides information about the processing of the payments to many stakeholders. It can be grouped in three categories:

- Customer reporting
- Internal reporting
- Regulatory reporting

Customer reporting aims to inform the customer about the processing of his orders and transactions. The customer gets the information about the outcome of the processing, if the orders were successfully processed or if they were partially or totally rejected. He can receive a SMS, an e-mail or a paper mail or view the status on the bank website. The account statement is another kind of reporting. It gives a detailed view of all the debits and credits entries made on a specific account. Customers can download the account statements from their bank websites and/or receive them through the mail.

Internal reporting is for bank employees. There are many types of internal reporting. They are created to provide specific information needed by the employees to perform their tasks and duties. An internal reporting is usually a list with orders and transactions that fulfill certain criteria:

- Orders / transactions that could not be processed because of exceptions
- Orders / transactions above a certain amount
- Orders / transactions for a particular type of account
- Orders / transactions for a particular type of customer
- and so on.

Internal reporting can be made available in paper or electronic formats. Payment engines provide some of the internal reporting directly through the GUI. When it is not possible, it feeds the systems responsible for generating the internal reports (Batch mode and asynchronous messaging).

Regulatory reporting is for financial regulatory agencies: Tax offices, central banks and other regulatory authorities. The kind and number of regulatory reports are country dependent. The payment engine provides part of the information required to create those reports.

Customer reporting, internal reporting and regulatory reporting are done in different systems. The payment engine can be interfaced with each of the system. But sometimes the payment engine can send all reporting information to a module or application which selects and forwards only the part of information required by the receiving system.

8.2.1.11 Data warehouse & Statistics

Payment statistics are measured in count and amount. Count is the number of transactions and amount is the total euro value of those transactions. Statistics are measured over a period, typically days, weeks, months, and years. The number and amount of payment transactions (credit transfers, rejects, normal returns, cancellation requests, positive responses and negative responses) in different statuses to/from a bank are made available in statistical reports. The reports thus provide information on different kind of transactions and the parties they are exchanged with inside the same bank, inside the bank group, outside the bank group and so on. These figures are good inputs for the analysis of payments processing and exchange, but not for the analysis of payment activity. For that, more data is needed. The analysis of payment activity requires connection with other areas of the bank like Marketing or Sales. That is where the data warehouse comes into play.

The Data warehouse is a central repository of integrated data from disparate sources. It stores current and historical data allowing the creation of analytical reports throughout the enterprise. All transactions processed in the payment engine are sent to the Data warehouse as well data from many other systems. The communication is asynchronous and the data is sent to the data warehouse at scheduled time during the day or as payments are being processed. Payment statistics can be easily retrieved from the data warehouse through simple queries. However, as already stated above, it is the combination of data from multiple sources that provides insight and better understanding of payment activities or customer habits. Creating the queries to achieve this requires specialized skills and capabilities.

The future of Data warehouse and statistics is *payment analytics*. Because of the data explosion, many tools used by banks today for the payment data analysis are becoming obsolete. You have certainly already heard about Big data. It is a term referring to data sets that are so large and complex that they make traditional data processing tools inadequate. Big data is bringing new challenges in payment reporting and data analysis. Payment analytics tools are the answers and many banks are implementing or will implement them in the coming years. In the bank's functional and application architectures, the box Data warehouse and statistics will then be replaced by payment analytics.

8.2.1.12 Monitoring

Monitoring is the act of observing, recording and checking the activity of the payment engine and its surrounding systems. The purpose is to ensure that the payment engine and its surroundings are performing well technically and functionally and that they are delivering the expected value to the business. When something goes wrong or if something is not performing as expected, it should be detected and the information should be pushed to someone to act upon. Monitoring is therefore a crucial operational activity.

The monitoring team uses tools to look after the whole system in other to be aware of its state and any change which may occur at any time. We distinguish three main types of monitoring:

- Technical monitoring
- Functional monitoring
- Business Process Monitoring (BPM)

Technical monitoring aims to oversee the technical infrastructure (hardware, software, network and applications). All components must be up and running. If a connection goes down or a server goes down or an application goes down, etc., an alert should be raised. Ping sensors and remote probes are used to verify the connection to one or more remote hosts by sending a packet to a specified IP address, and then waiting for a reply. The alert is triggered by a time out mechanism in case there is no response after an elapsed time.

Functional monitoring is about overseeing the different applications and ensuring that they are performing as they should. The applications should deliver the results they are supposed to deliver. Expected results are compared with actual results and if there is a difference, an alert should be raised. Let's take an example to make the things more concrete. The payment engine is supposed to create exactly 10 files every day at 4:00 pm and send it to one or more applications. For an unknown reason, only 8 files have been created and sent today. An alert is generated and someone must investigate. As you see, the payment engine is up and running, there is no technical problem. The issue is that it is not delivering the result it is supposed to deliver.

At last Business Process Monitoring (BPM) ensures that the system is delivering the expected quality to its internal and external customers. But it goes further that. It measures and analyzes the performance of end-to-end business processes to identify critical process problems pro-actively. That insight enables the management to make decisions in other to improve the speed, quality and efficiency of business processes.

Functional and business monitoring are always combined, but they are different things. Functional monitoring is confined to single applications without necessarily an overall consistency whereas BPM looks at end-to-end processes and looks for ways to improve things.

The technical, functional and business process monitoring is possible only if the payment engine and interfaced applications exchange information with the monitoring tools. The communications are asynchronous and can occur in batch or transactional mode. For critical services, communication must occur in relatively tiny time frame. In case of an incident, the monitoring team must become aware as soon as possible and act upon.

8.2.1.13 Scheduler

The scheduler is a software which launches jobs (or programs) to be executed at a specific time. The scheduler does not execute the job, but just sends a trigger to the application (payment engine for instance) that executes it. After the execution, the application replies to the scheduler if the execution was successful or not. The scheduler uses asynchronous messaging mostly in batch mode.

Many tasks are repetitive and would require a human intervention to be performed if there was no scheduler. Thanks to the scheduler, the programs are run automatically at specific times and the operational risk is reduced as no human action is needed. The frequency of execution can be many times a day, daily, weekly, biweekly, monthly, and so on. Examples of repetitive tasks for a payment engine are: data reception, data submission, directories upload, accounting events generation just to name a few. They can all be configured in the scheduler and executed automatically at specific times.

One key feature of any scheduler is the ability to indicate the dependency between two jobs or more. Sometimes a job A must be executed before the job B. That dependency can be put into the scheduler, so that the scheduler will not start the job B if the job A has not been completed successfully. Let us take an example. The payment engine generates a file at the end of the day and sends it to a surrounding application. But that file should be generated only if the last transactions of the day have been received from the CSM. In the scheduler the file generation job can be configured in such a way that it is executed only after the last job to receive the transactions has been completed successfully. If the job to receive the transactions is not completed successfully, the file generation job will not be started. In case a job does not terminate well, an alert must be sent to an operator for further investigations. We are back to the topic of the previous paragraph: monitoring. The scheduler is monitored like all other applications. This was a very brief introduction to jobs dependency management in a scheduler. There are other available dependency options. If you want to know more about this topic, you will certainly find detailed information in the documentation of your own scheduler.

In conclusion, the scheduler plays an important role and running a payment engine without it would be practically impossible. Finding out which jobs must be set up in the scheduler and at which frequency they must be executed is an important part of any payment engine implementation project. Start working on the scheduler and use it as soon as possible.

8.2.1.14 Investigations

As introduction to this paragraph, let's see why payment investigations tools are important. The processing of payments involves many applications in the bank. From the channels to the exchange via the order management, the number of applications is quite high. Now what to do when a customer calls and asks for the status of an order or transaction? One option is to go from one application to another to see if the order / transaction is there and what was the outcome of the processing. But we have a couple of issues here:

1) It takes time to navigate through all the applications and the customer may not appreciate.
2) The same user may not have the right to access all the applications and the involvement of more people may be required. As a consequence, the customer cannot get the information as quickly as possible.
3) You are not really interested in going through all the history of the order / transaction. What you really want is the final status and you do not know where to go to get it.

A good solution is the use of an end-to-end investigation tool. It is an application where you can easily get an overview of what has happened to a specific order / transaction. The user sees the last status of the transaction and can inform the customer rapidly. It is possible because the investigation tool accesses the required information located in different applications in the bank. So, the investigation tool must be connected to the payment engine as well as other applications.

One may think that the payment engine feeds the investigation tool with payment data. This happens sometimes but it is not the best practice. Data replication takes some time and might lead to inconsistencies between the payment engine and the investigation tool. That is why many investigation applications on the market provide solutions to connect directly to applications and view the transactions. You can consider it as a search engine where you can find orders / transactions in the different payment applications. Moreover, investigation tools convert customer or internal inquiries into investigative cases, trigger and manage resolution workflows. Investigations may also be carried out in connection with prosecutions or other legal actions.

In conclusion, an investigation tool brings many benefits. Among others, it eliminates time-consuming manual searches and therefore reduces the operational risk. It also lowers the operational costs and improves the customer service.

8.2.1.15 Payment Exchange platform

The payment processing application is interfaced with the exchange platform for the exchanges of transactions with the clearing systems and other banks of a bank group. This subject was already discussed in chapter 4.3 to which I refer you for more details.

8.2.2 Surrounding systems of Payment Exchange Platform

The figure below depicts the surrounding applications the payment exchange platform interacts with. As you can see, many surrounding applications are the same as for payment processing application. The interfaces are also of the same type, mostly batch mode with asynchronous messaging. Some differences do exist. There are highlighted later and in this paragraph and few explanations are provided.

Before that, I would like to underscore one point. The architecture below is an example of possible solutions that you may encounter in practice. It is not the best or the right architecture in all cases. For example, the screening application is connected to the payment platform. This is not always the case as many banks choose to interface the screening system with the payment processing systems as well. Generally, the interface with screening functions in the same way no matter if it is connected to the exchange platform or to a payment processing application.

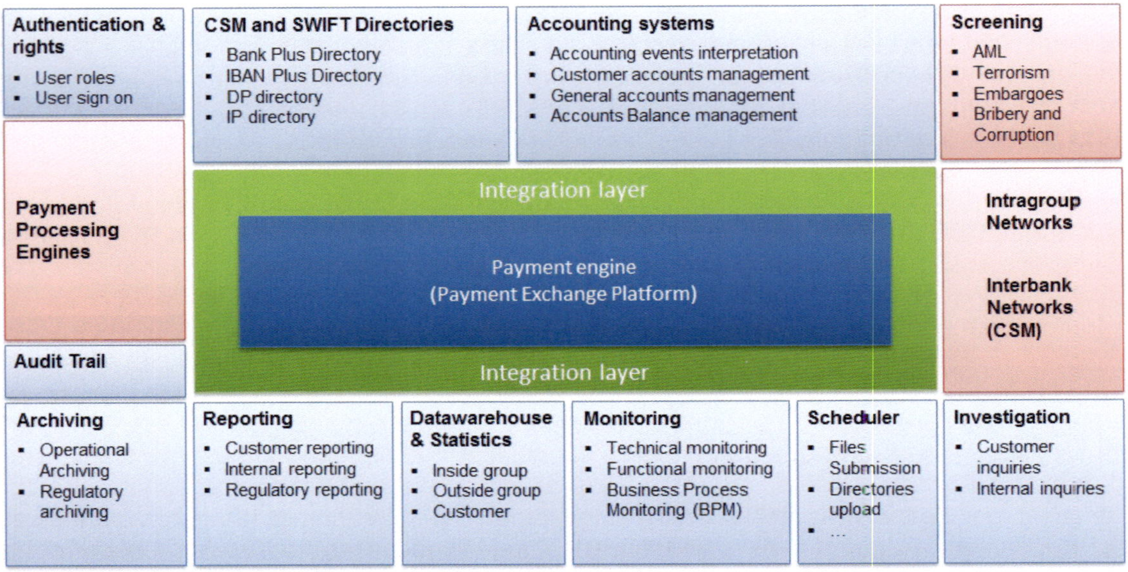

Figure 8.2: Surrounding systems of a payment exchange platform

The surrounding systems that did not appear on the picture of the previous paragraph are in another color (pink): Payment processing engines, the screening system, intragroup and interbank networks. The payment processing engines are connected to the exchange platform which itself is connected to the Interbank network and other banks of the group. If you read the paragraph 4.3 about the payment exchange, then you are familiar with that. Otherwise, I refer you to that part of the book.

If we consider the surrounding systems that were presented before, they are interfaced with the payment platform for almost the same reasons. The exchange platform must be monitored to ensure that it is up and running and that it is supporting the business processes. The platform exchanges transactions with CSM and other banks of the group. The related amounts are booked on internal and CSM accounts. Therefore, an interface to the accounting systems is required. The transactions processed in the exchanged platform must be archived as well. Users must authenticate themselves before accessing the exchange platform GUI. I will not cite all the systems again. Please just read to the previous paragraph (8.2.1) if you want more details about a specific surrounding system.

The screening is new and the connections to intragroup and interbank networks play a crucial role in the exchange of the transactions. They will be discussed in the subsequent paragraphs.

8.2.2.1 Screening

To comply with laws and regulations on Financial Crime, Banks must carry out many activities which include transaction screening during the payment processing. Financial crime prevention consists of the following main elements:

- Anti-Money Laundering (AML),
- Combating the Financing of Terrorism (CFT),
- Compliance with embargoes
- Anti-bribery and corruption.

Transaction screening implies going through all the information contained in the transaction and comparing that it with information available in the sanctions lists. It is carried out by screening engines that are specifically designed to check for possible matches between sanctions lists and transaction information. Some screening engines use sophisticated techniques to detect anagrams, missing letters, inversion of letters, misspellings, abbreviations and phonetic similarities. Sanctions lists are updated frequently. Banks must therefore ensure to update these lists as soon as they are published.

Before going into details on how the banks handle this compliance subject, let me first briefly explain the terms AML, CFT, Embargo, Anti-bribery and corruption.

- *Anti Money Laundering* is a set of procedures, laws or regulations designed to stop the practice of generating income through illegal actions. Money launderers generally hide their actions through a series of steps that make it look like money coming from illegal or unethical sources was earned legitimately. This definition shows that screening alone is not sufficient for AML and many other activities must be carried out for that.

- *Combating the Financing of Terrorism (CFT)* is straightforward. Terrorism financing is an activity that provides financial support to known terrorist groups. Initiatives to combat the financing of terrorism have increased especially since the terrorist attacks of 2001. There are many "Lists of designated terrorist groups"[19] published by countries or supranational organizations. Note that lists differ when you consider different countries. USA lists are not the same as Chinese lists which are also not the same as Russian lists.

  Remark: After defining AML and CFT, it is now worth mentioning the FATF[20] (Financial Action Task Force). It is an international organization whose purpose is to make recommendations in the fight against money laundering and against terrorist financing. The FATF has issued forty recommendations on anti-money laundering and nine special recommendations on the fight against the financing of terrorism.

- *An embargo* is the partial or complete prohibition of commerce and trade with a particular country or a group of countries. The restrictions and sanctions relate to economic, commercial or financial relations against a country but can also be applicable to goods or services, organizations, individuals like Politically Exposed Persons (PEP), moral persons or carriers in a country. Embargo lists are also country specific.

- *Anti-bribery and corruption*: Bribery is a specific offence which concerns the practice of offering money or other gratifications, to gain an illicit advantage. Corruption is an abuse of a position of trust in order to gain an undue advantage. PEP generally present a higher risk for potential involvement in bribery and corruption because of their positions and the influence that they may hold.

A payment transaction contains message elements like the BICs, IBANs, names and addresses of debtor and creditor, ultimate debtor and creditor, remittance information which are compared with information available in sanctions lists. In case of a match (the term HIT is also used), the processing of the transaction is put on hold and a decision must be taken after thorough investigations. The money can then be released, frozen or returned to the debtor. Money is released after manual investigations if there is no evidence that it is sent or received to/from a country, person, organization which is on a sanction list. This is called a false HIT.

---

[19] The Wikipedia article https://en.wikipedia.org/wiki/List_of_designated_terrorist_groups on the subject is quite interesting.

[20] The FATF website http://www.fatf-gafi.org/ provides useful resources for those who want to go further. You can access and download key publications under Publications in the menu.

To illustrate what I said, let us take an example of a politically exposed person (PEP) under sanction – officially since two weeks - with a bank account in the SEPA zone. First the bank must ensure that the sanctions lists used in the screening tool are updated. Now let's assume a debtor sends a credit transfer to that PEP who has an account in a SEPA country. The name of the person and postal address are mentioned in the payment. During the screening process, there is a match as the beneficiary name belongs to a list of PEPs under sanctions. So, the transaction is stopped and money is returned to the debtor. But this is quite simple to figure out. Isn't it? The PEP knowing that he is on a sanction list may ask his wife, brother or cousin to receive the money on his behalf. First names are different, but last names can still match. Or first and last names can be completely different, but addresses can match. Now consider the debtor knows that PEP is on a sanction list and purposely misspells his name or removes letter(s). In this case, there can still be a match after screening.

The screening belongs to last payment processing steps for outgoing transactions because transactions are not supposed to be modified after having undergone screening verifications. In case a transaction would be repaired for example after the screening, it would have to be rescreened again to comply with the regulation. This explains why screening is usually performed just before the transaction is sent to the clearing system or to the destination inside the Group.

Screening applies first to credit transfers. The cancellation requests and related negative responses are non-booking messages so they are not screened. The returns and positive responses contain almost the same information as the initial credit transfer, but can be sent many days after the credit transfers. Because of that, financial institutions are requested to screen pacs.004 transactions as well and not only the pacs.008.

To limit the number of interfaces and thus reduce the complexity of the IT landscape, the screening can be centralized by interfacing the screening application with the payment exchange platform. This brings other advantages: The bank can be sure that all transactions processed in the payment engine and sent to the market have been screened. Moreover, alignment and implementation of the screening rules are easier to achieve at Group level. So, interfacing the screening application with the payment exchange platform is not only cost efficient, but it also ensures overall consistency. All payments exchanged by the Bank with other banks inside or outside the group must go through the exchange platform and will be screened according to the rules defined at group level.

Historically many banks have not adopted a group level approach to deal with screening and compliance. As a result, many entities in the Bank have developed their own solution for screening based sometimes on completely different logics and software. A lot of money has been spent to finally realize that compliance holes remained in the bank. Today many organizations are putting solutions in place to solve those issues. The position of Group Chief Compliance Officer created a couple of years ago in many banks was an initiative to address this issue and make things move in the right direction.

8.2.2.2 Intragroup and Interbank networks

The Payment Exchange Platform connects banks of a group among themselves and the whole bank group to the clearing systems. All the banks of the group can then share the same connections to the CSM and reduce the related operational costs. This paragraph briefly explains what intragroup (inside group) and interbank (outside group) exchanges are all about.

Recipients of transactions are determined through BICs. The Debtor Bank uses the Beneficiary Bank BIC to figure out where a credit transfer should be sent. In case a Creditor Bank returns a credit transfer, it will use the Debtor Bank BIC to route it to the correct destination. We see that Debtor Bank BIC or Beneficiary Bank BIC can be used depending on the type of transaction. When we consider a Debtor Bank routing a credit transfer, there are the following possibilities:

1. The Beneficiary Bank BIC is the same as the Debtor Bank BIC.
2. The Beneficiary Bank BIC is a BIC of another Bank of the group or the BIC of an Indirect Participant of the group which does not belong to the group. Routing logic is almost the same in both cases.
3. The Beneficiary Bank BIC is a BIC of a Bank outside the Bank group.

In the first two cases, the Debtor Bank does not send the transaction to the CSM. The transaction is exchanged either inside the bank (intrabank exchange) or inside the group (intragroup exchange). Intrabank exchange is obviously a specific case of intragroup exchange. For the third case, the only way to reach the Beneficiary Bank is to send the transaction to the CSM. That is generally referred to as interbank exchanges. To be strict and avoid any misunderstanding, we can call them outside group exchanges as interbank may sometimes refer to exchange of transactions between banks of the same group.

Internal exchanges between banks of the same group occur in general instantaneously through messages. This is particularity the case when all the banks of the group and the exchange platform share the same application (See paragraph 4.4 on architectures). When the banks do not share the same application, the exchange platform sends and receives files to and from the bank processing applications.

External exchanges with CSM require protocols like SwiftNet FileAct or EBICS. This means as we saw in paragraph 4.1.3 that certificates must be used for the secure exchange of files. SWIFTNet FileAct is the protocol mostly used to exchange SEPA files with EBA / STEP2. On the SWIFT Network, the SWIFT Alliance Gateway (SAG) manages connectivity between customer applications and the SWIFT secure IP network. The SAG acts as a concentrator for SWIFTNet message flows. Consequently, the exchange platform does not send files directly to STEP2, but to the SAG. And then the SAG transmits them to STEP2. The incoming files from STEP2 are first received in the SAG which forwards them to the payment exchange platform.

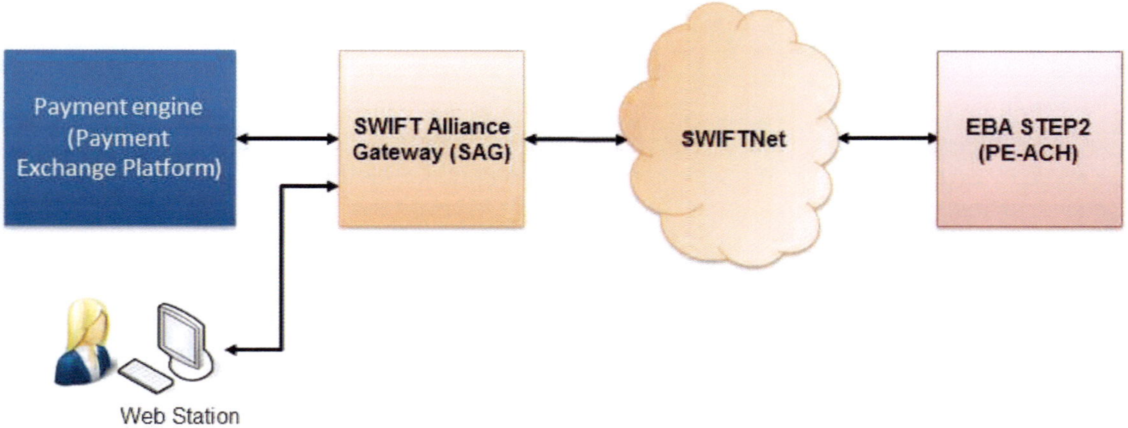

Figure 8.3: Connection of an exchange platform to EBA STEP2

The status of transactions from/to Bank in the STEP2 system can be viewed through a Web Station called Direct Participant Work Station (DPWS)[21]. As you see on the picture, the Web

[21] See https://www.ebaclearing.eu/services/step2-sct/key-features/

Station is directly connected to the SAG - via the SWIFTNet service Browse - and not to the exchange platform. The GUI of exchange platform application is used to see and monitor the transactions in the Exchange platform.

Each CSM communicates the cut-off after which transactions to clear and settle on the same day cannot be accepted anymore. These cut-offs are positioned beginning or middle of the afternoon. Banks must keep them for outside group transactions that they send to CSM. They don't have the choice. But Banks have more flexibility for inside group transactions where debtor and beneficiary are customers of the same bank or of two banks of the group. For these transactions, the cut-off can be positioned much later in the afternoon or even at nightfall. With the growing concentration of inside group transactions, many customers can benefit from this service and some do really appreciate it.

In conclusion, payment processing engines and payment exchange platform must be interfaced with many applications of the bank for the processing of transactions. The information exchange happens in batch mode with asynchronous messaging in the majority of cases.

Review Questions

- Explain the important concept of interface.
- Define and illustrate what synchronous and asynchronous messaging is
- Define and illustrate what batch and transactional mode means
- List the surrounding systems found in a typical Payment IT landscape
- Give a brief description of the main functions of each surrounding system
- What are ACH and SWIFT directories and what are they used for?
- Describe what customer referential are and how they interact with the payment processing platform
- Explain the differences between General accounts management system and Customer accounts management system. How are booking entries performed on both systems?
- Describe the differences between operational archiving and regulatory archiving. Can both be implemented in the same application?

Discussion Questions

- Imagine a payment engine without interface at all. Which features must be available for the payment processing?
- Why are interfaces with asynchronous messaging by far the most widely used?
- List the surrounding systems by complexity levels. Give the reasons why you have chosen this order.
- In a complex payments landscape, how to decide which functions to implement in which system?
- In this chapter, we presented the screening application as interfaced with the payment platform. Can you list the benefits and drawbacks of such an architecture?
- Running a payment engine without scheduler is not recommended. Why?

Congratulations !!!!

You have reached the end of the book. Now you know what the SEPA Credit Transfer is and you have strong foundations to understand domestic payments in any country in the world. The payment world is broad and fascinating and there are many other subjects that are as passionate as SCT:

- Other domestic payments like Cheques and SEPA Direct Debit,
- X-border payments
- Card payments
- Negotiable Instruments (Bill of exchanges and promissory notes)
- Trade finance
- Cash management
- Cash

If you are a payment professional or if you just want to extend your payment knowledge and skills without spending too much time on it, you can visit my blog regularly and subscribe to the newsletter.

www.paiementor.com

Annex 1: List of SEPA Countries

The table contains the list of SEPA countries as presented in the EPC409-09 EPC List of SEPA Scheme Countries v2.4 - April 2016.pdf document. For each country, you have the country code to use in the BIC, the country code to use in the IBAN and the currency code used in that country. All countries that used EUR as currency belong to the Euro zone.

Country	BIC	IBAN	Currency Code
Åland Islands	FI	FI	EUR
Austria	AT	AT	EUR
Azores	PT	PT	EUR
Belgium	BE	BE	EUR
Bulgaria	BG	BG	BGN
Canary Islands	ES	ES	EUR
Croatia	HR	HR	HRK
Cyprus	CY	CY	EUR
Czech Republic	CZ	CZ	CZK
Denmark	DK	DK	DKK
Estonia	EE	EE	EEK
Finland	FI	FI	EUR
France	FR	FR	EUR
French Guiana	GF	FR	EUR
Germany	DE	DE	EUR
Gibraltar	GI	GI	GIP
Greece	GR	GR	EUR
Guadeloupe	GP	FR	EUR
Hungary	HU	HU	HUF
Iceland	IS	IS	ISK
Ireland	IE	IE	EUR
Isle of Man	IM	GB	GBP
Italy	IT	IT	EUR
Jersey	JE	GB	GBP
Latvia	LV	LV	EUR
Liechtenstein	LI	LI	CHF
Lithuania	LT	LT	EUR
Luxembourg	LU	LU	EUR
Madeira	PT	PT	EUR
Malta	MT	MT	EUR
Martinique	MQ	FR	EUR
Mayotte	YT	FR	EUR
Monaco	MC	MC	EUR
Netherlands	NL	NL	EUR
Norway	NO	NO	NOK
Poland	PL	PL	PLN

Country	BIC	IBAN	Currency Code
Portugal	PT	PT	EUR
Réunion	RE	FR	EUR
Romania	RO	RO	RON
Saint Barthélemy	BL	FR	EUR
Saint Martin (French part)	MF	FR	EUR
Saint Pierre and Miquelon	PM	FR	EUR
San Marino	SM	SM	EUR
Slovakia	SK	SK	EUR
Slovenia	SI	SI	EUR
Spain	ES	ES	EUR
Sweden	SE	SE	SEK
Switzerland	CH	CH	CHF
United Kingdom	GB	GB	GBP

Overseas departments and territories (DOM-TOM) of France may use either the French country code or their own code in the IBAN.

DOM/TOM & Communities		Country code used in the IBAN
Metropolitan France		FR
DOM	Guyane	FR
	Guadeloupe	FR
	Martinique	FR
	Réunion	FR
Mayotte		FR or YT
Saint-Pierre and Miquelon		FR ou PM

Note that French Pacific communities (New Caledonia, French Polynesia and Wallis and Futuna) do not belong to SEPA.

Annex 2: IBAN calculation and validation algorithms

IBAN calculation and validation is an important topic since SEPA Payments use IBAN exclusively. You are probably interested in the algorithms used to compute and validate the IBAN check digits. That is the subject of this brief paragraph.

Generating IBAN check digits

According to the ECBS (European Committee for Banking Standards), "the generation of the IBAN shall be the exclusive responsibility of the bank/branch servicing the account". The ECBS document replicates part of the ISO/IEC 7064:2003 standard as a method for generating check digits in the range 02 to 98.

The steps of the preferred algorithm for the IBAN check digits generation is:

1. Check that the total IBAN length is correct as per the country. If not, the IBAN is invalid
2. Replace the two check digits by 00 (e.g. GB00 for the UK)
3. Move the four initial characters to the end of the string
4. Replace the letters in the string with digits, expanding the string as necessary, such that A or a = 10, B or b = 11, ... and Z or z = 35. Each alphabetic character is therefore replaced by 2 digits.
5. Convert the string to an integer (i.e. ignore leading zeroes)
6. Calculate mod-97 of the new number, which results in the remainder
7. Subtract the remainder from 98, and use the result for the two check digits. If the result is a single digit number, pad it with a leading 0 to make a two-digit number.

Example: We will consider the Belgium BBAN 510007547061 for which we can calculate the IBAN BEXX510007547061.

1. Total IBAN BEXX510007547061 length is 16. ➔ That is correct for Belgium.
2. Replace the two check digits by 00 ➔ BE00510007547061
3. Move the four initial characters to the end of the string ➔ 510007547061BE00
4. Replace the letters in the string with digits ➔ 510007547061111400
5. Convert the string to an integer ➔ 510007547061111400
6. 510007547061111400 mod-97 = 36
7. Subtract the remainder from 98 ➔ 98 – 36 = 62

The check digits are 62 and the IBAN is BE62510007547061.

Validating the IBAN

An IBAN is validated by converting it into an integer and performing a basic mod-97 operation (as described in ISO 7064) on it. If the IBAN is valid, the remainder equals 1. The algorithm of IBAN validation is as follows:

1. Check that the total IBAN length is correct as per the country. If not, the IBAN is invalid
2. Move the four initial characters to the end of the string
3. Replace each letter in the string with two digits, thereby expanding the string, where A = 10, B = 11, ..., Z = 35
4. Interpret the string as a decimal integer and compute the remainder of that number on division by 97. If the remainder is 1, the check digit test is passed and the IBAN is valid.

Example: We will consider the following IBAN GB82WEST12345698765432 of UK with sort code 123456 and account number 98765432)

- Total IBAN GB82WEST12345698765432 is 22. ➔ That is correct for UK.
- Move the four initial characters to the end of the string ➔ WEST12345698765432GB82

- Replace each letter in the string with two digits ➔ 3214282912345698765432161182
- Interpret the string as a decimal integer and compute mod 97 (remainder of the division by 97) ➔ 3214282912345698765432161182 mod 97 = 1

The IBAN GB82WEST12345698765432 is a valid IBAN.

You find more details about this topic under the chapter to the chapter CALCULATION AND VALIDATION OF THE CHECK DIGITS of the document EBS204 V3.2 — AUGUST 2003 that is easily downloadable on Internet.

Annex 3: How to read the SCT rulebooks and Implementation Guidelines

This annex is about the main documents published by the EPC: the Rulebooks and the implementation guidelines. For beginners, it might be unclear in which document to find which information. This annex provides an overview of these documents and their content. That knowledge is useful to know where to go to find the information you are looking for. We will consider the documents about the SEPA Credit Transfer, the topic of this book. However, what you read below is applicable for other SEPA schemes.

The three main documents published on the SCT scheme are:

- EPC125-05 SCT RB vX.Y Approved.pdf (SEPA Credit Transfer Rulebook Version X.Y)
- EPC115-06 Interbank CTIG vX.Y Approved November 20NN.pdf (SEPA Credit Transfer Scheme Inter-Bank Implementation Guidelines Version X.Y)
- EPC132-08 C2B CTIG V6.0 Approved November 20NN.pdf (SEPA Credit Transfer Scheme Customer-to-Bank Implementation Guidelines Version X.Y)

Take note that each EPC document is identified with a unique number preceded by the EPC symbol. The EPC publishes major versions (V7.0, V8.0, ...) of the rulebooks and associated implementation guidelines generally once every two years in November, to take effect in November of the next year. This gives one year to scheme participants to implement the changes of the new versions, before the deadline. Between major versions, the EPC may need to make small amendments or corrections. For that purpose, they will update the rulebook and publish a minor version (V8.1, V8.2, V8.3 ...). If a Rulebook remains unchanged from a functional or technical point of view, they can take effect few weeks later. If we consider for example the *EPC125-05 SCT Rulebook v8.3*, you see on the first page that date issued is 24 November 2016 and date effective is 24 December 2016. This means that the changes in the rulebook are taking effect one month after publication. The scheme participants cannot implement changes in one month. Therefore, the changes introduced into this version 8.3 do not have any operational impact.

Now let us look at each of document. The first on the list is the SCT rulebook. In that document, you find descriptions of processes and rules that all SEPA participants must comply with. Scheme definitions are also provided as well as right and obligations of participants. For beginners, this is undoubtedly the document to read first to acquire an overview about SEPA, the main actors involved and the business rules.

The other two documents (Implementation Guidelines) contain the specifications of the SCT scheme message formats. The Inter-Bank Implementation Guidelines are about the messages exchanged in the interbank space, so between one bank and another bank or between one bank and a CSM. The Customer-to-Bank Implementation Guidelines are about the messages exchanged in the Customer-to-Bank space. The messages sent from a (corporate) customer to a bank or received by a (corporate) customer from a bank are considered.

In the documents of the EPC, many references are made to ISO standard documents like:

- ISO 3166 Country Codes
- ISO 4217 Currency Code List
- ISO 9362 Business Identifier Codes (BIC)
- ISO 20022 Financial services – Universal Financial Industry message scheme
- ISO 11649 Structured creditor references to remittance information

If consultation of all these standards is highly recommended, a careful reading of the ISO 20022 standard is essential to understand the EPC Implementations guidelines. Indeed, all the messages used in SEPA, whether between different banks or between banks and customers are based on the ISO 20022 standard (https://www.iso20022.org/message_archive.page). The URL points to the ISO 20022 Payment Message Archive where you find all the message versions used in SEPA (Pain.001.001.03, Pacs.008.001.02, and so on). A search on your browser with the right message version is recommended to easily find the message you are looking for. Otherwise, you find other versions! Once you find the correct version, you have to download the document on the right (MDR hyperlink). These documents are called Message Definition Report (MDR). They contain more than the description of the messages. They are fairly comprehensive documents that indicate the context in which messages can be exchanged and the players involved. It is recommended to read the first two introductory chapters and then to look at the definition of the message you are interested in. By experience I would say that reading the message definition reports of SEPA messages is a must. Otherwise, it is very difficult to really understand the content of the EPC Implementation Guidelines and particularly the differences between the ISO 20022 and the SEPA requirements. In addition to MDR and the implementation guidelines, another interesting document to read is the following: *EPC217-08 Best practices SEPA Requirements for an Extended character set*. It contains a set of recommended best practices to be used when dealing with local language and special characters used in SEPA countries. Specific rules for some selected ISO 20022 XML data elements are outlined in that document as well. It is worth being aware of.

When you become used to SEPA and have already read EPC documents, the first thing you ask yourself when you see a new document version: what are the differences between this version and the previous one?. To find it out, you will agree with me that going through the documents is not the right approach. As already mentioned, major versions of the EPC documents are published every two years with minor versions in between. Between two versions, there may be more or less important modifications. The EPC recognized the need for users to see what changed compared to the previous version. Therefore, each document contains a section which provides the changes that have been made compared to the previous version. In the latest versions of the rulebooks, the changes are listed in Annex III (ANNEX III - RULEBOOK AMENDMENTS AND CHANGES). In the implementation guidelines, the changes are listed at the end of the document under the section List of changes in Credit Transfer C2B Implementation Guidelines Relative to previous version. So you now know where to go when you get a new version and are interested in the changes compared to the previous one.

Glossary

Terms	Definitions
Accounting Entry	An accounting entry is generated as a result of an accounting event processing. It is a debit or credit entry that is performed on a single account. An accounting entry is made using the double entry bookkeeping system, which requires you to make both a debit and credit entry. An accounting entry always have a counterpart of the opposite sign.
Accounting Event	Event generated by a payment processing engine indicating that an accounting entry must be created as a result of a step in the processing of a Payment entity. An accounting event creates two or more entries on different accounts. The total amount of debit entries must be equal to the total amount of credit entries.
Accounting System	The system used to manage the income, expenses, and other financial activities of a business. In payments, it is the system that performs the debits and credits on the accounts. Accounting systems are usually automated and computer-based, using specialised software and/or cloud-based services.
Agent	A generic name for any party, either financial or non financial, involved in the processing of a payment. It can be a bank, a clearing system, a settlement system ...
Agent Code	A text string that uniquely identifies an agent within a participation directory. In most cases, the agent code refers to the BIC code.
Asynchronous communication	Asynchronous communication describes information exchange between two applications or systems where one application places a message in a message queue and does not need to wait for a reply from the other application to continue processing. Asynchronous communication can be sent at any time without need for the sender and receiver to be time-synchronized.
Audit trail or Audit log	A security-relevant chronological record, set of records, that provide documentary evidence of the sequence of activities that have affected at any time a specific operation, procedure, or event.
Automated Clearing House (ACH)	An electronic clearing system in which payment orders are exchanged among financial institutions, primarily using magnetic media or via telecommunication networks, and handled by a data-processing centre. An ACH is usually used for high volume, low value retail payments.
Balance check	Service that determines if the customer has sufficient funds on his account for the order execution. Customer overdraft and lines of credit are usually taken into consideration.
Batch job	Batch jobs are planned and executed according to a defined frequency. Many batch jobs run during the night. Batch interfaces mostly use asynchronous communication with replies in seconds or minutes. But they can also use synchronous communication.
Cash management	Process of collecting and managing cash, as well as using it for short-term investing.

Terms	Definitions
Cash pooling	It allows companies to combine their credit and debit positions in various accounts into one account, and includes techniques like notional cash pooling and cash concentration.
Colleges of Signatories	Colleges of Signatories include users generally of the same level of authority who can validate and / or sign orders.
International Organization for Standardization (ISO)	International standard-setting body composed of representatives from various national standards organizations. Founded on 23 February 1947, the organization promotes worldwide proprietary, industrial and commercial standards. It is headquartered in Geneva, Switzerland, and works in 162 countries.
ISO 20022	An ISO standard for electronic data interchange between financial institutions. It describes a metadata repository containing descriptions of messages and business processes, and a maintenance process for the repository content. The standard covers financial information transferred between financial institutions that includes payment transactions, securities trading and settlement information, credit and debit card transactions and other financial information.
Batch Interface	It is a non-interactive user interface. All the details of the batch job are specified in advance in the batch processing, and the output is produced only after all the processing is done. There is no prompt for further user input after the processing has started.
Transactional Interface	It is an Interactive user interface. The user uses a transactional interface (graphical or not) to key in data as input for the processing. All the inputs of a transactional program are not known in advance. The user can provide input before and after the execution has started. Response time really matters here since the user wants to see the result of his actions as soon as possible, in few seconds generally.
Bankgroup	Large bank with many domestic and foreign subsidiairies. A bank group may have many brands in different countries. IT systems may be common or specific to some banks in the group.
Basic Bank Account Number (BBAN)	Identifier used nationally by financial institutions, ie, in individual countries, generally as part of a National Account Numbering Schemes, to uniquely identify the account of a customer. BBAN is part of the IBAN. The BBAN length = IBAN length - 4. Examples of BBAN: France 30004028370001095333394, Germany 370700600003619822.
Business Identifier Code (BIC)	Initially known as Bank Identifier Code, BIC now stands for Business Identifier Code. It is a unique identification code for both financial and non-financial institutions used to facilitate the automated exchange and processing of financial messages worldwide. The BIC was introduced by SWIFT which is the BIC registration authority. BIC is also called SWIFT-BIC, SWIFT ID or SWIFT code.

Terms	Definitions
Clearing	The process of transmitting, reconciling and, in some cases, confirming transactions prior to settlement, potentially including the netting of transactions and the establishment of final positions for settlement. Sometimes this term is also used (imprecisely) to cover settlement. For the clearing of futures and options, this term also refers to the daily balancing of profits and losses and the daily calculation of collateral requirements.
Clearing House	A multilateral system or arrangement that provides its participants with clearing services for payment instructions, securities transactions, derivatives transactions, and in some cases, settlement services.
Clearing system	A set of procedures whereby financial institutions present and exchange data relating to transfers to other financial institutions. The procedures often also include a mechanism for the calculation of participants" bilateral and/or multilateral net positions with a view to facilitating the settlement of their obligations.
Correspondent Banking	Correspondent banking is a method to settle a payment between two financial institutions. Two banks enter into an account relationship where one bank, called the correspondent bank, provides services to settle payments in a certain currency to another bank. The settlement of payments occurs via an account which a bank holds at the correspondent bank. Correspondent banking services are primarily provided across international boundaries, but are also known as agency relationships in some domestic contexts.
Interface	In computing, an interface is a shared boundary across which two or more separate components of a computer system exchange information.
Correspondent network	The total number of accounts in local and foreign currencies that a bank possesses in different currency zones is its correspondent network.
Credit risk	The probable risk of loss resulting from a borrower's failure to repay a loan or meet contractual obligations.
Credit transfer	A direct payment of money from one bank account into another. A credit transfer is a payment initiated by the payer. The payer sends a payment instruction to his/her payment service provider (PSP), e.g. a bank. The payer's PSP moves the funds to the payee's PSP. This can be carried out via several intermediaries.
Creditor	Party to which an amount of money is due. A creditor can be a consumer, a company, a financial institution, a NGO, etc. It owns the bank account where the funds are credited.
Creditor Agent	Financial institution servicing an account for the creditor. Same thing as creditor bank.
Customer-to-Bank Space	Space in which banks and customers exchange payment messages. Customers send instructions to Banks and Banks send reporting to customers.
Debtor	Party that owes an amount of money to the creditor. A debtor can be a consumer, a company, a financial institution, a NGO, etc. It owns the bank account that is debited.
Debtor Agent	Financial institution servicing an account for the debtor. Same thing as Debtor Bank.

Terms	Definitions
Direct Debit	A transfer initiated by the payee via his/her payment service provider. Direct debits are often used for recurring payments, such as utility bills. They require a pre-authorisation (or "mandate") from the payer. Direct debits are also used for one-off payments. In this case, the payer authorises an individual payment.
Direct Participant	A participant in a clearing system which has direct link to the clearing system and is responsible for the settlement of its own payments, those of its customers and indirect participants.
Enterprise Resource Planning	Integrated management of core business processes, often in real-time and mediated by software and technology. ERP often refers to a suite of integrated application that an organization uses to collect, store, manage, and interpret data from its many business activities.
Euro Banking Association (EBA)	Founded in Paris in 1985 by 18 commercial banks and the European Investment Bank, the number of EBA members has since then risen to almost 200. The institutions come from all member states of the European Union as well as from Norway, Switzerland, Australia, China, Japan, the United Arab Emirates and the United States. The EBA operates pan-european clearing systems for the processing of credit transfers and direct debits: EURO1, STEP1 and STEP2.
Graphical User Interface (GUI)	Type of user interface that allows users to interact with electronic devices through graphical icons and visual indicators such as secondary notation, instead of text-based user interfaces, typed command labels or text navigation. The actions in a GUI are usually performed through direct manipulation of the graphical elements
Indirect Participant	A type of participant in a clearing system. An entity that does not have direct access to the clearing system (CS), and is typically not directly bound by the rules of the CS, but whose transactions are cleared, settled, or recorded by the CS through a direct participant. An indirect participant has a bilateral agreement with a direct participant.
Initiating party	The party sending a payment message.
Instruction or Order	This term is used to refer to a remittance containing one or more individual credit transfers.
Interactive Voice Response (IVR)	Technology that allows a computer to interact with humans through the use of voice and Dual-tone multi-frequency (DTMF) signaling tones input via a keypad. IVR allows customers to interact with a Bank's host system via a telephone keypad or by speech recognition.
Interbank Space	Space in which banks exchange payment messages among themselves directly or though a clearing system (CSM).
International Bank Account Number (IBAN)	Identifier used internationally by financial institutions to uniquely identify the account of a customer. The IBAN consists of up to 34 alphanumeric characters comprising: a country code; two check digits; and a number that includes the domestic bank account number, branch identifier, and potential routing information. The check digits enable a sanity check of the bank account number to confirm its integrity before submitting a transaction. The IBAN is based on the standard ISO 13616:2007. All countries are not using the IBAN yet. But it is gaining wider adoption worldwide.

Terms	Definitions
LDAP	Lightweight Directory Access Protocol – An industry standard application protocol for accessing and maintaining distributed directory information services over a network.
NAR	Name, Address and Residence information.
Nostro (Mirror)	A copy of a local financial institutions" foreign currency accounts conducted with international correspondent banks to settle foreign currency transactions initiated by either the local Financial Institution or International Correspondent banks. The funds represented by the Nostro Mirror are held in a Vostro account at the bank that holds the currency being exchanged.
Operational risk	Risk of loss resulting from inadequate or failed internal processes, people and systems or from external events. When assessing operational risk, Employee errors, Systems failures, Fraud or other criminal activity, Any event that disrupts business processes should be considered.
Order or Instruction	This term is used to refer to a remittance containing one or more individual credit transfers.
Originating party	The party that owes the cash to the creditor as a result of receipt of goods or services.
Participation Directory	A list of the agent codes of financial institutions that participate in the execution of transactions
Payment status reports (PSR)	Reporting messages sent by banks to a customer to provide information about the progress of payment orders processing and execution. A PSR can be either positive (fully accepted message or order) or negative (fully rejected message or order) or partially positive (partially accepted message or order.
PEACH	Pan-European Automated Clearing House
Real-Time Gross Settlement system (RTGS)	A settlement system in which processing and settlement take place on an order-by-order basis (without netting) in real time (continuously).
Routing	It consists in determining the destination and delivery channel for a transaction.
SEPA Scheme	Set of rules, practices and standards to achieve interoperability for the provision and operation of a SEPA payment instrument agreed at interbank level.
Settlement	Act that discharges obligations in respect of funds or securities transfers between two or more parties. Settlement is the funds transfer that is carried out by one party to fulfill its obligations towards the counterparty in a financial operation. The settlement happens in general after bilateral or multilateral clearing.
Single Euro Payments Area (SEPA)	SEPA is a payment-integration initiative of the European Union for simplification of bank transfers denominated in euro. SEPA may be used to refer to the area which consists of 35 member states or to a specific SEPA payment scheme.
STEP2	PEACH-type clearing system operated by the EBA for the clearing of pan-european credit transfers and direct debits.

Terms	Definitions
Submission	Submission is the process by which transactions are created from information within OPF and delivered to a destination, with required controls.
SWIFT	SWIFT stands for It is the cooperative organization created and owned by banks which operates a network to facilitate the exchange of payment and other financial messages between financial institutions throughout the world.
SwiftNet	A group or messaging services provided by SWIFT: FIN: Messages using MT Standards InterAct: Messages and query-and-response services. "MX" XML message standards FileAct: File transfer for data-intensive applications. Store and Forward or Real Time Browse: Secure Browsing – Compliments InterAct, FileAct and FIN.
Synchronous communication	Synchronous messaging describes information exchange between two applications or systems where both parties work simultaneously in real time. Both applications must be present at the same time for the communication to take place. The sending application (also called client) waits for a reply from the receiving application (also called the server) and cannot initiate a new communication until it gets the reply.
TARGET 2	Trans-European Automated Real-time Gross Settlement Express Transfer
Transaction	This term is used to refer to an individual credit transfer. An order can consist of one or multiple transactions.
UNIFI	It stands for Universal Financial Industry Message Scheme (business modeling methodology and XML syntax). It is the same thing is ISO 20022.
VOSTRO Account	From a bank perpective, it is the account of another bank in its book. That account is in local currency most of the time and used to settle local currency transactions initiated by the other bank.
Work List Item (WLI)	An event that requires manual action on a transaction or order inside or outside the payment engine. This item appears in the work list of the payment engine GUI.
Zero balance account	Account in which a balance of zero is maintained by transferring funds from a master account. This is related to cash pooling.

Index

As a business analyst, solution designer, architect, tester, project or program manager working on SEPA Credit Transfer related projects, you want to understand the SEPA Credit Transfer and how banks implement it without having to read tons of documents. You are looking for answers to questions around SCT messages, the payment engines used to process them and the other applications and systems involved in SCT processing. This book provides you the answers to these questions and much more. Beginning with the underlying payment system model for the SCT, a thorough analysis of all the actors involved in SCT processes is made. Key concepts in payments like clearing, settlement, direct and indirect participants are presented. The ISO 20022 standard on which the SCT messages are based is introduced, and the differences between ISO standard and the SCT implementation guidelines are highlighted and made clear with examples. An overview of all SCT Additional Optional Services is also provided.

The processing of a SEPA Credit Transfer requires involvement of many applications of the Bank's IT environment. What are those applications? How do they interact with each other for the information exchange? Payment engines are of particular interest because they orchestrate the SCT processing. How do users interact with payment engines through the GUI? Which actions can they perform and how to ensure confidentiality? Get the answers to all these questions with practical examples.

Accounting and account balance management are crucial topics in payments and SCT processing. You get a step by step explanations of what they are and the underlying principles. You see how funds moves from the originating customer to the beneficiary and how the bank ensures availability of funds before execution of SCT orders.

This book will enable you to save precious time and move to the fast track in your career in banking and payment.

About the Author

Jean Paul acquired two engineering degrees from the University of Stuttgart in Germany and from Supélec in France. He has over 12 years of experience as consultant in banking and payments and has held many positions like Business Analyst, Functional Tester and Project Manager.

His journey with SEPA started in 2007 and since then he has carried out many projects internationally. With the time, Jean Paul has acquired a deep understanding of SEPA and the SEPA Credit Transfer. He wrote this book to share his knowledge, so that his readers can find everything they need to understand and implement SCT in one spot. On the other hand, this book also contains valuable information and insight that will change the way you see the SEPA Credit Transfer and add more value to your existing knowledge base.

Congratulations !!!!

You have reached the last page of the book. Now you know what the SEPA Credit Transfer is and you have strong foundations to understand domestic payments in any country in the world. The payment world is broad and fascinating and there are many other subjects that are as passionate as SCT:

- Other domestic payments like Cheques and SEPA Direct Debit,
- X-border payments
- Card payments
- Negotiable Instruments (Bill of exchanges and promissory notes)
- Trade finance
- Cash Management
- Cash

If you are a payment professional or if you just want to extend your payment knowledge and skills without spending too much time on it, you can visit my blog regularly and subscribe to the newsletter.

www.paiementor.com

Printed in Poland
by Amazon Fulfillment
Poland Sp. z o.o., Wrocław

23148224R00138